THE CAMBRIDGE COMPANION TO

DELEUZE

Each volume of this series of companions to major philosophers contains specially commissioned essays by an international team of scholars, together with a substantial bibliography, and will serve as a reference work for students and non-specialists. One aim of the series is to dispel the intimidation such readers feel when faced with the work of a difficult and challenging thinker.

Gilles Deleuze (1925–95) was an influential and provocative twentieth-century thinker who developed and presented an alternative to the image of thought found in traditional philosophy. This volume offers an extensive survey of Deleuze's philosophy by some of his most influential interpreters. The essays give lucid accounts of the fundamental themes of his metaphysical work and its ethical and political implications. They clearly situate his thinking within the philosophical tradition, with detailed studies of his engagements with phenomenology, post-Kantianism, and the sciences, and also his interventions in the arts. As well as offering new research on established areas of Deleuze scholarship, several essays address key themes that have not previously been given the attention they deserve in the English-speaking world.

New readers will find this the most convenient, accessible guide to Deleuze currently available. Advanced students and specialists will find a conspectus of recent developments in the interpretation of Deleuze.

Continued at the back of the book

The Cambridge Companion to
DELEUZE

Edited by

Daniel W. Smith
Purdue University

and

Henry Somers-Hall
Royal Holloway, University of London

CAMBRIDGE
UNIVERSITY PRESS

CAMBRIDGE UNIVERSITY PRESS
Cambridge, New York, Melbourne, Madrid, Cape Town,
Singapore, São Paulo, Delhi, Mexico City

Cambridge University Press
The Edinburgh Building, Cambridge CB2 8RU, UK

Published in the United States of America by Cambridge University
Press, New York

www.cambridge.org
Information on this title: www.cambridge.org/9781107002616

First published 2012

Printed and bound in the United Kingdom by the MPG Books Group

*A catalogue record for this publication is available from the British
Library*

Library of Congress Cataloguing in Publication data
The Cambridge companion to Deleuze / edited by Daniel Smith and
Henry Somers-Hall.
  p. cm. – (Cambridge companions to philosophy)
Includes bibliographical references and index.
ISBN 978-1-107-00261-6 (hardback) – ISBN 978-0-521-17571-5 (paperback)
1. Deleuze, Gilles, 1925–1995. I. Smith, Daniel W. (Daniel Warren),
1958– II. Somers-Hall, Henry.
B2430.D454C33 2012
194–dc23   2012013365

ISBN 978-1-107-00261-6 Hardback
ISBN 978-0-521-17571-5 Paperback

CONTENTS

CONTRIBUTORS

RONALD BOGUE, Distinguished Research Professor of Comparative Literature at the University of Georgia, is the author of *Deleuzian Fabulation and the Scars of History* (2010), *Deleuze's Way* (2007), and *Deleuze on Literature* (2003).

ROSI BRAIDOTTI is Distinguished University Professor at Utrecht University in the Netherlands and Director of the Centre for the Humanities. She is the author of a trilogy on nomadic thought: *Nomadic Subjects* (1994 and 2011 [second edn.]), *Metamorphoses* (2002), and *Transpositions* (2006) and has recently published a collection of papers entitled *Nomadic Theory* (2011).

MIGUEL DE BEISTEGUI is Professor of Philosophy at the University of Warwick. He is the author of *Truth and Genesis: Philosophy as Differential Ontology* (2005) and *Immanence and Philosophy: Deleuze* (2010). *The Joy of Proust* and *Aesthetics after Metaphysics: From Mimesis to Metaphor* are also forthcoming in 2012.

MANUEL DELANDA is Professor of Philosophy in the Department of Architecture at the University of Pennsylvania. He is the author of *War in the Age of Intelligent Machines* (1991), *A Thousand Years of Non-Linear History* (1997), *A New Philosophy of Society* (2002), *Intensive Science and Virtual Philosophy* (2006), and *Philosophy and Simulation: The Emergence of Synthetic Reason* (2011).

FRANÇOIS DOSSE is a Professor at the University of Paris 12, research associate at the IHTP, and historian. He is the author of works on intellectual history and historiography and of biographies of Paul Ricoeur (1997; 2008), Michel de Certeau (2002), Gilles Deleuze and

ix

Félix Guattari (2007), and Pierre Nora (2011). He has in addition published on the genre of biography itself: *Le pari biographique* (2005).

GARY GENOSKO, Professor of Communication at University of Ontario Institute of Technology, is the author of *Félix Guattari: An Aberrant Introduction* (2002), *The Party without Bosses* (2003), *Félix Guattari: A Critical Introduction* (2009), and editor of *The Guattari Reader* (1996) and *Deleuze and Guattari: Critical Assessments* (2001). He has edited a special issue of *Deleuze Studies* on *Félix Guattari in the Age of Semiocapitalism* (2012).

EUGENE W. HOLLAND, Professor and Chair of Comparative Studies at the Ohio State University, is author of *Baudelaire and Schizo-analysis* (1993), *Deleuze and Guattari's "Anti-Oedipus": Introduction to Schizoanalysis* (1999), and *Nomad Citizenship* (2011).

LEONARD LAWLOR is Edwin Erle Sparks Professor of Philosophy at Penn State University. He is the author of seven books: *Early Twentieth Century Continental Philosophy* (2011), *This is not Sufficient: An Essay on Animality in Derrida* (2007), *The Implications of Immanence: Towards a New Concept of Life* (2006), *Thinking Through French Philosophy: The Being of the Question* (2003), *The Challenge of Bergsonism: Phenomenology, Ontology, Ethics* (2003), *Derrida and Husserl: The Basic Problem of Phenomenology* (2002), and *Imagination and Chance: The Difference between the Thought of Ricoeur and Derrida* (1992). He is one of the co-editors and co-founders of *Chiasmi International: Trilingual Studies Concerning the Thought of Merleau-Ponty*.

BETH LORD is Senior Lecturer in Philosophy at the University of Dundee. She is author of *Kant and Spinozism: Transcendental Idealism and Immanence from Jacobi to Deleuze* (2011) and *Spinoza's Ethics: An Edinburgh Philosophical Guide* (2010), and has recently edited the collection *Spinoza beyond Philosophy* (2012).

DOROTHEA OLKOWSKI is Professor of Philosophy at the University of Colorado, Colorado Springs and Director of the Cognitive Studies Minor. Her publications include *Gilles Deleuze and the Ruin of Representation* (1999) and *The Universal (In the Realm of the Sensible)* (2007). Her most recent books are *Time in Feminist*

Phenomenology (with Christina Schües and Helen Fielding, 2011) and *Postmodern Philosophy and the Scientific Turn* (2012).

PAUL PATTON is Professor of Philosophy at the University of New South Wales in Sydney, Australia. He is the author of *Deleuze and the Political* (2000) and *Deleuzian Concepts: Philosophy, Colonization, Politics* (2010). He is the translator of Deleuze's *Difference and Repetition* (1994) and editor of *Nietzsche, Feminism and Political Theory* (1993) and *Deleuze: A Critical Reader* (1996). He is co-editor of *Political Theory and the Rights of Indigenous Peoples* (with Duncan Ivison and Will Sanders, 2000), *Between Deleuze and Derrida* (with John Protevi, 2003), and *Deleuze and the Postcolonial* (with Simone Bignall, 2010).

JOHN PROTEVI is Phyllis M. Taylor Professor of French Studies and Professor of Philosophy at Louisiana State University. He is the author of *Time and Exteriority* (1994), *Political Physics* (2001), and *Political Affect* (2009). He is editor of the *Edinburgh Dictionary of Continental Philosophy* (2005) and co-editor of *Between Deleuze and Derrida* (with Paul Patton, 2003).

DANIEL W. SMITH, Associate Professor in the Department of Philosophy at Purdue University, is the author of *Essays on Deleuze* (2012) and has published widely on topics in contemporary philosophy. He is the translator of Gilles Deleuze's *Francis Bacon: The Logic of Sensation* (2003) and *Essays Critical and Clinical* (with Michael A. Greco, 1998), as well as Pierre Klossowski's *Nietzsche and the Vicious Circle* (1997) and Isabelle Stenger's *The Invention of Modern Science* (2000).

HENRY SOMERS-HALL is Lecturer in Philosophy at Royal Holloway, University of London. He is the author of *Hegel, Deleuze, and the Critique of Representation* (2012) and the co-translator (with Nick Midgley, Alistair Welchman and Merten Reglitz) of Salomon Maimon's *Essay on Transcendental Philosophy* (2010).

JAMES WILLIAMS, Professor in European Philosophy at the University of Dundee, is the author of *Gilles Deleuze's Philosophy of Time* (2011), *Gilles Deleuze's "Logic of Sense"* (2008), *The Transversal Thought of Gilles Deleuze* (2005), and *Gilles Deleuze's "Difference and Repetition"* (2003).

ABBREVIATIONS

Works by Gilles Deleuze

ABC	Pierre-André Boutang (director), *Gilles Deleuze from A to Z*, 3-DVD set, trans. Charles J. Stivale (New York: Semiotext(e), 2011)
B	*Bergsonism*, trans. Hugh Tomlinson and Barbara Habberjam (New York: Zone Books, 1988)
DI	*Desert Islands and Other Texts 1953–1974*, ed. David Lapoujade, trans. Michael Taormina (Los Angeles: Semiotext(e), 2004)
DR	*Difference and Repetition*, trans. Paul Patton (New York: Columbia University Press, 1994)
ECC	*Essays Critical and Clinical*, trans. Daniel W. Smith and Michael A. Greco (Minneapolis: University of Minnesota Press, 1998)
EPS	*Expressionism in Philosophy: Spinoza*, trans. Martin Joughin (New York: Zone Books, 1990)
ES	*Empiricism and Subjectivity: An Essay on Hume's Theory of Human Nature*, trans. Constantin V. Boundas (New York: Columbia University Press, 1991)
F	*Foucault*, trans. Seán Hand (Minneapolis: University of Minnesota Press, 1988)
FB	*Francis Bacon: The Logic of Sensation*, trans. Daniel W. Smith (New York: Continuum, 2003)
FLB	*The Fold: Leibniz and the Baroque*, trans. Tom Conley (Minneapolis: University of Minnesota Press, 1993)
KCP	*Kant's Critical Philosophy: The Doctrine of the Faculties*, trans. Hugh Tomlinson and Barbara Habberjam (Minneapolis: University of Minnesota Press, 1984)

LS	*The Logic of Sense*, trans. Mark Lester, with Charles Stivale, ed. Constantin V. Boundas (New York: Columbia University Press, 1990)
M	*Masochism: Coldness and Cruelty*, trans. Jean McNeil (New York: Zone Books, 1989)
MI	*Cinema 1: The Movement Image*, trans. Hugh Tomlinson and Barbara Habberjam (Minneapolis: University of Minnesota Press, 1986)
NP	*Nietzsche and Philosophy*, trans. Hugh Tomlinson (London: Athlone, 1983)
PI	*Pure Immanence: Essays on a Life*, trans. Anne Boyman (New York: Zone Books, 2001)
PS	*Proust and Signs: The Complete Text*, trans. Richard Howard (London: Athlone, 2000)
SPP	*Spinoza: Practical Philosophy*, trans. Robert Hurley (San Francisco: City Lights Books, 1988)
TI	*Cinema 2: The Time-Image*, trans. Hugh Tomlinson and Robert Galeta (Minneapolis: University of Minnesota Press, 1989)
TRM	*Two Regimes of Madness: Texts and Interviews 1975–1995*, ed. David Lapoujade, trans. Ames Hodges and Mike Taormina (Los Angeles: Semiotext(e), 2007)

Works by Gilles Deleuze and Félix Guattari

AO	*Anti-Oedipus: Capitalism and Schizophrenia* I, trans. Robert Hurley, Mark Seem and Helen R. Lane (Minneapolis: University of Minnesota Press, 1977)
ATP	*A Thousand Plateaus: Capitalism and Schizophrenia* II, trans. Brian Massumi (Minneapolis: University of Minnesota Press, 1987)
K	*Kafka: Toward a Minor Literature*, trans. Dana Polan (Minneapolis: University of Minnesota Press, 1986)
WP	*What is Philosophy?*, trans. Hugh Tomlinson and Graham Burchell (New York: Columbia University Press, 1994)

Works by Gilles Deleuze and Claire Parnet

D	*Dialogues* II, trans. Hugh Tomlinson and Barbara Habberjam (London: Continuum, 2002)
N	*Negotiations*, trans. Martin Joughin (New York: Columbia University Press, 1995)

Introduction

Gilles Deleuze belongs to that group of philosophers, often taken to typify the continental approach to philosophy, for whom the difficulty we encounter in reading them is not simply one of the content of their claims and arguments, but also one of penetrating their style of writing itself. This difficulty is exacerbated by the fact that Deleuze not only seemingly employs language in order to destabilize and obfuscate his philosophical arguments, but also revises his basic philosophical terminology between his numerous writings, from the early work of intensive depth, virtuality, and pre-individual singularities, to the body without organs, machinic phylum, and plane of immanence of his collaborations with Guattari.[1] This leads us to the problem of how we read Deleuze. Do we see the obfuscation of language, the various appropriations of the sciences, and the experiments in philosophical writing as attempts to cover over a paucity of argumentation? Do we take up this rejection of traditional metaphysical language, seeing it as a rejection of the tradition of metaphysics itself, or do we strip the language away in the hope of finding underneath it a philosophical position that can be distinctly expressed in another, more palatable language? Similarly, we might ask what the reason is for the proliferation of philosophical systems developed by Deleuze, both in his historical monographs and his own philosophical writings. The continual reinvention of basic philosophical concepts might be taken to signal a failure of Deleuze's philosophical enterprise, an inability to formulate a definitive yet consistent philosophical outlook. Finally, Deleuze presents us with the problem of understanding the relation of these various projects. Deleuze's engagements with the history of philosophy, science, aesthetics, and ethics seem reminiscent of the

I

kind of grand systematic project of the nineteenth century exemplified by the works of Hegel. In spite of this similarity, there is a repetition of themes, and a recommencement of philosophical projects that is more akin to what we find in Schelling or Nietzsche. While *Difference and Repetition* and the *Logic of Sense*, for instance, were written at much the same time, they provide very different approaches to the questions of ontology and metaphysics. Key structures from Deleuze's early work, such as the simulacrum, disappear once he begins collaborating with Guattari, yet in his last, sole-authored project (*Immanence: A Life*), the early logic of multiplicities, together with the concepts of the virtual and the transcendental field, once again emerges.[2]

It is perhaps because of these difficulties that there are as yet so few attempts to provide a consistent general reading of Deleuze's whole *opus*.[3] Rather than deal with questions of Deleuze's specific engagements, which are masterfully explicated by the contributors to this volume, I want to focus in this Introduction simply on the question of how we approach reading, interpreting, and engaging with Deleuze's philosophy, and how we are to reconcile his approach with the seemingly antithetical aims we might attribute to our standard conception of the philosophical endeavor.

Deleuze's relationship to prior metaphysics is complex. While he wrote numerous monographs on figures from the history of philosophy, frequently analyses presented in these historical monographs reappear within Deleuze's own metaphysical systems. Thus, Deleuze's reading of Hume on habit in *Difference and Repetition* opens out onto a vitalist conception of nature that moves far beyond the psychological considerations of Hume himself. His reading of Spinoza's relations of speeds and slowness reappears in *What is Philosophy?* as the chaos that science, art, and philosophy are all preoccupied with. Deleuze is not so much interested in these cases in providing a historical analysis as in resurrecting the conceptual developments of his predecessors to bring them to bear on his own philosophical concerns. Deleuze makes this clear in perhaps his most famous, and most misunderstood, pronouncement on his relation to the tradition:

I imagined myself getting onto the back of an author, and giving him a child, which would be his and which would at the same time be a monster.

It is very important that it should be his child, because the author actually had to say everything that I made him say. But it also had to be a monster because it was necessary to go through all kinds of decenterings, slips, break-ins, secret emissions. (*N* 6)

In fact, Deleuze's borrowings from his predecessors make clear that what interests him in the philosophical systems of the past is not so much the systems themselves, but the concepts that each philosopher brings together to formulate their system. From his early years, Deleuze saw philosophical concepts as literary characters, having their own autonomy and style, and this preoccupation is reaffirmed in his last work with Guattari, *What is Philosophy?*, where they make the claim that "the philosopher is an expert in concepts and the lack of them. He knows which of them are not viable, which are arbitrary or inconsistent, which ones do not hold up for an instant" (*WP* 3). While the philosopher's expertise may extend to concepts more generally, the activity of philosophy itself is, however, something more specific. The activity of philosophy is, at root, the "creation of concepts" (*WP* 5). This characterization of the philosophical endeavor immediately raises three questions that I want to address in this Introduction. First, what does it mean to *create* rather than discover concepts? Second, how do we relate these concepts together? And finally, what does philosophy achieve through the creation of concepts? It is by answering these questions that we can provide at least a rough answer to some of the questions with which we began.

In *What is Philosophy?*, Deleuze and Guattari make the following provocative claim: "Plato said that Ideas must be contemplated, but first of all he had to create the concept of Idea" (*WP* 6). The assertion that Plato's philosophy is fundamentally creative appears radically at odds with Socrates' frequent claims, most notably in the *Meno* and *Phaedo*, that knowledge is attained through the reminiscence of our perception of real things prior to the soul inhabiting the body. Similarly, Descartes, in his *Rules for the Direction of the Mind*, does not understand the philosophical project as one involving innovation, but rather "entirely in the ordering and arranging of the objects on which we must concentrate our mind's eye if we are to discover some truth."[4] In both these cases, we do not appear to have a project of creation, but rather one of the reminiscence, recognition, or discovery of something that pre-exists our enquiry. Even a philosophical project such as Kant's, that gives a constitutive role to thought, still centers on the discovery of pre-existing rules of constitution. Understanding this claim is essential, both with respect to understanding Deleuze's engagement with the philosophical tradition, and with respect to his relationship to his own project.

Relating this claim to the philosophical tradition lets us know that for Deleuze, philosophical systems cannot simply be this relation to a pre-existing field of potential objects of knowledge: philosophy is not a science of discovery. We can understand this claim in the light of Deleuze's reading of Feuerbach, whose *Towards a Critique of the Philosophy of Hegel* was translated into French by Deleuze's friend Louis Althusser.[5] In this essay, Feuerbach makes the claim that the history of philosophy, including the grand systems of the eighteenth and nineteenth centuries, has been subject to a form of paralogism similar to the one Kant discovered in the philosophy of Descartes, but far more wide ranging.[6] As Feuerbach noted, the communication of philosophical concepts is not seen by philosophers to occur through some kind of affective relation (the philosopher "does not instil his thoughts into me like drops of medicine"),[7] but rather it relies on the listener actively taking up these ideas with his own intellect. Philosophical communication therefore relies on an abstraction from my own experience to that which is shared by every intellect (what Deleuze calls the "everybody knows" [DR 130]). Philosophy on this reading does not therefore concern itself with the active process of thinking itself, but rather with an image or representation of thought which can be recognized by and communicated to others. Furthermore, the concepts that it operates with are not concepts meant to capture the world, but rather those ready-made concepts that the intellect expects to find mirrored in others. Rather than exploring the metaphysical structure of the world, therefore, philosophy has instead produced a paralogistic image of a shared common sense. It is for this reason that it appears to be the case that we are remembering, discovering, or recognizing some objective state of affairs, while in fact we are merely mapping the structure of reason itself. Deleuze's response to this situation is twofold.[8] If we are to escape from this kind of paralogism, then first it is necessary to break with the image of thought. In order to do so, Deleuze introduces a certain obscurity into his language – a stuttering, or in his own words, a deterritorialization of language that prevents the kind of reliance on ready-made categories of thought that inhibits true philosophical engagement. It is this aspect of Deleuze's project that leads to the obscurity we find in much of his prose. This explains, further, his interest in writers of paradox such as Lewis Carroll. In this respect, Deleuze makes explicit affinities with the actor, dramatist, and poet, Antonin Artaud,[9] who also produces "defective" writing in order to forestall the kind of reflective enquiry Feuerbach is critical of:

This diffusion in my poems, these defective forms, this constant falling off of my ideas, must not be set down to lack of practice or control of the instrument I was manipulating, of *intellectual development*. Rather to a focal collapse of my soul, a kind of essential and fugitive erosion in thought, to a transitory non-possession of physical gain to my development, to the abnormal separation of elements of thought (the impulse to think at every stratifying endpoint of thought, by way of every condition, through all the branching in thought and form).[10]

If philosophy is not simply to fall into either sophistry or skepticism, it cannot simply remain at the level of stuttering, but instead needs to make this stuttering the foundation of a new method. It needs to think that which is outside of the intellect and reflect on that which has not been given to it ready-made. The notion that concepts are created is therefore intimately connected with the notion that philosophy begins with an encounter with that which is outside of it, whether this is "Socrates, a temple or a demon" (*DR* 139). In this sense, we can say that while there is a definite discipline of philosophy (the discipline of creating concepts), this discipline can only operate by reaching beyond itself, in encounter with that which is not philosophy. Deleuze's own work is exemplary in this respect, with its engagements with cinema, the arts, the sciences, and those aspects of philosophy itself that remain to be encountered (or re-encountered) beneath the sedimented structure of the image of thought: "each distinct discipline is, in its own way, in relation with a negative: even science has a relation with a nonscience that echoes its effects ... The plane of philosophy is prephilosophical insofar as we consider it in itself independently of the concepts that come to occupy it, but nonphilosophy is found where the plane confronts chaos" (*WP* 217–18).

This leads us on to the second question. What is the relationship between concepts, and what is it that makes the creation of concepts more than an arbitrary fancy? Throughout his career, Deleuze makes clear that he is not opposed to systematic philosophy, but only to a certain characterization of system: "In any case, the death of metaphysics or the overcoming of philosophy has never been a problem for us; it is just tiresome, idle chatter" (*WP* 9). The question is how to characterize the notion of system itself, therefore. Traditionally, systematic thought has relied upon building up a complete, or totalized, explanation of the world from a more basic set of principles, whether clear and distinct ideas or constitutive rules. Deleuze and Guattari's claim that philosophical concepts are "fragmentary wholes" opens up the possibility of an alternative conception of system. The concept's status as separable from its context is at best ambiguous on their reading. It is nonetheless the case that together they produce "a powerful Whole that, while remaining open, is not fragmented: an unlimited One-All, an 'Omnitudio' that includes all concepts on one and the same plane" (*WP* 35). A philosophical system is therefore a plane on which a collection of philosophical concepts can coherently coexist: a plane of consistency, or plane of immanence. This notion of a whole that is nonetheless open is central to Deleuze's conception of the philosophical project.[11] Deleuze presents this account in *What is Philosophy?* by noting that the plane of immanence is "a section of chaos" (*WP* 42); that which is outside of our conceptual schemata, and which escapes all rational consistency. We can make sense of this relationship between the plane of immanence (philosophical system) and the world by looking at an analogy Deleuze introduces in *Difference and Repetition*. Talking about Ideas, Deleuze claims that each Idea is like a conic section (*DR* 187). If we take a three-dimensional cone and cut it along a two-dimensional plane, then depending on the angle of the plane to the cone, we will obtain a different curve. If we take a section that is parallel to the cone, we will have a circle. Cutting the cone at a more skewed angle will give us an ellipse, then a parabola, and finally a hyperbola. Each of these planes is whole, in that it contains a whole curve, but yet it is not complete, as it is only a section of the cone. Likewise, the singular points of each curve (where the curve meets infinity, where the gradient of the curve = o) differ, but nonetheless all derive from the structure of the cone itself. Different philosophical systems are in the same manner object-ive presentations of the world that nonetheless are incommen-surate with one another, each presenting a perspective on chaos while leaving open the possibility of other perspectives. There is, for Deleuze, no possibility of a system that would reconcile all of these different planes in a grand Hegelian synthesis. Rather, each of the key concepts of Deleuze's predecessors, Nietzsche's will to power, Spinoza's substance, Scotus' intensive difference, selects and extracts a different plane or constellation of singular points from chaos. The relative merit of these philosophers is not governed by the number of true statements they make, but rather the adequacy of their selection of singularities. Even in the cases of Plato, Descartes, and Kant, there is a selection of singularities, albeit one which, unthematized, threatens to simply reiterate the structures of common sense.

If we return to Deleuze and Guattari's claim that Plato's Ideas must be created before they can be contemplated, we can now see why Deleuze appears to constantly recommence the philosophical endeavor from different perspectives. Given Deleuze's claim that project of *Difference and Repetition* is an inversion of Platonism,[12] Deleuze and Guattari's later claim can be read as a reflection on Deleuze's own philosophical development as much as on Plato's. The change in terminology between Deleuze's texts is not a super-ficial aspect of his writing, but signifies the attempt to develop new planes of immanence. None of these projects can be anything but provisional, as they open out onto that which cannot be con-sistently given all at once. This brings us to the last of our three questions about the nature of philosophy for Deleuze: what is the purpose of philosophy as the creation of concepts? Traditionally, the aim of metaphysics has been knowledge, and even Hegel, who emphasizes the need to understand the development of thinking, still prioritizes the endpoint of this development: absolute know-ing. If the best we can do is develop a plurality of wholes that are nonetheless still open, a fixed and final system of knowledge is not an attainable objective. In this context, Deleuze opposes know-ledge to learning. What is important is our success in formulating a plane of consistent concepts in the light of our own particular set of problems. These problems are themselves brought to light by the specific encounter that opens us up to thinking. In this respect, Deleuze comes close to Heidegger's insistence on the repetition of the question of the meaning of Being. For Deleuze, however, even the question itself changes, as this too arises from the particularity of the encounter. "Great authors of our time (Heidegger, Blanchot) have exploited this most profound relation between the question and repetition. Not that it is sufficient, however, to repeat a single question which would remain intact at the end, even if this question is 'What is being?' [Qu'en est-il de l'être?]" (DR 200). Ultimately, therefore, what is central to philosophy for Deleuze is a process of engagement with that which is outside of philosophy; a process that does not aim at a final result and end to the endeavor, but rather a continuous effort to safeguard our openness to the encounter capable of engendering thinking itself.

In explicating the key themes in *Difference and Repetition*, in his chapter James Williams notes the sheer number of references to other authors by Deleuze. While following Sauvagnargues in emphasizing the roots of Deleuze's transcendental empiricism in Kant's philosophy, he observes that even a "successful" interpretation of Deleuze's philosophy will occlude aspects of it while revealing others, depending on the reference points chosen. The essays in this collection provide a series of interpretations, each emphasizing a different theme of Deleuze's work, with the aim as a whole of providing a rich portrait of the range and sophistication of Deleuze's thinking.

Many explore Deleuze's complex relationships with his philosophical predecessors. Daniel W. Smith charts out the somewhat repressive role that the history of philosophy played in the formation Deleuze received in the French university system, and analyzes the way in which he developed a use of the history of philosophy that was neither historical nor eternal but "untimely," and which found its first expression in *Difference and Repetition* and its theoretical elaboration in *What is Philosophy?* Beth Lord and Dorothea Olkowski both provide accounts of Deleuze's ambivalent relationship to Kant. Lord shows that while indebted to Kant for a number of key insights (the rejection of rational theology, the paralogisms that "fracture" the "I," and the plane of immanence), Deleuze sees Kant as betraying these insights by ultimately reinstating God and the subject, and distorting the plane of immanence. She argues cogently for reading Deleuze as following Salomon Maimon in developing a genetic transcendental philosophy. Olkowski approaches Kant from the perspective of his aesthetics, noting the resonances between Kant's *Critique of Judgment* and Deleuze's own work on aesthetics, and showing how Deleuze's incorporation of insights from modern mathematics allows him to broaden the concept of aesthetics itself. Leonard Lawlor also takes up the theme of transcendental philosophy, but this time the transcendental philosophy of Husserl. Arguing that Husserl fails to provide a properly generative account of sense, Lawlor explores one of the most profound aspects of Deleuze's *Logic of Sense*: the reworking of the notion of a transcendental field to purge it of the form of consciousness. Miguel de Beistegui traces a different philosophical trajectory, showing how Deleuze's call to overturn Platonism leads not to a rejection of metaphysics, but rather to a series of creative readings of the non-Platonic aspects of the history of philosophy. His analyses of Lucretius and the Stoics render accessible an important but much neglected moment in Deleuze's reconstruction of the history of philosophy. Finally, Henry Somers-Hall explores Deleuze's relationship to his successor, Alain Badiou, arguing that both philosophers can be understood as attempting to continue the project of metaphysics after Heidegger's critique of metaphysics as onto-theology. For Deleuze and Badiou, what is needed is a new logic, but the question is whether this is to be a logic of the multiplicity or of the multiple.

Deleuze's references to other thinkers extend beyond philosophy itself, and several of the chapters explore Deleuze's engagements and appropriations in other fields. Manuel DeLanda and John Protevi both investigate Deleuze's complex appropriations of and interventions into science and mathematics. DeLanda explores Deleuze's attempts to replace an essentially Aristotelian model of species and genus (and its logical counterpart) with something more appropriate for capturing the dynamics of complex physical systems. In the process, he argues that Deleuze's account of the metaphysical commitments of such mathematical models resolves many of the current difficulties in Anglo-American attempts to understand different modalities (such as possibility). John Protevi's chapter looks at Deleuze's account of life, providing incisive readings of some of the more impenetrable discussions of organic life in *Difference and Repetition*, and giving lucid accounts of several of the key terms developed by Deleuze in his later collaborations with Guattari. Ronald Bogue explores Deleuze's emphatically philosophical engagements with literature throughout his career, tracing the development of Deleuze's thought through all of his major engagements with literature, from his early work on Proust to his later work with Guattari on Kafka, and showing why, despite the often indiscernible nature of the distinction between Deleuze's affective prose and literature, Deleuze still holds fast to such a distinction. Eugene W. Holland lays out Deleuze and Guattari's engagements with psychoanalysis, presenting their relationship to Freud and the often ignored influence of Jung, before presenting their own positive account of schizoanalysis. Paul Patton and Rosi Braidotti both explore the normative dimensions of Deleuze's thought. In Patton's account of Deleuze's politics, we find an advocation of micropolitics as an attempt to transform the institutions of democracy by enlarging the character of the majority. Braidotti draws out a nomadic ethics from Deleuze's neo-Spinozist ontology that emphasizes complexity, affirmation, and a reconception of the self as an assemblage of intensive forces.

Finally, Deleuze's collaborations with Guattari are discussed throughout the volume, but two pieces thematize this topic in particular. François Dosse's essay addresses Deleuze's relationship to structuralism, from his early quasi-structuralist sole-authored writings to his rejection and critique of it under the influence of Guattari. Tracing this history foregrounds the importance of Guattari for Deleuze's own development. Finally, Gary Genosko's chapter deals explicitly with Deleuze's work with Guattari, drawing on and explicating their attempt to replace a logic of predication ("x is p") with a logic of conjunction ("and ... and ... and").

NOTES

1   See the appendix to Manuel DeLanda, *Intensive Science and Virtual Philosophy* (New York: Continuum, 2002) for an attempt to correlate the terminology employed between Deleuze's work and his collaborations with Guattari.

2   See Gary Genosko's contribution to this volume for an account of Guattari's place in the work of Deleuze and Guattari. François Dosse's contribution shows how Deleuze's conceptual apparatus develops in response to his realization (once again, with the aid of Guattari) of the limitations of the structuralist paradigm.

3   There are very few detailed attempts to develop a consistent view of Deleuze's whole philosophy. Many, such as Alain Badiou, *Deleuze: The Clamor of Being* trans. Louise Burchill (Minneapolis: University of Minnesota Press, 2000) and Slavoj Žižek, *Organs without Bodies: Deleuze and Consequences* (London: Routledge, 2004), develop complete accounts of Deleuze's system only at the expense of ignoring Deleuze's later work with Guattari. Peter Hallward, *Out of This World: Deleuze and the Philosophy of Creation* (London: Verso, 2000) does provide a coherent reading of Deleuze's work as a whole, but at the price of introducing several fundamental flaws into the reading (see, for instance, Henry Somers-Hall, "The Politics of Creation: Peter Hallward's *Deleuze and the Philosophy of Creation*," *Pli*, 18 [2007], 221–36, and Gregory J. Seigworth, "Little Affect: Hallward's *Deleuze*," *Culture Machine* [2007], www.culturemachine.net/index.php/cm/article/view/166/147, site accessed July 6, 2012).

4   René Descartes, "Rules for the Direction of the Mind," in John Cottingham, Robert Stoothoff, and Dugald Murdoch (eds.), *Philosophical Writings of Descartes*, vol. 1 (Cambridge University Press, 1985), Rule 5.

5   See Dosse's contribution to this collection for an account of Deleuze's friendship with Althusser. As Deleuze notes in *Difference and Repetition*, "Feuerbach is among those who have pursued farthest the problem of where to begin" (*DR* 319).

6   A paralogism to the extent that the communication of philosophical ideas requires them to be expressed under the determinations of time.

7   Ludwig Feuerbach, "Towards a Critique of Hegelian Philosophy," in Lawrence S. Stepelevich (ed.), *The Young Hegelians: An Anthology* (Cambridge University Press, 1983), p. 105.

8   "Do not count upon thought to ensure the relative necessity of what it thinks. Rather, count upon the contingency of an encounter with that which forces thought to raise up and educate the absolute necessity of an act of thought or a passion to think. The conditions of a true critique and a true creation are the same: the destruction of an image of thought which presupposes itself and the genesis of the act of thinking in thought itself" (*DR* 139).

9   Deleuze's engagement with Artaud is principally to be found in *LS* and chapter 3 of *DR*, although he refers to him throughout his works.

10   Antonin Artaud, "Correspondence with Jacques Rivière," in Victor Corti (ed.), *Collected Works of Antonin Artaud*, vol. 1 (London: John Calder, 1968), pp. 25–48, at 30–31.

11   This notion of an open whole draws together the theme of encounter we find in Deleuze's early philosophy, and the concept of a rhizome Deleuze takes to exemplify the philosophical system in his later work.

12   "The task of modern philosophy has been defined: to overturn Platonism" (*DR* 59–64).

1 Deleuze and the history of philosophy

Deleuze began his philosophical career writing studies of various classic figures in the history of philosophy. His first book, published in 1953, was a study of Hume, and it was followed by a series of monographs on Nietzsche (1962), Kant (1963), Bergson (1966), and Spinoza (1968), which Deleuze continued in the 1980s, when he wrote his studies of Foucault (1986) and Leibniz (1988). In the intervening years he wrote his magnum opus, *Difference and Repetition* (1968), as well as his two-volume work of political philosophy, *Capitalism and Schizophrenia* (1972, 1980), co-authored with Félix Guattari. But what is the relation between these two sets of writings – one in the history of philosophy and the other in philosophy proper? Deleuze said that he considered *Difference and Repetition* to be a work in metaphysics. "I feel myself to be a pure metaphysician," he once claimed. "Bergson says that modern science hasn't found its metaphysics, the metaphysics it would need. It is this metaphysics that interests me."[1] Yet the history of philosophy seems to be littered with the detritus of outdated metaphysical systems, including some of the very systems that Deleuze analyzed in his historical monographs. "If we consider any scheme of philosophic categories as one complex assertion," Whitehead once wrote, "and apply to it the logician's alternative, true or false, the answer must be that the scheme is false."[2] Deleuze seems to have agreed with Bergson and Whitehead that metaphysics provides a schema of concepts adequate to both experience and science, and he attributed a complete positivity to "the power of the false" found in such systems. But what role did Deleuze's work in the history of philosophy play in the development of his heterogenetic and differential metaphysical system?[3]

THE HISTORY OF PHILOSOPHY IN THE
FRENCH UNIVERSITY

Deleuze's relation to the history of philosophy must be contextualized, in the first place, in terms of the French academic milieu in which Deleuze was trained as a philosopher.[4] Stephen Toulmin once quipped that the French do not "do" philosophy, but rather do the history of philosophy – a deliberately humorous exaggeration that nonetheless reflects an institutional reality. In order to pass the *agrégation* examination, which licensed students to teach in secondary schools, French philosophy students were required, primarily, to "do" close readings of classic texts in the history of philosophy, from Plato and Aristotle to Descartes and Kant and beyond, though the texts and names changed every year.[5] The history of philosophy was, in this sense, something imposed upon Deleuze, while a student at the Sorbonne, as a form of institutional reproduction, whose aim is always to perpetuate the institution through the reproduction of compliant young people. As such, it had an obvious negative function, against which the young Deleuze reacted strongly. "I belong to a generation," he would later write, "that was more or less bludgeoned to death by the history of philosophy. The history of philosophy exercises an obvious repressive function in philosophy: 'You dare not speak in your own name until you've read this and that, and that on this, and this on that.' Many members of my generation never broke free of this" (*N* 5). At its worst, the result was a form of philosophical thinking that devolved into a kind of scholasticism of texts: endless commentary and interpretation, one-upmanship with regard to knowledge of passages, the writing of perfectly conceived *mémoires*.

In other texts, Deleuze has evoked the specific effects this emphasis on the history of philosophy had on his own philosophical formation:

I was taught by two professors, whom I liked and admired a lot: Alquié and Hyppolite .... The former had long white hands and a stammer which might have been a legacy of his childhood, or there to hide a native accent, and which was harnessed to the service of Cartesian dualisms. The latter had a powerful face with unfinished features, and rhythmically beat out Hegelian triads with his fist, hanging his words on the beats. At the Liberation, we were still strangely stuck in the history of philosophy. We simply plunged into Hegel, Husserl and Heidegger; we threw ourselves like puppies into a scholasticism worse than that of the Middle Ages … After the Liberation, the history of philosophy tightened around us – without our realizing it – under the pretext of opening up a future of thought, which would also be the most ancient thought. The "Heidegger question" did not seem to me to be "Is he a bit of a Nazi?" (obviously, obviously) but "What was his role in this new injection of the history of philosophy?" … The history of philosophy has always been the agent of power in philosophy, and even in thought. It has played the role of a repressor: how can you think without having read Plato, Descartes, Kant, and Heidegger, and so-and-so's book about them? A formidable school of intimidation … So I began with the history of philosophy when it was still being prescribed. For my part, I could not see any way of extracting myself. I could not stand Descartes, the dualisms and the cogito, or Hegel, the triad and the operation of negation. (*D* 12–14)

One can discern in this passage several "reactions" on Deleuze's part. There is a reaction against Cartesian dualisms and Hegelian triads, which is as much a personal reaction against his teachers (Ferdinand Alquié and Jean Hyppolite) as a philosophical reaction. There is also a reaction against Heidegger, less because of his Nazism than his role with regard to this "injection" of the history of philosophy into the curriculum. Heidegger tended to read past philosophers as if they were his contemporaries (and not simply as moments in an ongoing dialectic, as did Hegel), and Deleuze certainly did the same. Yet he never shared Heidegger's (or even Nietzsche's) obsession with the Greeks and the Presocratics. His avowed preference for the Stoics and Lucretius was no doubt a reaction against this Hellenophilia, and he himself tended to prefer seventeenth-century philosophers, notably Spinoza and Leibniz. Heidegger famously wrote little on Spinoza, which would seem to be a surprising omission, since the *Ethics* is a work of pure ontology that poses the problem of ontological difference in terms of the difference between infinite substance (Being) and finite modes (beings). From this viewpoint, Deleuze's work on Spinoza can be read as his means of working through Heidegger's problematic of ontological difference in a new manner, just as *Difference and Repetition* could be read as a response to *Being and Time* (for Deleuze, Being is difference, and time is repetition). Where Heidegger returned to the Presocratics (the origin), Deleuze turned to Spinoza (the middle).

Finally, there is also a reaction against what he calls the "scholasticism" of "the three H's" – Hegel, Husserl, and Heidegger – which was prevalent after the Liberation. Many French philosophers – such as Levinas, Ricoeur, Derrida, and Lyotard – began their careers with books on Husserl. Significantly, Deleuze never wrote directly on any of "the three H's," though he was obviously immersed in their work, and instead wrote his first book on Hume (*Empiricism and Subjectivity*, which was published in 1953), as if he wanted to add a fourth "H" of his own to the list. In fact, the decision to write on Hume as a student is a good example of the generally heterodox tendencies of the young Deleuze. Vincent Descombes, in his 1980 analysis of *Modern French Philosophy*, characterized the entire generation of philosophers to which Deleuze belongs – which includes Jacques Derrida, Michel Foucault, Jean-François Lyotard, and Michel Serres – by their reaction against Hegel, and in particular against Alexandre Kojève's reading of Hegel.[6] Foucault had already noted in his 1970 inaugural lecture at the Collège de France: "Whether through logic or epistemology, whether through Marx or Nietzsche, our entire epoch is struggling to disengage itself from Hegel."[7] Deleuze's early work on Hume was an instance of what he himself would later call a "generalized anti-Hegelianism" (*DR* ix). English philosophy, led by Bertrand Russell, had already gone through its own reaction against Hegel (at least as represented by Bradley) a full half-century earlier than did the French, but for quite specific reasons (*NP* ix). Drawing on the recent developments in logic stemming from the work of Frege and Peano, Russell developed the empiricist theme that relations are external to their terms, which became one of the standard criticisms laid against Hegel (for whom, like Leibniz, relations are internal to their terms). In France, this aspect of Anglo-American philosophy had been taken up by Jean Wahl, whom Deleuze would often cite, in his later writings, with regard to the priority Wahl gave to the conjunction "and" over the copula "is."[8] Throughout his career, Deleuze remained a great admirer of Russell, and was strongly antagonistic to the effects Wittgenstein's work had had on Anglo-American philosophy (*ABC W*). Writing on Hume, and declaring himself to be an empiricist in the British mold, in other words, was already a direct anti-Hegelian provocation. For Hegel, empiricism itself was almost a non-philosophy, because it tried to grasp "this," "that," "here," and "now" in an immediate manner, whereas such indexical are universals that can never grasp sensible experience in an unmediated way.[9] Deleuze dedicated his Hume book to his teacher Jean Hyppolite – "a sincere and respectful homage," reads the dedication – and the provocation could hardly have been clearer: the twenty-six-year-old student "respectfully" presenting to his Hegelian teacher a thesis on the greatness of empiricism.

Nonetheless, it could be argued that *Empiricism and Subjectivity* occupies a somewhat marginal position within Deleuze's corpus: Deleuze would eventually turn Hume's empiricism into what he would later come to call a "transcendental empiricism." This change was effected in the years between the publication of *Empiricism and Subjectivity* in 1953 and the appearance of *Nietzsche and Philosophy* in 1962, in which Deleuze's reaction against Hegel appears at its most intense. Deleuze has called this an "eight-year hole" in his life (1953–61), during which he published very little. "I know what I was doing, where and how I lived during those years," he would later say, "but I know it almost abstractly, rather as if someone else were relating memories that I believe in but don't really have ... That's what I find interesting in people's lives, the holes, the gaps, sometimes dramatic, but sometimes not dramatic at all. There are catalepsies, or a kind of sleepwalking through a number of years, in most lives. Maybe it's in these holes that movement takes place" (*N* 138). Externally, during these eight years, Deleuze married and had his first child, and moved through a series of temporary academic posts, from the lycée in Orleans to the Sorbonne and CNRS in Paris. But a profound "intensive" movement of thought took place as well: Deleuze emerged pursuing a singular philosophical trajectory that would be worked out in a series of monographs on individual figures – Nietzsche (1962), Kant (1963), Proust (1964), Bergson (1966), Masoch (1967), and Spinoza (1968) – and that would culminate in *Difference and Repetition*, which was the first book in which Deleuze spoke in his own name. "After I studied Hume, Spinoza, Nietzsche, and Proust, all of whom fired me with enthusiasm, *Difference and Repetition* was the first book in which I tried to 'do' philosophy" (*DR* xv), having finally extracted himself from the history of philosophy. In this sense, Deleuze's early monographs in the history of philosophy can be seen, as Michael Hardt has argued, as a long period of "apprenticeship" to philosophy.[10]

THE LINE OF FLIGHT

Deleuze's situation as a student in the 1940s, however, was no different from that of any student anywhere. Students in Anglo-American philosophy find themselves faced with a similar "school of intimidation," oriented less around historicism than a certain logicism and naturalism. As Michel Serres says, "freedom of thought always has to be reinvented. Unfortunately, thought is usually only found constrained and forced in a context rigid with impossibilities."[11] To be sure, Deleuze's training in the history of philosophy stood him in good stead, since he thought naturally in terms of that history, and in his seminars he would return to and reread many of the same classic texts he had studied at university. As a result, readers of Deleuze's works are often faced with the opposite challenge: constructing for themselves a familiarity with the history of philosophy that Deleuze could take for granted. But the question remains: how did Deleuze manage to escape this conformity and institutional reproduction, and make use of the history of philosophy in pursuit of his own creative project? "We have to see creation as tracing a path between impossibilities," Deleuze would later write. "A creator who is not grabbed around the throat by a set of impossibilities is not a creator ... Without a set of impossibilities, you won't have a line of flight, the exit that is creation, the power of falsity that is truth" (N 133). Students who managed to break free of the history of philosophy did so, Deleuze suggests, "by inventing their own particular methods and new rules, a new approach" (N 5–6). If they wanted to do "creative" work in this institutional context, philosophy students necessarily had to devise inventive readings that adhered to the institutional requirements, but moved in new directions. François Châtelet, a fellow student at the Sorbonne and later a colleague at Vincennes, recounts a story that illustrates the manner in which Deleuze, as a student, was already negotiating this tension between the university's requirements and his own interpretive invention:

I cherish the memory of a reading by Gilles Deleuze, who had to treat I don't know what classic theme of Nicholas Malebranche's doctrine before one of our most profound and most meticulous historians of philosophy, and had constructed his demonstration, solid and supported with peremptory references, around the sole principle of the irreducibility of Adam's rib. At the expression of this adopted principle, the master turned pale, and obviously had to keep himself from intervening. As the exposition unfolded, the indignation was changed into incredulity, and then, by the end, into admiring surprise. And he justly concluded by making us all return the next week with our own analysis of the same theme.[12]

The novelist Michel Tournier, another fellow student, similarly recounted that, while at the Sorbonne, Deleuze already "possessed extraordinary powers of translation and rearrangement: all the tired philosophy of the curriculum passed through him and emerged unrecognizable but rejuvenated, with an air of freshness, undigestedness, and raw newness, utterly startling and discomfiting our weakness and laziness."[13]

It is not by chance, therefore, that the works of Deleuze and Jacques Derrida, for example, are frequently indexed on creative readings in the history of philosophy. (Both thinkers persistently return to the history of philosophy, even after "experiments" such as Derrida's *The Post Card* or Deleuze and Guattari's *A Thousand Plateaus*.) "Deconstruction" can be seen as the new approach that Derrida developed to escape from these institutional constraints, while nonetheless remaining within their parameters – an approach Deleuze appreciated, even though he himself moved in a different direction. "As for the method of deconstruction of texts," he once remarked, "I see clearly what it is, I admire it a lot, but it has nothing to do with my own method. I do not present myself as a commentator on texts. For me, a text is merely a small cog in an extra-textual practice. It is not a question of commentating on the text by a method of deconstruction, or by a method of textual practice, or by other methods; it is a question of seeing what use it has in the extra-textual practice that prolongs the text."[14] Instead of asking of a text, "What does it mean?," Deleuze asked, "How does it work" (Where does it take you? What comes through, and what doesn't?) (N 7–8). Indeed, Deleuze's explanation of his own means of escape is one of the most cited texts in his corpus:

I suppose the main way I coped with it at the time was to see the history of philosophy as a sort of buggery or (it comes to the same thing) as an immaculate conception. I saw myself as taking an author from behind and giving him a child that would be his own offspring, yet monstrous. It was really important for it to be his own child, because the author had to actually say all I had him saying. But the child was bound to be monstrous too, because it resulted from all sorts of shifting, slipping, dislocations, and hidden emissions that I really enjoyed. (*N* 6)

This image of philosophical "buggery," while provocative and easily misused, nonetheless has a precise sense. As had often been noted, when reading Deleuze's monographs – whether on Nietzsche, Spinoza, Leibniz, Kant, or Bergson – one has the distinct impression of entering a "zone" in which Deleuze's own project and that of the author at hand seem to become indiscernible. They constitute what Deleuze himself calls a "zone of indiscernibility": on the one hand, there is a becoming-Deleuze of the thinker at hand, as it were; and on the other hand, there is a kind of becoming-Spinoza on Deleuze's part, for instance, or a becoming-Leibniz, a becoming-Bergson, and so on. This is what Bakhtin called a "free indirect style" of writing, which "testifies to a system which is always heterogeneous, far from equilibrium" (*MI* 73).

This by now familiar style, however, makes for some acute difficulties of interpretation: where does Deleuze end and, say, Spinoza begin? Where does an explication become an interpretation, and an interpretation, a creation (to use hermeneutical terms which Deleuze avoided)? These are not easy questions; such distinctions are, as Deleuze says, indiscernible. Put crudely: in all Deleuze's readings, one moves from a fairly straightforward "explication" of the thinker at hand, to a more specifically Deleuzian "interpretation," which often makes use of concepts incorporated from outside thinkers. For instance, Deleuze interprets Spinoza in terms of Duns Scotus' concept of "univocity," and Leibniz in terms of the mathematical theory of "singularities," although neither of these terms appears in Spinoza's or Leibniz's texts). Finally, one reaches a kind of "creative" point where Deleuze pushes the thought of the thinker at hand to its "differential" limit, purging it of the three great terminal points of metaphysics (God, World, Self), and thereby uncovering the immanent movement of difference in their thought. This is the point where Deleuze's own "system" would begin. Evaluating where these different points lie is one of the most challenging and difficult tasks in reading Deleuze – precisely because there are no clear-cut points where the transition is made.

Sometimes, however, interpreters have contented themselves with a quite different task: identifying Deleuze with (or distancing him from) certain philosophers in the history of philosophy, separating his "friends" from his "enemies." For instance, one could easily imagine drawing up the following four lists. The first would be a list of Deleuze's "canonical" philosophers, those to whom he devoted separate monographs: Hume, Nietzsche, Bergson, Spinoza, Leibniz. To this, one could then add a list of secondary names, philosophers Deleuze loves and refers to often, even though he never wrote a separate monograph on them: Lucretius, the Stoics, Duns Scotus, Maimon, Whitehead. Then there would be the list of Deleuze's ostensible enemies, which would include Plato, Kant, and Hegel. And finally, one could identify certain "hidden" thinkers that Deleuze confronts in a fundamental manner, but who are not frequently discussed directly – most notably Heidegger. With these lists in hand, one could begin to debate, for instance, about who Deleuze's "true" master is. Is it "really" Bergson, as Alain Badiou wants to claim?[15] Is it Nietzsche? Is it Spinoza? Deleuze's own comments in certain texts (such as the "Letter to Michel Cressole") tend to encourage this approach: he says he detested Hegelianism, sought a way to overturn Platonism, thought of his study of Kant as "a book on an enemy," and that his work tends toward "the great Spinoza-Nietzsche identity" (*N* 125).

But the distinction between Deleuze's friends and enemies, or the identification of Deleuze's "true" masters, is at best a preliminary exercise: necessary, perhaps, but certainly not sufficient. The fact is that Deleuze reads every philosopher in the history of philosophy – friend or enemy – in the same manner, following the same strategy, pushing each thinker, so to speak, to their differential limit. (Indeed, this is a point of affiliation with Hegel: Hegel pushes thought to its point of contradiction; Deleuze, to the point of difference.) Deleuze indeed describes his Kant book as "a book on an enemy," but elsewhere he notes, more accurately, that Kant was one of the great philosophers of immanence, and Deleuze unhesitatingly places himself squarely in the Kantian heritage, even if Kant was unable to push the thought of immanence to its necessary conclusion, that is, to its differential conclusion (see *N* 145). Conversely, and for the very same reason, Deleuze often departs from his "friends": he rejects Bergson's critique of intensity in *Time and Free Will*; his Leibnizianism is a Leibnizianism minus God; his Spinozism is a Spinozism minus substance; and Spinoza himself defined determination as negation – a position from which Deleuze broke strongly in his earliest work. But this does not mean that Deleuze is "anti-Spinoza" or "anti-Leibniz" or "anti-Bergson" – any more than he is simply "anti-Hegel." Such characterizations, while not entirely inaccurate, are far too simplistic; they miss the movement and "becoming" of Deleuze's thought, both in itself and in its complex relation to the history of philosophy.

PHILOSOPHY AS THE CREATION OF CONCEPTS

If one considers the books Deleuze wrote on the history of philosophy, abstracted from their specific contents, one can distinguish several common traits. First, Deleuze considered each of the figures he wrote on to be a "minor" philosopher – not in the sense that they were secondary, but that they challenged the "major" conception of the canon, and what Deleuze would come to call its "dogmatic" image of thought (DR 131). "I liked writers who seemed to be a part of the history of philosophy, but escaped from it in one respect or altogether ... I see a secret link between Lucretius, Hume, Spinoza, and Nietzsche constituted by their critique of negativity, their cultivation of joy, the hatred of interiority, the externality of forces and relations, the denunciation of power" (D 14–15; N 6). Bergson had faded into obscurity by the time Deleuze wrote on him: Lévi-Strauss is said to have remarked that "Bergson reduced everything to a state of mush in order to bring out its inherent ineffability,"[16] and Bertrand Russell had penned a number of influential critiques of Bergson, to the point where Deleuze noted "there are people these days who laugh at me simply for having written about Bergson at all" (N 6). For Deleuze, this rejection of Bergson was no doubt a sign of the importance of his heterodox work, and Deleuze's 1966 book Bergsonism is now credited with having led to a revival of interest in Bergsonism. Second, and perhaps more importantly, each book presented a systematic analysis of the thinker at hand, which considered their work as a whole. In the Abécédaire interviews, Deleuze recalls that when he was quite young, he liked the idea of reading an author's work in its entirety, the complete works, whether in philosophy or literature, and that he considered literary writers to be great thinkers. As a result, he initially tended to have an affection for authors who had written little – he found enormous corpuses, like Hugo's, to be somewhat overwhelming (*ABC* L). Deleuze retained this emphasis on reading complete works. Unlike Foucault, for instance, whose early work analyzed broad but historically specific "epistemic formations," Deleuze's early writings were focused primarily on the *singularity* of a particular author. Third, Deleuze ultimately located the singularity of philosophers he wrote on in the *concepts* they had created, and the linkages they established between these concepts. "I sometimes dream of a history of philosophy," Deleuze later mused, "that would list only the new concepts created by a great philosopher – his most essential and creative contribution" (*ES* ix). This was the basis for the definition of philosophy that Deleuze and Guattari would propose in their late work, *What is Philosophy?* (1991): "philosophy is the art of forming, inventing, and fabricating concepts" (*WP* 2). Yet this understanding of the task of philosophy had already been implicit in Deleuze's earliest writings. In *Expressionism in Philosophy: Spinoza*, which was largely written in the 1950s but not published until 1968, Deleuze had written that "the power of a philosophy is measured by the concepts it creates, or whose sense it alters, concepts that impose a new set of divisions on things and actions" (*EPS* 321). Hume, for instance, created the concepts of habit, belief, and association; Spinoza gave an entirely new distribution to the concepts of substance, attribute, and mode; Nietzsche created the concepts of will to power and the eternal return; Bergson invented the notions of duration, *élan vital*, and intuition, and so on.

It is this conception of philosophy as the creation of concepts that lies at the heart of Deleuze's approach to the history of philosophy, although it was only late in his career that Deleuze would finally lay out the principles, so to speak, of his approach. In *What is Philosophy?* Deleuze argued that concepts can be analyzed under the double rubrics of their *exo-consistency* and *endo-consistency* (*WP* 19–10). For Deleuze, no concept is ever simple: not only does it link up with other concepts (exo-consistency), but each concept also has its own internal components (endo-consistency), which in turn can themselves be considered as concepts. Descartes' concept of the *cogito*, for instance, can be said to have three components, namely, thinking, doubting, and being: "I (who doubt) think, and therefore I am (a thinking being)." A concept is therefore always a multiplicity: it is composed of a finite number of distinct, heterogeneous, and nonetheless inseparable components or variations; the concept itself is the point of coincidence, condensation, or accumulation of these component elements, which it renders consistent *in itself*; and this internal consistency in turn is defined by the zones of neighborhood (*voisinage*) or indiscernability that it creates between these components. But like a hypertext, the concept of the *cogito* is an open-ended multiplicity that contains the potential for bridges that provide links or crossroads to other Cartesian concepts. The idea of infinity is the bridge leading from the concept of *cogito* to the concept of God, a new concept that has three components forming the "proofs" for the existence of God. In turn, the third proof (ontological) assures the closure of the concept but also throws out a new bridge or branches off to a concept of extended being, insofar as the concept of God guarantees the objective truth value of our other clear and distinct ideas.

This exo-consistency of concepts extends to the history of philosophy as well. When Kant later criticized the Cartesian *cogito*, he did so in the name of a new problematic field: Descartes could not say under what form the "I think" is capable of determining the "I am," and this determinable form, Kant argued, is precisely the form of time. In this way, Kant introduced a new component into the Cartesian *cogito*. Yet to say that Kant "criticized" Descartes is simply to say that Kant constructed a problem that could not be occupied or completed by the Cartesian *cogito*. Descartes created the concept of the *cogito*, but he expelled time from it as a form of *anteriority*, making it a simple mode of succession sustained by a continuous divine creation. If Kant introduced time as a new component of the *cogito*, he did so on the condition of *creating a new concept* of time: time now becomes a form of *interiority* with its own internal components (succession, but also simultaneity and permanence). Similarly, to ask if there are precursors to the *cogito* – for instance, in Augustine – is to ask: "Are there concepts signed by previous philosophers that have similar or almost identical components, but from which one component is lacking, or to which others have been added, so that a cogito does not crystallize, since the components do not yet coincide in a self?" (*WP* 26). Concepts, in short, possess an *internal* history, a potential for transmutation into other concepts, which constitutes what Deleuze likes to call the "plane of immanence" of philosophy.

Creating concepts is constructing some area in the plane, adding a new area to existing ones, exploring a new area, filling in what's missing. Concepts are composites, amalgams of lines, curves. If new concepts have to be brought in all the time, it's just because the plane of immanence has to be constructed area by area, constructed locally, going from one point to the next. (N 147)

It is precisely through this kind of analysis that one can account for the various kinds of conceptual becomings that one finds in Deleuze's own work, and the transformations he himself introduced into concepts drawn from the history of philosophy. "The history of philosophy," Deleuze writes, "means that we evaluate not only the historical novelty of the concepts created by the philosopher, but also the power of their becoming when they pass into one another" (WP 32).

HISTORY AND BECOMING

In proposing an "analytic" of concepts oriented around their endo- and exo-consistency, Deleuze was not being "historicist" in the usual sense of the term. He did not attempt to "situate" thinkers, or the concepts they created, within their historical period, though he did not deny the determinative role of their historical context. Deleuze's book on the painter Francis Bacon, subtitled *The Logic of Sensation*, is an interesting case in this regard, even though it is not a study of a philosopher. For Deleuze, artists and writers are as much thinkers as philosophers are – they simply think in terms of percepts and affects rather than concepts: painters think in terms of lines and colors, just as musicians think in sounds, writers think in words, film-makers think in images, and so on. In his book on Bacon, Deleuze therefore attempted to create a series of philosophical concepts (the Figure, rhythm, chaos, force, the diagram, and so on) that each relate to a particular aspect of Bacon's paintings, but which also find a place in a general logic of sensation. Rather than analyzing a philosopher's concepts, Deleuze here created his own philosophical concepts that parallel Bacon's artistic work. The text is organized in quasi-musical fashion, divided into seventeen sequences that develop concepts as if they were melodic lines (endo-consistency), which in turn enter into increasingly complex contrapuntal relations that, taken together, form a kind of conceptual composition that parallels Bacon's sensible compositions (exo-consistency). Yet readers who approach the book expecting a work of art criticism will be disappointed: there is little discussion of the socio-cultural milieu in which Bacon lived and worked; nor of his artistic influences or contemporaries, such as Lucian Freud or Frank Auerbach; nor of his personal life (his homosexuality, his lovers and friends, his drinking and gambling, his nights at the Colony Room club), which played such an evident role in Bacon's work and in his choice of subjects. The reason for this omission, Deleuze explains elsewhere, lies in the distinction he makes between history and becoming.

"I became increasing aware," Deleuze said in an interview with Antonio Negri, "of the possibility of distinguishing between becoming and history ... Becoming is not part of history: history only designates the set of conditions, however recent, that one leaves behind in order to 'become', that is, to create something new. This is exactly what Nietzsche called the 'untimely'" (N 171). Bacon's personal and social-cultural background constitutes the historical conditions that make his artistic work possible, yet there is nothing in this background that determined Bacon to become a painter, or to paint in a Bacon-esque style. Others shared this background without becoming either artists or painters. In philosophical terms, one could say that history provides the necessary conditions of Bacon's artistic work (history), but says nothing about its sufficient conditions (becoming). Moreover, the very search for conditions, whether necessary or sufficient, always takes place in a retrograde manner: faced with the singularity of Bacon's paintings, one then seeks, after the fact, to "explain" them by elucidating the conditions that led to their production. But the reverse is never the case: one can never, through an examination of current conditions, "explain" that someone is about to write a certain opera or a certain treatise on astronomy. Bacon's work is the creation of something new, the eruption of a becoming, that is to say, an *event* (in Deleuze's sense of this term). What history grasps in an event is the way it was actualized in particular circumstances, but the becoming of the event itself is beyond the scope of history. Events "cannot be explained by the situations that gave rise to them, or into which they lead. They appear for a moment, and *it is that moment that matters, it's the chance we must seize*" (N 176). This, then, is how Deleuze wound up approaching the works of philosophers, and the concepts they had created, including his own created concepts: as events. He neither sought to explain them in terms of their historical context, nor to extract eternal and timeless truths from them (or to critique them for *not* being "true"). In this, he took his cue from the French poet Charles Péguy:

In a major philosophical work, *Clio*, Péguy explained that there are two ways of considering an event: the first consists in following the course of the event, examining its effectuation in history, how it is conditioned by and passes away within history, but the second consists in going back into the event, installing oneself within it as in a becoming, growing both young and old in it at once, passing through all its components and singularities. (*N* 170–71; cf. *DR* 189)

But what then does it mean to consider philosophical concepts in their "becoming," in a way that is irreducible to either their historical conditions or their eternal truth? In *What is Philosophy?* Deleuze provides an instructive analysis of the difference between the history of philosophy and the history of science. Often, ideas of "progress" (the before and the after) in both science and philosophy are derived from archaic religious conceptions that are dramatized in the use of the calendar: before Christ and after Christ. At a certain moment, everything stops and we start counting over again from zero, assigning negative numbers to the preceding era. Before the Greeks, no one thought, or only thought mythically; then came the Greek miracle, which invented philosophy. The same schema is appealed to when one speaks of the so-called Copernican or Galilean Revolution in science: reason later, unreason before. The Age of Enlightenment was instrumental in categorizing as irrational any reason not formed by science – it was the bid of science to take over the totality of reason, and to remove all rationality from anything that was not science (even though reason is statistically distributed everywhere, and no one can claim exclusive rights to it). The idea of the birth of a new time, or the advent of a new era, is one of the most archaic and quasi-religious conceptions of temporality, yet it is also one of the most persistent. Just as we once situated the earth and ourselves spatially at the center of the universe, we still tend to position ourselves temporally at the cutting edge, at the state-of-the-art of development – a temporal schema that allows us not only to be right, but to be more right than was ever possible before, since the present is always the last word on time and truth.[17]

Deleuze rejects this popular temporal schema. Neither science nor philosophy can be reduced to a simple linear succession, but each can be seen to be structured by a different form of temporality, that is, a different relation between the before and the after. Consider an example from science often invoked by Deleuze: the history of number. In one direction (from before to after), the history of number can be defined by a series of breaks or ruptures with previous conceptions: the fractional number breaks with whole numbers, the irrational number breaks with rational numbers, and Riemannian geometry breaks with Euclidean geometry (*WP* 124; cf. *DR* 232). But in the other direction (from after to before), one can say that the whole number appears as a particular "case" of the fractional number (2 = 2/1), or the rational number as a "cut" in a linear set of points (Dedekind), or Euclidean geometry as a case of abstract metrical geometry. From this second perspective, one can say that there is indeed a unifying progress to science, but one that works in a retrograde direction (as when Newtown is derived from Einstein). Science can thus be said to operate within a temporality that is *serial* and *ramified*, in which the "before" designates bifurcations and ruptures to come, and the "after" designates retrospective reconnections.

But the same is not true of philosophy. To simply say that Kant breaks with Descartes, or that the Cartesian *cogito* is a particular case of the Kantian *cogito*, says Deleuze, "is hardly satisfying, since this is, precisely, to turn philosophy into a science" (*WP* 125). In science, there is no need to work through a named equation; one simply uses it. In philosophy, however, Kant does not simply use Descartes' concept of the *cogito*; rather, he is forced to work through the concept again in order to alter its components (endo-consistency), as well as its relation to other concepts (exo-consistency) – whence the impression that philosophers are always starting over again. "Philosophical time," Deleuze writes, "is thus a grandiose time of coexistence that does not exclude the before and after but superimposes them in a *stratigraphic* order" (*WP* 50). The temporality of philosophical concepts, in other words, is like the temporality of geological strata: layers deposited eons apart lie on top of or next to each other; intermittent earthquakes produce dramatic breaks and ruptures in these layers, driven underneath by continuous and barely perceptible molten movements that propel the surface crust – a coexistence of superimposed strata in space and multiple scales of time. Mathematics provides a similar model in the field of topology: I can mark out points on a flat piece of paper, but if I crumple or fold the paper, two distant points may find themselves in the neighborhood of each other, or even superimposed; and if I tear the paper at certain places, two points that were close can become very distant. Whereas metrical geometry is the science of stable points and well-defined distances, topology is this science of neighborhoods and tears – whence Deleuze's interest in the concept of the fold. It is as if the temporality of philosophical concepts has an extraordinarily complex variety, with stopping points, ruptures, shafts, chimneys of acceleration, rifts, and lacunae, with their multifarious interactions.

It was this new model of temporality that Deleuze utilized in his analyses of the becoming of philosophical concepts as events. Similarly, in his preface to *Difference and Repetition*, Deleuze commented on his "untimely" use of the history of philosophy that rejected the alternatives of temporal/nontemporal or historical/eternal: "There is a great difference between writing history of philosophy and writing philosophy. In the first case, we study the arrows or the tools of a great thinker, the trophies and the prey, the continents discovered. In the second case, we trim our own arrows, or gather what seem to be the finest arrows, only to shoot them in other directions, even if the distance they travel is relatively short rather than stellar" (*DR* xv). The book is filled with numerous examples of topological transformations of concepts drawn from the history of philosophy, all of which are now put in the service of Deleuze's own "heterogenetic" metaphysics. Deleuze, for instance, develops a theory of Ideas that draws on both the Platonic and Kantian notions of the Idea, folding them together, as it were, into a single plane that constitutes a new concept (*DR* 168–70). Similarly, when Deleuze takes up Duns Scotus' concept of univocity – like a very old stratum rising to the surface again (*WP* 58) – and claims that there is a tradition of univocity that extends from Parmenides to Heidegger, passing through Spinoza and Nietzsche, he is bringing these otherwise distant thinkers together in a single "neighborhood" that allows them to communicate with each other (*DR* 35–42). Conversely, when he formulates his concept of intensity, he opens up a distance between his own concept and the Bergsonian critique of intensity, which he finds unconvincing (*DR* 239). Using Deleuze's own image, the history of philosophy plays a role in the book that is roughly analogous to that of *collage* in painting (*DR* xxi), bringing together disparate elements and tracing out lines "that crosscut history without being confused with it" (*WP* 59).

One can thus trace out a complex trajectory in Deleuze's relation to the history of philosophy. As a student, he experienced the required curriculum in the history of philosophy as "a formidable school of intimidation that manufactures specialists in thought" (*D* 13), and he combated this conformism by choosing to write on authors "who seemed to be part of the history of philosophy, but who escaped from it in one respect or another: Lucretius, Spinoza, Hume, Nietzsche, Bergson" (*DR* 14). In the process of writing on these philosophers, he developed a use of the history of philosophy that was neither historical nor eternal, but "untimely," and which found its first expression in *Difference and Repetition* and its theoretical elaboration in *What is Philosophy?* Looking back on this line-up of favored philosophers, Deleuze later noted:

These thinkers have few relationships with each other – apart from Nietzsche and Spinoza – yet they do have them. One might say that something happens between them, at different speeds and at different intensities, which is not in one or the other of them, but truly in *an ideal space*, which is no longer a part of history, still less a dialogue among the dead, but an interstellar conversation, between very irregular stars, whose different becomings form a mobile bloc which it would be a case of capturing. (*D* 15–16)

This is where Deleuze's work in the history of philosophy and his development of a differential metaphysics became one and the same thing, since it is precisely in this ideal space that, as Deleuze puts it, "philosophy is becoming, and not history; it is the coexistence of planes, and not the succession of systems" (*WP* 59).

Yet one must add that the trajectory Deleuze followed does not necessarily imply a prescription for others. To diagnose the becomings of the present is the task Nietzsche assigned to the philosopher as "the physician of civilization," and Deleuze often spoke of the difficulties faced by young philosophers. "What part can philosophy play in resisting a terrible new conformism?," Deleuze asked in a 1980 interview.

The generation to which I belong was, I think, a strong one (with Foucault, Althusser, Derrida, Lyotard, Serres, Faye, Châtelet, and others). What now seems problematic is the situation of young philosophers, but also all young writers, who are involved in creating something. They face the threat of being stifled from the outset. It has become very difficult to do any work, because a whole system of "acculturation" and anti-creation specific to the developed nations is taking place. It's far worse than censorship. Censorship produces a ferment beneath the surface, but reaction seeks to make everything impossible. (*N* 27)

But it is precisely in such impossible situations, with their choked passages, that creation takes place. The creation of concepts itself is an appeal to a new earth and a new people who do not yet exist. To think the past, in order to act on the present, in favor (one hopes) of a future to come – such is the task of the philosopher. "But there is no general prescription ... Nothing can be known in advance" (*D* 144; *ATP* 461).

NOTES

1   From Deleuze's interview with Arnaud Villani in the latter's *La guêpe et l'orchidée: essai sur Gilles Deleuze* (Paris: Belin, 1999), p. 130.
2   Alfred North Whitehead, *Process and Reality*, corrected edition, ed. David Ray Griffin and Donald W. Sherburne (New York: The Free Press, 1978), p. 8.
3   The reflections in the paragraphs that follow are adapted in part from material developed in an earlier article, "Deleuze, Hegel, and the Post-Kantian Tradition," *Philosophy Today* (Supplement 2001), 126–38.
4   The French academic milieu has been analyzed by Pierre Bourdieu in works such as *Homo Academicus*, trans. Peter Collier (Stanford University Press, 1988) and *The State Nobility: Elite Schools in the Field of Power*, trans. Lauretta C. Clough (Stanford University Press, 1988).
5   For an analysis of the role of the *agrégation* examination in determining the direction of philosophical work in France, see Alan Schrift's *Twentieth-Century French Philosophy: Key Themes and Thinkers* (Oxford: Blackwell, 2006), pp. 201–4 (202n discusses the tension between competence and creativity in the exam assessments, as evidenced by the tension between the Sorbonne and the École normale supérieure). Schrift also edited the magisterial eight-volume *History of Continental Philosophy* (University of Chicago Press, 2011), which is an indispensible guide to the many complexities of twentieth-century European philosophy.
6   See Vincent Descombes, *Modern French Philosophy*, trans. L. Scott Fox and J. M. Harding (Cambridge University Press, 1980), p. 12: "In 1945, all that was modern sprang from Hegel ... In 1968, all that was modern was hostile to Hegel."

7   Michel Foucault, "The Discourse on Language," in *The Archaeology of Knowledge and the Discourse on Language*, trans. A. M. Sheridan Smith (New York: Pantheon Books, 1972), p. 235.

8   See *ATP* 526, n.32: "Jean Wahl's works contain profound reflections on this sense of 'and,' on the way it challenges the primacy of the verb 'to be.'"

9   See G. W. F. Hegel, *Phenomenology of Spirit*, trans. A. V. Miller (Oxford University Press, 1979), section on "Sense Certainty." See also Deleuze's comment in *NP* 4: "Hegel wanted to ridicule pluralism, identifying it with a naive consciousness which would be happy to say 'this, that, here, now' – like a child stuttering out its most humble needs."

10   See Michael Hardt, *Gilles Deleuze: An Apprenticeship in Philosophy* (Minneapolis: University of Minnesota Press, 1993), which analyzes Deleuze's readings of Nietzsche, Bergson, and Spinoza.

11   Michel Serres, with Bruno Latour, *Conversations on Science, Culture, and Time*, trans. Roxanne Lapidus (Ann Arbor: University of Michigan Press, 1995), p. 43.

12   François Châtelet, *Chronique des idées perdues* (Paris: Éditions Stock, 1977), p. 46; the professor referred to was probably Ferdinand Alquié.

13   Michel Tournier, *The Wind Spirit: An Autobiography*, trans. Arthur Goldhammer (Boston: Beacon Ness, 1988), pp. 127–28; see also pp. 134–35 and 157.

14   Deleuze was responding to a question posed to him during the Cerisy colloquium on Nietzsche in 1972; see *Nietzsche aujourd'hui*, vol. I, *Intensities* (Paris: Union Générale d'Éditions 10/18, 1973), pp. 186–87.

15   Alain Badiou, *Deleuze: The Clamor of Being*, trans. Louise Burchill (Minneapolis: University of Minnesota Press, 2000), p. 39: "Deleuze is a marvelous reader of Bergson, who, in my opinion, is his real master, far more than Spinoza, or perhaps even Nietzsche."

16   Richard Rorty, "Unsoundness in Perspective" [review of Gilles Deleuze, *Nietzsche and Philosophy*], in Times Literary Supplement, 17 June 1983, p. 619. Rorty seems to have been thinking of the following passage by Claude Levi-Strauss in *Tristes Tropiques* [1955], trans. John and Doreen Whiteman (London: Jonathan Cape, 1973), pp. 55-56: "Rejecting the Bergsonian acts of faith and circular arguments which reduced beings and things to a state of mush, the better to bring out their ineffability, I came to the conclusion that beings and things could retain their separate values without losing the clarity of outline which defines them in their relation to each other and gives an intelligible structure to each."

17   On all these points, see Serres, *Conversations on Science, Culture, and Time*, pp. 48–51, 138–39.

2   *Difference and Repetition*

Press send
You know you want to ...

Gilles Deleuze's *Difference and Repetition* is at the center of his philosophical works, not only chronologically but also methodologically and in terms of interpretation. This does not mean it is his most important book. This depends on the problems and questions driving any given reading. Political studies are more likely to focus on the later collaborations with Félix Guattari.[1] Interpretations more interested in art will be drawn first to *Proust and Signs* or to the book on Francis Bacon, *The Logic of Sensation*.[2] More pure philosophical enquiry does not have to start with *Difference and Repetition*, since *The Logic of Sense* is the better starting point for the study of Deleuze's philosophies of language and of the event.[3]

Close reflection on the history of philosophy or on Deleuze's ontology need not emphasize the difference book, since works such as *Nietzsche and Philosophy* and *The Fold: Leibniz and the Baroque* offer more comprehensive accounts of Deleuze's version of those authors and, for instance, his concepts of world or creation. Nonetheless, as a reading goes deeper into any of these areas, extensive reference to *Difference and Repetition* will prove necessary. It is the keystone to Deleuze's philosophy, but as we shall see, even the notion of such a secure foundation is challenged in the book.

I want to argue for the value and necessity of Deleuze's major book around two questions. First, why is *Difference and Repetition* a great work of philosophy, able to stand alongside Descartes' *Discourse on*

Method, Kant's *Critique of Pure Reason,* and Heidegger's *Being and Time?* One answer to this first puzzle leads to my second question. These great works introduce novel and ground-breaking methods into philosophical practice. This justifies not only their influence but also their status as revolutionary in content and effect. What, therefore, is the new method developed in *Difference and Repetition?*

An answer to the question of method has now begun to be suggested among Deleuze scholars worldwide. The revolutionary method behind Deleuze's philosophy is to be called "transcendental empiricism." My aim here will therefore be to draw together the many strands of his book around a critical assessment of the two claims implied by this answer: transcendental empiricism is Deleuze's methodological innovation; it is a great method worthy of comparison to the Cartesian method of doubt, to Kantian critique, and to Heideggerian hermeneutics.

My guide through the first claim will be the most important piece of interpretation on Deleuze's work and on *Difference and Repetition,* Anne Sauvagnargues' *Deleuze: L'empirisme transcendantal.*[4] The title explains my interest, but more significantly her book is the most deep and broad interpretation of Deleuze's oeuvre currently available.[5] It is a tour de force in Deleuze's tradition, a manner of philosophizing inherited from his masters Gueroult, Wahl, and Hyppolite, whom he met very early on, in his last years of lycée, and then worked with at the Sorbonne.[6] This tradition is the French close reading seeking to draw a work together around its most potent conceptual and methodological innovations, yet always following the principle of the greatest possible faithfulness to an author's texts, to their place in the history of philosophy, and to the logical consistency of an author's ideas.[7] It is an immanent reading following a thinker's concepts, arguments, and references while minimizing external presuppositions.

Yet Deleuze's influence goes well beyond this French academic practice with its remarkable scholarly and intellectual values. The French academy has strong parochial boundaries too, not only in styles of critical method and analysis, but also in its sense of the place of philosophy as a historical undertaking situated above other disciplines, even as they inform it. Such rigorous commitments to place and internal form have the great advantage of building on classical wisdom and practice. They impose disciplines formed and tested over time. They also, though, run the risk of falling behind the times into irrelevance or exercises designed to maintain a privileged yet embattled position against a changing world. One of the merits of Deleuze's work is its mastery of disciplines but as expanded through an exploration beyond disciplinary limits and through deliberately risky experimentation, for instance in Deleuze's love of adventure in English and American literature, or in his taste for those living life on the edge, such as Artaud or Nietzsche.[8]

This hybrid form explains the style of *Difference and Repetition*. On the one hand, it is his French long doctoral thesis, his *doctorat d'état*, the culmination of many years of strict academic training. As such it involves extended scholarly readings of many major historical and contemporary philosophical figures around an original thesis about difference and repetition. On the other hand, it is a major work of philosophical invention and as such it also introduces a novel style and accompanying modes of thought and ideas into philosophy.

Both aspects contribute to the fearsome difficulty of the book, which, like many revolutionary works, must not be dismissed with hasty accusations of obscurity or mystification. The ideas set out in *Difference and Repetition* make heavy demands on the reader because they are radically new. They therefore enforce a break with common expectations, language, and values. This break is an intrinsic part of the book's arguments. For example, Deleuze suggests a revolutionary transformation of all of time around the idea of a caesura or split in time at the introduction of the new: "[The image of a unique and formidable event adequate to the whole of time] exists itself in torn form, in two unequal portions; and yet therefore it draws together the assembly of time" (*DR* 89, translation modified). An event breaks time in two unequal parts: the past before the event and the future ahead of it. Yet we decode the past and the future through this event, which is therefore adequate to the whole of time. The split in time is therefore also its assembly.[9]

It is a duty for interpreters and teachers to alleviate the demand of Deleuze's work, but this should not be confused with the thought that the ideas have easier forms than the ones he sets out. Each simplifying reading, like this one here, loses something of the richness and complexity of Deleuze's text. So though sections of this essay will follow Anne Sauvagnargues and other interpreters in tracing the definition of the apparently paradoxical method of transcendental empiricism, further sections will consider critical points against this emerging orthodoxy.

The conjunct of "transcendental" and "empiricism" is historically incongruous and analytically paradoxical because it combines two historical movements apparently at odds with each other.[10] It links Hume's philosophical empiricism and its scientific and philosophical heirs with the later Kantian critique. It draws out the contradiction of a philosophy seeking to bring no subjective and dogmatic presuppositions to enquiry with a philosophy also attempting to avoid dogmatism but through the deduction of the necessary conditions for any appearance in intuition.[11]

For radical empiricism, to hold to the existence of such conditions prior to experiment is dogmatic. Setting down one of the main tenets of this empiricism, Hume therefore states that all ideas must follow from impressions, from experience.[12] However, for transcendental critique, to fail to take account of the a priori conditions for such impressions is to misunderstand the nature of our faculties of thought and sensibility. Every appearance in intuition requires a synthesis of time which therefore allows us to deduce universal categories for any appearance.

From his earliest book on Hume, Deleuze's interest in these debates has been practical rather than abstractly theoretical. We employ faculties in all our everyday activities, for instance, in our connected feelings around a send button and our impulses towards pushing it, as our muscles tense in expectation and dread. They are also used more intellectually and introspectively, when seeking to understand our thoughts about the action of pressing, the significance of doing so, and the rightness, wrongness, beauty, and ugliness of our actions. Yet these faculties are the locus for ongoing and thorny questions about the priority of universal conditions or of empirical facts, captured by discussions around Deleuze's transcendental empiricism.

Are there universal conditions for appearances in thought and sensation? Are we subject to a universal legislation of our faculties? Or is each faculty discovered through tentative, varied, and probabilistic experiment? Is the encountered world subject to conditions holding for any possible experience – the same for all? Or is it radically pluralistic and always open to disproval by new facts, against all theoretical underpinning? Are the natural sciences the only source of knowledge or is there a place for philosophical truths in their own right? One way of understanding Deleuzian transcendental empiricism is as an attempt to avoid the oppositions between these options. It seeks to be transcendental and empirical but must therefore redefine both terms away from their contradiction of each another.

My critical remarks on transcendental empiricism will therefore span two thoughts. Is transcendental empiricism a viable candidate for a method meant to mark a great philosophy? Even if it is, what are the restrictions imposed on Deleuze's philosophy in giving it the distinguishing mark of "transcendental empiricism"? For both aspects of the essay, the secondary aim will be to draw in many of the features of *Difference and Repetition* that are either downplayed or discarded in the search for its defining method. These include its style, its main images and examples, its more minor reference points and relations to other disciplines, its governing concepts, and historical debts.

DIFFERENCE IN ITSELF AND REPETITION FOR ITSELF

I just can't do it
Coward ...

Difference and Repetition is distilled from many major and minor movements in the history of philosophy. The variety and number of thinkers covered in the book are demonstrated by its eclectic index of names and subjects. Each entry is listed with a short comment by Deleuze explaining its place in the new versions of ideas of difference and of repetition he argues for. The overall thesis is that we must think of difference "in itself," as pure difference defined not in relation to identity, in accordance to the negation of an identity (not-X), or according to a difference between two identities (X different from Y). Instead, difference is to be an ideal or virtual potential for the transformation of identities (the differing between X and Y). This pure difference does not have fixed identity. It is an ongoing variation of relations, rather than any given object, substance, or quality.

For example, we could think of this virtual potential in human terms as a reserve of shifting relations of pliable moods and passions we embody at different degrees of intensity. For instance, when we mock another's incapacities, we force potentials of rage, humiliation, revenge, and sadness on to them. These are then expressed in a singular form. The potentials are pure differentials of relations of passions because they can be expressed differently in many individuals. The differentials transform those individuals or reveal them to be processes of individuation (*how could I know it would hurt you so much?*). According to Deleuze's definitions of difference and repetition, and the accompanying definitions of the virtual and the actual, all passions remain as pure virtual potential until they are expressed in actual processes of becoming at different degrees of intensity.

This potential is actualized in series of repetitions and determined by them. Thus repetition is defined as a differential variation across series. So repetition too is defined against identity and representation as repetition "for itself." This is not the repetition *of* another same thing (not the repetition of X, X, X ...) but the variation along differences (X, X', X"...). We could, for example, think of repetition as a variation along a series of shades of a color. For Deleuze there is repetition when there is difference in the shades resisting definition according to a fixed identity.

A puzzling thought to hold, but an important one for Deleuze, is that there can never be a repetition of the same thing. This is because there is always a novel series of differences each time a "same" thing is repeated. Sameness is then illusion because difference is the condition for repetition. We *never* encounter the same color. These statements could not come from radical empiricism, given the categorical assertion pertaining to a matter of fact. It is a transcendental claim about necessary conditions. It is also an assertion at odds with even the possibility of the experimental falsification of the statement about difference in any repetition. There is hence a deep challenge to the commitment to truth as determined exclusively and probabilistically by the empirical sciences.[13]

For Deleuze the real always presupposes difference in itself, and when we define reality under the opposing condition of sameness we foster an illusion. One of the aims of *Difference and Repetition* is to criticize claims which support the illusion: "It is because nothing is equal, because everything bathes in its difference, in its dissemblance and its inequality, even with itself, that everything returns" (*DR* 243). This statement reflects the great importance of Nietzsche's doctrine of eternal return for *Difference and Repetition*: only difference returns and never the same.

Difference in repetition explains why the book names difference AND repetition. For Deleuze, there is no difference without series of repetitions; and no series without difference. Another difficult claim is that these series of repetitions occur in pairs, where difference is released across series (for instance from the series of pure virtual passions to the series of actual expressions at given intensities). The rage released in the victim following a humiliating taunt runs with a twin in the increased erotic intensity felt by the tormentor. Paired differences explain the relation between two series as processes of transformation. It also explains why difference appears in a series at all. This is because no series of repetitions is unique. It is in a dynamic relation to all other actual and virtual series.

These ideas about series, structures, and differences are developed most fully in *The Logic of Sense*. This explains the complex interaction between the two near-contemporary books. Where *Difference and Repetition* sets out Deleuze's ontology of difference in repetition, *The Logic of Sense* shows their structural processes in moral and linguistic practice. Note the importance of the concept of explanation in understanding Deleuze, where to explain is to describe consistent connections within a system, as a response to apparent contradictions or lacunae in a part of the system. Deleuze is not only creator of a novel methodology but also of an explanatory system. The key critical question is whether the explanatory power of the system as a multiple series of explanations and connections is attenuated by the imposition of the restricted logic of transcendental conditions and terms.

DELEUZE'S SOURCES

> *Explain yourself*
> *Even my dark precursors?*

The index of names at the end of *Difference and Repetition* divides thinkers according to their positive and negative stand with respect to Deleuze's novel definitions of difference and repetition. Aristotle is listed for ontological and logical difference, but where they are subordinated to the identity of species and genera. Bergson is there for repetition and memory, as well as biological difference, repetition in physics, and the important concept of intensity (difference is differentiated by Deleuze according to differences of intensity, such as the intensity of light in shades of colors). Freud earns a place thanks to his work on repetition and the unconscious. While Hegel, like Aristotle, is named for a logic and ontology of difference as negation, opposition, and contradiction.[14] These brusque distinctions between the saved and the damned are a perplexing facet of Deleuze's writing.[15]

This abruptness need not be seen as a flaw. It is a sign of two important aspects of his philosophy and live practice. Deleuze values the fraught and passionate relation of master to apprentice. He also values humor, above what he sees as romantic and ultimately nihilistic subject-centered irony (due to the way irony reflects back on to the privileged position of the ironist, which itself proves to be hollow).[16] Often, Deleuze's tough judgmental statements are humorous lessons for apprentices, meant to strike back later filtered by the unconscious (*how stupid of me to have sought and found a final judgment on Hegel ...*). A fascinating problem is then how far we should take account of humor when reading Deleuze and how far humor and other affects are designed to be seeded in our unconscious for later effect by a playful master: killing our stupid seriousness with stealthy blows to the unconscious.

To develop a sense of these problems about interpretation, humor, provocation, and ambivalence in *Difference and Repetition*, we can look at the place of error in the work. It might seem that Deleuze's critique is aimed at the error of adopting a dogmatic image of thought, that is, of received ideas and of common sense. Deleuze, though, writes of the "problem" of stupidity. Ideal problems have a very important role in his philosophy. They generate questions which seek to respond to the problem but instead transform it and bring it into actual worlds around questions of Who? Why? How? The questions can be answered, but the problem will recur in a different form. An ideal problem is then an irresolvable driver of creative responses in individual situations. This is something like the dialogical search in the Socratic method of Elenchus, taking us on an endless philosophical *practice* around the discovery of stupidity but not with an arrival at secure truths. These would be but another stupidity for Deleuze, which is why I treated even the foundational role of *Difference and Repetition* for his work with caution.

In *Difference and Repetition* he draws Socrates towards the sophists and Nietzsche and away from Plato. Like Socrates he wants to show how error is at its most dangerous when we think we have done with it or are immune from it:

[B]ut the sophist does not distinguish himself from Socrates, and thereby calls into question the legitimacy of such a distinction. Twilight of the Icons. Is this not to designate the point where the identity of the model and the resemblance of the copy are errors, where the same and the similar are born from the function of the simulacrum? (*DR* 128, translation modified)

There is a critique of judgment in accordance with external images, models, and standards in *Difference and Repetition*. They are false idols present in philosophy when it gives itself timeless images and postulates of what constitutes true and good thinking.

The third chapter of the book charts eight postulates defining this image of thought. These can be summed up as postulates of the natural good will of the thinker and rectitude of thought; of a shared common sense; of a faculty of recognition regulating all others according to an object; of representation as determining the object; of error as the negative of thought; of designation as determining the truth of a proposition; of solutions as resolving problems; and of knowledge as the result of thought, as opposed to an endless apprenticeship to thought (*DR* 167). Accordingly, thought is defined as inherently good and as well directed when it proceeds as a common sense which recognizes its proper objects.

These objects must in principle be representable and are designated by true propositions. When exercised properly thought avoids error and solves problems, arriving thereby at knowledge. For Deleuze these propositions of thought are to be criticized. They are guided by false idols because each one serves to deny the role of difference and of repetition in thinking and in the constitution of the real. These images and idols will return even in a philosophy designed to be critical of them. So philosophy must think upon the conditions of possibility of error, rather than towards its eventual elimination or about a pure thought free of it: "It would have been enough for philosophy to adopt this problem with its own means and with necessary modesty. To consider stupidity not to be that of others, but rather the object of a properly transcendental question: How is stupidity (and not error) possible?" (*DR* 151, translation modified). Error supposes an opposite: error-free truth. For Deleuze truth and error are instead intertwined due to the ever-present possibility of stupidity. This arises from the way in which individual thought has to construct itself on an obscure and indistinct ground of unconscious drives and processes of becoming.

The unavoidable relation of thought to error is replicated in Deleuze's account of subjects of thought. Subjects are determined by dark precursors connecting conscious acts and representations to determination by an unconscious, shifting, and insecure ground. This allows for a transcendental critique of the subject that Sauvagnargues places at the core of Deleuze's transcendental empiricism. Instead of a subject defined through a transcendent identity, for example, thanks to a self-identity remaining the same through time, Deleuze argues for "a subject thought in function of immanent coordinates, and not a transcendent substance; it does not pre-exist its material conditions of individuation, and must be thought as variable and plural."[17] This plurality and immanent malleability is shown through concepts such as dark precursor: "We call the dark precursor disparate, that difference in itself, at the second degree, putting heterogeneous or disparate series themselves into relation" (*DR* 120, translation modified). All things are processes of individuation, individual becoming, which are themselves series of repetitions communicating through dark precursors, that is, through elements crossing from one series to another though recognized in neither: precursors of change the system cannot foresee or represent.

Deleuze owes many of his ideas on unconscious processes not to Freudian psychoanalysis, but to Nietzsche's will to power. In the index to *Difference and Repetition* Nietzsche receives the high praise of a citation for the ontology of difference and repetition, whereas Plato is listed for the ontology and logic of difference. It is important to note Deleuze's special use of logic, here, as practical art of the systematization and selection of different processes according to difference and repetition, rather than simply formal rules of implication. Duns Scotus is included due to the importance of his work on immanence for Deleuze. Schelling provides the opportunity to cover the relation between difference and power, but also the ideas of ground, removal of ground, founding, and foundation in *Difference and Repetition* (as we have just seen in relation to error and stupidity). Kierkegaard is accorded a place for repetition and difference in positive senses related to freedom, though this is mitigated by the necessity of Kierkegaard's leap of faith. Heidegger, a thinker in the background of many parts of the book, is cited for his ideas of ontological difference close to Deleuze's.[18] Lévi-Strauss and the distinction between static and dynamic repetition testify to Deleuze's continued interest in transforming rather than denying structuralism, where static repetition in a system in balance does not allow for the movement afforded by repetition in dynamic systems.

Deleuze's contemporaries also play key roles, notably Lacan around the death drive and Klossowski for his interpretation of Nietzsche's eternal return. Michel Foucault, Deleuze's friend, is present because of his critique of difference, resemblance, and identity through a positive use of difference and repetition in the idea of the simulacrum (a thing that is always becoming what it is not and whose identity at any given point cannot be referred to an original).[19] Derrida allows Deleuze to connect repetition and the unconscious to language and to the work of art.[20] Whereas Milner, Leclaire, Ricoeur, and Miller all demonstrate Deleuze's work on repetition in psychoanalysis, an interest that becomes more oppositional in the later works with Guattari. Althusser (and Balibar, Establet, Macherey, and Rancière) extend Deleuze's quite short reference to Marx's *18th Brumaire*.

This extensive list of philosophical references is testimony to Deleuze's astonishingly productive engagement with philosophy, past and present.[21] It is a distortion, though, because to refer only to philosophers is to miss four all-important sources for Deleuze: literature, biology, physics, and mathematics. The last three are perhaps the least well known, partly due to the uptake of French thought primarily in literary and critical theory disciplines outside France. Many English-language interpreters of Deleuze are based in literature or politics departments, rather than in the sciences or philosophy.

However, the importance of the sciences for the understanding and influence of Deleuze will grow once more interpreters register the function played by differential calculus, dynamic systems, and the biology of individuals in Deleuze's account of the determination of difference and genesis. In mathematics, this is developed in relation to singularities in the work of Wronski, Abel, Carnot, and Bordas-Demoulin. However, it is arguable that questions of structure and problems in number theory and meta-mathematics are equally influential through the works of Plato, Février, Ghyka, Heyting, Russell, and, above all, Lautman. In biology the major figure is Simondon, for his work on individuation, set critically alongside other works by Lalande, Osborn, Dalcq, and Geoffroy Saint-Hilaire.[22]

The index and text of *Difference and Repetition* also testify to the importance of novelists and poets and of the literary imagination for Deleuze. It is tempting to cite Blanchot as the major figure here, due to his influence on Deleuze's understanding of literary theory and his ideas about death. However, other writers are equally important, notably Borges, Gombrowicz, Artaud, Proust, Robbe-Grillet, Tournier, Butor, Sollers, and Joyce, as well as literary philosophers such as Péguy. Literature is not included in the book simply as a source of examples or as a topic of study. It is thought itself, as the imaginary, that Deleuze values and turns to in literature; for instance, when Borges allows him to explain how all worlds subsist beyond the selection of a particular one according to a dice throw, itself driven by a death drive (*DR* 115–16) or when Gombrowicz allows him to determine the relation between ideas of cosmos and chaos.[23] According to Deleuze's metaphysics, it is an illusion to hold the common-sense idea that we can either have the real or fiction, as if they are clearly delineated and to be valued differently. For him, the virtual is real and it is accessed best through expressive signs encountered in art and literature. This virtual and the expressive "fictions" communicating with it are more real than any set of possible scenes traced on a well-identified and well-represented actual world.

It would be easy to conclude from the mixture of authors, topics, and disciplines covered in *Difference and Repetition* that the book cannot take in all of them, perhaps any, with a high degree of depth and seriousness. The book would then be dilettante: an essay in spurious and self-indulgent commentary. That this is not the case is due to the fit of style, critical and creative modes of thought, and set of ideas achieved by Deleuze. These can be summed up through the concepts of variations of speed, multiplication of modes of thought, and consistency within novelty of ideas. Rhythm is very important for Deleuze. He means a variation of different speeds such that each one enhances and expresses the others while undermining any claims to self-sufficiency or supremacy. Thought is about great speed in slowness and great reach in intense concentration or contemplation. His book includes intricate tangles of long and slow passages of critical exposition with much shorter, faster, and condensed definitions and insights.

To follow the speed it is often important to observe its effects over the critical and expository moments, for instance, where Deleuze's definition of difference allows for a critical reflection on the concept of being in Aristotle (*DR* 30–35). Or when the whole of Chapter 3 of the book, on the image of thought, unfolds and explicates how error and illusions are a necessary side of any mode of thought, yet one we should seek to avoid through the critique of representation: "[The eight postulates of the image of thought] crush thought under the image of the Same and of the Similar in representation. This image is the deepest betrayal of what thought signifies, which is to ally the two powers of difference and repetition, of philosophical commencement and recommencement" (*DR* 167, translation modified). In order to avoid this crushing way of thinking, Deleuze drops lines of escape within each critical reading.

To work with these powers of escape and flight it is necessary to multiply modes of thought and create novel concepts, in order to free thought from the dominance of any one of them. This explains the alternation of poetic expression, conceptual clarification, philosophical interpretation, the glossing and transformation of scientific and mathematical ideas, and the borrowing from all of the arts. This accounts for why dramatization is an essential idea for *Difference and Repetition*. Yet even after taking account of this rhythm of styles and modes the question remains: how do all these different speeds and topics cohere? To use one of the ideas from the book, how do they create a cosmos? Given Deleuze's commitment to difference and repetition against forms of established yet illusory order, this must be a cosmos teetering perpetually on the edge of chaos, yet a cosmos nonetheless. The answer is that whichever part of the cosmos we select must dramatize or replay all the others in its own way.

Deleuze's book and his style do not conform to the idea that there should be one proper style or that a book should set out the steps of an argument without repetition or redundancy. On the contrary, his work repays interpretations combining aleatory selections with jumps and connections across sections, topics, and ideas. Does it mean it lacks the seriousness, terminological economy, ontological parsimony, and logical consistency expected of philosophy? No. It involves a rejection of all of these, if they are taken as settled and natural, because they fail their own tests once exclusions, concealments, and omissions are revealed. One of the greatest strengths of Deleuze's apparent eclecticism and preparedness to throw subjects and ideas together is to dramatize the errors and illusions implied by claims to their independence, purity, or natural hierarchies.

HISTORICAL SELECTIONS AND THE PROBLEM OF INTERPRETATION

What are you afraid of?
It is never "What?" it is "Why?", "Who?" and "How?"

A further point to make when considering *Difference and Repetition* as the keystone of a new method of transcendental empiricism is about selection among its historical influences and antecedents, given the range and style of Deleuze's work. The book was first published in French in 1968 by the pre-eminent academic press Presses Universitaires de France in a collection edited by Jean Hyppolite. It is the same collection in which Deleuze published his first book, on Hume, in 1953. *Difference and Repetition* is a turning point in Deleuze's published works, since it is the first not written as an essay on another philosopher, with the exception of the books on novelists Proust and Sacher-Masoch (though arguably they are also read as philosophers of, respectively, sensation and subjection under the guises of Eros and the sensual apprenticeship to signs). All the books prior to *Difference and Repetition* were single-subject works, on Hume (1953), Nietzsche (1962), Kant (1963), Proust (1964), Bergson (1966), and Sacher-Masoch (1967). Each of the philosophers studied in Deleuze's earlier works appears again in *Difference and Repetition*, but each time in a more restricted and precise role.

It is important, though, to note Deleuze's early lessons and essays, alongside his published books. A gifted teacher, Deleuze was a master of dense yet suggestive and far-sighted thought when speaking and when writing. His recorded lessons and essays show the development of his ideas and the extraordinary range of interests leading to *Difference and Repetition*. Among these, the most important for the understanding of the later master-work might be the essay "The Method of Dramatization." It is a difficult yet rewarding paper, demonstrating Deleuze's thinking about the original nature of his philosophy as method but also as conceptual and practical innovation. This line of thought continued after *Difference and Repetition* and attained a further level of conceptual clarity in the book co-written with Guattari, *What is Philosophy?* It is tempting therefore to interpret the earlier book through the more clear distinctions of the later, for instance around art, philosophy, and science, or through the concepts of plane of immanence, geo-philosophy, and conceptual personae. This is not an approach I favor, because the later book adopts negation and definitions according to conceptual identity for polemical reasons around conflicts within philosophical movements and with the sciences. These characteristics make it a more accessible but philosophically less innovative book.

The profound influence of Deleuze's encounters with Hume, Nietzsche, Kant, and Bergson mean *Difference and Repetition* enters into a critical and creative dialogue with them. There are three more to add to the list determined by Deleuze's earlier works: Plato, Leibniz, and Spinoza. The latter was given a book in parallel to *Difference and Repetition*, *Spinoza and the Problem of Expression* (1969). Leibniz remained unfinished business until *The Fold: Leibniz and the Baroque* (1988). Plato is discussed at length in the appendices to *The Logic of Sense* but, like Marx, Deleuze's definitive encounter with him is lacking. There is a plausible case to be made for the many significant references to Plato in *Difference and Repetition* to constitute Deleuze's final view on his "reversal of Platonism."[24] It is instructive to remark upon Deleuze's references to Plato, alongside Nietzsche, in the closing passages of two of the main chapters of his book and at the heart of two others. Though transcendental empiricism places Kant at the heart of a filial dispute with Deleuze, another interpretation could argue for the importance of his creation of a fearsome hybrid of Nietzsche and Plato.

The setting within the history of philosophy is problematic, therefore, since each interpretation of *Difference and Repetition* and each account of his method implies a selection within his fore-runners. More significantly, each of these readings is also a selection within possible versions determined by Deleuze's Hume, or Deleuze's Bergson, or his Nietzsche, or Plato. However, as soon as Deleuze's method is defined as transcendental empiricism, Kant takes on the central role. This consequence is not without its difficulties, since as Sauvagnargues demonstrates, although Deleuze owes his dedication to transcendental critique to Kant, this is at the cost of a critical reading. In giving one of her many definitions of the method of transcendental empiricism, Sauvagnargues stresses both the debt to and departure from Kant: "Transcendental empiricism is defined thus: to recast transcendental critique while expurgating its conformism; to dissolve Kantian idealism in a renewed empiricism."[25] According to this definition, the point of the new method is to preserve critique based on the transcendental conditions of the given, while avoiding Kant's formal presuppositions.

If we accept Sauvagnargues' account, Kant remains an idealist through these presuppositions because they commit him to the ideal form of any possible experience, which in turn sets limits (categories) for the given.[26] Instead, Deleuze's empiricism is to be radically experimental in seeking to be struck by the given by going beyond the limits set by an orthodoxy.[27] The given is therefore not something appearing within a general pure form of representation and in the identity of the appearance, but rather an event occurring when such forms break down: "As experience, as actualized performance, according to its proper mode, art realizes that which a philosophy fascinated by identity and unity has such trouble achieving: a critique of representation, condition for a transcendental empiricism."[28]

This language of revolutionary purification is therefore not mere rhetoric. Transcendental empiricism is a reaction against a perceived philosophical conformism which is literally a commitment to formal presuppositions but also, socially and politically, a commitment to established forms set by common sense and "cliché."[29] Expurgation is to be attained through an experimental method where experiment is taken in the strong sense of adventure and creativity outside the boundaries of established knowledge and against a true and "proper" image of thought.[30] Here, the experimental is extended beyond its association with the empirical sciences and into artistic and aesthetic creativity: "Transcendental empiricism is therefore presented as a true transcendental aesthetic, simultaneously a science of the sensible and a philosophy of art, or, as Deleuze will say in 1981: a logic – of sensation."[31]

This extension is guided by other thinkers from Deleuze's early books: "Hume and Nietzsche, Proust, Bergson and Spinoza are the successive interlocutors of such a transformation of Kantian critique."[32] The selection of Kant as the main protagonist in the development of Deleuze's thought and method is not therefore done through the exclusion of other thinkers, but rather occurs through an ordering of them in terms of priority and function. According to Sauvagnargues' complex and authoritative definition of transcendental empiricism, Kant becomes the central figure in Deleuze's philosophy: both saint and sinner. Other thinkers then occupy roles in relation to this struggle with the Kantian legacy.

This in turn shows some of the risks in interpreting *Difference and Repetition* through its historical relations in philosophy but also in relation to the rest of Deleuze's oeuvre. The dialogue entertained with the tradition has many voices and the voice selected as dominant then conditions not only the place of all the others, but also our understanding of the main terms of the book. There is a different *Difference and Repetition*, when Nietzsche, Bergson, Plato, or Hume is taken as the main influence or opponent. There is also therefore the potential for different accounts of Deleuze's method. I will go on to show some of these possible readings while following Sauvagnargues' analysis more closely in relation to the subject and to time.

If we take Plato as the main inheritance and opposition for Deleuze, then the notions of condition and the concept of transcendental take a lesser role in his philosophy. This does not mean these notions disappear. Instead, Deleuze transforms Platonic idealism through a reversal where Plato's Ideas switch into pure becoming and intensities. This means the Idea no longer fulfills the role of timeless anchor and test for poor copies and false pretenders, such as the Idea of virtue against which virtuous citizens are found wanting. Instead, the Idea generates difference and dissimilarity, rendering true copies obsolete and legitimate pretenders illegal:

Among Plato's most strange pages, manifesting the anti-Platonism at the heart of Platonism, there are those suggesting that difference, the dissimilar, the unequal, in short, becoming could not just be faults affecting the copy, as a cost of its secondary quality, a counterpart to its resemblance, but would themselves be models, terrible models of the pseudo where the power of the false is developed. (*DR* 128, translation modified)

In this passage, Deleuze is discussing six of the most important themes of *Difference and Repetition*. First, difference is to be seen as primary and resistant to representation and to identification. Difference is dissimilar in itself and hence impossible to represent. Difference is always unequal; it cannot be equated to its identity. Second, difference is change. It is always in a process of becoming. Third, difference is generative. It forces things to become different, thereby making them different to what they are. The being of a thing – past or present or future – thereby becomes a falsehood. Fourth, then, everything is a model, not a copy of an original but rather a simulacrum. So – fifth and sixth themes – such simulacra exist in ever-changing series, not regulated according to the repetition of the same, but rather by the creation of difference through the repetition of becoming.

Deleuze allies this reversal of Platonism not to anything found in Kant, but rather to Nietzsche's model of eternal return. Plato operates according to a circle based on the truth and identity of the Idea (over time all new false pretenders to virtue are found out by the recurrence of the true Idea). This circle is replaced by Nietzsche's eternal return, according to which only difference returns and never the same. The Kantian focus on the given and on its conditions then becomes a moment in a wider set of metaphysical processes, such as eternal return. The process is very hard to interpret in post-Kantian transcendental terms because the return of difference cannot be deduced but is instead posited speculatively. The return is the only process that remains the same: "It is not the Same that returns. It is not the Similar that returns. The Same is the return of that which returns, that is of the Different. The Similar is the return of that which returns, that is of the Dissimilar" (*DR* 384). In this passage, as elsewhere in the book, the use of capitals indicates the idea rather than any particular manifestation. Taken on this Nietzschean and Platonic basis, Deleuze's method becomes speculative. It is still empirical in Sauvagnargues' sense. Now, though, it is so right down to

Deleuze's method itself, which instead of being characterized once and for all as transcendental idealism, becomes a succession of creative speculative systems.

No doubt this has the disadvantage of losing the self-critical and anti-dogmatic rigor of radical critique. It has a double gain, though, of releasing the concept of experiment from its post-Kantian conditions and of allowing interpretations of Deleuze and of his work with Guattari as a series of metaphysical experiments, rather than a single line on transcendental empiricism, from its birth pangs in Deleuze's historical studies to its refined apogee in his last essay, "Immanence: A Life ..." There is still place for Kantian critique, for instance where Deleuze introduces Kant's idea of a transcendental illusion for types of thought after Plato, where representation takes over from the copy and the model: "Representation is the place of transcendental illusion. This illusion has many forms, four interpenetrated forms, corresponding particularly to thought, to the sensible, to the Idea and to being" (*DR* 265, translation modified).

Against the ubiquitous application of transcendental empiricism to Deleuze's work, the transition from Platonic copy to Aristotelian representation shows each critical method to have a well-defined role: "A slippage occurred from the Platonic world to the world of representation (which is why, there too, we could present Plato at the origin, at the crossroads of a decision)." Every method, every system, and hence every critical move is the result not of a transcendental deduction regarding legitimate conditions, but rather of a dice throw at a crossing. They are selections rather than deductions. For Deleuze, a transcendental illusion, for instance regarding thought, involves the imposition of illusory figures on a process. These figures deny the essence of the process while claiming to embody it. In continuing to interpret Deleuze in the transcendental line we release the full potential of this critique and renew the line of empiricism drawn from Hume. The problem remains, though, of whether this allows the full force of Deleuze's other methods to come through, notably, though not exclusively, his pragmatism and his creative and speculative legacies.

Did you press send?
It will never have been me

NOTES

1   See Paul Patton, *Deleuze and the Political* (London: Routledge, 2000), pp. 11–12.

2   See Miguel de Beistegui, *Immanence: Deleuze and Philosophy* (Edinburgh University Press, 2010), pp. 172–74.

3   See Jean-Jacques Lecercle, *Deleuze and Language* (Basingstoke: Palgrave Macmillan, 2002).

4   Anne Sauvagnargues, *Deleuze: l'empirisme transcendantal* (Paris: Presses Universitaires de France, 2009).

5   For the most extensive discussion of transcendental empiricism other than Sauvagnargues', see Levi R. Bryant, *Difference and Givenness: Deleuze's Transcendental Empiricism and the Ontology of Immanence* (Evanston: Northwestern University Press, 2008). Sauvagnargues' interpretation takes the development of Kantian critique as her main lead whereas Bryant emphasizes the given and its encounter as ways of responding to problems of transcendental empiricism (pp. 15–17). This does not mean the two views are incompatible, but rather that transcendental empiricism allows for different accentuation dependent on whether we emphasize its critical relations or its internal tensions. Sauvagnargues and Bryant of course take both approaches but accentuate one or the other. For a related but slightly different take on transcendental empiricism, see Joe Hughes' very helpful introduction, *Deleuze's "Difference and Repetition": A Reader's Guide* (New York: Continuum, 2009). The contrast with Sauvagnargues and Bryant can be found in an approach where Kant's transcendental philosophy is contrasted with Husserl's phenomenology (pp. 8–12).

6   For a detailed account of these early years among the Parisian intellectual elite in the last years of the Second World War and immediately after, see François Dosse, *Gilles Deleuze et Félix Guattari: biographie croisée* (Paris: La Découverte, 2007), pp. 114–27.

7   For an alternative approach from within the tradition that emphasizes the problem rather than transcendental conditions, see Pierre Montebello, *Deleuze* (Paris: Vrin, 2008), pp. 47–51.

8   There is a detailed account of the spread of Deleuze's thought outside France in Dosse, *Gilles Deleuze et Félix Guattari*, pp. 556–83. See also Deleuze's remarks on English and American literature in *Dialogues* and his essays in *Essays Critical and Clinical*.

9   *Difference and Repetition* introduces a new philosophy of time constructed around three syntheses of time. For a critical account of this philosophy see James Williams, *Gilles Deleuze's Philosophy of Time: A Critical Introduction and Guide* (Edinburgh University Press, 2011)

and Nathan Widder, *Reflections on Time and Politics* (University Park, PA: Pennsylvania State University Press, 2008).

10 Sauvagnargues, *Deleuze: l'empirisme transcendantal*, p. 30.

11 For a helpful discussion of Deleuze and dogmatism in relation to Kant, see Bryant, *Difference and Givenness*, pp. 174–78.

12 Jeffrey A. Bell has a good analysis of transcendental empiricism in relation to Hume: Jeffrey A. Bell, *Deleuze's Hume: Philosophy, Culture and the Scottish Enlightenment* (Edinburgh University Press, 2009), pp. 15–18.

13 For two strong collections taking different approaches to Deleuze and science, see John Marks (ed.), *Deleuze and Science*, special number of *Paragraph*, 29:2 (July 2006) and Peter Gaffney (ed.), *The Force of the Virtual: Deleuze, Science, and Philosophy* (Minneapolis: University of Minnesota Press, 2010).

14 The most helpful and deep study of Deleuze's critical relation to Aristotle is by Henry Somers-Hall in *Hegel, Deleuze, and the Critique of Representation: Dialectics of Negation and Difference* (Albany, NY: SUNY Press, 2012), chapter 2 *passim*.

15 One of the best discussions of this somewhat Manichean relation to the history of philosophy can be found in Catherine Malabou's essay "Who's Afraid of Hegelian Wolves?," in Paul Patton (ed.), *Deleuze: A Critical Reader* (Oxford: Blackwell, 1996), pp. 114–38.

16 For an introduction to Deleuze's transcendental empiricism that takes account of his work on the subject and literature, and connects it well to the later works with Guattari, see Claire Colebrook, *Gilles Deleuze* (London: Routledge, 2002), esp. pp. 84–89.

17 Sauvagnargues, *Deleuze: l'empirisme transcendantal*, p. 27.

18 For work drawing on Heidegger and Deleuze, see Miguel de Beistegui, *Truth and Genesis: Philosophy as Differential Ontology* (Bloomington: Indiana University Press, 2004). The reading of Deleuze through conceptual connections with Heidegger allows Beistegui to give a more strongly ontological reading of Deleuze than found in proponents of the post-Kantian transcendental empiricism. This is significant because it allows Beistegui to make good use of the idea of genesis in drawing a philosophy of nature and science from Deleuze that is much harder to develop through the Kantian critical heritage. Beistegui uses the term transcendental empiricism, but stretches it thanks to analyses of genesis through, for example, biological differentiation in Deleuze (pp. 292–93).

19 For a discussion of Deleuze and friendship see Charles J. Stivale, *Gilles Deleuze's ABCs: The Folds of Friendship* (Baltimore: Johns Hopkins University Press, 2008), pp. 70–71.

20 For a collection on Deleuze and Derrida, see Paul Patton and John Protevi (eds.), *Between Deleuze and Derrida* (London: Continuum, 2003). The essays by Smith, Alliez, and Lawlor are particularly helpful in explaining the importance of the Deleuze and Derrida, for, respectively studies of method, language, and death.

21 For a more comprehensive collection on Deleuze's many connections to other philosophers see Graham Jones and Jon Roffe (eds.), *Deleuze's Philosophical Lineage* (Edinburgh University Press, 2009). The best work on the underestimated and more arcane references for Deleuze, in critical relation to Kantian transcendental empiricist interpretations, is Christian Kerslake, *Immanence and the Vertigo of Philosophy: From Kant to Deleuze* (Edinburgh University Press, 2009). See, in particular, Kerslake's discussion of immanence through Spinoza (pp. 264–67).

22 See Simon Duffy (ed.), *Virtual Mathematics: The Logic of Difference* (Manchester: Clinamen Press, 2006), for discussions of Deleuze and mathematics by Duffy, DeLanda, Salanskis, Durie, Badiou, Plotnistky, Evens, Smith, and Webb. See in particular David Webb's study of mathematics and the transcendental (pp. 103–12). See also Manuel DeLanda, *Intensive Science and Virtual Philosophy* (New York: Continuum, 2002), for an interpretation of Deleuze in relation to mathematics and to science that yields as little as possible to any notion of transcendental empiricism (p. 177).

23 For work on Deleuze and literature see Ronald Bogue, *Deleuze on Literature* (New York: Routledge, 2003). Bogue is good at explaining concepts such as chaos and cosmos through Deleuze's work on literature (p. 188).

24 The most important work on Deleuze and the overturning on Plato is Daniel W. Smith, "The Concept of the Simulacrum: Deleuze and the Overturning of Platonism," *Continental Philosophy Review*, 38:1–2 (2006), 89–123.

25 Sauvagnargues, *Deleuze: l'empirisme transcendantal*, p. 35.

26 *Ibid.*, pp. 45–46.

27 *Ibid.*, p. 32.

28 *Ibid.*, p. 48.

29 *Ibid.*, p. 32.

30 *Ibid.*, p. 33.

31 *Ibid.*, p. 49.

32 *Ibid.*, p. 35.

3 The Deleuzian reversal of Platonism

Of the many books that Deleuze devoted to the history of philosophy, none focuses on ancient philosophy. And yet, one could argue that few thinkers of the twentieth century have engaged with ancient philosophy, and drawn from it, as much and as systematically as Deleuze. Naturally, one could think of Heidegger as another twentieth-century philosopher whose thought was shaped through his confrontation with Greek philosophy. But where Heidegger eventually mobilizes the Presocratics against Plato and Aristotle, and seeks to extract from them possibilities of thought beyond the "closure" of metaphysics, Deleuze doesn't envisage the history of philosophy in the same terms, and simply refuses to identify what he calls "the metaphysics of representation," or "Platonism," with metaphysics *as such*. That being said, it would be difficult to ignore that his entire philosophy – up until *Logic of Sense* at least – unfolds under the Nietzschean injunction to reverse, overturn, and overcome Platonism, stressing all the while the need to construct another "image of thought." Most striking, perhaps, is the extent to which his effort to produce another image of *thought* requires a new thought of the *image*, one that he finds already at work in Greek philosophy itself. My goal, here, is threefold: to return to the source of Platonism by following the thread of the image, and show the extent to which philosophy is, from the start, and irreducibly, a matter of ethics, aesthetics, and politics; to reveal the extent to which Deleuze saw resources to overturn Platonism in ancient, and even Platonic, philosophy itself; to indicate the manner in which, drawing on those resources, Deleuze develops an anti-Platonism based on the concepts of "difference" and "repetition."

WHAT IS PLATONISM?

Before we can understand *why* Deleuze equates the task of philosophy with that of the overthrow of Platonism, and *how* he intends to
bring it about, we need to begin by asking *what* defines Platonism.
The idea and the task of inverting or reversing Platonism initially
came from Nietzsche. In an early sketch for *The Birth of Tragedy*,
Nietzsche writes: "My philosophy an *inverted Platonism*: the further removed from true being, the purer, the more beautiful, the
better it is. Living in semblance [*Schein*] as goal."[1] As is well known,
Nietzsche later complicated this task by asking about the sense and
status of semblance itself, once it has been freed from its subordination to the super-sensuous. For him, the question became one of
knowing how to think and live in a world that is *only* and purely
sensible: "We have abolished the true [*wahre*] world," Nietzsche
famously claims in the section of *Twilight of the Idols* entitled
"How the 'True World' finally Became a Fable."[2] Having announced
the abolition of the true world, he asks: "what world is left? The illusory one, perhaps?" To which he responds emphatically: "But no! *We
got rid of the illusory world along with the true one!*"[3] Following
Nietzsche's own clue, Deleuze insists that Platonism is not redu-
cible to the mere distinction between the world of essences and the
world of appearances, or the intelligible and the sensible (*DR* 166,
340; *LS* 292). There is another, more fundamental distinction, which
characterizes Platonism proper, and which is to become the object
of the reversal. It is that distinction which, ultimately, reveals the
fundamental *motivation* behind Platonism as a whole. The distinction, internal to the world of appearances (φαινόμενα), is that between
icons and phantasms, or images and simulacra.[4] We should note
from the start that Plato introduces this distinction in Book 10 of
the *Republic*, that is, in the very specific context of a critique, and
even the outright condemnation, of mimetic art in relation to politics and the construction of the ideal city state. The distinction,
along with its eminently political context, is affirmed once again in
the *Sophist* (236b, 264c). To that distinction, we need to add another,
between the copy and the model, which Plato introduces only to be
able to distinguish between true and false images, or between icons
and simulacra. We should be careful, then, not to confuse the two
types of images (εἴδωλα) or image-making (εἰδωλοποιικὴ τέχνη), namely,

likeness-making (εἰκαστικὴ τέχνη), such as that of the cabinetmaker, which "produces an image [εἰκών] or imitation by following the proportions of the original, of the paradigm, and by giving the right color to each part," and mere semblances (φαντάσμα), which require a technique that Plato characterizes as *phantastic* (φανταστική τέχνη). Whereas the copy is defined in relation to the original, which it resembles more or less, or which it imitates to a greater or lesser extent, the simulacrum is defined by the fact that it *seems* to conform to the original, or the model, but in reality unfolds outside the relation between original and copy. It is of the utmost importance, then, to emphasize the essential ambiguity of the image itself, which has the power to disclose the original, or the model, but also to conceal it, and deceive us into believing that it is the original. The images of the artist, like those of the sophist, only *simulate* being (*Republic*, 596d–e): they *are* nothing (real), yet pretend to be, thus giving rise to the problem that Plato seeks to solve. Between the two types of images, there is not so much a difference of degree as of kind. The task of Platonism is to reveal that difference and provide the philosophical tools that will allow one to discriminate between them.

What characterizes Platonism – at least that of the *Sophist* and the *Republic* – is that, whilst recognizing the existence of such untamed differences, or such a multiplicity without tutelage, it sees it as a threat to thought, morality, politics, and art, and finds in it the seeds of anarchy: "the will to eliminate simulacra or phantasms has no motivation apart from the moral" (*DR* 265). To be more specific, Platonism is a response and a solution to a problem brought about by the birth of Athenian democracy, in which, in the words of a commentator, "anyone could lay claim to anything, and could carry the day by the force of rhetoric."[5] Such is the reason why Platonism seeks to nip this anarchy and rebellion in the bud, by hunting down, as Plato says, simulacra and rogue images of all kinds. At the heart of Platonism lies the desire, which Deleuze will not cease to attack and try and overturn by revealing another type of desire, and another type of life, to introduce Judgment in philosophy (in the plane of immanence), and give it a (preferably bad) conscience. Platonism is the effort to establish a definitive authority and a transcendence (different, Deleuze insists in *Essays Critical and Clinical*, from the "imperial or mythical transcendence" [171] that predates the emergence of the Greek *polis* and philosophy), to which ultimately everything can be referred: "The poisoned gift of Platonism is to have introduced transcendence into philosophy, to have given transcendence a plausible philosophical meaning (the triumph of the judgment of God)" (*ECC* 137). Like Nietzsche, Deleuze sees in Platonism the source of our sadness, our decadent values, and our most deeply entrenched illusions, extended and radicalized in Christianity, which Nietzsche defined precisely as "Platonism for 'the people'".[6] But, Deleuze argues, transcendence should have no place in philosophy; it is not a philosophical invention, but a religious, moral, and political distribution of power. Deleuze goes even further by claiming that the distinct opportunity or destiny of philosophy is bound up with the emergence of immanence as a political "event" in the broad sense of the term, which presupposed the advent of democracy as a society of equals, and of philosophy as a society of friends (*WP* 43–44, 86–88).[7] It's that political transformation which, in the absence of the old hierarchy, generates the problem of Platonism; and it is to that potential anarchy and crisis of power that Plato responds by turning philosophy into the ultimate source of authority. Subsequently, Deleuze insists, "the world of representation will more or less forget its moral origin and presuppositions" (*DR* 265). But that origin will continue to shape and orient it, and even determine its most metaphysical concepts and onto-theological hierarchies. If there is a forgetting at the heart of metaphysics, then, it is not that of Being, but that of the moral values and attitude underlying it. As a result, the overcoming of Platonism is itself a matter of moral genealogy and political critique, not ontology (or at least not primarily).

How, exactly, does Plato manage to avoid anarchy and "exorcise simulacra?" With the help of a remarkable tool, a *concept*, which is also, and above all, selective. It is precisely with a view to bringing a certain order and hierarchy in the visible world, including the world of the City, for which, in the *Republic*, Plato is concerned to provide an ideal constitution, that he creates the most formidable and arguably successful concept of the entire history of philosophy, namely, the Idea. In doing so, however, he reintroduces transcendence in philosophy. The force of the Idea, which any anti-Platonism will have to reckon with, and substitute with another, equally powerful concept, is that it is at once a political weapon, a moral tool, and an aesthetic ideal. Ideas designate beings (ὄντα) in their truth. Semblances, on the other hand, are nothing real. As such, the Idea is the principle of selection that allows one to distinguish between images, and especially between likenesses and semblances. The Idea enables one to discriminate between, and select, those images we can count on, as they set us on the way to truth, and those images that lead us astray and onto the path of error and illusion. In other words, Ideas help us distinguish between those images that *resemble* the original, and those that are mere *semblances* of the original. The Idea is itself the origin of all appearances. It is itself not an image, but the model after which all images are forged. To the extent that it can be apprehended, it is not through the senses (αἴσθησις), as an image, but through thought (νόησις). If all images are derived from the original, which they imitate, or only simulate, it is only fitting that the only type that can distinguish between images and simulacra by looking at the original, namely, the philosopher, be the custodian of that order that extends between the visible and the invisible. It is only fitting that the philosopher rule the City according to that natural order and hierarchy. Artists, sophists, and other simulators, on the other hand, whose power of deception is a source of corruption for all citizens, will be banned from the City, or closely watched.[8] For once in the grip of such deceiving images, the souls are riveted to non-being, and oblivious of truth. They, in turn, become a danger and a threat – to truth, and to the possibility of constructing a city that would be built on truth. With Platonism, philosophy becomes a police operation. And the greatest police operation we find in Plato, one that involves a strategy of shadowing, tailing, and results in a relentless manhunt, is against the Sophist, considered to be the greatest enemy of the ideal city. But the no less remarkable feature of Plato's *Sophist* is the extent to which the Sophist, precisely as a shadow or semblance of truth, as a false pretender, continuously escapes the hunt, snare, or trap of the Eleatic Stranger, and in such a way that, at the very end of the dialogue, after what seems like an interminable chase, the matter of the difference between the Sophist and the Philosopher isn't entirely resolved.[9]

Still, the *raison d'être* of the Idea is its ability to discriminate, eliminate, select, and choose. It is only superficially that the Platonic method involves dividing something according to its natural articulations, that is, according to genus and species.[10] In other words, the

operation of specification, from genus to species and all the way
to what Aristotle calls "differences," with which Plato's work is
sometimes associated, is only a preliminary step towards a more
significant goal. Or, to put it differently, the Aristotelian operation
of division and specification is itself an effect of, and a response to,
the image of thought that Plato had identified for philosophy. The
Platonic method is a dialectic not of contradiction and contraries
(antiphasis), but of rivalry (amphisbetesis). It is concerned with the
need to select rivals and suitors. The ultimate goal of the division is
to distinguish the real thing from the illusion of the imposture and
to establish a hierarchy between types. And where there is no longer
a genuine relation of resemblance or imitation, but only a simulation or simulacrum of imitation, the philosophical, moral, and
political procedure of exclusion of the claimant is introduced. Once
the Idea – of the Good, Justice, Beauty, Love, the Statesman, etc. –
has been established, it becomes a question of presenting the rivals
before its tribunal, and asking them the extent to which they resemble the Idea, or "participate" in it.[11] The greater the degree of participation, the purer or more authentic the claim and the pretender:

> Undoubtedly, one must distinguish all sorts of degrees, an entire hierarchy,
> in this elective participation. Is there not a possessor of the third or the
> fourth rank, and on to an infinity of degradation culminating in the one
> who possesses no more than a simulacrum, a mirage – the one who [like
> the sophist] is himself a mirage and simulacrum? (LS 255)

But the Idea alone possesses something firsthand, and it's only in
relation to it that the hierarchy can be established.

   What are the constitutive features of the Idea? How does it work?
By contrast with the image, which is *only* an image, that is, secondary, derivative, and always changing, the Idea is the thing itself, in
its being and truth. It is itself and nothing else (*auto kath'auto*). In
other words, the Idea is the very figure of *sameness*, or self-identity,
and defines being as identity. It is also characterized, from the point
of view of the image, by a relation of internal *resemblance* and likeness: identity defines not only the original, but also the relation
between the original and the copy; only the relation of likeness, and
thus of identity, is recognized as a genuine relation. The threat of
those images that Plato defines as simulacra comes precisely from
the fact that they cannot be contained within such a paradigm:

the only differences that can be recognized, in every sense of the term, are those differences defined as *non*-identities, or as situated at a distance from, but still in relation to, identities. Pure differences, or simulacra, can only be rejected, expelled, or neutralized. And yet, Deleuze's entire enterprise consists in showing how such "pure" or "oceanic" differences continue to proliferate and bubble beneath the surface of fixed identities: "An entire multiplicity rumbles underneath the 'sameness' of the Idea" (*DR* 274). The challenge that Deleuze set for thought was that of accommodating, and subordinating itself to, those differences, thus altering its image and goal, and reversing its course. Thirdly, because the resemblance is internal, the copy must itself have an internal relation to the true, or being, which is itself *analogous* to that of the model. Finally, the copy must be identified by means of a method which, given two *opposed* predicates, selects the one that agrees with the model. The copy, then, can be distinguished systematically from the simulacrum by subordinating its own difference to this fourfold principle of the Same, the Similar, the Analogous, and the Opposed (*DR* 265). To be sure, Deleuze goes on say, "with Plato these instances are not yet distributed as they will be in the deployed world of representation (from Aristotle onwards)" (*DR* 265). No doubt, "in the transition from the Platonic world to the world of representation," "a slippage occurs" (*DR* 265). The sameness of the Platonic Idea, guaranteed by the Good, gives way to the *identity of the concept*, oriented towards the *form of identity in the object*, and grounded in a *self-identical thinking subject*. But, Deleuze insists, "it is the moral vision of the world that is thereby extended" (*DR* 266) and affirmed as *common sense*: the image of thought as recognition (*récognition*) requires the concordance and collaboration of all faculties (perception, memory, reason, imagination, judgment, etc.) in the presentation of the *same* object, or the object in the form of *self-identity*. Far from breaking with the *doxa*, and becoming *paradoxical*, the dominant image of thought inherited form Platonism solidifies into an *orthodoxy*, all the more difficult to shake off in that its hidden, underlying presupposition is moral through and through. It is the discourse that says or, more often, implies: "Everybody knows that … or recognizes that … Nobody can deny that …", as if thought were the most natural and consensual activity, as if a bit of good will and the right method were enough to arrive at the truth. This is how the moral vision of the world, which grants thought a good nature, and the philosopher with good will, continues to orient and shape the most abstract philosophical concepts and systems, and to generate "transcendental illusions."

HOW TO OVERTURN PLATONISM?

Having established the origin and fundamental meaning of Platonism, we need to ask about its possible reversal: what can it possibly mean, and how can it be brought about? How can one distinguish between appearances without subordinating them from the start to the self-sameness of Ideas, and introducing the problematic of imitation and participation? How can one select without judging, or at least without introducing a transcendent point of view within the immanent plane of appearances? How, in other words, can one think without Ideas, and overturn the doxic image of thought? If, as I have tried to show, the Platonic Idea is a political tool, a moral concept, and an aesthetic ideal, the question is one of knowing what image of thought, and what concepts, can be developed as a genuine alternative. Those questions take us to the very heart of the Deleuzian project and intimate the extraordinarily difficult task that awaits those who wish to create an image of thought, and a philosophy, devoid of idealism and transcendence. It cannot be a question, here, of providing a detailed account of such a project. Nor can it be a question of reviewing the various attempts that, according to Deleuze himself, have developed in the margins of Platonism, threatening it all along, opening up possibilities of thought and life unknown to it. Whilst dominant, and deeply entrenched in Western thought, Platonism is a porous substance, from which thought escapes in all sorts of ways.

In a way, the overturning of Platonism begins to unfold in the Platonic text itself, and in the *Sophist* in particular. For there, we arrive at the paradoxical and eminently open-ended situation where the art of the Sophist is brought to a point of almost absolute proximity with that of the genuine philosopher. The conclusion that we are invited to draw is that, ultimately, there is no absolute criterion for the distinction between images and simulacra. Deleuze doesn't fail to mention the irony, pushed to its very limits, that is, to the point of *humor*, which is at work in the Platonic dialogue: Plato is "the first to indicate this direction for the overthrow of Platonism" (*LS* 295). By confronting "sophism as its enemy, but also as its limit and its double" (*ECC* 136), Platonism reveals a force it cannot contain.[12] It is precisely from that standpoint, internal to Platonism, that Deleuze will attempt to overturn it. Deleuze's strategy, then, is not to construct a system of thought outside Platonism. Rather, it is to show that its reversal takes place at the very moment at which it is set up, and to see the entire system from the point of view of the simulacrum itself. Some have gone as far as to describe the Deleuzian project "as a rejuvenated and even a completed Platonism."[13] Ultimately, I would like to suggest that Deleuze's own formidable philosophical activity and creation of concepts in the 1960s, and those of "difference" and "repetition" in particular, can be attributed to such a strategy and to the need to invent new possibilities of thought and new forms of life. As a preliminary stage, however, I would like to indicate how Deleuze identifies resources to overturn Platonism within the post-Platonic age of the Greeks, and most notably in the naturalisms of Lucretius and Stoicism.

Lucretius' naturalism

In his essay, "The Simulacrum and Ancient Philosophy," Deleuze presents the naturalism of the author of *De Rerum Natura* as a speculative as well as practical enterprise that is specifically anti-Platonic. It consists of an investigation into the nature of things, and the laws of nature, the ultimate goal of which is to identify the conditions under which the human can achieve the highest degree of fulfillment, which Lucretius defines as pleasure:

The speculative object and the practical object of philosophy as Naturalism, science and pleasure, coincide on this point: it is always a matter of denouncing the illusion, the false infinite, the infinity of religion and all of the … myths in which it is expressed. To the question "what is the use of philosophy" the answer must be: who else would have an interest in holding forth the image of a free man, and in denouncing all of the forces which need myth and troubled souls in order to establish their power? … One of the most profound constants of Naturalism is to denounce everything that is sadness, everything that is the cause of sadness, and everything that needs sadness to exercise its power. From Lucretius to Nietzsche, the same end is pursued and attained. (*LS* 278–79, translation modified)

On one level, Lucretius' point of departure is remarkably close to that of Plato, and everything happens as if he placed himself on the very terrain that Plato had chosen for philosophy. Like Plato, Lucretius develops a theory of the image, and emphasizes the need to distinguish between different types of images. As in Plato, the ultimate goal of such a distinction is moral, or, better said perhaps, ethical. Yet the context is entirely different from that of Platonism: the image is not opposed to the phantasm or the simulacrum, and is not thought in relation to an original, a model, or an Idea. In fact, by translating the Epicurean εἴδωλον with the Latin *simulacrum*, which he also refers to images as *imagines*, *effigiae*, and *figurae*, Lucretius blurs the distinction that Plato had introduced between copies and simulacra. Insofar as simulacra "are everywhere" and "we do not cease to be immersed in them, and to be battered by them as if by waves" (*LS* 275), the question becomes one of knowing how to see through them, and of identifying the criterion by which such a distinction can be made. If there is a need to distinguish between such semblances or "impressions," then, it is not with a view to establishing how far from or how close to an original, posited as Idea, they are nor indeed to separate images from simulacra, but to distinguish between images and illusions, or false representations.

By contrast with the Platonic account, Lucretius' explanation doesn't consist of a comparison between an image, and its (more or less successful) imitation of the original, and the simulacrum, as bearing no relation whatsoever with the original. Rather, it consists of an immanent and purely materialist method, which moves from the core and depth of the natural entity in question to its surface, and what can be apprehended at the surface. In place of a vertical and transcendent structure, governed by the Idea's relation to its many instances, we have an immanent structure, governed by a complex play of depth and surface. In place of an eidetic core, appre-hended through our faculty of intellection, we have a material core, apprehended through the senses. In addition, the relation between depth and surface, atoms and effects, is not one of imitation and resemblance, but of production through combination: every body produces images and simulacra which do not reproduce the exter-nal appearance of its smallest constitutive elements; although we do not see or perceive matter at the atomic level, we always perceive it *as it is*, in the way in which it is combined and composed. Near the beginning of Book 4 of *De Rerum Natura*, Lucretius writes the following: "[T]here exist what we call images [*simulacra*] of things; which, like films [*membranae*] drawn from the outermost surface of things, flit about hither and thither through the air" (4: 30–32). Insofar as those effects, produced by things at their surface, affect the mind (*animus*) and the soul (*anima*), they account for sensible qualities. To be more precise, and in Deleuze's words: "Sounds, smells, tastes, and temperatures refer especially to the emissions from the depths, whereas visual determinations, forms, and colors refer to the simulacra of the surface" (*LS* 273). In fact, the situation is even more complex, "since each sense combines information of the depth with information of the surface" and emissions from the depth necessarily pass through the surface (*LS* 273). In any case, Deleuze goes on to write, "emissions and simulacra are grasped not as atomic compounds, but as qualities apprehended at a distance on and in the object; the distance is given by the stream of air that emissions and simulacra push before them, as it passes through the sensory organ" (*LS* 274). In other words, it is all a matter of the speed with which those emissions traverse space. Many images, Lucretius writes, "arise in brief space, so that there is good reason to call the origin of these things rapid" (4: 159–60). It is moments of time itself that we feel and apprehend. Simulacra, for example, are "swifter than emanations, as if there were, in the case of sensible time, differentials of diverse orders" (*LS* 275).

There is yet another kind of image – images that enjoy a high degree of independence with respect to objects and an extreme mobility. It is as if, with those images, and as a result of their independence, a certain confusion could arise, and thus, also, a certain danger. Clouds, for example, of which Lucretius recognizes that no man can say what they are an image of (4: 174–75), as they are carried by the wind, can take on various shapes, such as that of a giant, or a monster (4: 136–42). Being very far from the objects from which they emanate, and having lost with them any direct connection, clouds form these grand autonomous figures, in which we are tempted to read all sorts of signs and project false ideas. Our belief in gods, in a hidden meaning and will, stems from such false conclusions regarding physical impressions. Equally deceiving and misleading are those images that are made of "particularly subtle and agile simulacra, coming from various objects, and able to merge together, condense and dissipate" (*LS* 276, translation modified). No doubt, Deleuze goes on to explain, they are too swift and too tenuous to be actually *seen*, yet stable enough to supply the *animus*, or the mind – of which Lucretius says that it is "itself thin and wonderfully easy to move" (4: 748) – with visions of its own: "centaurs, Cerberus-like creatures, and ghosts; all of the images which correspond to desire or, again, and especially, dream images."[14] Images produced by the imagination, then, or by dreams, aren't of a different nature from those that we simply see: they too are simulacra that emanate from objects, the only difference being that they are more subtle and thinner than those of vision; rapidly passing through the senses, they reach the mind more quickly, and affect it more vividly.

The third and final type of image, also potentially deceiving, which Deleuze emphasizes, broaches the question of (erotic) desire and its problematic relation to pleasure. In a passage from *De Natura Rerum*, Lucretius compares the "thin images" of love with a thirst that cannot be quenched. Whereas "the desire of water or bread is easily fulfilled," "from man's aspect and beautiful bloom nothing comes into the body to be enjoyed *except thin images* [*simulacra tenvia*]," "as when in dreams a thirsty man seeks to drink, and no water is forthcoming to quench the burning in his frame, but he seeks the image [*simulacra*] of water, striving in vain, and in the midst of a rushing river thirsts while he drinks: so in love Venus mocks lovers with images [*simulacris*]" (4: 1084–101). In the case of erotic love, then, we succumb to a certain illusion, which makes us believe in the reality of something, and the possibility of a sat-isfaction, when the image that we hold on to is actually severed from what we seek to achieve. We seek something stable, definitive, which we hope to achieve by grasping the most fleeting images.

Those three types of simulacra or, better said perhaps, of phan-tasms, and the illusions to which they lead, are all due to the fact that we project infinity into something finite, and are unable to relate the visions of our mind to perceptions of actual simulacra, or surface and depth images. Lucretius' materialism is a systematic effort to dissolve all illusions – religious, dreamlike, and erotic – and denounce all uses of the bad infinite. In the end, everything comes down to this distinction, which is also the basic principle of selection, between the infinite and the finite, as well as the true infinite and the bad infinite. As Deleuze puts it: "*simulacra produce the mirage of a false infinite in the images which they form;* they give birth to the double illusion of an infinite capacity for pleasure and an infinite possibility of torment" (*LS* 277).

Stoicism

The naturalism of Epicurus and Lucretius is often opposed to the Stoic tradition. There are historical reasons for such an opposition: whereas the uncompromising materialism of Epicureanism amounted to an open war against religion, Christian theology and morality made use of Stoicism, and of its asceticism in particular. On Deleuze's reading, however, Stoicism and Epicureanism share a common ground and aspiration, namely, their anti-Platonism, and a common question, namely, that of the relation between bodies and their surface, effects of surfaces, and events. In the second series of *Logic of Sense*, Deleuze claims that, with their theory of the event, to which we shall turn very shortly, "the Stoics bring about the first great and radical reversal of Platonism" (*LS* 6, translation modified). In the same series, we are told that the Epicureans themselves had a theory, albeit never fully developed, of the event, which was very close to that of the Stoics.[15] With the Stoics, then, we encounter once again the question of the surface, and its relation to depth – a question which the Epicureans summarized with their concept of the simulacrum, and which the Stoics refer to as "incorporeals," or "events." Let me begin by summarizing the Stoic theory of the event, before turning to the philosophy of time that Deleuze extracts from it, and which will open up the distinctly Deleuzian concept of repetition.[16]

Stoicism also begins with a distinction, which Deleuze sees as a powerful alternative to the Platonic distinction between images and simulacra, or Ideas and phantasms. The distinction in question is that between bodies (σώματα) and the effects produced by those bodies – effects that are themselves incorporeal entities (ἀσώματα). The crucial point, with respect to our overall problematic and goal, is that, ultimately, this distinction corresponds to a temporal distinction, or a distinction between two modalities of time.

Let me elaborate further on the distinction between bodies and incorporeals, and weave the temporal distinction into it. Firstly, then, there are bodies, "with their tensions, physical qualities, actions and passions, and the corresponding 'states of affairs'" (LS 4). "States of affairs" (états de choses) here translates the Greek τὸ τύγχανον. These states of affairs, actions and passions, are the result of the various ways in which bodies mix together. The time of bodies is the present: the living present is the exact temporal extension, or the duration, which accompanies and measures the action of the agent and the passion of the patient. Bodies are connected together as causes (but not as effects), which exist (ὑπάρχει) in space and in the living present, and the unity of which is called "Destiny." The modality of being of bodies is existence. Another way of saying this is to say that all that exists is corporeal. Such a statement would seem to point to an irreducible materialism. And yet, as we shall see in a moment, bodies don't exhaust the real.

Secondly, bodies, insofar as they are causes, produce *effects*, which are of an entirely different nature: the effects are incorporeal entities. It is this difference in kind between bodies and incorporeals that Deleuze is concerned to investigate. Formulated in such a schematic way, however, the distinction seems dangerously close to the Platonic distinction between images and Ideas, or the Aristotelian distinction between substances and essences. And, as we shall see, Deleuze increases the potential misunderstanding when he equates the incorporeal with the ideal. It is all the more important, then, to show how radically different the two distinctions are. Their difference is ultimately temporal: whereas the Platonic and Aristotelian distinctions aim to grasp the permanent and stable behind the fleeting and becoming, the Stoics understand the incorporeal as the eventful, which opens up a different modality of time. Of incorporeals, we cannot say that they *exist*, nor even, and especially not, that they *are*. Rather, we need to say that they "insist" or "subsist" (ὑφεστάναι). Besides existence, then, which designates the reality of bodies, there is at least another sense of being, that of the incorporeal. Incorporeals are neither agents nor patients, but effects of actions and passions – "impassive results." Because they are neither substances nor simply accidents, we need to treat them not as substantives, or adjectives, but as *verbs*. This distinction between the corporeal and the incorporeal draws on the Stoic theory of causality. Following the Platonic definition of being as power (δύναμις),[17] the Stoics understand the body as what can act or be acted upon. By contrast, they define the incorporeal as

essentially inactive and impassive: "According to them, the incorporeal neither acts on anything, nor is acted upon by anything."[18]
This view implies that whilst incorporeals do not interact with bodies, nor bodies with incorporeals, bodies do interact with another.
Yet a body can cause an incorporeal effect in another body, such as
"being burnt" or "being cut." It is clear, therefore, that the Stoics
draw a radical distinction between two planes of being: on the one
hand, real or profound being, force (δύναμις); on the other, the plane
of effects, which take place on the surface of being, and constitute
an endless multiplicity of incorporeal beings, which the Stoics refer
to as *attributes* (and distinguish from properties).

This new dualism between bodies or states of affairs and incorporeal events carries decisive consequences for the metaphysics
of representation. For the Aristotelian tradition, all categories are
said of, and in relation to, Being. Difference itself is recognized and
located "between substance as the primary sense and the other categories which are related to it as accidents" (*LS* 7). For the Stoics,
on the other hand, accidents, states of affairs, qualities and quantities *are*, or are a part of substance. They *exist* like the substance.
In that sense, like the Epicureans, the Stoics can be seen to force
the simulacrum back onto the substance, or, should we privilege
the Platonic vocabulary, the image. Their distinctive move, however, consists in understanding the effects produced by bodies as
incorporeals, and therefore as outside or otherwise than being (or
existence). This is how, for them, the highest term is not Being, but
Something (*aliquid*), not in the sense of *a* being, or entity, but in the
"non-personal" sense of the *event* that precedes and exceeds every
subject or substance, and every noun. This apparently innocuous
move amounts, as already suggested, to "the first major reversal of
Platonism" (*LS* 7). Why? Precisely insofar as the Idea, which Plato
posited as primary and permanent, and from which the image and
the sensible world as a whole emerges, through imitation, is now
identified with the incorporeal, which is nothing but an "impassive,
sterile and inefficacious" effect that takes place at the surface of
bodies (substance and accidents, image and simulacra), without
resembling them (*LS* 7). In other words, the incorporeal, or ideal, is
only secondary and *produced* by the material interaction of bodies.

In this new configuration, it is no longer a question of neu-
tralizing the simulacra that elude the ground (the Idea) and leave

Socrates perplexed regarding their ontological status: in response to Parmenides, Socrates claims that it would be absurd to think that things "as vile and paltry as hair, dirt, and even mud" could each have a corresponding Idea. And yet, he goes on to admit, "I sometimes get disturbed, and begin to think that there is nothing without an Idea."[19] The Stoic concern, by contrast, is to free those effects that manifest themselves and unfold at the surface of things, without ground or limit (*LS* 7). It is the open and unlimited totality of those effects – effects that are not only causal, but also sonorous, linguistic, visual, etc. – that Deleuze now calls Idea, or ideality. With the Stoics, simulacra cease to be "subterranean rebels" that the Idea needs to hunt down and suppress; they rise to the surface and thrive at the surface, freed from all paradigms and norms, and are now able to unfold (to "insist"), not as particular instances of universals (of categories), but as *singularities*: "To reverse Platonism is first and foremost to remove essences and to substitute events in their place, as throws [*jets*] of singularities." By distinguishing between states of affairs (and their corresponding essences) and events, the Stoics are able to point to an entire dimension of reality, populated not by substances, accidents, and essences, but by what, following the language of mathematics, and of Lautman in particular, Deleuze calls "singular" (as opposed to "ordinary") or "sensitive" points:[20] boiling point, points of fusion, condensation, crystallization; points of tears and joy, illness and health, hope and anguish, etc. In the margins of the logic of states of affairs and actual bodies, there is a logic and chain of events, which is not causal. In that chain, all events communicate and are held together in a single Event, which bodies, including our own, arrest, freeze, and divide up, thus giving the impression of a world that is discontinuous and fragmented, oblivious of the fact that it is a continuous multiplicity.

This is the point at which we need to turn to the Stoic theory of time. To the classical view of time, which sees past, present and future as three parts of the same temporality, and privileges the present as the origin of time, the Stoics oppose two different and mutually exclusive temporalities, a temporality of depths ("Chronos"), and a temporality of surfaces ("Aion"): on the one hand, there is "the *always limited* present, which measures the action of bodies as causes and the state of their mixtures *in depth* (Chronos)"; on the other hand, there is "the *essentially unlimited* past and future, which gather incorporeal events, *at the surface*, as effects (Aion)" (*LS* 61).[21] The present incarnates itself in a state of affairs. It is, quite literally, a matter of incorporation. Incorporeals, on the other hand, are not living presents, but what escapes and eludes the present by dividing time infinitely in past and future: pure events are always about to take place, and have already taken place, *at the same time*. The two regimes of time are always intertwined, yet ontologically distinct: the time of succession, which defines being as existence, is chronological; but traversing that time, or cutting through it, is the time of *becoming*, which defines being as "insistence," or "subsistence." Since, according to Chrysippus, time is a pure continuum, and can thus be divided *ad infinitum*, it is never present strictly speaking. It always escapes the present. This, in turn, means that the present or the instant is itself nothing temporal, but is always limited. It is, if you will, the limit or measure of time, and of action in particular, as Aristotle claimed before the Stoics. Such is the reason why the Stoics say that time doesn't exist, that it is incorporeal, or that it is nothing actual.

According to Deleuze, those two "readings" of time are as necessary as they are mutually exclusive.[22] This means that they do not correspond to two different interpretations of time, but two different temporalities (something that, once again, the Stoics would dispute, insofar as, for them, the order of the present is not a temporal order). According to the first reading, it will be said that only the present exists, that it reduces or "contracts in itself the past and the future" (*LS* 61). The only reality, then, would be that of the present, and of its contractions. From contraction to contraction, and "with ever greater depth," the present "reaches the limits of the Universe and becomes a living cosmic present" (*LS* 61). Time is composed only of interlocking presents. But then, if all the presents contract in one living cosmic present, the order is entirely reversible, and, from relaxation to relaxation, the Universe can start all over again, and its infinity of presents can be restored. This is how, whilst limited, "the time of the present," as Deleuze calls it, is infinite. Its infinity is cyclical and animates a physical eternal return of the Same (*LS* 61). According to the second reading, which Deleuze is most concerned to emphasize, "it will be said that only the past and future subsist, that they subdivide each present, *ad infinitum*, however small it may be, stretching out over their empty line."[23] This movement is exactly opposed to the contraction of past and future in the living present: every present is now extended, stretched out, in two directions at once, and *ad infinitum* – like Alice in *Alice in Wonderland*, who becomes shorter and taller at the same time. It is not the cyclical, yet limited, infinity of the eternal return of the Same, but the unlimited infinity of a line that extends and spreads outward, from the middle. The eternally neutral, empty, and *infinitive* form of time undoes the material, cyclical, and limited form of actual time:

> Through its unlimited subdivision in both directions at once, each event runs along the entire Aion and becomes coextensive to its straight line in both directions. Do we then sense the approach of an eternal return no longer having anything to do with the cycle, or the entrance of a labyrinth. (*LS* 64, translation modified)

Time is still a line, and the line is still made of points. But the points are the singular points of events, and not the ordinary points of states of affairs. This is the point at which the line becomes far more labyrinthine, uncanny and threatening, far more difficult to accept, and more difficult still to *affirm*, than the infinity of the recurring present. As will become apparent in the following section, this is the point at which, extending the Stoic conception of time, and connecting it with Nietzsche's concept of eternal recurrence, Deleuze sees time as the object of a new kind of affirmation, a new test, and a new principle of selection, opposed to the moral image of thought of Platonism.

THE NEW PRINCIPLES OF SELECTION: "DIFFERENCE" AND "REPETITION"

Deleuze's own systematic attempt to overturn Platonism draws on the Stoic theory of incorporeality and time, as well as on the naturalism of Lucretius, and his theory of the simulacrum in particular. Deleuze celebrates the philosophy of pure becoming and affirmation of the former, whilst characterizing the latter as this "sensualism connected with the joy of the diverse," and this "critique of all mystifications" (*LS* 279). In his own way, Deleuze seeks to liberate philosophy from sadness, from the illusions and traps generated by the transcendent image of thought and the power of

Judgment. *Difference and Repetition* goes as far as to define itself as a "system of simulacra," that is, as a nomadic and fluid system of differences freed from the grip of Ideas and the logic of identity. The question is still one of knowing how to think diversity and multiplicity. It is still, as Deleuze says, a matter of knowing how beings are distributed or organized, how "being is distributed among beings" (*DR* 285). Playing on the many meanings of the word '*distribution*' in French, which applies also to card games, Deleuze raises the question of the rule of the game that presides over the dealing of beings as a whole: is the rule of the game given in advance, and once and for all, or is the rule the very object of the game? Is being distributed among beings through imitation, participation, or even analogy – that is, ideally and categorially, in what amounts to a movement from diversity, multiplicity, and difference, to increasing decrees of unity and identity, and culminating in the Good and God? Or is it distributed *univocally* through chance and the endless, inexhaustibly repetition of difference? Is philosophical thought oriented towards the identity of the object, or towards the differential system of multiplicities?[24]

Deleuze defines the simulacrum as "the system where different [*le différent*] relates to different through difference itself" (*DR* 277). To the formula, "only that which resembles differs," he opposes the formula, "only differences can resemble each other" (*LS* 261). Each corresponds to a different reading of the world, and a different perspective. The first, connected with the thoughts of Plato and Aristotle, thinks difference from the standpoint of a previous similarity or identity. The second, on the other hand, suggests that we think of similarities, and even identity, "as the product of a deep disparity" (*LS* 261). By saying that identity is a product of difference, Deleuze not only reverses the *terms* of Platonism. He also, and most significantly, replaces the metaphysics of representation with a metaphysics of production, which Lucretius had already intimated: difference, he claims, is essentially productive, and the only engine or principle of production. The world does not unfold through imitation and reproduction, but through a rigorous dynamic of production. If there is an origin of production, it is not identity, but *disparity*: it is as a result of disparities between elements and series, and at every level (physical, biological, psychological, aesthetic, social and political, etc.), that the world is shaped and events take place. It is only because of differences and differentials – of potential, energy, pressure, level, temperature, tension, in short, differences of *intensity*[25] – that new phenomena emerge. The first formula defines the world as a world of copies or representations, and posits it as image. The second formula, on the other hand, "defines the world of simulacra" and "posits the world itself as phantasm."[26] According to this reading of the world, phenomena are not the manifestation of a hidden essence, which they would reveal and conceal at the same time, but the expression or product of a communication between heterogeneous and disparate series, which results in a temporary solution. In such a reading of the world, there is no longer any room for icons or images: the only reality is that of simulacra, that is, phenomena generated through difference. The simulacrum is no longer a degraded copy. It is no longer a matter of distinguishing between essence and appearance, or model and copy. Rather, it is a matter of distinguishing between copies and simulacra, but with a view to affirming the rights of the latter, and subverting the distinction constitutive of representation: "Crowned anarchies are substituted for the hierarchies of representation; nomadic distributions for the sedentary distributions of representation" (*DR* 278). The system of simulacra does not force one to choose and judge *between* appearances, but to affirm the world *of* appearances and celebrate it as "a condensation of coexistences and a simultaneity of events" (*LS* 262).

In place of the system of representation, dominated by the paradigm of imitation, resemblance, and participation, and the systematic exclusion of simulacra, Deleuze construes a system of difference, insisting all along that such a system is the only reality, and that the world of representation is itself an illusion. Were it not for the connection between difference and repetition, however, the reversal of Platonism would remain incomplete. Why? Because representation itself presupposes a concept of repetition. Whether in the Platonic theory of imitation, the Neoplatonic theory of participation, or the Aristotelian theory of truth, a certain type of repetition is at stake. It is the repetition of the same in the other, the identical in difference, or the model in the copy, but in a way that signals a loss, however minimal. In other words, it is a model of repetition as degradation. The Deleuzian concept of repetition is entirely different, and aimed at wresting production from representation. Re-petition, he claims, is opposed to re-presentation. If the two concepts share a prefix, its meaning is radically different in both (*DR* 57). In the first instance, difference is said only in relation to the identical, whereas in the other it's being itself – the *being* of the simulacrum – which is said in relation to difference. That which is repeated, or returns, in the system of the simulacrum, and that which makes (a) difference, is not the self-identity and self-presence of the paradigm, but difference itself. All that returns, and returns always, and always differently, is difference. Were it not for this return, the world would repeat itself identically, or perhaps slightly differently, but always as the world that unfolds from an identical origin. There would be no possibility of anything new emerging in the world, no possibility of creation or evolution. In that sense, repetition is opposed to re-production. The world is produced as a result of a principle of difference that never ceases to return. The only thing that reproduces itself, and always differently, is difference.

In following Nietzsche's effort to overturn Platonism, Deleuze also follows Nietzsche's most extreme and demanding thought, namely, that of the eternal return. Yet, as with the definition of Platonism, Deleuze interprets Nietzsche's thought of the eternal return in a specific way. If Nietzsche's thought of the eternal return is able to reverse representation and destroy the icons (as well as the model), it is to the extent that he does not presuppose the Same and the Similar, but shows them to be produced by the system of the simulacrum, and thus, at the same time, reveals the illusion of the Same as the origin and foundation of everything that is, as the Being beneath beings. But the only Being is that of difference, and its productive repetitions:

Returning is being, but only the being of becoming. The eternal return does not bring back "the same", but returning constitutes the only Same of that which becomes. Returning is the becoming-identical of becoming itself. Returning is thus the only identity, but identity as a secondary power, that is, the identity of difference, the identical which is said of the different, or which gravitates around the different. Such an identity, produced by difference, is determined as "repetition". (*DR* 41)

It is a mistake, therefore, to claim that *everything* – every single thing, every being – returns. Insofar as what returns is difference,

the power of the simulacrum, the chaos of a world without beginning or end, repetition is itself a principle of selection, albeit a
paradoxical one: "What is selected are all the procedures opposed
to selection" (LS 265). What is excluded is selection in the sense
of Platonism – selection based on similarity and identity. "Not
only does the eternal return not make everything return, it causes
those who fail the test to perish ... The Identical does not return.
The Same and the Similar, the Analogous and the Opposed, do
not return" (DR 299). Everything that doesn't withstand the test
of the eternal return is expelled, excluded, negated. What returns,
what is selected, is precisely everything that Platonism excludes,
namely, "that which pretends to correct divergence, to recenter the
circles or order the chaos, and to provide a model or make a copy"
(LS 265). Far from being merely a theoretical representation of the
world, then, repetition "carries out a practical selection among differences according to their capacity to produce," and this means,
ultimately, their capacity "to pass the test of the eternal return"
(DR 41). Difference returns insofar as it can produce; production
is itself a result of a process of differentiation. The new principle
of selection is one that affirms the reality of becoming, or chaos,
over the fixed order and hierarchy of representation. And if it is
"practical," it is not just in the ontological, but also in the ethical sense of the term. As Nietzsche himself emphasized, repetition is a test for us, and a principle to which our entire existence
should be subjected as the most demanding, extreme, and beautiful thought. For it is the thought through which we affirm the
reality of becoming and difference over the illusion of being and
identity, the desire for a world of creation over the world as imitation, the love of the abyss over the longing for secure foundations,
the celebration of new values over the reproduction of old values.
Repetition is selective in the ontological *and* ethical sense. But
the point is that, for Deleuze, as for Spinoza or Nietzsche, there is
no longer any difference between the ontological and the ethical:
the ethical is nothing outside our ability to realize or maximize
our ontological potential, nothing, that is, outside our capacity to
extend ourselves to the limit of our power (*puissance*), to reach
that extreme limit or point at which our energy is able to transform itself. As such, repetition signals the possibility of a life that
is no longer governed by the ordinary and the average, but by the

extreme, the liminal, the singular. Those categories aren't moral, but, first and foremost, ontological, physical, mathematical, *as well as* ethical. If they can be understood as values, it is not insofar as they belong to a faculty of judgment, but insofar as they correspond to a type of existence, and signal a measure, a desire to measure and describe intensities, or energies. They signify a life beyond good and evil, an existence that is no longer defined by its ability to judge. To live, to exist, now becomes a matter of experimenting, creating, in short, *becoming*.

By focusing on Deleuze's account of Platonism, and his effort to overturn it, we were able to extract the origin of, or the fundamental motivation behind, the metaphysics of representation, and reveal another image of thought, which is at once genealogical and constructive. Platonism is the name of a solution to a problem that is at once moral, aesthetic, political, and metaphysical. The notion of image, especially as distinguished from that of the simulacrum, crystallizes all those aspects, initially unified. The Deleuzian overturning of Platonism doesn't remain content with reversing the terms of the Platonic distinctions, nor even, as the tradition has done, with dismantling the distinction between appearance and essence. Rather, it extracts from Platonism that which the Platonic text sought to neutralize and set aside, but which keeps returning, disrupting that text, undermining the efforts of representation. It doesn't offer a different solution to an old problem – how to select genuine images and exclude simulacra – but reverses the terms of the problem itself, and asks: how to select simulacra and reveal the extent to which they escape the play of the original and its copies? How to think images outside the framework of representation? How to produce an image of *thought* that is based on a different thought of the *image*? How to think and live without transcendence? In the end, we can wonder whether those questions, initially triggered by Deleuze's confrontation with the history of Platonism, continued to orient and shape his thought, despite the fact that the notion of simulacrum more or less disappeared from his work after the publication of *Difference and Repetition* and *Logic of Sense*.[27] Even though Deleuze's later thought no longer focuses on the distinction between copies and simulacra, and the need to select the latter in place of the former, it is still concerned with the possibility of distinguishing between images, of drawing a typology of images, to which specific images of thought correspond. Whether in connection with Francis Bacon or the history of cinema, it is now a matter of distinguishing between mere clichés and genuine images, between *organic* images and fragmentary or *crystal*-images. It is a matter of revealing the gap that separates the orthodox conception and practice of art *and* philosophy as representation, that is, as the effort to produce an organic and harmonious image via the convergence and accord of all faculties, and the hetero- or para-doxical image of thought and art, which is set in motion, and quite literally provoked, through the experience of an image that tears the world of familiar images apart, brings about a conflict of the faculties that results not in harmony and beauty (as symbols of the moral good), but in an unsettling pathos that draws thought out of its dogmatic sleep, laziness, stupor, and stupidity, and opens the way to what, in his later thought, Deleuze calls the body without organs, or the life of pure immanence.

NOTES

1   Friedrich Nietzsche, *Werke: Kritische Gesamtausgabe*, ed. Giorgio Colli and Mazzino Montinari (Berlin: Walter de Gruyter, 1969), III, iii, p. 207.

2   Friedrich Nietzsche, *The Anti-Christ, Ecce Homo, Twilight of the Idols, and Other Writings*, eds. Aaron Ridley and Judith Norman, trans. Judith Norman (New York: Cambridge University Press, 2005), p. 171.

3   *Ibid.*

4   For a brief account of the concept of the simulacrum in twentieth-century French thought, see Daniel W. Smith, "The Concept of the Simulacrum: Deleuze and the Overturning of Platonism," *Continental Philosophy Review* 38 (2006): 89–90. Whilst the concept of the simulacrum is not Bergsonian, I would be tempted to include Bergson's thought in a discussion of its impact and use in twentieth-century French philosophy. Henri Bergson, *Matter and Memory*, trans. Nancy Margaret Paul and W. Scott Palmer (Mineola, NY: Dover Publications, 2004), begins with the claim that the world as a whole consists of "images, in the vaguest sense of the word" (p. 1), yet in a sense that does not presuppose an original, of which they would be the copy.

5   Smith, "The Concept of the Simulacrum," p. 93.

6   Friedrich Nietzsche, *Beyond Good and Evil: Prelude to a Philosophy of the Future*, eds. Rolf-Peter Horstmann and Judith Norman, trans. Judith

Norman (Cambridge University Press, 2002), p. 4. In the still stronger words of *The Antichrist*: "Christianity has taken the side of everything weak, base, failed, it has made an ideal out of whatever contradicts the preservation instincts of a strong life" (Nietzsche, *The Anti-Christ, Ecce Homo, Twilight of the Idols, and Other Writings*, p. 5).

7 For a precise account of the historical sources behind Deleuze's claim, see Smith, "The Concept of the Simulacrum," pp. 91–93.

8 It is not by chance that Deleuze saw in modern, and especially pop art an anti-Platonic move within the history of art, one that philosophy, in its quest to move beyond representation and produce another image, could draw inspiration from: "The theory of thought is like painting: it needs the revolution which took art from representation to abstraction" (*DR* 354). On the relation between Deleuze's anti-Platonism and his views regarding modern art, see Paul Patton, "Anti-Platonism and Art," in Constantin V. Boundas and Dorothea Olkowski (eds.), *Gilles Deleuze and the Theater of Philosophy* (New York and London: Routledge, 1994), pp. 141–55. From Duchamp to Warhol, Patton remarks, modern art "has come to see its task not as the representations of appearances, but as their repetition; not as the production of copies, but as the production of simulacra" (p. 143).

9 See Plato's *Sophist*, 264b–268d.

10 The three major dialogues that present this method of division are the *Phaedrus* (265d–266b), the *Statesman* (258b ff.), and the *Sophist* (218a–232a; 252e–254b).

11 "To participate" (μετέχω) is, quite literally, "to have after," and means to enjoy a share of, share in, take part in. It has the sense of having something, then, but second-hand.

12 For a more detailed account of the Sophistic overturning of Platonism, see Gregor Flaxman, "Plato," in Graham Jones and Jon Roffe (eds.), *Deleuze's Philosophical Lineage* (Edinburgh University Press, 2009), pp. 18–24.

13 Smith, "The Concept of the Simulacrum," p. 105.

14 *LS* 276. Lucretius, *De Rerum Natura*, trans. W. H. D. Rouse (Cambridge, MA, and London: Harvard University Press, 1992), 4: 732ff.

15 *LS* 335, n.4. Since Deleuze himself doesn't elaborate on this connection beyond the footnote mentioned, we can only speculate as to what the Epicurean theory of the event might be. As a result, an unresolved tension runs through Deleuze's analysis: whereas Epicureanism is a radical materialism, and would envisage a theory of the event and, as we saw briefly, of time, only as matter, Deleuze insists that the time of the event, which he distinguishes from the time of bodies, is independent of all matter (*LS* 62).

16 Deleuze follows and interprets freely two main secondary sources: Émile Bréhier's concise but illuminating *La théorie des incorporels dans l'ancien stoïcisme* (Paris: Vrin, 1997 [1928]), and Victor Goldschmidt's more substantial *Le système stoïcien et l'idée de temps* (Paris: Vrin, 1998 [1953]). On the question of time, which Bréhier discusses briefly in his final chapter, and which is the focus of Goldschmidt's monograph, it is important to note that Deleuze selects freely between various Stoic positions, and seems to privilege Plutarch's over Chrysippus' (at least as presented by Arius). See Bréhier, *La théorie des incorporels*, p. 58.

17 Plato, *Sophist*, 247e.

18 Sextus Empiricus, *Adversus Mathematicos*, trans. R. G. Bury (Cambridge, MA: Harvard University Press, 1997), VIII, 263.

19 Plato, *Parmenides*, 130d.

20 See Albert Lautman, *Essai sur les notions de structure et d'existence en mathématiques* (Paris: Hermann, 1938), vol. II, pp. 148–49.

21 My emphasis. See also Bréhier, *La théorie des incorporels*, pp. 57–59.

22 Deleuze follows Goldschmidt's analysis in *Le système stoïcien*, pp. 36–40.

23 *LS* 61. This is what Plutarch means when, in *Against the Stoics on Common Conceptions* (chapter 41), he writes that "in the time that is present, one part is to come, and the other past" (*Plutarch's Moralia*, trans. Harold Cherniss, Loeb Classical Library, vol. XIII, part II [Cambridge, MA: Harvard University Press, 1976]). In a very similar way, Diogenes Laertius claims that "in time past and future are unlimited but the present is limited" (*Lives and Opinions of Eminent Philosophers*, book VII, chapter VII, 140). Both are cited in Bréhier, *La théorie des incorporels*, p 58.

24 According to Alain Badiou's *Deleuze: The Clamor of Being*, trans. Louise Burchill (Minneapolis: University of Minnesota Press, 2000), Deleuze fails to answer those questions convincingly. In fact, Badiou argues, far from overcoming and overturning Platonism, Deleuze's thought consists in "a metaphysics of the One." Despite his emphasis on multiplicities, difference, and diversity, Deleuze remains committed to the univocity of being and a "Platonism of the virtual" which subordinates the actual to a new figure of transcendence. For a further exploration in support of Badiou's thesis, see Peter Hallward's *Out of This World: Deleuze and the Philosophy of Creation* (London: Verso, 2000). For a critical assessment of Badiou's claim, see Nathan Widder, "The Rights of Simulacra: Deleuze and the Univocity of Being," *Continental Philosophy Review*, 31:4 (2001), 437–53, and Miguel de Beistegui, "The Ontological Dispute," in Gabriel Riera (ed.), *Alain*

Badiou: Philosophy and Its Conditions (Albany, NY: SUNY Press, 2005), pp. 47–58.

25 An intensity, Deleuze argues, is "constituted by a difference which itself refers to other differences (E–E' where E refers to e–e' and e to ε–ε')" (*DR* 117).

26 *LS* 261–62; *DR* 126.

27 In 1993, Deleuze wrote the following: "It seems to me that I have completely abandoned the notion of the simulacrum" (*TRM* 362).

4   Deleuze and Kant

How are things determined to be what they are? Kant's answer to this question defines transcendental idealism, and forms the core of Deleuze's lifelong fascination with Kant.[1] He criticizes Kant for reducing determination to the external application of concepts to the given. Yet what preoccupies Deleuze is a deeper account of determination in Kant: the determination of the being of the self ("I am") by its own thinking activity ("I think"). Because this determination happens in time, the being that is *determined* is different from the being that is *determinable*. The latter, by definition, is not thought and cannot be thought, and yet it is precisely what *is to be* thought. Here is what, above all, fascinates Deleuze about Kant: the very act in which the I thinks its own being requires that being to squirm out of thought's reach. Through its thinking activity the I generates difference from its being, indicating that the being of thought is both what *must* be thought and what *cannot* be thought.

The difference of thought from its being recurs throughout Deleuze's writings on Kant. An early version of it appears in *Empiricism and Subjectivity* (*ES* 111); in an essay of the following year, Deleuze speaks of Kant in terms of "the difference internal to the Being which thinks itself" (*DI* 17, translation modified).[2] It is a rich presence in *Difference and Repetition* (*DR* 58, 85–86, 276), in the essay "On Four Poetic Formulas That Might Summarize the Kantian Philosophy" (*ECC* 27–35, cf. *KCP* vii–xiii), and in his 1978 lectures.[3] Finally, this difference is evoked in terms of the plane of immanence:

Perhaps this is the supreme act of philosophy: not so much to think THE plane of immanence as to show that it is there, unthought in every plane, and to think it in this way as the outside and inside of thought, as the not-external outside and the not-internal inside – that which cannot be thought and yet must be thought, which was thought once, as Christ was incarnated once, in order to show, that one time, the possibility of the impossible. Thus Spinoza is the Christ of philosophers, and the greatest philosophers are hardly more than apostles who distance themselves from or draw near to this mystery. (WP 59–60)

Deleuze appears to be an apostle among apostles, attempting to draw ever nearer to the mystery of *thought that thinks its own being*. This activity both makes possible and relies on the difference of being and thought. Thought thereby generates its own differing from itself, its own "unthought" or "outside" that is nevertheless internal to it, "as if thought was worked over from the inside by something that it cannot think."[4] This is significant for Deleuze's understanding of philosophy itself, the non-philosophical core of which is the origin of thought that necessarily escapes thought.

This may come as a surprise to those who take Deleuze's relation to Kant to be largely critical, partly on the basis of Deleuze's own remarks.[5] Certainly Deleuze is disparaging about Kant's empiricism and his idealism, and he is eager to break the bounds within which Kant restricts "the transcendental" and "ideas." Incontestably, Spinoza, Nietzsche, and Bergson do more than Kant to advance a philosophy of difference. Yet a strong body of critical literature presents Deleuze as a post-Kantian, and for good reason: Deleuze's work extends Kant's critical project and Copernican revolution.[6] With respect to the discovery of this specific problem – that of how thought is to think its own being – Kant is second only to Spinoza in Deleuze's estimation. We cannot reduce the Deleuze–Kant relation to one of rivalry or criticism, but should instead see Kant as Deleuze's co-apostle, trying to reveal the same mystery.

In this chapter I will show how Deleuze upholds Kant's recognition of the difference of being and thought as an internally determining and ontologically productive difference.[7] It is because of this discovery that he criticizes Kant's tendency to conceal this difference and to make determination an external, merely epistemic procedure. Kant discovers the differing of thought from its own being, but covers over this internal difference with the identity of the subject, leading him to affirm only the external separation of conceptual thought from the being of the given. Thus a pure, productive, internal difference is suppressed in favor of a restrictive external separation reliant on a self-identical subject. This separation, a defining move of transcendental idealism, is for Deleuze a betrayal of transcendental philosophy, which on Kant's model does not delve deeply enough into the differential conditions it briefly identifies. This tension between revealing and concealing difference is the subject of the first two sections.[8] In the third section we see how this tension is indicative of both the Kantian plane of immanence and of Deleuze's conception of what philosophy is.

EXTERNAL DIFFERENCE AND DETERMINATION

Kant's *Critique of Pure Reason* aims, among other things, to destabilize the rationalist assumption that thought is necessarily adequate to being. For the rationalist, *to be* is *to be conceived* in a complete concept by God's infinite intellect, and to be thus conceived is to be brought into being. Rationalism thereby provides a unified account of the genesis of beings and of their determination to be what they specifically are. Fundamental to transcendental idealism, by contrast, is the denial of the intelligibility of the genesis and complete determination of beings (cf. *KCP* 13–14). The finite thought of a human mind is not only inadequate to being; it cannot even be certain that there is an infinite intellect that would generate, determine, and know being adequately. The human mind has an *idea* of such an intellect, and ideas about how being is generated and completely determined. These "transcendental ideas," as Kant calls them, can be thought but not known. Such ideas regulate the procedure by which the human mind overcomes its metaphysical ignorance: the procedure of applying concepts to intuitions. For the human mind is not like the idea of an infinite intellect, which would produce its objects in thinking them; the human mind "can only think," and it must apply its stock of concepts to given things that affect it from the outside.[9] Pure a priori concepts – Kant's categories – neither generate beings nor internally determine them to be what they are. The categories are applied externally to the given, determining it as an "object in general" that can be represented and known. Determination is a matter of applying to intuited material the concepts which make it an object of possible experience. The genesis and internal determination of that material are inaccessible to us, and must "remain undetermined."[10]

Deleuze criticizes transcendental idealism on the grounds that in separating thought and being, it blocks every attempt to investigate the genesis of being. Deleuze is critical of Kant's "empiricism" in considering structures of thought only as they are applied externally to received givens: neither the concept nor the idea has any internal connection to being. Kant's transcendental idealism is not transcendental enough for Deleuze, because it cannot show how the structures of thought are really and internally connected to the given, nor how thinking can apply itself to anything other than its own representations. Thinking, trapped amongst its concepts, is fundamentally at odds with the being whose means of production it cannot know. The Transcendental Aesthetic, "the science of the sensible," becomes founded on "what *can* be represented in the sensible," and not on the "being *of* the sensible" (*DR* 56–57).

This problem was identified in Kant's own day by Solomon Maimon, a critic of Kant and an important source for Deleuze. In Maimon's 1790 *Essay on Transcendental Philosophy*, the claims of the *Critique of Pure Reason* are subjected simultaneously to rationalist and empiricist scrutiny.[11] Maimon argues that Kant has established neither the fact of experience (*quid facti*) nor our right to apply concepts to it (*quid juris*). The fundamental problem is the separation of sensibility from understanding: "How can the understanding submit something (the given object) to its power (to its rules) that is not in its power? In the Kantian system, namely where sensibility and understanding are two totally different sources of our cognition, this question is insoluble."[12] Maimon believes that to overcome this problem, transcendental idealism must investigate not the conditions of *possible* experience, but the conditions of *real* experience: the genesis of qualitative sensations. Drawing on Spinoza and Leibniz, Maimon argues that the finite understanding is a mode of the infinite intellect and operates in the same way, producing its objects in intuiting them. Real experience is thus the product of a genesis that takes place within the understanding, based on rules for generating qualities called "differentials." From these pure differences flow intensive qualities called "ideas of understanding," which are finally "fixed" as objects of sensibility through imagination and representation. There is no problem about applying concepts to the content of sensibility since the latter is produced by the finite understanding and is not fundamentally different from the content of thought.

Maimon reinstates the adequacy of thought to being in order to assert that being is the product of thought, and pushes transcendental philosophy further by investigating the genesis of the real from the idea. It might be contested that this is rationalism in the service of absolute idealism, but Maimon is committed to the transcendental nature of experience, and so is Deleuze. Maimon's *Essay* is therefore an important source for *Difference and Repetition*, which takes on this same project while avoiding its idealist conclusion.[13] Deleuze says that it is Maimon "who proposes a fundamental reformulation of the *Critique* and an overcoming of the Kantian duality between concept and intuition" (*DR* 173). For Kant, the concept is applied to the intuition from the outside, such that the transcendental moment is one of conditioning, and the requirement to account for the genesis of the given is renounced. The determination of things through concepts is, similarly, a process external to those things that relies on mere empirical differences. These differences enable us to determine things relative to one another or "negatively," but they do not account for how they are positively determined in the first place. Through their external differences things differ merely in degree, because they all resemble each other at some level of generality. Kant's categories are the terms of highest generality that render objects of experience the same in their objectivity in general, but different in the degree of their spatial extent, temporal duration, qualitative intensity, causal efficacy, and so on. The determination of the given takes place through applying the terms of highest generality to it from the outside.

It is in this sense that the mistake of empiricism is "to leave external what is separated," while that of dogmatism is to fill it (*DR* 170). Dogmatism fills the gap between a determinable object and its conceptual determination either by arguing for the a priori complete determination of the former by the latter (Leibnizian rationalism) or by showing that they necessarily collapse into a new indeterminate unity (Hegelian idealism). But empiricism leaves the determinable object and its conceptual determination separate, such that the determinable–determinant relation is external to the thing to be determined. A more profound transcendental philosophy must consider how determination, and the crucial relation between determinable and determinant, operates internally to the thing, such that the determination of the thing is no broader than the thing itself. Externally determining conditions will only give us "objects in general" that differ in degree, and the mass of possible experience. Kant's approach is "too empirical," investigating merely the superficial relation of concepts to representations, and never delving into the "depth" of what makes those representations what they are.

Deleuze's "transcendental empiricism" is worked out in contrast to this.[14] It is concerned with what is *immanent* to the empirical, the transcendental conditions that generate the real (where "real" is understood in the Kantian sense of qualitative or intensive, that which can only be sensed and not known a priori). In seeking what lies within and gives rise to real experience, Deleuze wants to recover a more determinate version of Kant's noumenon: one that does not have a transcendent relation to phenomena. He seeks "the noumenon closest to the phenomenon" which is *internal* to it and produces it *immanently* (*DR* 222). Whereas Kant's noumenon is the indeterminate thought of an intelligible ground, Deleuze's is the being *of* the sensible which is both determinable and determining, and which can only be *sensed* or encountered, not represented. The object of encounter which "forces us to think ... is not a sensible being but the being *of* the sensible. It is not the given but that by which the given is given" (*DR* 139–40). The sensible is Kant's "empirically real" world of possible experience, whereas the encounter is the real of sensation – "just that element which cannot be anticipated."[15] The encounter is forced into the sensible realm by intensity, a real (but not empirically real) transcendental condition (but not of possible experience). Intensity is insensible in terms of representation, and unthinkable in terms of concepts. But the fact that it cannot be grasped by the empirical exercise of the faculties of "common sense" does not render it unintelligible; rather, the intensive condition of the given is internal to thought and *must* be thought. This is not conceptual thought applied to an already-given object; it is the thought that is forced on us in the encounter, in the *giving* of the given (*DR* 192–94).

Deleuze makes the Kantian "real of sensation" the product of a Maimonian genesis immanent to thought. For Deleuze as for Maimon, the real transcendental conditions of the given are *ideas*, within which intensities flow and surge. Kant also locates the conditions of the given in ideas: our thoughts of what produces and completely determines being are the transcendental ideas of the infinite intellect and the sum total of reality. These ideas are conditions that cannot be experienced, but that force themselves upon our thought. But while Kant's ideas can legitimately be thought as the conditions of our *thinking* of the genesis of being, they cannot be assumed to be the *real* conditions of that genesis. Furthermore, transcendental ideas are legitimate only when they regulate conceptual thought. For Kant, attempting to investigate the genetic conditions of being brings us to transcendental ideas whose explanatory power is limited to the realm of concepts of possible experience. Once again we are closed off from the conditions of the real of sensation.

Kant's transcendental ideas are important but frustrating for Deleuze.[16] They are "problems" concerning the genesis of being, expressed in the paralogisms, antinomies, and ideal of pure reason. But these problems are "solved" only in relation to represented appearances and concepts of understanding. Problems that cannot be solved in relation to these external conditions are "false problems" that generate transcendent objects as their illusory solutions (*DR* 168–70, 161–62).[17] The antinomies, for instance, are insoluble if we assume their ideas relate to the real being of a complete universe, first cause, and so on. They are resolved only when their ideas are restricted to regulating our thinking about possible experience. Deleuze thinks this makes the truth of the Kantian idea dependent on the possibility of finding a solution in its external relation to representation, and not on its internal power (*DR* 161–62). The constitutive power of the idea to determine and generate being is distrusted and suppressed by Kant, leaving it only a regulative power to determine thinking. It is not that transcendental idealism is unwilling to investigate the conditions of being in the idea, Deleuze thinks; rather, it is unable to do so, for it cannot trust the power of ideas except insofar as they are considered *not* to be constitutive of being.

Deleuze's criticism that Kant's transcendental idealism is "too empirical" has four targets: Kant's failure to account for the genesis of beings, his "external" account of determination, his reliance on a conception of difference in degree, and his denial that the idea has any real constitutive power. Deleuze's transcendental empiricism is proposed as a corrective to these limitations: it looks into the depth, interior, or *being* of experience and does not remain on its surface. Deleuze wants to find there a concept of difference in itself, where *differences in kind* affirmatively determine and individuate things, and *Ideas* are the internally determining conditions that produce intensive real objects that differ in kind. Difference must be *internal* to determination, which takes place between determinable and determinant elements in the *idea*. The relation will then not be one of externally conditioning the object of experience, but of internally generating and determining the real object, yet without relying on an infinite intellect.

INTERNAL DIFFERENCE AND DETERMINATION

Deleuze's critique of Kant risks the objection that it misses the point. Kant's intention – indeed his innovation – is precisely to instate the "external" determination of judgment in the place of the internal ontological determination of rationalism, which relies on dogmatic claims about the infinite intellect. What makes Deleuze a significant reader of Kant is his insistence that Kant *does* thematize internal determination, in a way that avoids dogmatism and approaches transcendental empiricism. In chapter 1 of *Difference and Repetition*, Deleuze says:

Rather than being concerned with what happens before and after Kant (which amounts to the same thing), we should be concerned with a precise moment within Kantianism, a furtive and explosive moment which is not even continued by Kant, much less by post-Kantianism ... For when Kant puts rational theology into question, *in the same stroke* he introduces a kind of disequilibrium, a fissure or crack in the pure Self of the "I think," an alienation in principle, insurmountable in principle. (*DR* 58)

Kant "puts rational theology into question" by making God a regulative idea in the Transcendental Dialectic. God no longer has the power to *think* the sum total of reality, nor to generate or determine being internally in thought. Instead, the subject has the power to think the idea of God, and to determine objects externally through the categories. It has this power thanks to its spontaneity, the "active" part of the subject that applies concepts to the given objects taken up by the subject's receptivity. Thus in asserting the spontaneity of the subject, Kant puts rational theology into question, and gives the power of internal determination to the subject. The "moment" in question is one that makes the spontaneous self an other to itself in section 25 of Kant's B-edition Transcendental Deduction.[18] Here, the difference between the given and the concept that grounds the external determination of possible experience reveals a more profound difference between being and thinking that grounds the internal determination of the real.

The Transcendental Deduction is where Kant justifies the application of the categories to the given. He does this by way of an analysis of the complex moves through which experience, and both the subject and object of experience, are formed. The sections under consideration here concern how the manifold of intuition – including intuition of our own existence – is synthesized, and thereby determined, by our spontaneous understanding. In section 24 Kant shows that inner sense on its own contains only the form of intuition without a combined manifold, and therefore contains no determinate intuition. The understanding, through the spontaneous act that relates the manifold to the "I think," combines the manifold and determines it. In this way, indeterminate intuitions are produced as determinate representations that can be thought. Even time (the pure form of inner sense) cannot be represented, determined, or thought unless its manifold is combined, in the drawing of a line for instance. The self, insofar as it is intuited in inner sense, is equally indeterminate unless its manifold is combined by the understanding. The indeterminate self and the self that determines it are the same subject, and yet they are distinct. But there is no difficulty here, Kant says: since I am an appearance in space and time, I must be "given" to my own passive receptivity, and synthesized by my own active spontaneity, just like any other object.[19]

The complexity of this position is drawn out in section 25. In the activity of combining the manifold, "I am conscious of myself, not as I appear to myself, nor as I am in myself, but only that I am. This *representation* is a *thought*, not an *intuition*."[20] That is, the "I think," which is responsible for *determining* intuitions, involves the *indeterminate* thought of my existence. My existence is not immediately determined by the "I think," for it can be determined only through a combination of the manifold of inner sense. The consciousness of my existence that arises with the "I think" gives me no knowledge of my existence. "Accordingly I have no knowledge of myself as I am but merely as I appear to myself."[21]

Deleuze rightly points out that this is Kant's response to Descartes' *cogito*, which states that determination ("I think") directly implies an undetermined existence ("I am") determinable by it ("I am a thing that thinks").

The entire Kantian critique amounts to objecting against Descartes that it is impossible for determination to bear directly upon the undetermined. The determination ("I think") obviously implies something undetermined ("I am"), but nothing so far tells us how it is that this undetermined is determinable by the "I think" … Kant therefore adds a third logical value: the determinable, or rather the form in which the undetermined is determinable (by the determination). This third value suffices to make logic a transcendental instance. It amounts to the discovery of Difference – no longer in the form of an empirical difference between two determinations, but in the form of a transcendental Difference between the Determination as such and what it determines; no longer in the form of an external difference which separates, but in the form of an internal Difference which establishes an *a priori* relation between thought and being. (*DR* 85–86)

In Kant's rejection of the immediacy of "I think therefore I am," Deleuze finds that Kant adopts transcendental empiricism – just for an instant – and discovers the pure difference internal to the relation of determination. This difference establishes an original relation between thought and being that is deeper than the relation between concept and given.

To understand Deleuze's point, we need to look at Kant's important footnote to section 25. Kant reiterates that while my existence is already given with the "I think" that determines it, my existence cannot be immediately determined. For the mode in which I am to determine my existence – that is, the manifold to be combined by the "I think" – is not immediately given. It must be intuited in time, which makes my indeterminate existence determinable by the "I think." But the "I think" thereby determines something different from itself: it determines its existence *as it is given in time*. Thus "I cannot determine my existence as that of a self-active being; all that I can do is to represent to myself the spontaneity of my thought, that is, of the determination."[22]

The "I think," in the act of determining its existence, *prevents* the determination of its own activity. And so the determination of my existence is a movement of self-differing. Determination is not here a matter of subsuming some given being in general under an external concept that would determine it as my being. It is a matter of *producing* my being by internally differentiating it from my thinking. This is the moment in which Kant approaches a theory of immanent differential genesis: the "I think" generates itself from its own differential relation to itself. The difference means there is no possibility of adequately thinking my spontaneity; it can only be *represented* insofar as receptivity experiences the spontaneity of my thought being exercised upon it, as if from outside it. The self cannot enact or *be* its own thinking activity. For this reason, Deleuze characterizes this moment with Rimbaud's phrase, "I is an other" (*DR* 86; *KCP* vii; *ECC* 29). Time is the condition of determinability of the self, and the hinge on which I generate my difference from myself. I cannot experience or know the spontaneity of my thought; I can only experience its effects in time.

Kant's "fractured I" grounds determination in an original difference of undetermined being and determinant thinking. The fractured I *is* undetermined being, the determinability of that being, and the activity of determining it. In this sense, it has the same problematic unity as the "Idea" in Deleuze's sense:

> Ideas ... present three moments: undetermined with regard to their object, determinable with regard to objects of experience, and bearing the ideal of an infinite determination with regard to concepts of the understanding. It is apparent that Ideas here repeat the three aspects of the [fractured] Cogito: the *I am* as an indeterminate existence, *time* as the form under which this existence is determinable, and the *I think* as a determination. Ideas are exactly the thoughts of the Cogito, the differentials of thought. (*DR* 169)

This passage, from the opening to chapter 4 of *Difference and Repetition*, suggests that Deleuze's Idea has its roots not only in Kant's transcendental ideas but also in the fractured I and Maimon's ideas of understanding. The spontaneous activity of Kant's fractured I remains undetermined as it determines its being, thereby producing itself as that which can only be represented as an other. Correspondingly, Deleuze's Idea, in its activity of determining itself with regard to objects of experience, remains undetermined with regard to its object. The object of the Idea is the virtual *problem*, and its self-determination is its integration into actual solutions.

As the Idea determines itself through actual solutions in the realm of the sensible, its virtual object, the problem, "must be represented without being able to be directly determined" (*DR* 169). The problem becomes determined *by analogy* with the objects of experience it relates to. So the Idea *is* its differing from itself. It produces itself as the determinate solutions (singularities and events) that make its problematic being fundamentally undeterminable, and thinkable only in terms of representation. As a result, problems can be represented in terms of experience and concepts, though the problematic being of the Idea is fundamentally undetermined and unrepresentable. Just as Kant's passive self "receives the activity of [its] own thought as an other" (*ECC* 30), Deleuze's actualized Idea receives the activity of the problem as an other. This other has a powerful capacity to shock: it is the "being of the sensible" that can only be sensed; the unthinkable that must be thought (*DR* 199–200).

The Idea, like the "fractured I", indicates the priority of time in the determination and genesis of real experience. "Ideas are exactly the thoughts of the [fractured] Cogito" because they enact the activity of thinking determining its own being *as* the unfolding of time. Time is the form of the determinability of being by thought. For Kant, it is the form internal to the I that continually *produces* the I as differing from itself. For Deleuze, time is internal to the Idea: its unfolding is the activity of the Idea determining itself and preserving its own indeterminacy. Time is understood here as the pure difference that establishes the a priori relation between thinking and being (*DR* 86).[23] It is not that thinking determines being *in time*, as if thinking and being were concept and object standing opposed to one another in a temporal container. Rather, time is the difference internal to both the fractured I and the Idea: thought determining being *is* the unfolding of time and the operation of difference ("Time itself unfolds … instead of things unfolding within it" [*DR* 88]). This indicates an original and irreducible relation that does not merely condition but *generates* experience: the relation of the difference of thinking and being that can be formulated "thinking-time-being" or "determinant-determinable-undetermined." Ideas contain these "dismembered moments" as "an internal problematic objective unity" (*DR* 170).

It is clear that this determination does not take the form of a judgment between a concept and an object, and that the thinking and being spoken of here do not refer to a subjective mind or actual objects. Rather, this is a deeper ontological relation that forms the internal structure of Deleuze's virtual, pre-individual Idea and Kant's pre-subjective I. The original relation of the determination and genesis of the real is the relation of being and thinking differentiated by time. Deleuze thinks Kant is wrong to locate this differential relation in a subject, where the difference and its generative power become covered over. The fracture in the I is "quickly filled by a new form of identity" and obscured by the external difference between spontaneity and receptivity (*DR* 87). Yet in this moment of the Transcendental Deduction, which even the post-Kantians do not recognize, Kant discovers pure difference. "For a brief moment we enter into that schizophrenia in principle which characterises the highest power of thought, and opens Being directly onto difference, despite all the mediations, all the reconciliations, of the concept" (*DR* 58).

Thus the fractured, self-differing I is, for Deleuze, the essence of Kant's Copernican revolution and "constitutes the discovery of the transcendental" (*DR* 86). For here Kant discovers *the genetic condition of real experience in the pure difference of being and thinking*. In this, Kant overcomes rationalism and even supersedes Maimon. For without this difference, experience and determination would be grounded in the identity of an infinite intellect for which there is no being that cannot be thought. Actual experience would be nothing more than a copy of a "possible reality" determined in advance. Both the content of experience and the space in which it plays out would be predetermined, and the future would be foreseeable (*DR* 198, cf. *LS* 105–6). Where experience is grounded in the pure difference between being and thinking, however – either in Kant's fractured I or in Deleuze's Idea – the sensible is determined *as it is generated*. Experience is produced as surprising and unforeseeable: from pure difference emerge the real encounters that "cannot be anticipated" and that shock us into thinking.

ORIENTATION ON THE PLANE OF IMMANENCE

Kant's Copernican revolution rests on the discovery of internal difference, but also on the transcendent subject that covers it over. Kant both reveals and conceals that experience is transcendentally conditioned by pure, determining difference. This tension between revealing and concealing is intrinsic to transcendental idealism. The "concealing" move of conceptual judgment is necessarily grounded in the fractured I. But the internal difference of the self cannot remain openly "revealed" lest the whole critical enterprise collapse in on itself; Kantian critique requires a self-identical subject that can reliably think about itself and its projects. The subject, in order to be a subject, necessarily conceals the differential conditions of its own genesis: no wonder, then, that Kant cannot, or will not, inquire into the genetic conditions of the real. This interplay of revealing and concealing amounts to the Kantian plane of immanence, a discussion of which will complete the Deleuzian portrait of Kant.[24]

In *What is Philosophy?* Deleuze and Guattari tell us that

the history of philosophy is comparable to the art of the portrait. It is not a matter of "making lifelike," that is, of repeating what a philosopher said but rather of producing resemblance by separating out both the plane of immanence he instituted and the new concepts he created. (*WP* 55)

The Kantian plane of immanence needs to be separated and isolated from Kant's new concepts, a task which is partly achieved in the diagram of a proposed "machinic portrait" of Kant (*WP* 56). In this diagram, the "I think" (an ox head) loudly proclaims its self-identity by repeating "Self = Self" while powering a waterwheel that generates experience through categories. Neither the machine nor the diagram includes the difference of the "I think" from its being, for even if that difference could remain open, it could not be represented materially or diagrammatically. However, immanent to the "I think" and binding the image together is a broken line representing "the transcendental field of possible experience," a line which unifies the portrait and draws a boundary around it (*WP* 57). (Significantly, the transcendental ideas extend outside the boundary.)

Immanence and the transcendental are neatly conjoined for Kant. Things that appear to us have conditions of possibility that are transcendental – pertaining to representational and conceptual thought – but not transcendent. This means that the principles that serve as transcendental conditions, and our search for and use of those principles, are "immanent" in a Kantian sense: they remain within the bounds of possible experience.[25] Principles that profess to pass beyond those bounds are transcendent, and generate transcendental illusions. So for Kant, concepts and representations are immanent as long as they apply only to objects of possible experience, and ideas are used immanently as long as they only regulate and determine thinking. The act of externally determining givens through concepts is immanent, but an attempt to account for their genesis would not be.

This sense of immanence is almost the opposite of Deleuze's. Yet the "plane of immanence" is a partly Kantian idea, discussed in *What is Philosophy?* in Kantian terms. Distinguishing the plane from the concept, Deleuze and Guattari state "the plane of immanence is not a concept that is or can be thought but rather the image of thought, the image thought gives itself of what it means to think, to make use of thought, to find one's bearings in thought" (*WP* 37). As becomes explicit in the next paragraph, this refers to Kant's "What is Orientation in Thinking?," the 1786 essay in which he stresses the importance of recognizing the limits of reason. Kant draws an analogy between spatial and logical orientation: we orient ourselves in an unfamiliar landscape or room by relating fixed objects to the difference we feel "within [our] own subject" between left and right.[26] We similarly orient ourselves in thought by means of "a subjective principle of reason where objective principles of reason are inadequate."[27] When reason ventures beyond the "frontiers" of possible experience, it too orients itself by means of a subjective feeling – in this case, its own need for a concept of an unconditioned being to ground the concept of possible experience as a whole. Instead of left and right, reason makes use of a distinction between its own theoretical and practical employment, which determines whether an object is a matter of knowledge or rational belief. With the understanding that God is a matter of rational belief and not knowledge – a regulative and not a constitutive idea – the thinker has a "compass" with which to "orient himself on his rational wanderings" beyond possible experience.[28]

Kant's image of what it means to find one's bearings in thought is spatial and geographical: it is the image of reason wandering in a field, crossing the boundary line of possible experience into the dark and unfamiliar land of the supersensible, orienting itself by means of its need for the unconditioned and the internal compass that tells it how to reflect upon it. Put otherwise, "reason gives the orders" as to what is immanent and includable in conceptual thought, and what is transcendent and excluded (*KCP* 14; *NP* 92). This is the Kantian plane of immanence, "the image thought gives itself of what it means to think": thinking means excluding that which cannot be thought in representational and conceptual terms. These excluded things can be thought – they are ideas – but they are objects of speculation and symbolization. Every element of the plane is in the subject: the subject constitutes the field, the conditions of what appears inside the boundary line, where the boundary line is drawn, the need to venture beyond it, and the tools for orientation. Danger, too, comes from the subject: thought is no longer threatened by error or "holes in the path" as it was for Descartes, but by illusions that issue from reason's own "internal arctic zone where the needle of every compass goes mad" (*WP* 52–53). Kant's assumption that reason can identify and assess its own conditions, structures, and errors is known as "immanent critique": the notion that reason can orient itself without reference to anything outside it (*KCP* 3; *NP* 91).[29]

The Kantian plane is an image of immanence *as* the transcendental. This plane is constituted by the subject, as the condition of possibility of all cognitive thinking as such. Kant says at the end of his life: "transcendental philosophy precedes the assertion of things that are thought, as their archetype, [the place] in which they must be set."[30] Kant called his plane transcendental philosophy and believed he had thereby avoided transcendence and illusion. But by making the plane immanent to a subject, Kant "discovers the modern way of saving transcendence": the transcendence of "a Subject to which the field of immanence is only attributed by belonging to a self that necessarily represents such a subject to itself" (*WP* 46). What the subject transcends is the unthinkable, which is either *made* thinkable through synthesis and judgment, or is pushed off the plane. In affirming itself as the center and legislator of immanence, in deciding what is to stay "inside" conceptual thought, reason creates an "outside" to which it is transcendent.

Yet there is another 'outside' at work here. The "best" plane of immanence – perhaps discovered only by Spinoza – is one in which immanence is not immanent *to* anything, transcendence is not restored, and the unthinkable "outside" of thought is not external to thought itself (*WP* 59–60). The same idea is expressed in Deleuze's essay "Immanence: A Life ...":

Without consciousness the transcendental field would be defined as a pure plane of immanence since it escapes every transcendence of the subject as well as of the object. Absolute immanence is in itself: it is not in something, not *to* something; it does not depend on an object and does not belong to a subject. [... In Kant] immanence is deformed and ends up being contained in the transcendent. Immanence does not relate to a Something that is a unity superior to everything, nor to a Subject that is an act operating the synthesis of things: it is when immanence is no longer immanence to anything other than itself that we can talk of a plane of immanence.[31]

Just as Deleuze criticizes Kant's suppression of difference, he criticizes Kant for deforming immanence and containing it within a transcendent subject. But equally, just as the suppression of difference conceals an original discovery of internal difference in the fractured I, the "subjection" of immanence conceals the "unthinkable" at the heart of conceptual thought. Deep within the transcendent subject – indeed, immanent to it – is the impossibility of thought thinking its own being. This "unthinkable" is not an idea to be cordoned off by reason into the realm of rational belief; it is an "unthinkable" that originates all conceptual thought, that *must* be thought if representation and concepts are to get off the ground in the first place.

Kant's plane of immanence reveals and conceals THE plane of immanence, the one that

is, at the same time, that which must be thought and that which cannot be thought. It is the nonthought within thought. It is the base of all planes, immanent to every thinkable plane that does not succeed in thinking it. It is the most intimate within thought and yet the absolute outside – an outside more distant than any external world because it is an inside deeper than any internal world: it is immanence ... the incessant to-ing and fro-ing of the plane, infinite movement. (*WP* 59)

In this to-ing and fro-ing is the rhythm of revealing and concealing. "The nonthought within thought," the very being of thought, is precisely what Kant finds at the heart of the transcendental, which cannot represent or conceptualize this being and so "does not succeed in thinking it." The unthinkable is revealed in the process of the self analyzing its own conditions – "immanent critique" – but must necessarily be concealed in order for critique *by* a self to be possible at all. The condition of possibility of critique is that the *being* of thought, "that which cannot be thought," must be concealed in order to be revealed, and vice versa. Kant's critical philosophy itself rests on this paradox.

Deleuze's own conception of *what philosophy is* is far too complex to summarize here. But I want to close by suggesting that it is related to the revealing–concealing structure at the heart of Kant's critical philosophy. The condition of possibility of philosophy is something that "cannot be thought and must be thought," something non-philosophical that comes from outside. The non-philosophical is revealed in the shock of the encounter, and cannot be accommodated to representation or conceptualization. Thought can only give itself an image of what it means to think, an image of what it is to be affected by the unthinkable. For this reason, "the supreme act of philosophy" is not "to think THE plane of immanence" but to *show*, in an image, that it is there (*WP* 59–60). Philosophical "showing" reveals "that which cannot be thought and yet must be thought," but this act of showing and *thinking* the unthinkable is surely also a concealment of the unthinkable spur to thought.

The dimension that shapes thought most decisively is also the dimension that escapes thought, that thought is never quite able to bend backwards towards its own presupposition, and make its own image transparent to itself. All that thought could ever hope to do would be to intimate its own image, to approach it, asymptotically as it were.[32]

Deleuze and Guattari's *What is Philosophy?* shows us *what philosophy is* by playing out the impossibility and the exigency of thinking its own unthinkable sources. Kant's *Critique of Pure Reason* similarly shows us *what philosophy is* in a Deleuzian sense. This is also *what philosophy is* in a Kantian sense: asking into the conditions of possibility of thinking as such. Kant and Deleuze mutually illuminate each another's thought through their shared commitment to the "unthought" that generates thought. For this reason, Kant is crucial for understanding Deleuze, and Deleuze is a significant interpreter of Kant.

NOTES

1   This was matched by a thorough knowledge of Kant's texts: Deleuze writes not only about Kant's three *Critiques*, but also about his essays and lectures, and the little-read *Opus Postumum*. This chapter focuses on Deleuze's engagement with Kant's *Critique of Pure Reason*. Deleuze discusses Kant's *Critique of Practical Reason* and *Critique of Judgment* in *KCP* 28–75; *DI* 56–71; and *Anti-Oedipus* (which Daniel W. Smith argues is "derived from [Kant's] second critique": "Deleuze, Kant, and the Theory of Immanent Ideas," in Constantin V. Boundas (ed.), *Deleuze and Philosophy* (Edinburgh University Press, 2006), pp. 43–61, p. 53).

2   For discussion of this 1954 essay, "Jean Hyppolite's *Logic and Existence*" (*DI* 15–18), see Christian Kerslake, "The Vertigo of Philosophy: Deleuze and the Problem of Immanence," *Radical Philosophy*, 113 (2002), 10–23.

3   Gilles Deleuze, "Cours Vincennes" (14 March–4 April 1978), "Les Cours de Gilles Deleuze," transcripts in translation, at www.webdeleuze.com, last accessed June 22, 2011.

4   *Ibid.* (21 March 1978), p. 8.

5   For instance, "Kant … is the perfect incarnation of false critique: that's why he fascinates me" (*DI* 139, cf. *NP* 89–90); "My book on Kant … I wrote it as a book on an enemy" (*KCP* xv).

6   Important recent contributions include Levi R. Bryant, *Difference and Givenness: Deleuze's Transcendental Empiricism and the Ontology of Immanence* (Evanston: Northwestern University Press, 2008); Christian Kerslake, *Immanence and the Vertigo of Philosophy: From Kant to Deleuze* (Edinburgh University Press, 2009); and Anne Sauvagnargues, *Deleuze: l'empirisme transcendantal* (Paris: Presses Universitaires de France, 2009).

7   In arguing that *the difference of being and thought* is what matters, I disagree with Descombes and McMahon, who suggest that the difference between concept and intuition is the real difference for Kant and Deleuze. My interpretation is in line with that of Beistegui, who takes the being–thought difference to be crucial for Deleuze. Vincent Descombes, *Modern French Philosophy*, trans. L. Scott-Fox and J. M. Harding (Cambridge University Press, 1980); Melissa McMahon, "Immanuel Kant," in Graham Jones and Jon Roffe (eds.), *Deleuze's Philosophical Lineage* (Edinburgh University Press, 2009), pp. 87–103; Miguel de Beistegui, *Truth and Genesis: Philosophy as Differential Ontology* (Bloomington: Indiana University Press, 2004).

8   This chapter's first two sections include material previously published in Beth Lord, *Kant and Spinozism: Transcendental Idealism and Immanence from Jacobi to Deleuze* (Basingstoke: Palgrave Macmillan, 2011).

9 Immanuel Kant, *Critique of Pure Reason*, trans. Norman Kemp Smith (London: Macmillan, 1929), B135 (references are to the 1781 [A] and 1786 [B] editions, as is standard).

10 *Ibid.*, B145.

11 Solomon Maimon, *Essay on Transcendental Philosophy*, trans. Nick Midgley, Henry Somers-Hall, Alistair Welchman, and Merten Reglitz (London: Continuum, 2010). I discuss Maimon's *Essay* at length in Lord, *Kant and Spinozism*, pp. 105–29.

12 Maimon, *Essay*, pp. 37–38.

13 Smith suggests that the two exigencies set by Maimon for transcendental philosophy – the search for the genetic elements of the real, and the positing of a principle of difference to account for it – are the primary components of Deleuze's transcendental empiricism (Smith, "Deleuze, Kant, and the Theory of Immanent Ideas," p. 49). For further discussion of Deleuze's relation to Maimon see Daniel W. Smith, "Deleuze's Theory of Sensation: Overcoming the Kantian Duality," in Paul Patton (ed.), *Deleuze: A Critical Reader* (Oxford: Blackwell, 1996), pp. 29–56; Graham Jones, "Solomon Maimon," in Jones and Roffe (eds.), *Deleuze's Philosophical Lineage*, pp. 104–29; and Sauvagnargues, *Deleuze: l'empirisme transcendantal*, pp. 223–31.

14 There is considerable literature on Deleuze's transcendental empiricism, notably: Bruce Baugh, "Transcendental Empiricism: Deleuze's Response to Hegel," *Man and World*, 25 (1992), 133–48; Beistegui, *Truth and Genesis*, pp. 241–47; Bryant, *Difference and Givenness*, pp. 15–48; Kerslake, *Immanence*, pp. 80–92; and Sauvagnargues, *Deleuze: l'empirisme transcendantal*, pp. 17–36.

15 Kant, *Critique of Pure Reason*, A167/B209.

16 On Kantian and Deleuzian "ideas," see the books listed in note 14 above, and also Jean-Michel Salanskis, "Idea and Destination," in Patton (ed.), *Deleuze: A Critical Reader*, pp. 57–80; Smith, "Deleuze, Kant, and the Theory of Immanent Ideas"; and James Williams, *The Transversal Thought of Gilles Deleuze Encounters and Influence* (Manchester: Clinamen, 2005), pp. 29–31.

17 Cf. Kant, *Critique of Pure Reason*, A328/B384–85, A476–84/B504–12.

18 *Ibid.*, B157–59.

19 *Ibid.*, B154–56, cf. B131–33.

20 *Ibid.*, B157.

21 *Ibid.*, B158.

22 *Ibid.*, B158n; cf. B407.

23 See Bryant, *Difference and Givenness*, pp. 178–84.

24 The evocation of Heidegger here is intentional, for Heidegger similarly finds in Kant's transcendental deduction a tension between

revealing and concealing being that defines Kant's ontology. Martin Heidegger, *Kant and the Problem of Metaphysics*, trans. Richard Taft (Bloomington: Indiana University Press, 1990); on Heidegger and Deleuze see Beistegui, *Truth and Genesis*.

25 Kant, *Critique of Pure Reason*, A295–96/B352–53.

26 Immanuel Kant, "What is Orientation in Thinking?," trans. H. B. Nisbet, in Kant, *Political Writings*, ed. Hans Reiss (Cambridge University Press, 1991), pp. 237–49, p. 238.

27 *Ibid.*, p. 240.

28 *Ibid.*, p. 245.

29 See Kant, *Critique of Pure Reason*, A763/B791, and Christian Kerslake, "Deleuze, Kant, and the Question of Metacritique," *Southern Journal of Philosophy*, 42:4, 481–508.

30 Immanuel Kant, *Opus Postumum*, trans. Eckart Förster and Michael Rosen, ed. Eckart Förster (Cambridge University Press, 1993), p. 256.

31 Gilles Deleuze, "Immanence: A Life ...," trans. Nick Millett, *Theory, Culture and Society*, 14:2 (1997), 3–7, p. 4.

32 Miguel de Beistegui, *Immanence: Deleuze and Philosophy* (Edinburgh University Press, 2010), p. 11.

5 Phenomenology and metaphysics, and chaos: on the fragility of the event in Deleuze

Deleuze is frequently characterized as a critic of phenomenology. Yet, Deleuze's thought cannot be understood unless we recognize its similarities to phenomenology. There are in fact *three* similarities. *First,* phenomenology takes up what Deleuze in *Difference and Repetition* calls "the task of modern philosophy"; that task is to reverse Platonism (*DR* 59). Through the epoché, phenomenology reduces any transcendent world or transcendent thing in itself to a phenomenon; anything transcendent comes to be located *within* experience. *Second,* through the preposition "within," we see that the reversal of Platonism amounts to a reduction to immanence. No greater debt to phenomenology appears in Deleuze's thought than in his use of the word "immanence." Immanence in both Deleuze and in phenomenology refers to a transcendental (but not transcendent) ground. A *third* similarity appears in the fact that the grounding relation in both phenomenology and in Deleuze's thought is paradoxical. All transcendental philosophy results in a paradoxical relation: the ground of experience must remain within experience (the ground must not be separate from the grounded) and the ground must be at the same time different from what it grounds (the ground must not resemble what it grounds). In other words, the ground must remain immanent and yet, as immanent, not result in a vicious circle. It must be the case that what is being grounded is not presupposed in the ground.

This chapter extends my "The End of Phenomenology: Expressionism in Deleuze and Merleau-Ponty," in Leonard Lawlor, *Thinking through French Philosophy* (Bloomington: Indiana University Press, 2003), pp. 80–94.

103

It is in relation to the third similarity – the paradoxical relation of ground and grounded – that we can see Deleuze's specific
criticism develop.[1] Both phenomenology and Deleuze seek the
elimination of all transcendence; both seek to arrive at a plane
of immanence. Despite the similarity however, phenomenology
defines immanence by a dative relation; it relates the plane of
immanence back *to* – in this "to," we have the dative relation – a
subject or consciousness that constitutes the given (*WP* 46).[2] In
order, however, for there to be a *pure* plane of immanence, a plane
with no transcendence whatsoever, there must be no dative relation. In other words, the plane of immanence must not be an image
of something else. In particular, it must not be an image of what
it is attempting to ground. There must be a difference or a heterogeneity – a non-resemblance relation (*LS* 99) – between ground
and grounded, between condition and conditioned, or between origin and derivative. According to Deleuze, the phenomenological
reduction merely moves the phenomenologist from the natural
attitude (*doxa*) back to what Husserl calls *Urdoxa*.[3] In other words,
there is a resemblance of opinions, with no difference between
natural opinion and proto-opinions (*WP* 149–50; *DR* 137). Despite
Husserl's attempt to escape, phenomenology falls into a "vicious
circle" (*LS* 105).

Deleuze's criticism of phenomenology resembles those found
at roughly the same time in the works of Foucault and Derrida.[4]
Although Deleuze is unique among his generation of French philosophers because he embraces (at least at the moment of the end
of the 1960s) the term "structuralism," his criticism of phenomenology arises, like Derrida's and Foucault's, from reflections on structuralist concepts like the floating signifier.[5] Moreover, like Derrida,
Deleuze links the criticism of phenomenology to the criticism of
metaphysics, of "the old metaphysics." Once again, the task of modern philosophy is to reverse Platonism. However, unlike Derrida,
Deleuze criticizes both phenomenology and metaphysics together
(phenomenology as metaphysics) by means of the concept of the
event: to reverse Platonism, for Deleuze, is first and foremost to
depose the old metaphysical essences with events (*LS* 53). Yet, the
concept of event appears not only as a reaction against phenomenology and metaphysics. It is also a reaction against (a "counter-
effectuation" of) chaos. Deleuze's thought is always in a two-front

battle, at once against already formed ideas and concepts (clichés); this is the battle against "phenomenology and metaphysics." But his thought also battles against the undifferentiated abyss of chaos (such as the experiences of schizophrenia, alcoholism, and madness disclose). Hence, the title of this essay: "Phenomenology and Metaphysics, and Chaos." However, it is the subtitle – "On the fragility of the event" – that indicates the primary thesis of this essay. We shall argue that the event, in Deleuze's precise sense of the term, is unlimited (he says "eternal"). The unlimitedness of the event will lead us into the problem of potency and impotence, power and inability. Despite its singularity and novelty, the event does not end; it is incessant (Deleuze negates the French verb, *cesser*, at crucial points in his discourse).[6] The event has a potency that cannot be stopped ("il ne cesse pas"). As the word "cannot" already implies, what calls forth the event's unlimited potency is the fragility, indeed, the impotence of the event, the inability to make it stop. What cannot be stopped is dying. What cannot be stopped, nevertheless, must be stopped; what cannot be grasped must be grasped. And that imperative – given in a vision – tells us that all events are like battles. As we shall see, Deleuze wages a two-front war on clichés and chaos because he is precisely a thinker of the event as a struggle.

We shall be able to see this two-front war develop only if we examine Deleuze's 1969 *The Logic of Sense*; in fact, the entire following essay takes place within the confines of this book. In *The Logic of Sense*, we find Deleuze's most explicit criticism of phenomenology (of Husserl's 1913 *Ideas I*) coupled with his strongest appropriation of the idea of structure. More importantly, however, in this book, we find Deleuze's most developed concept of event. In fact, as we shall see, the concept of event that Deleuze invents in *The Logic of Sense* contains four inseparable features: (1) novelty; (2) effectuation; (3) counter-effectuation; and (4) unlimitedness. It is the last feature – unlimitedness – that will lead us to the battle. As title of Deleuze's book indicates, we shall be able to reach the concept of event as struggle, and therefore reach Deleuze's two-front battle, indeed, we shall be able to reach his very concept of philosophy (laying out a plane of immanence and creating concepts), only if we pass through "the logic of sense." This is a logic inspired by "phenomenology and structuralism."

PHENOMENOLOGY AND STRUCTURALISM

The logic of sense (or the requirements for a true genesis)

To write a logic of sense ("sens" is the French word, "Sinn" in German; both terms mean "meaning" as well as "direction" and both are connected to words like "sensibility") means to write a transcendental philosophy (*LS* 105). Above, when we spoke of the paradoxical grounding relation, we summarized what we might call Deleuze's "principle of all principles" for transcendental philosophy ("the principle of all principles" being a phrase coined by Husserl). Here is the principle in more detail: the ground – sense or what is expressed by a proposition or a sentence – must not be posited as existing outside of the grounded or expression; and at the same time the ground must not resemble the grounded (see especially *LS* 21 and *LS* 99 for the two clauses of the principle).[7] The first clause of inseparability removes sense from "the old metaphysics," while the second clause of resemblance removes sense from anything subjective such as universals or general concepts and from anything objective like things or states of affair. This "principle of all principles" is the principle of immanence. The ground cannot be a second world, a world of essences; it cannot be separate from this world; it must be within, immanent. Yet, as immanent, it must not be immanent *to* anything else, not grounded on anything, not copied off anything else. For Deleuze, this principle is not a principle of conditioning (as in Kantian transcendental philosophy), but a principle of genesis. The logic of sense is a logic of genesis (and for Deleuze as for Derrida there is no conflict between structure and genesis).[8] Indeed, what is at issue in *The Logic of Sense* is what Husserl calls "the donation of sense" or constitution (*LS* 71). What is at issue is the determination of the "transcendental field" (*LS* 105) or "true genesis" (*LS* 98). What is required for true genesis, according to Deleuze? Sense must generate the other dimensions of the primary element in discourse, that is, the proposition. In other words, sense must generate (1) the state of affairs denoted by the proposition (denotation); (2) the signified concepts and classes of the proposition (signification); and (3) the states of the subject manifested by the proposition (manifestation). All of these aspects of the proposition are aspects of belief, of *doxa*. As the genetic source, however, sense must not duplicate *doxa* (or opinions). Sense must be *neutral* in regard to all the modes of the proposition, and yet it must be productive, it must generate those propositional modes.

Phenomenology (or Deleuze's criticism of Husserl's theory of constitution in Ideas I)

Deleuze is interested in phenomenology because, as he says, "phenomenology [might] be the rigorous science" of sense for which he is seeking (*LS* 21).[9] To determine whether phenomenology is this "rigorous science," Deleuze focuses, as we said, on Husserl's 1913 *Ideas I*.[10] Husserl seems to "discover sense" in *Ideas I* through the idea of the noema (*LS* 96, also *LS* 32).[11] As the Greek word indicates (from "noein," to think), the noema is the thought-object, which is correlated to what Husserl calls "noesis" (thinking). At first glance, it seems, according to Deleuze, that the noema – the entire apparatus of intentionality laid out in *Ideas I* – satisfies the requirements for a true genesis. The noema in Husserl looks to be "independent" and "neutral" because Husserl distinguishes the noema from the physical object, from the psychological or from lived experience, from mental representations, and from logical concepts (*LS* 101). In other words, the noema seems to differ from denotation, manifestation, and signification. It does not seem to resemble what it is supposed to generate.

As the word "seems" suggests, however, Deleuze argues that Husserl's genesis occurs only in "appearance" (*LS* 100); it is a "sleight of hand" (*LS* 97). In fact, Deleuze's criticism of Husserl's genesis takes place in *three steps*. *First*, Deleuze notices that, when Husserl discusses the noema, he uses the image of a core; the noema or sense has, according to Husserl, a nucleus.[12] As Deleuze says, "Nucleus metaphors are disquieting; they envelope what is in question" (*LS* 98, also *LS* 212). What Husserl has done, according to Deleuze, is determine the nucleus of sense as a "predicate" (*LS* 97). Determining sense as a predicate (the greenness of the tree in the proposition "the tree is green"), Husserl understands the nucleus as a concept or a generality. If sense is a generality, then it gives itself, ready-made, the form of signification – rather than generating it. The nucleus of sense, being determined as a generality, is related, for Husserl, to "a something = X," which is an object in general. So, as

Deleuze stresses, just as signification is given ahead of time ready-made, denotation is given ahead of time ready-made. In relation to both signification and denotation, the donation of sense remains within a "vicious circle" (*LS* 105). *Second*, Deleuze stresses that Husserl determines the something = X as an Idea in the Kantian sense (an approximation to an ideal). The idea in the Kantian sense maintains reason as the basic form of genesis. More precisely, by maintaining reason, Husserl seems to be presupposing "an originary faculty of common sense"; the originary faculty of common sense accounts for the identity of the object in general (the identity is what is held in common by all the possible objects) (*LS* 97, also *LS* 116, *LS* 119). According to Deleuze, Husserl even seems to be assuming a good sense; good sense (this is the Ideas in the Kantian sense as a *telos*) accounts for the process of identification of all the objects in general to infinity (the process is always seeking the identification of all objects as if that identification is the good) (*LS* 97).[13] Always seeking the same commonality, always seeking the same identification, the genesis once again falls into a vicious circle. Finally, *third*, Husserl maintains the form of consciousness (*LS* 102, also *LS* 122).[14] According to Deleuze, Husserl divides consciousness – a "radical separation" – between actual doxic (or believing) consciousness, which is productive (it posits that something exists and makes judgments), and a merely "thinking of" consciousness, which is neutral and non-productive (its neutrality means that it posits no existence and makes no judgments).[15] Actual consciousness (or the actual *cogito*) is under the "jurisdiction of reason," while the consciousness that merely thinks is not. Deleuze stresses that Husserl determines the relation between the two kinds of consciousness as a relation of proper and improper and he provides an image of this relation. For Husserl, the neutral, that is, improper consciousness is the shadow, while the proper and rational consciousness is the thing that casts the shadow. Thus, according to Deleuze, Husserl, through the "separation," makes a "disjunction" within consciousness, endowing the form of actual consciousness with the potency of genesis (productivity), while the neutralized consciousness has no productive potency. However, in order to have a genuine genesis, the generating sense must be at once neutral and productive. In other words, Husserl's genetic source is not neutral in relation to the generated forms of consciousness that are actually manifested in the proposition. Once again, Husserl falls into a vicious circle since he makes one actual form of consciousness (the rational form) be the genetic source of those forms of consciousness that are manifested. Overall therefore, in these three steps, what Deleuze shows is that the forms of *doxa* (a nucleus of *proto-doxa*), of reason (common sense and good sense through the Idea in the Kantian sense), and of consciousness (proper consciousness) are used as the genetic source and then these same forms appear in what is generated. In other words, although the noema is Husserl's great discovery, it is *not truly* neutral.

Structuralism (or true genesis)

In *The Logic of Sense*, Deleuze clearly takes inspiration from the entire apparatus of intentionality that we find in Husserl's *Ideas I*. As have seen, however, there are three ways, according to Deleuze, in which Husserl (or phenomenology) makes transcendental genesis (constitution or sense donation) false or be only apparent. First, by giving himself the forms of the object and the concept (generality) ready-made, genesis in Husserl remains a vicious circle. Second, by maintaining the form of reason and the direction of an Idea in the Kantian sense, Husserl presupposes a common sense and a good sense (the *Urdoxa*). Thanks to the *Urdoxa*, genesis functions by means of identity and teleology. What is produced is distributed hierarchically in relation to the identity and oriented purposively. Again, the vicious circle appears. Finally, by determining neutral consciousness as only a shadow, only as improper consciousness, Husserl maintains the form of consciousness as the model for what is generated. Fundamentally, the criticism that Deleuze levels against the apparatus that Husserl sets up in *Ideas I* is that genesis is a kind of copying. The noema is not neutral in relation to the dimensions of the proposition. Based in intentionality, genesis is not an event; sense is not a singularity. As Deleuze says, "Only when the world, teeming with ... impersonal and pre-individual singularities, opens up, do we tread at last on the field of the transcendental" (*LS* 103, translation modified).

We now enter into one of the most complex parts of Deleuze's thought, the determination of the transcendental field. In order to designate the transcendental field, Deleuze employs several negative terms: nonsense; paradox; anti-generality; informal; incorporeal; indetermination; indifference; infinitive; a-conceptual; anonymous; immediate; impersonal; impenetrable; impassible; non- (or pre-) individual; counter-God; unlimited; and unconscious. These negative terms function as a guardrail to steer us toward the fact that the ground in Deleuze does *not* resemble – no copying relation – the grounded. And yet, their negative function is supposed to open onto something positive (*LS* 136, 123). What the negative function opens out onto is something *smaller* than beliefs (*doxa* or opinions arrived at by consensus); generalities; forms; bodies; *smaller* than determinate, differentiated, or finite terms and concepts; *smaller* than what has a name; *smaller* than mediation; persons; individuals; than what can be penetrated; than what is either active or passive; *smaller* than God (or man); a limit; and consciousness (*LS* 63–64).[16] What is a singularity? It is no larger than a point or an instant. Husserl, in Deleuze's eyes, remains at the level that is too large, as it is itself constituted by the smaller processes of singularities. But, insofar as Husserl does not reduce to the small, he also does not reach the really large, that which does not stop, the *eventum tantum* (*LS* 151).

For Deleuze, the singularities that populate the transcendental field form a *structure*. Deleuze tells us that there are "three minimal conditions" for a structure (*LS* 50). *First*, there must be two heterogeneous series; a single series does not make a structure. Here, as to be expected since *The Logic of Sense* appears in 1969, Deleuze makes use of structuralist terminology, saying that the one series is the "signifier" (a repeatable phonic or graphic form), while the second is the "signified" (what the form means). Throughout *The Logic of Sense*, Deleuze refers to dualities such a signifier–signified, but also word–thing, and, as we shall see, bodies–incorporeals. The heterogeneity of the two series is due to a "perpetual relative displacement" or "perpetual disequilibrium"; the two series are always "out of step with one another" ("décalage") (*LS* 52–54). The "décalage" ensures that, fundamentally, there is no resemblance between the two series. Second, as in structural linguistic, the terms in the series are determined in relation to one another, that is, by the difference in value between the terms. To these relations or to the value of these relations "very particular events correspond, that is, *singularities*" (*LS* 50, Deleuze's emphasis).[17] Each series, then, has a distribution of singular points, that is, of events. As already indicated (mentioning Derrida as well), Deleuze stresses that it is a mistake to oppose structure to event. What a structure registers is events, and what a structure produces is more events. Structure is genesis.

The third condition concerns genesis. The two heterogeneous series converge toward what Deleuze calls a "paradoxical agency" ("instance paradoxale": also paradoxical instance, paradoxical last court of appeal) (*LS* 40, 98).[18] The inspiration for what Deleuze calls a paradoxical agency comes from Lacan. One example of the paradoxical agency, then, is a phantasm, that is, a child's real or unreal representation of the parental coitus (*LS* 7, 210). The psychoanalytic example indicates that the paradoxical agency is a representation of something real but separated from that reality; it is imaginary too. Another example, this time from Lévi-Strauss' structural anthropology, is the "floating signifier" (*LS* 48–49).[19] A signifier (a phonic or graphic form) such as the Polynesian term "mana" does not possess a determinate signified (or meaning); not having a determinate signified this signifier "floats" between the series of signifiers (it differs from the rest of the signifiers since it lacks a determinate signified) and the series of signifieds (it seems to be its own signified). The paradoxical agency belongs, then, to neither series (neither the real nor the imaginary, neither the signifiers nor the signifieds), although it is situated between or (just above) the two series. The paradoxical agency articulates or differentiates the two series, reflects the one into the other, makes them communicate, coexist, and resonate (*LS* 51). In short, the paradoxical agency donates sense onto the two series. The paradoxical agency is able to endow the two series with sense because it is equally present in the signifying series and in the signified series; it is "two-sided, "at once word and thing, name and object" (*LS* 40). The paradoxical agency, by its very nature, is split apart in relation to itself, incomplete. As Deleuze says, there is nothing stranger than "this two-sided thing with two unequal or uneven 'halves'" (*LS* 41).[20] What makes the agency strange is the fact that it is in default, defective, or lacking ("défaut"). The paradoxical agency is defective, the signifier "floats" because it lacks a determinate signified; it includes non-sense (*LS* 68–71).[21] Since it includes non-sense, the paradoxical agency lacks ultimate determination and a unique direction or one sense (*LS* 77). Precisely because it lacks sense, it is able to give too much sense. The combination of not enough and too much explains why, for Deleuze, the paradoxical agency is defined by a question, a question with too many answers because there is no one ultimate answer (*LS* 56). The combination also explains why the paradoxical agency is problematic; it is a problem with too many solutions because there is no one ultimate solution. Most importantly, the paradoxical agency "does not stop circulating" ("ne cesse de circuler") within the two series (*LS* 40). It never stops, it has no end (no determinate direction); the paradoxical agency is unlimited, infinite, and therefore it has, as Deleuze says, an "eternal truth" (*LS* 63). Because the paradoxical agency is two-sided, it is neither denotation nor signification. Lacking a determinate sense, the paradoxical agency is a "something = X," but this X is not an Idea in the Kantian sense (*LS* 66). The paradoxical agency "destroys" both good sense and common sense (*LS* 3). Finally, because it is a structure, and an unlimited structure, it does not have the form of consciousness. The paradoxical agency does not endow sense only apparently, *but truly*. Structuralism's discovery of the paradoxical agency results in the idea of true genesis. It produces sense as an event. Thus structuralism for Deleuze in *The Logic of Sense* belongs to the movement of reversing Platonism.

WHAT IS AN EVENT?

Earlier we claimed that Deleuze had taken inspiration from Husserl's phenomenology in his logic of sense. Then we saw how he appropriates structuralist thinking (Lacan's psychoanalysis and Lévi-Strauss' anthropology). The real inspiration for Deleuze's conception of sense as an event, however, comes from Stoic logic (which he sees operating in Lewis Carroll's writings). As he says, "the Stoics undertake the first great reversal of Platonism, the radical reversal" (*LS* 7). The genius of Stoic philosophy, according to Deleuze, lies in the new "cleavage" it makes in the causal relation. Unlike Aristotle and Kant, who distinguish types of causality, the Stoics "dissociate" the causal relation; they make a "border" where there never was one before: between cause and effect. On the one hand – this is one of the many dualities in *The Logic of Sense* we have already noticed – there are bodies and mixtures of bodies; the mixtures are the causes. The interaction between bodies is called "mixture" because the interaction is accidental. It is, however, the accident that turns what happens into an event. But the accident itself is not the event. On the other hand, there are the effects that the causes bring about. Being dissociated from the causal bodies, the effect is not bodies (*LS* 19). The effects of the corporeal causes are non-bodies, what the Stoics call "the incorporeals" (*LS* 4). The incorporeals are "ideal [or irreal] events" (*LS* 52). The Stoics not only make a cleavage between cause and effect, they also make a cleavage between accident and event. Accidents are corporeal, while events are incorporeal or ideal.[22]

Deleuze uses the word "event" in two ways. That Deleuze, in *The Logic of Sense*, uses the same word to refer to two phenomena indicates how closely connected (inseparably connected) the two are. Indeed, Deleuze distinguishes between the two uses only by means of lower case and upper case: event versus Event. Event (with an upper-case "e") is not depth; it is opposed to the abyss of chaos; chaos is the unforeseen mixtures of bodies, the rumbling of bodies in the depths (*LS* 164, 106–7, 156–57). The Event is the surface (the word "surface" appears countless times in *The Logic of Sense*). Insofar as it is the surface, the Event is an incorporeal. Or, more precisely, it is the limit between bodies and incorporeals. Deleuze always qualifies the Event (with an upper-case "e") with the phrase "one and the same": "un seul et même Événement" (*LS* 11, 64, 114). Even though the Event of the surface being laid out happens as one and the same, it ramifies into many dualities, more than the ones that we have seen, between bodies and incorporeals, between signifier and signified; there is always more than one surface. This claim about multiple surfaces explains why Deleuze says that what is at issue is neither monism nor dualism (*LS* 24). The ramification of dualities means that one and the same Event contains potentially a multiplicity of events (now with a lower-case "e"). Written with a lower-case "e," events are not the surface (not the Event), but "surface effects" of the mixtures of bodies. Yet, as we have seen, the Stoics make a cleavage between cause and effect. What makes the surface effects differ in nature from the causes is that events (still written with a lower-case "e") in Deleuze are always events of language (or of expression) (*LS* 12). The linguisticality of events is what makes the events ideal; it is what gives them a "minimum of being," a kind of "extra-being" (*LS* 22, 180, 7). The minimum of being, however, is not separate being. The events do not reach the height of metaphysical essences and Platonic ideas; they are not generalities or universals. Events (with a lower-case "e") do not *exist*, but rather *insist*. Not being facts (or bodies) and not being generalities, events (lower-case "e"), according to Deleuze, are verbs (*LS* 3, 21, 214–15). For example, the event expressed in the proposition "the tree is green" is not found in the predicate "green," but in the infinitive "to green" (*LS* 214). Since the event is expressed in an infinitive, the verb has the potency or power to divide itself into other tenses and numbers. This power – it is this power that defines a "pure event" for Deleuze (*LS* 136) – makes the event unlimited. Unlimited, the event (still written with a lower-case "e") "follows the border" or "skirts along the surface" (*LS* 10).²³ Then, the event (lower-case "e") is virtually identical to "the one and the same Event." The event is always said twice (*LS* 34).

We anticipated these two senses of the event in Deleuze – Event as surface and event as surface effect – when we spoke of the paradoxical agency. In fact, there is no difference in Deleuze between paradoxical agency and event. The event is paradoxical, it is two-sided; it is always both incorporeal and corporeal, ideal and factual, surface and surface effect at once (*LS* 8). Despite the doubleness, what, *first and foremost*, defines the event, just as for the paradoxical agency, is singularity. This is the list that Deleuze produces of what counts as a singularity: "turning points or points of inflection; bottlenecks, knots, foyers, and centers; points of fusion, condensation and boiling; points of tears and joy, sickness and health, hope and anxiety, 'sensitive' points" (*LS* 52). On the basis of the list, we see that what makes something be a singularity lies in its being caused, effectuated, or realized by mixtures of bodies.²⁴ Bodies mix and there is contagion, which causes illness; bodies mix and there is heartbreak, which causes tears. That an event results from an "effectuation" means that an event is always at first an effect, always at first a fact or an accident. For Deleuze, there can be no event, no singularity that does not *begin* as an accident. What happens, what has happened, is that, when bodies mix (again contagion or poison), the mixture has an effect. *Then*, it is possible that something of the effect is selected (*LS* 151). What is selected is what there is "in principle" or "by right" ("en droit") in the event (*LS* 22, 17). For instance, and we shall return to this example below, what is selected from the accident of a wound is the idea of a scar that at once disjoins and joins. These two features – referring to a "no longer" whole and referring to a "not yet" whole – are made consistent in the selection.[25] In other words, the selection transforms the factual accident into an ideal event, becoming neutral (indifferent) in relation to the ways it is effectuated through bodies. Yet, because the selection of what is "by right" is *within* the effect (inseparable from the effect), the event remains at once corporeal and incorporeal. *Most importantly,* for Deleuze, this doubleness affects the temporal status of the event. The event is a singularity because it is effectuated in the present instant. In this regard, the event is really singular, unlike anything else, unlike any other event; it is a novelty. Yet, when the "by right" features of the event are selected, when they are expressed, the minimum of being that those features acquire turn the event into a "counter-effectuation." The event is "against" effectuation because the features selected have, as we mentioned earlier, "eternal truth," or the temporal status of being "eternal." They are "eternal" not in the sense of an eternal present that never changes or of a circle of time that constantly returns to the present. Events (lower-case "e") are "eternal" in the sense of being non-present, that is, they refer, like a verb, to an unlimited past and future (*LS* 61).[26]

Once more, it is necessary to stress that the event is a singularity, a novelty. However, even though it is not separable from the cause (it is once again not a Platonic idea) – it has only extra-being – the effect is expressed in language. For Deleuze, linguistic expression means minimally that the effect takes on a form. The minimum of being means a minimum of language, nothing more than the "stuttering" of the infinitive (*LS* 24). Nevertheless, the minimal formalization differentiates the event from the effect. When formalized, the event becomes repeatable. It is a caused, factual, by chance accident, and, at the same time, something that can be repeated. The repeatability is the power or potentiality of the event. With this power it "skirts along the surface," and becomes almost identical to the Event (with an upper-case "e"). As almost identical to one and the same Event, the event becomes larger than any of its corporeal effectations. Then, the form of the event "supervenes" ("survient") on bodies and their mixtures (*LS* 24). The relationship of supervenience means that the event, now ideal, an ideal form, takes on the characteristic of being an a priori condition for its own factual or empirical effectuation. It appears to be originless or self-originating, having no beginning, opening out onto an unlimited past. The event is, nevertheless, itself a singularity and thus caused. The event is a first that is a second and a second that is a first. Being caused and yet prior to its own cause, the event is a repetition without an origin. Like the paradoxical agency, the event is based on a lack, on nothing, on no sense. The lack explains why Deleuze defines the event in this way: "the event is the identity of form and emptiness" (LS 136). It explains his use of all the negative terms that we have seen, but especially this one: "the informal" (LS 107). It is formal (minimally formal), although it lacks an ultimate form. The emptiness or void refers to the surface having no limit in the past, having no stopping point in that direction. But, the event is always bi-directional (it has no good sense or common sense). It is a question for which the answer was not given ahead of time and for which no one answer will ever fully respond. Not only does the event supervene on the mixtures of bodies (functioning as their prior condition in the past), but also the event "soars over" ("survoler") the mixtures (functioning as what exceeds them into the future) (LS 155). In this second direction, into the future, the event's power is excessive. It never stops being able to be repeated beyond any limit or over any stopping point; it is incessant and endless (LS 40, 51, 62, 63, 150, 167). Instead of one determinate end, it possesses an unlimited number of ends.

CONCLUSION: PHENOMENOLOGY AND METAPHYSICS, AND CHAOS

We are able to summarize the concept of event that we just developed in the following way. The event is a singularity; it is a novelty. What makes the event new is that it is caused, accidentally or by chance, by a mixture of bodies. The event is always effectuated. The source of effectuation is chaos, depth, or the abyss. However, it is possible that something of the effect is selected. The selection of what is "by right" or "in principle" in the effect is not effectuation (it is no longer what is by chance or accidentally), but counter-effectuation. Counter-effectuation makes what was in the depth rise to the surface. Counter-effectuation produces the surface and the surface effects: the one and the same Event and ideal events. Although above the depth, the Event and the ideal events are still lower than the height of Platonic ideas and generalities. We have seen that Deleuze's concept of ideal events resembles the psycho-analytic phantasm and the structuralist floating signifier. But Deleuze, in fact, models the concept on literature. The one and the same Event is a story ("une histoire") composed of turning points, boiling points, points of crisis (LS 50). The question posed by the paradoxical agency is the question of the tale and the novella (LS 63): what happened, what is going to happen?[27] These questions cannot be answered with causes. Even more, we must recognize that the event implies that there are no ultimate answers to these questions. These questions remain answerless because the Event or paradoxical agency is "eternal" or, more precisely, unlimited. The paradoxical agency is a repeatable form that lacks a determinate origin. Lacking a determinate origin, it becomes repeatable incessantly; it has a potency that is endless. To be as concise as possible, we can say that the Deleuzian concept of event contains these four insep-arable features: (1) novelty; (2) effectuation; (3) counter-effectuation; and (4) unlimitedness.[28] Similarly, here is the list of the examples of the Deleuzian event that we have seen so far: (1) the psychoanalytic phantasm; (2) the structuralist floating signifier; (3) the infinitive (the verb); and now (4) the tale and novella.

Besides these four examples, there is one more. Indeed, it is the most important example. We anticipated it above when we spoke of the wound and the scar. Deleuze says, "the battle is not one example of an event among others … [it is] the Event in its essence" (LS 100). The battle is the Event in its essence because it fits the definition of the event that we have seen so far. Due to the chance mixtures of bodies on the battlefield, each battle is novel, singular, and differ-ent from all the others. The mixtures of bodies cause or effectuate the battle. But also, the battle fits the definition because the battle "soars over" ("survole") its own battlefield (LS 100). That the battle soars over the battlefield means that it can be the subject of a coun-ter-effectuation. The counter-effectuation (the selection of by-right features) makes the battle be neutral in relation to all its effectua-tions in the present, indifferent in regard to the victor and the van-quished, the brave and the cowardly. Because counter-effectuation takes place in language, Deleuze mentions famous novels about war by Stendhal, Hugo, Tolstoy, and Stephen Crane. The counter-effectu-ation in the novel makes the battle "eternal." It is no longer simply the present of effectuation; instead, the battle is "always to come and already passed" (LS 100). That is, as an ideal sense, battle appears to lack an origin; but also, as an ideal sense, it exceeds all possible fulfillments. Deleuze says that the non-present temporal status makes the event "all the more terrible" (LS 100). It is all the more terrible because the linguistization of the battle (as in a novel), the grasping of the battle (as in a philosophical concept), is the unlimiting of life, or, more precisely, the unlimiting of life in its struggle with death. The example of the battle (but really the battle shows what the event truly is) therefore provides us one more feature of the event. This feature is really why it is the Event in its essence. It shows that every event is like a plague, war, or death (LS 151).

For Deleuze, the battle's effectuation and counter-effectuation – indeed, effectuation and counter-effectuation in general – are like the ambiguity of death. Here, in regard to the ambiguity of death, Deleuze follows Blanchot.[29] Blanchot had shown that death is not only personal, me dying, my life being too weak when the moment comes; it is not only a, so to speak, "big death." But also, death is impersonal, without a relation to me, with me being too weak for life which as it exceeds limits is like a series of "little deaths." In other words, there is the portion of the event that is accomplished and realized (personal death: me, as a soldier, with a proper name, I am dying); then there is the portion that cannot realize its accomplishment (impersonal death: other soldiers whose names I do not know, they are dying and never stop dying). The lack of accomplishment means that impersonal death is incessant: "they never finish up with dying" ("on n'en finit pas de mourir") (LS 152). Behind the emptiness of the question, behind the answerlessness of what happened and what is going to happen, there is always dying. It is this endless death that has risen up from the depths of the battle's chaos to the surface. The surface is fragile (LS 82, 94, 120, 167). It is fragile because the soldier is mortally wounded, personally "in his own flesh" (LS 101, see also LS 156). He has risked his life in the abyss of the battle. In this moment of grace between life and death, however, the battle in its unlimitedness hovers above the battlefield enough for the soldier to "see" it.[30] What does the soldier see? It is the vision of so many singularities dying (not just soldiers with unknown names dying, but also animals perishing and countrysides and cities being destroyed). It is the vision of life in its endless struggle with death: chaos, or, as Deleuze sometimes calls it, "Bichat's zone."[31] It is this vision that cannot be "grasped" (LS 156). It is this vision of death never ceasing, never ending, never accomplishing itself, never making itself be over once and for all, this vision cannot be thought. The inability to stop ("il ne cesse pas, ne cesse jamais") is the impotence of the event. And yet, from this powerlessness comes power. The unthinkable must be thought, the ungraspable must be grasped. Responding to the vision, the mortally wounded soldier, "in a single act of violence" includes all violence and all mortal events in one single Event, in a plane of immanence that denounces and deposes all violence and all death (LS 152–53). The mortally wounded soldier must write the story of the battle – in order to liberate it "always for other times" and "to make us go farther than we would have believed possible" (LS 161).[32] As Deleuze (and Guattari) would say in *A Thousand Plateaus*, the vision of the battle is grasped (some part of it) in order to make us *become*.

Perhaps the mortally wounded soldier's vision of the battle's surface (the vision of this plane of immanence) is like a phenomenological intuition. We do not know.[33] What we know, however, is that Deleuze connects his criticism of phenomenology to another criticism. Like Derrida at the same moment, Deleuze associates phenomenology with metaphysics. Deleuze says, "Metaphysics and transcendental philosophy," that is, phenomenology, "have reached an agreement" (LS 106). Metaphysics and phenomenology set up an alternative (LS 106). *On the one hand*, metaphysics has God as a sovereign Being, completely and infinitely, analytically, determined by its concepts. *Yet*, still *on the first hand*, transcendental philosophy (that is, phenomenology) has the finite form of the Person which synthesizes representation. We see what is on the first hand: it is God and man. What is *on the other hand*, in distinction from God and man, is "an undifferentiated ground, a groundlessness, formless non-being, an abyss without differences and without properties" (LS 106). It is this alternative – *either* the analytic form of the sovereign being plus the synthetic form of the person *or* chaos – that Deleuze is criticizing, and continues to criticize throughout his entire career. Only if we recognize Deleuze's rejection of this alternative do we understand the philosophy, and the conception of philosophy, that emerges from his criticisms of both phenomenology and "the old metaphysics." Philosophy, in

Deleuze, is a two-front fight, against already constituted forms (clichés) and against the chaos of no form at all. What emerges from this two-front fight is the conception of philosophy presented in *What Is Philosophy* as concept creation and the laying out of a plane of immanence. But only with this two-front battle in mind do we see that the purpose of concept creation lies in the fight against clichés, while the purpose of the laying out of a plane of immanence lies in the fight against chaos. What is still at issue in *What Is Philosophy* is surface effects and the surface. The purpose or end of philosophy, for Deleuze, really means that what is required in philosophy is to "grasp" the event in its singularity, a singularity that verges on the formless chaos on the one hand and on the forms of the ready-made on the other. Philosophy's specific power is to create concepts, to "grasp" the event, but this power is based on a vision of immanence that cannot be grasped.[34] As Deleuze says in *What Is Philosophy* (with Guattari), "We will say that THE plane of immanence is, at the same time, that which must be thought and that which cannot be thought. It is the nonthought within thought" (*WP* 59). Imitating Deleuze's capitalization of "THE plane of immanence," we are tempted to write this final sentence: "THE plane of immanence, it can NOT be thought."

NOTES

1   Alain Beaulieu has written an excellent essay on Deleuze's criticisms of, and his relation to, phenomenology. Alain Beaulieu, "Edmund Husserl," in Graham Jones and Jon Roffe (eds.), *Deleuze's Philosophical Lineage* (Edinburgh University Press, 2009), pp. 261–81. James Williams' *Gilles Deleuze's "Logic of Sense"* also has a precise summary of Deleuze's criticisms of Husserl; overall, it is an excellent introduction to *The Logic of Sense*. James Williams, *Gilles Deleuze's "Logic of Sense"* (Edinburgh University Press, 2008), pp. 129–34. Joe Hughes has also written an excellent discussion of Husserl and *The Logic of Sense* in his *Deleuze and the Genesis of Representation* (London: Continuum, 2008).
2   See also *ES* 87.
3   Edmund Husserl, *Experience and Judgment*, trans. James S. Churchill and Karl Ameriks (Evanston: Northwestern University Press, 1973), section 13, p. 59. Deleuze also has in mind Merleau-Ponty. See Maurice Merleau-Ponty, *The Phenomenology of Perception*, trans. Colin Smith

and rev. Forrest Williams (London: Routledge and Kegan Paul, 1962, rev. 1981), p. 61.

4   Foucault's criticisms of phenomenology are found in *The Order of Things* and in *The Archaeology of Knowledge*. *The Order of Things* criticizes phenomenology for thinking in a circularity ("a vicious circle," as Deleuze would say), in a "dialectic of the same" between all the doublets that determine the modern concept of man, while *The Archeology of Knowledge* criticizes phenomenology's teleological thinking in favor of a thinking of the event. See Michel Foucault, *The Order of Things: An Archaeology of the Human Sciences* trans. anon. (New York: Vintage, 1994), and *The Archeology of Knowledge and the Discourse on Language*, trans. A. M. Sheridan Smith (New York: Pantheon Books, 1972).

5   For structuralism in Deleuze, see also "How Do We Recognize Structuralism," *DI* 170–92. For structuralism generally, see François Dosse's *History of Structuralism*, trans. Deborah Glassman (Minneapolis: University of Minnesota Press, 1997).

6   See *LS* 40, 51, 62, 63, 150, 161, 167.

7   Deleuze presents the logic of this principle in *EPS* 46–47.

8   Here we are focusing only on what Deleuze calls "static genesis," which he opposes to "dynamic genesis." In *The Logic of Sense*, Deleuze says, "The expressed makes possible the expression. But in this case, we find ourselves confronted with a final task: to retrace the history which liberates sounds and makes them independent of bodies. It is no longer a question of a static genesis which would lead from the presupposed event to its effectuation in states of affairs and to its expression in propositions. It is a question of dynamic genesis which leads directly from states of affairs to events, from mixtures to pure lines, *from depth to the production of surfaces*, which must not implicate at all the other genesis" (*LS* 186, Deleuze's emphasis). The final third of *The Logic of Sense* concerns dynamic genesis (Series Twenty-Seven to Thirty-Four). For more on genesis, see *DR* 183.

9   By calling phenomenology a "rigorous science," Deleuze of course is referring to the well-known work by Husserl: "Philosophy as a Rigorous Science, in *Phenomenology and the Crisis of Philosophy*, ed. Q. Lauer (New York: Harper, 1965)."

10   Edmund Husserl, *Ideas Pertaining to a Pure Phenomenology and to a Phenomenological Philosophy, First Book*, trans. Fred Kersten (The Hague: Martinus Nijhoff, 1983). Kersten's translation uses the Husserliana volume, while Ricoeur's uses the third edition (1928) of the original Max Niemeyer publication. The first English translation (by Boyce Gibson) also uses the Niemeyer edition. See Edmund Husserl, *Ideas: General Introduction to Pure Phenomenology*, trans.

W. R. Boyce Gibson (New York: Collier Books, 1975 [1931]). Making use of Paul Ricoeur's 1950 French translation, Deleuze cites or alludes to the following specific paragraphs: 88, 89, 90, 98 99, and 124 (on the noema); 103 and 104 (on *Urdoxa*); 110 and 114 (on neutrality modification); and 129, 135 and 143 (on the Idea in the Kantian sense).

11   The criticism that Deleuze presents here in *The Logic of Sense* should be compared with the one Derrida presents at basically the same time. In an early essay, "'Genesis and Structure' and Phenomenology" (collected in *Writing and Difference*), Derrida, like Deleuze, recognizes the innovation that the Husserlian idea of noema represents. Yet, Derrida, again like Deleuze, thinks that Husserl retreats from this innovation insofar as Husserl conceives of history as teleological (the Idea in the Kantian sense). In *Voice and Phenomenon*, Derrida might appear at first to be at odds with Deleuze since in this book Derrida criticizes the Husserlian idea of expression. Yet, what Derrida criticizes is the restriction that the Husserlian concept of expression seems to impose on sense. In other words, like Deleuze, Derrida conceives sense as an infinite (unlimited becoming), not to be reined in by a *telos* of "the relation to an object" (the Idea in the Kantian sense again). Derrida sees the unlimited nature of sense in what Husserl calls indication (*Anzeichen*), rather than in expression. Neither Derrida nor Deleuze is satisfied respectively with Husserl's difference between and conception of indication and expression. The lack of satisfaction implies a community of conception between Derrida and Deleuze. Notice in this formula of a "relation to the object," we see the dative. Derrida's criticism of "the relation to the object" implies that he does accept the dative relation. See Jacques Derrida, *Voice and Phenomenon*, trans. Leonard Lawlor (Evanston: Northwestern University Press, 2011), p. 84. He cannot therefore be easily classified among the so-called "philosophers of transcendence." The other (of any sort) is internal and not a transcendence that puts a break (not a stopping point) on becoming. Both Derrida and Deleuze are thinkers of infinite, continuous variation (multiplicity or dissemination). See Jacques Derrida, "'Genesis and Structure' and Phenomenology," in *Writing and Difference*, trans. Alan Bass (University of Chicago Press, 1978), pp. 162–63; also Derrida, *Voice and Phenomenon*, Introduction and chapter 7.

12   Deleuze is referring to *Ideas I*, sections 90, 99, and especially 129. Ricoeur translates Husserl's "*Kern*" with the French "*noyau*"; Kersten renders "*Kern*" in English as "core." The English translators of *The Logic of Sense* render "*noyau*" as "nucleus." The old Boyce Gibson translation of *Ideas I* uses "nucleus" to render "*Kern*." We are using "nucleus" here, which allows one to see the image better.

13   The definition of good sense given in *The Logic of Sense* is: "good sense affirms that in all things there is a determinable sense or direction" (*LS* 1). Deleuze frequently refers to good sense and common sense. The most thorough discussion occurs in *Difference and Repetition*, chapter 3.

14   Deleuze refers to *Ideas I*, sections 110 and 114.

15   Kersten renders Husserl's "*radikalen Scheidung*" as "radical separation"; Ricoeur renders it as "*coupure radicale.*" Deleuze then uses "*coupure radicale,*" which is rendered in the English translation of *The Logic of Sense* as "radical cleavage" (*LS* 102).

16   Here, Deleuze also speaks of "large differences." See also *Difference and Repetition*'s discussion of Leibniz and Hegel (*DR* 42–50).

17   To explain this idea of a singularity referring to the value of a relation, Deleuze refers to differential calculus (*LS* 65, 52).

18   Deleuze appropriates the idea of the paradoxical agency from Lacan (*LS* 38–40). Deleuze cites Jacques Lacan, "Seminar on 'The Purloined Letter'," in *Écrits: The First Complete Edition in English*, trans. Bruce Fink (New York: Norton, 2007), pp. 6–49. In *The Logic of Sense*, Deleuze distinguishes the phantasm from the simulacrum. See *LS* 94, 216. The simulacrum remains bound to the causality of bodies in depth, while the phantasm is a surface effect. For more on the simulacrum, see Deleuze's "Letter-Preface to Jean-Clet Martin," in *DI*, 361–63. Of course, Deleuze's major study of psychoanalysis appears in *Anti-Oedipus* (written with Guattari).

19   "The floating signifier" comes from Lévi-Strauss. Deleuze cites Claude Lévi-Strauss, *Introduction to the Work of Marcel Mauss*, trans. Felicity Baker (London: Routledge and Kegan Paul, 1987), pp. 61–62.

20   Stressing the two sides of the paradoxical agency, Deleuze says, "For, what is in excess on one side is nothing other than an extremely mobile *empty place*. What is in default on the other side is a rapidly moving object, an *occupant without a place*, always supernumerary and displaced" (*LS* 41, Deleuze's emphasis). This quotation anticipates Deleuze's idea of a people to come and a land (*une terre*) to come.

21   Nonsense in Deleuze has nothing to do with the philosophy of the absurd, which had defined nonsense simply as the absence of sense (*LS* 71). In contrast, for Deleuze, nonsense is not in a simple oppositional relation to sense (*LS* 71); rather, sense and nonsense exist in "an original type of intrinsic relation, a mode of co-presence" (*LS* 68).

22   François Zourabichvili's *Deleuze, une philosophie de l'événement* (Paris: Presses Universitaires de France, 1996) presents an excellent summary of Deleuze's thought, with particular attention to the concept of event. See especially p. 89 for a discussion of the relation of incorporeals to bodies.

23 When the event (lower-case "e") starts to skirt the surface, the event becomes a kind of "refrain" (LS 57). The idea of a refrain will play an important role in *A Thousand Plateaus*. See *A Thousand Plateaus*, the eleventh Plateau: "1837: Of the Refrain ["ritournelle"]." "Ritournelle" is the French translation of the Italian "ritornello," which in Baroque music refers to a recurring passage in music.

24 This is the problem of the "third order" in Spinoza. See *EPS* 235–54 and 317. The English translation of *Logique du sens* renders the French word "effectuation" as "actualization." This translation is correct, but it loses the direct connection to the idea of an effect. So, we are rendering it here as "effectuation."

25 In *What is Philosophy?*, consistency of "distinct, heterogeneous and yet not separable" features is the definition of a concept. See *WP* 19.

26 The temporal status of events is what Deleuze calls "Aion." Deleuze opposes Aion to Chronos. But he also stresses that Aion and Chronos amount to two different "readings of time." As two "readings," Aion and Chronos have an inseparable relation, just as the event contains inseparably the features of effectuation and counter-effectuation. For "two readings," see *LS* 5, 61, 162, 164.

27 These questions are taken up in *A Thousand Plateaus*, Plateau 8.

28 For a helpful summary of the Deleuzian concept of event, see François Zourabichvili's *Le vocabulaire de Deleuze* (Paris: Ellipses, 2003), pp. 36–40.

29 Deleuze cites Maurice Blanchot, *The Space of Literature*, trans. Ann Smock (Lincoln: University of Nebraska Press, 1982), p. 123.

30 Deleuze speaks of how Stendhal, Hugo, and Tolstoy make their heroes "see" the battle; then he speaks of a "volitional intuition" of the battle in regard to Crane's "young man" (*LS* 100–1).

31 He says this in reference to Foucault's work, especially *The Birth of the Clinic*. See *F* 121. I have developed this idea in my *Implications of Immanence* (Bronx, NY: Fordham University Press, 2006).

32 The importance of writing in Deleuze (and Guattari) is seen in the first Plateau of *A Thousand Plateaus*. I have argued for the importance of writing (either a story or a philosophical concept) in Deleuze's thought, and in particular to his concept of becoming in my "Following the Rats: An Essay on the Concept of Becoming-Animal in Deleuze and Guattari," in *SubStance*, 117, *The Political Animal*, 37:3 (2008), 169–87.

33 Unfortunately, it is beyond the scope of this chapter to compare this sort of intuition, which Deleuze says is different from all "empirical intuitions" to what Husserl calls "eidetic intuition." Such a comparison would require an investigation of Bergson's concept of intuition.

But the investigation would be guided by this comment from Foucault's *Hermeneutics of the Subject*: "Meditating death (*meditari, meletan*), in the sense that the Greeks and Latins understand this ... is placing oneself, in thought, in the situation of someone who is in the process of dying, or who is about to die, who is living his last days. The meditation is not therefore a game the subject plays on his own thought, with the object or possible objects of his thought. It is not something like eidetic variation, as we would say in phenomenology. A completely different kind of game is involved: not a game the subject plays with his own thought or thoughts, but a game that thought performs on the subject himself. It is becoming, through thought, the person who is dying or whose death is imminent." Michel Foucault, *The Hermeneutics of the Subject: Lectures at the Collège de France, 1981–1982*, trans. Graham Burchell (New York: Palgrave Macmillan, 2005), pp. 359–60. In Husserl, an eidetic variation results in an eidetic intuition. What Foucault is implying here is that the phenomenological eidetic intuition does not transform the subject doing the variation and having the intuition. In contrast, the volitional intuition, like meditation in this sense, transforms the subject.

34 In *What is Philosophy?*, Deleuze (and Guattari) compare the plane of immanence to an intuition (*WP* 40).

6   Deleuze and structuralism

INTRODUCTION

In the years between 1966 and 1969, Deleuze was close to the work of the structuralists, while at the same time he was aware of their impasses, rejecting any closure of sense or any reduction to a binary mode of thought that would be closed to both the process of temporalization and the pragmatic dimension of language. Deleuze's encounter, in 1969, with his friend Félix Guattari itself constituted a veritable war machine against structuralism. Guattari, as a Lacanian and a member of the Freudian school, participated fully in the propagation of structuralism in his form of psychoanalysis. As for Deleuze, his desire to leave the history of philosophy made him very receptive to the ongoing tumult in the humanities. For him, the figure of the schizophrenic became a question in both its clinical form and its literary form. But neither Deleuze nor Guattari could be satisfied with a simple adherence to the dominant theories of the time. Just before their encounter in 1969, the position they were both expressing was already a lively critique of structuralism.

MACHINE *CONTRA* STRUCTURE

By the time Guattari spoke before the members of the Freudian School of Paris in 1969, he had already broken with Lacan's formalist and logicist development of it. He was no longer the heir apparent of the Master, who preferred his son-in-law Jacques-Alain Miller and his circle at the École normale supérieure on rue d'Ulm, which had just launched the *Cahiers pour l'Analyse*. Guattari

This article was translated by the editors Daniel W. Smith and Henry Somers-Hall.

called his talk, whose title alone evokes his target, "Machine and Structure," although it might as well have been called "Machine *contra* Structure."[1] In his lecture, Guattari locates blind spots in the grid of structural analysis, and he puts forward the notion of the "machine" in an attempt to think what has been repressed by structuralism, namely, the joint processes of subjectification and the historical event. This is the first text by Guattari that references Deleuze, whom he has not yet met, although he had read and enjoyed Deleuze's doctoral thesis, *Difference and Repetition* (1968) as well as his *Logic of Sense* (1969), which Guattari cites at the beginning of his paper, utilizing the Deleuzian definition of structure. Against structure, which is defined by its ability to exchange its particular elements, the machine would stress repetition, but in the sense in which Deleuze understands it – that is, repetition as difference, "as a conduct and as a point of view [that] concerns non-exchangeable and non-substitutable singularities" (*DR* 1). Given his reading of Deleuze's thesis, Guattari feels that he needs the concept of machine in order to introduce this differential element that reintroduces the event and movement: "Temporalization penetrates the machine on all sides and can be related to it only after the fashion of an Event. The emergence of the machine marks a date, a change, different from a structural representation."[2] One is struck here by the proximity of their positions and their discourse, which already exists before Deleuze and Guattari even meet. Guattari is the spokesman for a philosophy of the event, which is the primary topic of Deleuze's *Logic of Sense*.

Within the matrix of this lecture, we find another concept, derived from the concept of the machine, which will also become central to the Deleuzo-Guattarian system – the concept of the "war machine." Guattari takes up, in his own manner, the Deleuzian orientation toward a philosophy that breaks with the idea of representation, and he situates his concept of machine within this point of view: "The essence of the machine is precisely this function of detaching a signifier as a representative, as a 'differentiator', as a causal break, different in kind from the structurally established order of things."[3] In order to escape the impasse of the pan-linguism of structural semiotics, Guattari suggests restoring the speech act as a signifier: "The voice, as speech machine, is the basis and determinant of the structural order of language, and not the other way round."[4] He therefore completely reverses the structuralist perspective, which upheld the system of language as the only scientific level, thereby excluding speech, which was dismissed as purely contingent.

What interests Guattari is the *subject*, and he sees it as split, torn, at the intersection, in the in-between, in tension between structure and machine. "The human being is caught where the machine and the structure meet."[5] Still remaining within Lacanian categories, while trying to put them in motion, Guattari takes up Lacan's analysis of partial objects, the object-*a*, and uses it as a war machine against structural equilibrium. The object-*a* in effect creates an eruption where one least expects it, like a true "infernal machine."[6] The object-*a* becomes what is irreducible or inassimilable in the structure, and is renamed by Guattari the "objet-machine petit 'a'."[7] It is the impeding element of circular thinking ("penser en rond") and the deconstructor of structural balances, which undermines attempts at self-representation and decenters the individual "outside itself, on the boundaries of the other."[8]

Guattari's search for a type of connection that would be a group connection, or a connection of collective entities, not only links his thought to one of Deleuze's primary concerns (the question of the institution and its ambivalent relationship with desire),[9] but would turn out to have a fecund future in Deleuzo-Guattarianism with their notions of the group-subject and the collective assemblage of enunciation. For Guattari, this critical putting-into-perspective of structuralism had a significance that was not only speculative but also eminently political. It was necessary to draw lessons from May 68, and to revitalize the structures that had been shaken by the eruption of the event. How can one revive the revolutionary machine whose capacity for creating openings was clearly demonstrated in May 68? This was Guattari's specifically political question: "The revolutionary program, as the machine for institutional subversion, should demonstrate proper subjective potential and, at every stage of the struggle, should make sure that it is fortified against any attempt to 'structuralize' that potential."[10] If May 68 facilitated the institutional triumph of structuralism at the university,[11] the 68-event also gave rise to a 68-thought that would have nothing structuralist about it, and that on the contrary would put into crisis, in a decisive manner, a paradigm that was rather quickly abandoned by those who had seen in modernity the expression of a new worldview, and who now claimed never to have dined at the structuralist banquet.

If Guattari found material for his arguments in the two books published by Deleuze in 1968 and 1969, it was because Deleuze's philosophical orientation distinguished him from the dominant and undivided paradigm of the time. In his thesis, *Difference and Repetition*, Deleuze had remained vigilant with regard to any reduction of the event to insignificance, as was practiced by structuralism. He argued instead for a refusal of the alternative between structure and event, in favor of their joint articulation: "There is no more opposition between event and structure or sense and structure than there is between structure and genesis" (*DR* 191). Deleuze nevertheless recognizes the effectiveness of structuralism in accounting for multiplicities. His theatre has nothing to do with representation; it is rather a "theatre of multiplicities" (*DR* 192), which, rather than seeking an ideal synthesis of recognition and representation adequate to the identical, tracks the problems at the very heart of the movements of experimentation.

According to Deleuze, however, structuralism remains a prisoner of the categories of identity and opposition, and fails to pose the right problems. Thus linguistics – the pilot science of the structuralist paradigm in its Saussurean-Jakobsonian form, which turned the rules of phonology, in their structural aspects, into a heuristic model – is enclosed in a binary logic, and privileges negative terms by "assimilating the differential relations between phonemes to relations of opposition" (*DR* 204). Saussurean structuralism mutilates the potential positivity of difference, and Deleuze opposes to it the work of another linguist, Gustave Guillaume, who was marginal in the world of linguists, but on whose importance Deleuze would constantly insist. "The fundamental lesson of Guillaume's work is the substitution of a principle of *differential position* for that of distinctive opposition" (*DR* 205). In Guillaume, there is a veritable transcendental exploration of the Idea of the linguistic unconscious which, in Guillaume's case, does not lack its object. In his seminar on the semiotics of the cinema on March 19, 1985, Deleuze affirms his enthusiasm for Guillaume's theories: "What is the signified of power for Guillaume? It is movement: what confirmation! It is a day of celebration. What an encounter!"[12] He presents Guillaume as the last of the great linguistic philosophers, whose thesis, rejected by most linguists, is to maintain that a word, as the minimal signifying unit, has only one sense, which he calls the "signified of power."[13] This dimension refers to an ideal material that pre-exists discourse, but which we cannot avoid: "This is the resurrection of a philosophy that arrives behind the back of linguistics, and is detested by linguists."[14] Guillaume, as the "psycho-mechanic" of language, is indeed not far, in his hypotheses about language, from Deleuze's own schema, and he constantly reproached other linguists for remaining at the level of visible facts.

The affirmation of an ontology of difference led Deleuze, in his thesis, to take careful account of the theories advanced by those thinkers who had presented themselves as the masters of structuralism, in all its facets, during the 1960s. He recognized the merit of Freud for having insisted on a pre-genital sexuality consisting of partial drives, and of Lacan for having extended this discovery with his object-*a*. For Deleuze, Lacan also had the merit of separating the relation with time of the real object and virtual object, the latter having the property of both being and not being where it is. Yet despite these advances, psychoanalysis, according to Deleuze, remained the prisoner of a philosophy of the representation of the subject, subordinating its theory of repetition to a principle of identity in the past or a principle of analogy of resemblance in the actual.

HOW DOES ONE RECOGNIZE STRUCTURALISM?

Just as he commended the contribution of Lacan, Deleuze also welcomed the reading of Marx's work found in Althusser and the Althusserians. "Althusser and his collaborators are, therefore, profoundly right to show the presence of a genuine structure in *Capital*, and in rejecting the historicist interpretations of Marxism" (*DR* 186). The relations between Althusser and Deleuze were rather good. In 1964, Althusser invited Deleuze to teach at the École normale supérieure at the rue d'Ulm. Deleuze declined the offer because he was moving to Lyon:

Thank you for your letter and your proposal. Alas, alas. I have not been appointed in Grenoble, who received me badly ["qui m'accueillait mal"]. I am doing an about-face and going to Lyon to take up the strange position of a professor of morals. I'm going to move there. So although I would have loved to, I will not be able to teach a course at the *École*. I am touched that you and students at the *École* wanted to have me, tell them this. Warm regards.[15]

In 1965, Althusser sent Deleuze his own works as well as those of his group, and Deleuze's reaction was very positive.

I am touched that you sent me your three books. You could not have given me greater pleasure. I am not finished yet, but already, not only articles I had read and admired, but everything I did not know (your elucidation of the concept of "problem," a common concern of mine and yours), and then the fetish and the analysis of the exact role of alienation, it all seems so important that I feel its influence. Of your collaborators, I knew Macherey a little, whom I hold in some esteem. All three of these books and your style impress me ... (Yes, I think these books are of a great depth and beauty. I would like very much to talk about them with you).[16]

The beautiful text by Deleuze, "How Do We Recognize Structuralism?," which his friend Francois Châtelet published in his *History of Philosophy* in 1972, was in fact written in 1968 and submitted to Althusser.

I am sending you enclosed the text, which I told you about, on structuralism. I had told you that my ambition here was for a more rigorous popularization than is usually done. But I am not satisfied with it, even modestly. For sometimes it seems that everything is totally obscure, and sometimes that it is complete bullshit ["de déconner complètement"] (particularly in the final paragraph on the "last criteria"). But I am sending it to you because, on the one hand, it concerns you, and on the other, for you to tell me if it's publishable. Do me the favor of reading it, in a very personal manner. To write something bad can always be formative, but to publish it – no. Maybe the final part should be removed.[17]

Published in 1972, but written before 1968, and thus before his encounter with Guattari, what Deleuze published in Châtelet's *History of Philosophy* was an extremely fundamental text in which he analyzed the structuralist paradigm in a text he had submitted in advance to Althusser.[18] Beyond the diversity of the areas explored, Deleuze attempted to identify a number of common criteria for structuralist studies, which at the time preoccupied the linguistic, literary, anthropological, sociological, and psychoanalytic fields. The first characteristic is the centrality of the symbolic dimension, which forms the link between the real and the imaginary, and Deleuze attributes the discovery of this third term to structuralism. In this domain, as in others, it is linguistics that played the role of a pilot science. The second criterion is localization or position. The meaning of the elements of the structure is due solely to their position, and Deleuze hails the "rigorous" manner in which Lévi-Strauss has shown this. One can find here the very foundations of structuralist ambition, which is to become a topology, a logic of relations. On this point, Deleuze feels very close to this way of valorizing what he would later call the plane of immanence. The third and fourth criteria – the valorization of the differential and singular – demonstrate even more Deleuze's affinity with the structuralist paradigm: "Every structure is a multiplicity" (*DI* 177), says Deleuze, who on this basis provides a reading of the structural paradigm that brings it close to his own ontology of difference. This is evident when he says that "of structure one will say: *real without being actual, ideal without being abstract*" (*DI* 179). He praises Lévi-Strauss for conceiving that the unconscious is always empty and tributary to its own structural laws. Here again, we are far from the negative assessment that will be given later, after Deleuze's encounter with Guattari, when both thinkers would stigmatize Lévi-Strauss' structuralism by describing it as the anorexic conception of the unconscious. We are still at a moment when structuralism is being presented in its positivity. The fifth criterion is seriality, which gives movement to a structure. On this point, Deleuze feels himself to be close to structuralism, and he will organize his book, the *Logic of Sense*, into thirty-four different series. The sixth criterion, extremely important for structuralism, is the principle of the empty case, the famous degree zero of both language and the unconscious. Deleuze notes that it lacks in its own place, and that it is this *lack* that causes the movement: "No structuralism is possible without this degree zero" (*DI* 186).

In the 1969 *Logic of Sense*, one can sense the ambivalence towards structuralism that was already present in the 1968 thesis, which is mixed with a fascination for a method that allows sense to circulate, on a surface plane, around a zero point or an empty case. Deleuze still sees structure as equivalent to a machine. Guattari's text, "Machine and Structure," would fascinate Deleuze all the more in that it seemed far more advanced in its critique of structuralism.

In 1969, Deleuze was still saying: "Structure is in fact a machine for the production of incorporeal sense" (*LS* 71). These linguistic, anthropological, and psychoanalytic studies that turn around an empty case – which can also be the place of death, the zero value, the floating signifier – put into question the schema of causality, since the cause is absent from its place. Deleuze thus proclaims that "the importance of structuralism in philosophy, and for all thought, is that it displaces frontiers" (*LS* 71). "It is thus pleasing that there resounds today the news that sense is never a principle or an origin, but that it is produced. It is not something to discover, to restore, and to re-employ; it is something to produce by a new machinery. It belongs to no height or depth, but rather to a surface effect" (*LS* 72). Deleuze sees in this orientation a liberation from transcendence, a valorization of the plane of immanence, and finds in it the possible productive machinery of sense that he wants to see deployed in a free proliferation in order to make pre-individual singularities emerge.

In the *Logic of Sense*, Deleuze adheres closely to the structuralist project, to which he devotes many chapters characterized as series, but always in pursuit of his own metaphysical exposition. Notably, he draws on the work of Benveniste to distinguish the three forms that a proposition can assume: firstly, the relation of *denotation* to an individual thing, which is the indexical; secondly, *manifestation*; and only thirdly, *signification*. To these three levels investigated by linguists, Deleuze adds a fourth dimension, which is that of sense. The Stoics discovered sense along with the question of the event: "Sense, the *expressed of the proposition*, is an incorporeal, complex, and irreducible entity, at the surface of things, a pure event which inheres or subsists in the proposition" (*LS* 19).

In the approach suggested by Deleuze – which is inspired in part by the works of linguists, who are then connected to his own philosophical orientation – sign and sense are no longer two different strata or two alternative horizons; on the contrary, they are indissolubly linked. "As Bergson said, one does not proceed from sounds to images, and to images from sense: one is established 'from the outset' within sense" (*LS* 28). The fact that we find ourselves immersed in an already-there of sense, towards which we regress in a limitless proliferation, had already been made clear by Frege, on the plane of logic, and by Carroll, on the plane of literary writing. What Deleuze was responding to, in a critical fashion, was the alternative between, on the one hand, an indefinite regression and, on the other, a sterile duplication as a final determination of sense: the "one or the other" (LS 32) that still prevailed in Husserl's phenomenology. The characteristic of the pure event is precisely that it overcomes all dualisms and opens up the horizon of impossible objects, of paradoxes that lead to the absurd, and of oxymorons of the type the round square, unextended matter, mountains without valleys ... "which are objects 'without a home', the outside of being ... They are of 'extra-being' – pure ideational events, unable to be realized in states of affairs" (LS 35). Affirming the paradoxical nature of regression, Deleuze suggests that force can only be serial. If he repeats the structural distinction between signifier and signified, he gives it another acceptation by calling the signifier a sign, since the latter has an element of sense, and by calling the signified that which serves as the correlate to this aspect of sense: "what is signified is never sense itself" (LS 37), but the concept.

What Deleuze insisted on – always with the desire to affirm a philosophy of paradox, the double, the tension maintained in the oxymoron – was the co-presence of sense and nonsense, which are not in a relation of exclusion (of the false by the true). Deleuze brought about a reversal with regard to the "panlinguism" of the epoch. At a time when everybody was proclaiming that everything is structured like a language, or that everything is a part of language, Deleuze gave far less importance to language compared to what language relies on, namely, the *event*. "Events make language possible" (LS 181). What we find at the beginning is not the order of the system of language, but the speech act. Deleuze thus distances himself from the dominant Saussureanism through his rehabilitation of speech as signifier: "We always begin in the order of speech" (LS 181). For Deleuze, the event becomes the transcendental horizon of language, its condition of possibility.

THE DELEUZE AND GUATTARI ASSEMBLAGE

The "Deleuze-Guattari assemblage" that begins in 1969 will radicalize the critical stance of both thinkers, but in the early 1970s it will take a marked turn towards polemic by being deployed *together*. The first words of *Anti-Oedipus* are significant for their refusal of any structural closure, even if they indicate the irrelevance of the topic of the subject, the "I," in favor of a machinic polymorphic logic. They affirm the absolute primacy of multiplicities in relation to structural binarism. *Anti-Oedipus* is conceived as a veritable war machine against structuralism, and it will contribute greatly to the acceleration of the deconstruction of the current paradigm that had been in process in 1967/68. It will operate as an infernal machine, exploding the structuralist paradigm from within.

Deleuze and Guattari would oppose to the formalism of structural studies, by their collaborative writing itself, the counterpoint of experimentation. Their project in the early 1970s was to oppose the social sciences to the structuralist paradigm. They relied primarily on a rereading of the advances made in anthropology, semiotics, psychoanalysis, and history – when all these disciples were following paths traced out by the structuralist schema – precisely in order to undo it. Together, they would practice the method of "perversion," developed by Deleuze, in order to escape the structuralist closure.

According to Deleuze and Guattari, there are various orders of machines: technical machines, cybernetic machines, war machines, economic machines, signifying machines, institutional desiring-machines, as well as literary machines. "Machine" is a veritable catchphrase that was meant to dethrone another catchphrase of the time: the notion of "structure." The concept of machine became so central that when Deleuze published a new edition of *Proust and Signs* in 1970, he added a second part entitled "The Literary Machine," which included a description of the 'three machines' found in *In Search of Lost Time*.

Anti-Oedipus begins with a chapter devoted to desiring-machines, a concept that will be abandoned by its authors a few years later in *A Thousand Plateaus*, almost certainly because the concept had done its job of undermining the concept of structure, which no longer needed to be challenged in 1980, when the structuralist paradigm was little more than a memory. By contrast, Guattari's notion of transversality was used more and more extensively in order to grasp "cuts" in the flows, through which the desiring machine had been defined. The romp through the human sciences found in the two volumes of *Capitalism and Schizophrenia* had been a way of exploding the structuralist paradigm in order to free multiplicities and singularities from their closure.

The designated adversary of *Anti-Oedipus* – the "structuralized" psychoanalysis of Lacan – is based on the Saussurean conception of language. Deleuze and Guattari thus undertake a violent critique of the Saussurean theory of the sign. They even denounce the "shadow of Oriental despotism. Ferdinand de Saussure does not merely emphasize the following: that the arbitrariness of language establishes its sovereignty, as a servitude or generalized slavery visited upon the 'masses'" (*AO* 207); moreover, the signifier/signified relation is asymmetrical in Saussure, to the benefit of an absolute prevalence of the signifier. What was once described as positive – the empty case operating by successive folding in numerous orders – is now considered to be dependent on a conception of a linguistic field defined by Saussure as a transcendence turning around a master signifier.

To this linguistics of the signifier, Deleuze and Guattari will oppose a completely different type of linguistics: a linguistics of flow. On this point, the contribution of Guattari is clear, as evidenced in the preparatory notes he wrote for *Anti-Oedipus*.[19] In fact, Hjelmslev, the inventor of what he himself called "glossematics," initiated a linguistics that is even more formal than Saussure's. Deleuze and Guattari use of it has little to do with glossematics, and the meanings of Hjelmslev's notions are blithely altered. Their real objective is to use this reading as an anti-Saussurean war machine leaving space for a truly pragmatic linguistics. To do this, they believe they see in Hjelmslev the advent of a real plane of immanence, which corresponds to their call for a linguist who aims "to establish an algebra immanent to language."[20]

What Deleuze and Guattari take most of all from Hjelmslev, interpreting him in their own way, is his distinction between the plane of expression and the plane of content, which function in an entirely reversible manner: "Their functional definition provides no justification for calling one, and not the other, of these entities *expression*, or one, and not the other, *content*."[21] This distinction reveals strata, or planes of consistency, that break the Saussurean binarism. There would in effect be a single plane of consistency being deployed in multiple strata. Hjelmslev would have had the merit of liberating the study of language from its shackles, opening it up to a theory of the sign that is intended to embrace everything. Guattari also saw in Hjelmslev's *Essays* a Prolegomena to their theory of the collective agent of enunciation, and hence the supersession of the Saussurean dichotomy between language and speech. Hjelmslev is thus enlisted in the construction of the semiotic machine built by Deleuze and Guattari against structural semiotics – a program that had already been made clear in the text of *Anti-Oedipus*: "Louis Hjelmslev's linguistics stands in profound opposition to the Saussurean and post-Saussurean undertaking. Because it abandons all preferred reference. Because it describes a pure field of algebraic immanence that no longer allows any surveillance on the part of a transcendent instance, even one that has withdrawn" (*AO* 242). This is a purely immanent theory of language that "causes form and substance, content and expression, to flow according to the flows of desire, and that breaks these flows according to points-signs or figures-schizzes" (*AO* 242–43).

Between 1972 and 1980, the date of the publication of *A Thousand Plateaus*, Deleuze and Guattari discovered another theorist of language to oppose to Saussure, the semiotician Charles Sanders Peirce, the founder of pragmatism, who defined thinking as a sign.[22] According to Peirce, thought is deployed within a semiotic triangle (sign–object–interpretant) that refers to an indefinite dialogic of interpretations. Peirce thereby constituted a decentering of linguistics, which became little more than a partial subset of a general semiology, and subordinated the rules of language to their use. Sense thus reveals its practical function. Peirce's other major reversal is to think of the world no longer as merely physical, but as fundamentally semiotic. For their part, Deleuze and Guattari would reject the alternative between physics and semiotics.

In *A Thousand Plateaus*, this pragmatic orientation, in particular, was appealed to as an alternative to Saussure. In this case, speech functions as an expression of a doing, and the utterance, as the elementary unit of language, is conceived of as an "order-word" (*ATP* 75). Language presents itself as essentially informative, whereas it is first and foremost performative. Deleuze and Guattari rely heavily on J. L. Austin's theories on the interrelationship of action and speech performance, as well as the work of Oswald Ducrot.[23]

Although Deleuze and Guattari establish their correlation with a particular socius, these semiotics are not yet identified with a particular historical moment, and there is no question of opposing to a static and purely synchronic structuralism an evolutionary continuum. Rather, Deleuze and Guattari assert the primacy of mixtures or hybrids. These are *assemblages*, which are the very conditions of intelligibility of these regimes of signs. What allows the passage from one regime of signs to another is always the founding event that cuts the flows, and sets them in motion again on unforeseen paths. For this reason, there are two dates in the epigraph of the "fifth plateau": 587 BC and AD 70, the two dates of the destruction of the Temple that obliged the Jewish people to leave. The Jewish prophet thus embodies the passage, necessitated by the destruction of the Temple, from thought to action, inciting the movement of the Israelite people. The prophet becomes the eponymous character of a concrete case of transformational semiotic analysis, able to move from a signifying semiotics to a semiotics of subjectivity. Pragmatics is not considered by Deleuze and Guattari to be a mere supplement to the soul of linguistics, but rather is the basic element on which everything else depends.

THE DESIRING-MACHINE *CONTRA* THE MASTER SIGNIFIER

The desiring-machine must make its way into the structures in order to explode the master signifier defended by the Lacanians. The psychoanalytic interpretation begins with the notion of a primary lack, of absence, whereas according to our authors, subjective cuts, the real cuts of flow, on the contrary, begin with a full excess. Epistemologically, on the side of its object, psychoanalysis is stigmatized as an enterprise of normalization and repression, continuing the work of confinement and circularity ["repli sur soi"] that characterized psychiatry in the nineteenth century. "Instead of participating in an undertaking that will bring about genuine liberation, psychoanalysis is taking part in the work of bourgeois repression at its most far-reaching level" (*AO* 50).

In reality, psychoanalysis would be a familialism endowed with a pseudo-scientific discourse. In this regard, the desiring-machine has to escape the Oedipal straitjacket in order to better release the productive forces of the unconscious and schizophrenize them. Alongside the argumentative developments opposing the theories of psychoanalysis, we find in the writings of the two authors slogans taken straight from the May 68 movement: "We are all schizos! We

are all perverts! We are all libidos that are too viscous and too fluid"
(*AO* 67). The constant conversion by analysts of any unconscious
manifestation in Oedipus shows that psychoanalysis bears within
itself a metaphysics that must be subjected to a materialist critique.
Proponents of a method of conjunctive disjunction, our authors criticize the systematic use of "either ... or ..." exclusive disjunctions in
psychoanalytic practice, totally ignoring the schizophrenic, who is
made an outsider to the Freudian discourse.

Schizoanalysis aims to reconnect the unconscious to the social
and the political. The grid of the Oedipal reading would be subject both to a form of mechanistic reductionism and a process of
simple application. The function of the structural apparatus of
Lacanianism would actually serve to repress desire to make sure
that it is renounced, and thereby to perfect the therapeutic work
of the apparatus of repression. "By placing the distorting mirror
of incest before desire (that's what you wanted, isn't it?), desire is
shamed, stupified, it is placed in a situation without exit, it is easily
persuaded to deny 'itself'" (*AO* 120).

Putting desire back in motion, and making it productive, becomes
the primary function of the desiring-machine, which must be substituted for the confining Oedipal structure. The postulated structural unity of the machine must also be undone. The difference lies
at the level of molar machines and molecular machines, the essential point being that desire is of the order of production, whether it
occurs at the micro or macro level. However, the structural unity
around the theory of lack imposes a molar aggregate: "Such is the
structural operation: it distributes lack in the molar aggregate"
(*AO* 307).

This polarity between the molar and molecular was introduced
by Guattari, and was derived primarily from his practice in the field
of institutional psychotherapy at the La Borde clinic. It began as a
way to subvert the molar logic of stratification, bureaucratization,
and routinization of organizations by liberating, at every moment,
molecular flows and intensities capable of weakening the codes of
the molar pole. "The distinction between macro and micro is very
important, but it belongs perhaps more to Guattari than to me. For
me, it is rather the distinction between the two multiplicities. That's
the key for me."[24] Guattari suggests that Deleuze contrast molecular alterity and molar alterity to the imaginary alterity of Lacan,

who said: "There was a linguistization of molar sets, a refusal of the usual geneticism ... Everything is reduced to structuralism on a linguistic model. It's absolute, structural, linguistic alterity with no guarantees: the A (there is no Other of the Other)."[25]

Even if Lacan had the immense merit of discovering the object-*a* – something of the order of the molecular that, as a partial object, always escapes and exceeds the structure – he nonetheless remained a prisoner of structure. Defining itself as a materialist approach, schizoanalysis instead opposes to the endogenous play of structure the signifying the intervention of an outside. The schizoanalyst presents himself primarily as a supporter of a mode of experimentation, and not in order to interpret using the grid of a reading or appealing to the primal scene. As a "mechanic, a micro-mechanic" (*AO* 338), what must be grasped in everyone is not a deeply buried secret but desiring-machines that operate in a singular manner, with their failures, their accelerations, their cuts of flow, their becomings. "In the unconscious it is not the lines of pressure that matter, but on the contrary the lines of escape" (*AO* 388).

Defining the unconscious as a multiplicity of intensities and excess, Deleuze and Guattari put back into circulation what had been repressed by structuralism. On this score, one might claim, following Joël Burman, that the clinical practice ["clinique"] defended by Deleuze and Guattari aims to reintroduce the economic problematic of Freudian metapsychology, namely, the theory of the drives eliminated by Lacanianism. On the face of it opposed to the formalist and purely symbolic conception of an unconscious functioning as a structure according to the linguistic model, Deleuze and Guattari "argued in *Anti-Oedipus* that the unconscious is traversed from one end to another by drives, or, in other words, that the unconscious cannot exist without intensities."[26] The desiring machine puts drives back into the circuit with their excesses, their mobility and their failures, their disjunctive capacities. Schizophrenia, in this context, is doubly interesting in that it demonstrates the inability of even a structuralized psychoanalytic discourse, with its Oedipus squared, to be able either give an account of it or to be able to treat the pathology. But the schizophrenic also incarnates the figure of singular impersonality that Deleuze and Guattari look to in order to oppose both the de-singularized structure and personalism.

THE CRITIQUE OF CLAUDE LÉVI-STRAUSS

The relationship with Lévi-Strauss is far less polemical than the relation with Lacan in *Anti-Oedipus*, whose primary target is the practice of psychoanalysis. Nevertheless, Deleuze and Guattari obviously distance themselves from structural anthropology. They appeal to Edmund Leach, for whom the absence of structure characterizes an entire set of directly observed empirical givens – which does not mean that there is no structure in Leach, but only that the structure is the principle of its own disequilibrium.

Deleuze and Guattari thus reject the idea of cold societies, primitive societies without history, grounded in a simple reproduction of the same. "The idea that primitive societies are without history, dominated by archetypes and their repetition, is particularly weak and inadequate" (*AO* 150). Even if Lévi-Strauss is not held responsible for this conception, it is he who divided civilizations into hot societies, operating on the model of thermodynamics, and cold societies, with the mechanical functioning of a watchmaker, sheltered, through repetition, from any aleatory element that might bring about change.

Deleuze and Guattari also work to overturn Lévi-Strauss' classic demonstration that the universality of the exchange of women would derive from the desire to avoid the closure of society into itself. "Far from being the extension of a system at first closed, the opening is primary, founded in the heterogeneity of the elements that compose the prestations and that compensate for the disequilibrium by displacing it" (*AO* 150). Deleuze and Guattari challenge the universal law of the prohibition of incest discovered by Lévi-Strauss, which was taken to be an inviolable law of every society in every latitude. They argue that the very idea of such prohibition is not relevant, since "incest does not exist" in numerous primitive societies.[27]

They base this claim on research by Meyer Fortes on territorial logics that are more basic than the exchange of women. "The problem is not that of the circulation of women ... A woman circulates by herself. She is not at one's disposal, but the legal rights of the offspring are determined in favor of a specific person."[28] The earth, with its territorial segmentarities, is then primary in relation to marriage exchanges and parental structures. Systems of alliances and kinship rules are thereby relegated to a second plane compared to territorial encodings of the socius. Contrary to Lévi-Strauss' argument, Deleuze and Guattari state: "A kinship system is not a structure but a practice, a praxis, a method, and even a strategy" (AO 147).

The very idea of a potential closure of a kinship system is derived from the mistaken perspective that consists in cutting off marriage practices from their economic and political substrate. Pierre Clastres has shown, in relation to the Guayaki Indians, that there are no pure nomads because there is always an encampment where a stock is stored, even in small quantities – in order to eat, to get married, and so on.[29] The critique of the epistemological order that Deleuze and Guattari address to the proponents of structural anthropology, as well as to structural semiotics, is the privileging of the sphere of exchange and circulation at the expense of production and social reproduction. However, for them, once again, the machinic is opposed to the structural because it is the hard link: "The soft structure would never function, and would never cause a circulation, without the hard machinic element that presides over inscriptions" (AO 188).

All these activities run through lived experience in order to segment it spatially or socially, combining different types of segmentarity – linear, binary, or circular. However, it is the nonstructural Africanists such as Fortes, Evans-Pritchard, and others who have succeeded in showing how the political system of primitive societies without a state has managed to incorporate territorial systems and segmentarities, building and appropriating kinship relations according to a hybrid and supple system. Deleuze and Guattari indeed see a binary at work, but they oppose the supple segmentarity of primitive societies to the hard segmentarity of modern societies. To support their thesis, they evoke the reform of Cleisthenes the Athenian in ancient Greece, who built a political space of citizenship by overcoding the lineal segments in order to produce a homogeneous space. But these two types of segmentarity are intertwined with each other: as Kafka showed, one can find suppleness at the heart of the most rigid bureaucratic systems; by contrast, one can also observe kernels of arbrification and hardening in the most primitive societies. These lines of segmentarity are characteristic of every society and every individual, and they ground the dominant character of politics: "Everything is political, but every politics is simultaneously both a *macropolitics* and a *micropolitics*" (*ATP* 213). The micropolitics that results from these observations, along with the primacy given to the political dimension, becomes a major concept with the publication of *A Thousand Plateaus*, where it replaces the concept of schizoanalysis and functions as its equivalent.

In *Anti-Oedipus*, Deleuze and Guattari oppose to structural anthropology an entire historical and political anthropology, which is deployed in accordance with the bipolarity between the logic of flows of decoding and the logic of processes of recoding. If structuralism is not a good approach for studying primitive societies, functionalism succeeds no better when it inquires into the use of this or that institution, believing it will find meaning in their function. Ethnologists, however, are credited with being far in advance of the psychoanalysts, who remained ensconced in the question, "What does it mean?" To these false questions, the schizoanalysis substitutes a focus on uses: "How it works is the sole question" (*AO* 180).

This is the question posed by Deleuze and Guattari, and it leads them to differentiate between three types of societies: Savage, Barbarian, and Civilized, according to degrees of deterritorialization of flows. They thus construct a genuine political anthropology in which the driving role is attributed to the process of decoding, which is at once both progressive and discontinuous, the weakness of codes and the liberation of flows. At each step, the central state structures, whether despotic or feudal, are shown to be incapable of resisting the forces of decoding that subordinate the institutional state forms in order to enslave them. Little by little, flows of numerous types impose their laws: "Flows of property that is sold, flows of money that circulates, flows of production and means of production" (*AO* 223). The fundamental characteristic of the capitalist machine is that it will be able to connect all these decoded flows, to make them play together in a single score, to make them function together in a system. The restitution of a universal history of humanity is in no way presented as a new teleology, since it is animated by the contingency of events that make social becomings bifurcate in one direction or another.

"It is certain that, even and especially in their manifestations of extreme force, neither capitalism nor revolution nor schizophrenia follows the paths of the signifier" (AO 244). What defines civilizations is their degree of codification or decodification of flows. What differentiates the capitalistic flow from the schizophrenic flow is that the latter remains blocked, since capitalism recodifies and imposes limits that cannot be crossed. Capitalist modernity did not go wrong with its policy of "the great confinement," as analyzed by Foucault. If capitalism sees in schizophrenia the characteristic traits of its own tendency to decode and to deterritorialize, it also sees schizophrenia as its external limit, and it "can function only on the condition that it inhibit this tendency" (AO 246). Like any society caught in the tension between these two major poles – the tendencies to deterritorialization and reterritorialization – capitalism remains fundamentally ambivalent.

According to Deleuze and Guattari, there would therefore be three successive social machines that would have each their dominance. The first one, that of the savage, is the underlying territorial machine that endeavors to code the flows over the full body of the earth. The imperial machine of the barbarians then overcodes these flows with the body of the despot and his bureaucratic apparatus of power. Finally, the civilized, modern, capitalistic machine decodes flows and achieves immanence. It thereby exemplifies, in the concrete plane of the historical realization of humanity, the deployment of a generalized theory of flows and multiplicities, and the primacy of productive machinery, having regained a dynamic and an axiomatic, and thus having broken free from purely structural, synchronic interpretations that value invariants and permanence, and reduce events to insignificance.

CRITIQUE OF THE SEMIOLOGY OF CINEMA

Later, in the early 1980s, when Deleuze took film as the object of his studies, he was once again confronted by the structuralist paradigm, for what appeared to be the deepest critical perspective was a semiology of cinema, which was the heir to the structuralist paradigm. It found its theoretician in the person of Christian Metz, who participated actively in the development of linguistic semiotic readings. In 1968, Metz published a book that would inaugurate an entirely new trend in semiotics, the *Essais sur la signification au cinema*.[30]

According to Metz, cinema is a language system without a language ["un langage sans langue"] whose characteristics are narration, the film-image being approximately equivalent to a statement: "The filmic shot resembles a statement rather than a word."[31] Finally, if one asks under what conditions this image becomes a statement, one is led to define rules of use, and this is the project of a semiology of cinema, along the lines of a Saussurean linguistics.

Metz moves from cinephilia to a new approach to the cinema, where he applies the conceptual grid that he formulates with his "great syntagmatic": "The object of my intellectual passion was the linguistic machine itself."[32] In 1964, his first semiological writing begins with a reaction against any cinematographic criticism that ignores the linguistic renaissance and remains untouched by the advances in semiotics, while multiplying the invocations of a specific cinematographic language: "In this manner, I left behind the Saussurean notion of language ... It seemed to me that film could be compared to a system of language ["langage"] and not a language [langue]."[33]

This extreme formalization of a system of cinematic language finds its linguistic source essentially within the work of Hjelmslev, whose definition of the concept of expression defines very clearly, according to Metz, the basic unit of the filmic "language," whereas its codification amounts to an approach that is purely formal, logical, and relational. "In the sense intended by Hjelmslev [form of content + form of expression], a code is a field of commutability, of differential signifiers. Thus, there may be several codes within a single system of language."[34]

Deleuze instituted a radical rupture with this orientation, which dominated the campus of the University of Paris III, the high place of theoretical studies on cinema in France. For him, the cinematic image cannot be defined as a language because it leaves to the side everything that specifies the image as movement and as time. Deleuze describes Metz as "Kantian," a rather laudatory adjective, but he adds that Metz does not seem to be able to carry the project to its completion. It was Kant who sent the Platonic metaphysical question, "What is ...?" to the pre-critical past in order to substitute for it another question, that of the conditions of possibility. The classical duality of an essence revealed behind an appearance is succeeded by the duality of attested facts and the conditions of their possible emergence. However, Metz remains Kantian to the degree that he dismisses, as a false problem, the question of knowing if, as the pioneers claimed, cinema reveals a universal language. He displaces this question in a Kantian manner by asking: "Under what *conditions* can cinema be considered a system of language?"[35]

Deleuze commends Metz's prudence when he supports his argument with an attested historical fact – the domination of Hollywood cinema as the matrix of narrative cinema. Where Deleuze does not follow Metz is in the price he has to pay: "As soon as the image is replaced by a statement, the image is given a false appearance, and its most authentically visible characteristic, movement, is taken away from it" (*TI* 27). The language system, with its rules, is folded over everything, and for Metz it is narration that marks the difference between photography and the cinema-image: "To go from one image to two images is to go from the image to language."[36] Metz's disciples pursue a similar path that leads to the suspension of movement in what is defined as a "semio-critique."

Metz's ambition, then, is to construct a "great syntagmatic" – an ambition that makes Deleuze smile: "It makes me laugh, because I hear Bossuet saying, 'The great lady is dead!'"[37] Still in an amused manner, Deleuze says to wait, after the great syntagmatic, for the great paradigmatic, but Metz agrees that, for the cinema, the paradigmatic is of little importance, since it remains infinite in its possibilities.

Deleuze opposes to Saussurean semiotics another source of inspiration, one that allows him to pursue his desire to construct harmonics between signs, in continuity with what he had already undertaken with Proust. When he talks about cinema, he has in mind a classification of signs. Announcing to his students on November 2, 1982 that he is going to continue his previous year's course on cinema, and ruminate on it, he adds, "like a cow," he starts from his intuition that he is on to something important, which he intends to pursue through a systematic exploration of signs: "I'm not saying that it will change the world if I get to this classification, but it will change me, and it would give me great pleasure."[38] Deleuze ambition is not to establish, in film, an equivalent of Mendeleyev's table. Rather than Saussure, it is the inventor of semiotics, Charles Sanders Peirce, who will play the role of toolkit, and who will give a completely different direction to Deleuze's research: a pragmatic direction, which privileges action and uses.[39] Peirce insists on the fact that each stage contains previous stages. But above all, his primary interest, in Deleuze's eyes, is his conception of signs, which has a completely different logic than the logic of language. Indeed, his trilogy basically starts with the movement-image, and it therefore allows him to think the cinematographic image according to its endogenous logic. Deleuze, however, does not allow himself be hemmed in by Peirce's "drive" toward classification. In the first place, he has a completely different concept of what a sign is; but above all, he rejects Peirce's idea of closing the system with Thirdness. The Saussurean model was not suitable for Deleuze because it was synchronic, negating all movement in the name of the law that governs the system; and moreover it excluded speech on principle, as an object of linguistic science, to the sole benefit of the language system.

The majority of specialists in film theory gave a very critical, if not caustic, reception to Deleuze's work. If Metz, in his seminars, was able to accept the principle that lay at the base of Deleuze's critique of his views, he nonetheless argued that he and Deleuze were not speaking about the same thing, which allowed him to avoid a direct confrontation. When *The Movement-Image* was published, Metz was no longer the leader of a growing group devoted to generalized semiology, and he was becoming increasingly isolated. His reaction of withdrawal reinforced in his inner circle – Michel Marie, Roger Odin, Marc Vernet, François Jost, and all the regulars of his seminar – a violent rejection of Deleuze's theories. This academic reaction was to continue for a long time. With a few exceptions, it was not until the 1990s that students forced Deleuze's cinema books on their teachers. It is this type of experience that made Jacques Aumont rethink his initial negative impressions – primarily because of the research of his students, notably the thesis of Dork Zabunyan.[40] Dominique Castle, by contrast, would remain very critical and polemical through the 1990s, seeing Deleuze as a guardian of the philosophical temple, concerned above all to maintain a monopoly on the concept, and having a "cannibalistic" conception of philosophy.[41] He added that the two books Deleuze devoted to cinema did little more than provide philosophical clothing to a purely Bazinian conception of cinema, ignoring Metz's contributions to filmolinguistic theory: "Deleuze rejects the linguistic hypothesis to return to simplistic Bazinian (and Bergsonian) assumptions."[42]

VITALISM *CONTRA* STRUCTURE

The culmination of Deleuze and Guattari's joint work appeared in the form of a highly classical metaphysical question that the two friends seem to have rejected earlier by asserting the primacy of "and" over "is." In 1991, however, *What is Philosophy?* was published, to widespread surprise.

Philosophy shares the domain of creativity with art, but here again, their objects differ. Art is the domain of affects and percepts, which are distinguished from affections and perceptions by their ability to be conserved, to go beyond the moments when they are experienced. The function of art is to make possible this conservation and transmission beyond the finitude of existence and experience. If the philosopher creates concepts, the artist creates percepts and affects, by various means.

The objective is to liberate vital forces wherever they are imprisoned, to rediscover their virtuality by an operation of destratification. Insofar as there is no determinism to be discovered on the plane of immanence, every moment and every place can be a rich source of experimentation. Whence the generalized constructivism suggestive of a creative "bricolage" that could push all expressions of life into other arrangements and measure whether the results are interesting.

The fundamental gesture consistently championed by Deleuze and Guattari is the setting-in-motion of the natural, animal, and human world. Through a close observation of the way things happen, they attempt to grasp Being in its becoming. This implies a philosophical style that is always on the lookout for new assemblages and new concepts.

NOTES

1   Félix Guattari, "Machine and Structure," in *Molecular Revolution: Psychiatry and Politics*, trans. Rosemary Scheed (New York: Penguin Books, 1984), pp. 111–19.
2   *Ibid.*, p. 112

3 *Ibid.*, p. 114.

4 *Ibid.*

5 *Ibid.*

6 *Ibid.*, p. 115.

7 *Ibid.*

8 *Ibid.*

9 See *Instincts et institutions*, ed. and introduced by Gilles Deleuze (Paris: Hachette, 1953, in the "Classiques" series).

10 Guattari, "Machine and Structure," p. 119.

11 See François Dosse, *Histoire du structuralisme*, vol. II, *L'institutionnalisation: la conquête de l'université* (Paris: Livre de Poche, 1995), pp. 173–82.

12 Gilles Deleuze, seminar at the University of Paris 8, March 19, 1985, sound archives of the Bibliothèque Nationale de France (BNF).

13 According to Guillaume, the "signified of power" is the unconscious dynamic that organizes the polysemy of a given lexeme. The signification of a word in discourse is thus always an assemblage or an arrangement between the word of the language (the signified of power) and the context.

14 Deleuze, seminar at the University of Paris 8.

15 Gilles Deleuze, letter to Louis Althusser, October 29, 1964, Fonds Althusser in the archives of the Institut Mémoires de l'Édition Contemporaine (IMEC).

16 Deleuze, letter to Louis Althusser, February 28, 1966, Fonds Althusser in the archives of IMEC.

17 Deleuze, letter to Louis Althusser, February 24, 1968, Fonds Althusser in the archives of IMEC.

18 Gilles Deleuze, "How Do We Recognize Structuralism?," in *DI*, pp. 170–92.

19 Félix Guattari, *The Anti-Oedipus Papers*, trans. Kélina Gotman, ed. Stéphane Nadaud (New York: Semiotext(e), 2006).

20 Louis Hjelmslev, *Prolégomènes à une théorie du langage* (Paris: Minuit, 1968 [1943]), p. 11. English translation: Louis Hjelmslev, *Prolegomena to a Theory of Language*, trans. F. J. Whitfield (Madison: University of Wisconsin Press, 1961).

21 Hjelmslev, *Prolégomènes*, p. 60.

22 Charles Sanders Peirce, *Écrits sur le signe* (Paris: Seuil, 1978).

23 J. L. Austin, *How to Do Things with Words* (Oxford: Clarendon Press, 1962).

24 Gilles Deleuze, "Réponse à une série de questions," November 1981, in Arnaud Villani, *La guêpe et l'orchidée*: essai sur Gilles Deleuze (Paris: Belin, 1999), p. 131.

25 Guattari, *Anti-Oedipus Papers*, p. 129.

26 Joël Birman, "Les signes et leurs excès: la clinique chez Deleuze," in Eric Alliez (ed.), *Gilles Deleuze: une vie philosophique* (Paris: Institut Synthélabo, 1998), pp. 477–94, p. 485.

27 Alfred Adler and Michel Cartry, "La Transgression et sa derision," *L'Homme*, 11:3 (July 1971), 5–63.

28 Meyer Fortes, "Colloque sur les cultures voltaïques," in *Recherches Voltaïques* 8 (Paris: CNRS, 1967), pp. 135–37.

29 Pierre Clastres, *Chronicle of the Guayaki Indians*, trans. Paul Auster (New York: Zone Books, 2000).

30 Christian Metz, *Film Language: A Semiotics of the Cinema*, trans. Michael Taylor (University of Chicago Press, 1990).

31 *Ibid.*, p. 116.

32 Christian Metz, interview with Marc Vernet and Daniel Percheron, *Ça Cinéma* (May 1975), p. 26.

33 Christian Metz, interview with Raymond Bellour, *Semiotica*, 4:1 (1971), p. 3.

34 *Ibid.*, p. 266.

35 Gilles Deleuze, seminar at the University of Paris 8, February 26, 1985, audio-visual archives of the BNF.

36 Metz, *Film Language*, p. 46

37 Gilles Deleuze, seminar at the University of Paris 8, March 5, 1985, audio-visual archives of the BNF.

38 Gilles Deleuze, seminar at the University of Paris 8, November 2, 1982, audio-visual archives of the BNF.

39 Peirce, *Écrits sur le signe*.

40 Dork Zabunyan, *Gilles Deleuze. Voir, parler, penser au risque du cinema* (Paris: Presses de la Sorbonne nouvelle, 2006).

41 Dominique Château, *Cinéma et philosophie* (Paris: Nathan, 1996), p. 107.

42 *Ibid.*, p. 142.

7 Deleuze and Guattari: Guattareuze & Co.

PREFACE

It is perhaps a testimony to their influence and notoriety that Deleuze and Guattari can be located at a number of stations along the continuum between parody and homage. I want to briefly consider three seemingly distant stations, each with its own humorous elements, but deployed to different ends. These prefatory considerations will open onto questions and demonstrations of how to characterize Deleuze and Guattari's collaborations, that is, how they, and others, posed and answered such questions, and what these tell us about their joint work. The emphasis in this contribution is less on the content of the books they wrote together than on characterizations of their process and how these characterizations have been deployed and redeployed to different ends.

The late French cartoonist and illustrator Gérard Lauzier (1930–2008) was known, among other things, for his parodies of intellectuals and the Left, including Deleuze and Guattari. Lauzier collapsed Deleuze and Guattari into a third figure of "Gilles Guatareuze" (one "t" only), described tentatively by François Dosse in terms of the rather neutral "coalescence."[1] Dosse provides some dialogue from a single panel – the final one – of Lauzier's illustrations of 1978, and quotes François Fourquet, somewhat tangentially, in order to explain how an already fragile Guattari was deeply wounded by such cruel commentary:

Mad drama. 5 policemen wounded at Saint-Tropez. Gilles Guatareuze called the police to have his mistress interned. The least surprising wasn't seeing the famous theoretician of antipsychiatry running after the police chief of Saint-Tropez pleading, "You aren't going to put her at La Borde or with the nice people, right! They could screw up and let her escape! They could screw up and let her escape! No, no a serious place, right? A padded cell and everything."[2]

Dosse has not actually seen these illustrations. But the cartoon panel continues in this way: "Otherwise the next time she may tear me to bits." Over the course of a few lurid color pages, the fear experienced by Guatareuze of Solange, his hysterical mistress, whose desire is rendered explicit as she bites and scratches him after he tries to convince her that she is an imposter who has replaced his true lover (the name "Solange" parodies both the shepherdess-saint and the region where La Borde is located). Guatareuze is pompous, fat, grey-haired, and bespectacled; his arrogance is palpable; he is manipulative, complaining that his desire has become a gulag, that he has been reduced to a slave. His face reddens in exasperation at his hitherto oblivious lover before she finally attacks. The final panel is a news report, from which the above quotation is taken.[3] The comic strip works a number of acute angles of highly vicious parody, mocking Guatareuze as "the Lenin of the libido" and referring to trees as having "tellurian erections," but concludes with Guatareuze's betrayal of his own principles (even if, strictly speaking, those of anti-psychiatry were decidedly not Guattari's own since he considered it too easily recuperated by reformist concessions and its maintenance of familialism).

The label of anti-psychiatrist remains attached to Guattari, at least in the popular imagination of French cartoonists. Lauzier is not alone in this. Consider Pierre-François Beauchard – pseudonym of David B, author of *Epileptic* – a graphic novel drawn in black and white. Centered around namesake Pierre-François – and told from his point of view – his younger sister Florence, and older brother Jean-Christophe, this novel recounts the family's struggle with J.-C.'s seizures and the "endless round of doctors" that defined their lives together from childhood through adulthood. Faddish macrobiotic treatments, hopes and letdowns, guilt and escape merge in Pierre-François' entry into the world of drawing comics, a dimension populated with totem animals and magical beings where he finds some respite. Inspired by May 68 as an epic scene of violence seen through the pages of *Paris-Match*, young Pierre-François at nine years of age defines his drawing style in densely detailed battles, indebted to the psychedelic mysticism of middle-brow French journal *Planète*. At the same time, his parents struggle with another hope – the leading lights of the anti-psychiatry movement: "The anti-psychiatry movement begins, propounded in France by people like Gilles Deleuze, Félix Guattari, Roger Gentis." Sitting in bed Pierre-François' mother says: "These are the kind of people Jean-Christophe should be seeing." And to this his father replies: "You think?"[4] Nothing comes of it. Much of *Epileptic* explores the structures of misrecognition in the family, as well as the stereotypes of the series of alternative communities and healers they come into contact with in search of a treatment for Jean-Christophe. Including Deleuze in the anti-psychiatry movement is based on a misunderstanding, perhaps an overly hopeful interpretation of his support for German anti-psychiatrists.[5] The irony is lost that Guattari's criticisms of the movement include that its best experiments were short-lived and largely a literary phenomenon.[6] By the same token, the Alternatives to Psychiatry Network in which he was active from the mid 1970s to the early 1990s made few substantive inroads outside of Italy,[7] even though it exposed horrendous conditions in psychiatric facilities that still existed in southern Europe.

There is another "Guatareuze" in circulation, but this time it is neither in France nor a parody. Rather, it is an *homage*, and a heroic one at that. As Nick Thoburn observes the Bolognese pirate radio station "Radio Alice … used the composite 'Guattareuze' (double 't') to characterize their practice."[8] In a section concerning the characteristics of a "minor music" in the Collectif A/traverso textual collage *Radio Alice, radio libre*,[9] the formulation is attributed: "as Guattareuze would say." Homage to Guattari, whose little essay "Millions and Millions of Potential Alices" sought to transfer some of the energy (with a strong coefficient of deterritorialization, flush with politics, and collectively assembled enunciations) that the free radio station catalyzed; and also to the creative deviation of minoritarian becoming that Guattari developed with Deleuze, but stretching beyond literature. While "Bifo" did not coin the word "Guattareuze," he recalls that it dates from the A/traverso magazine of September 1977. Its origin remains embedded in a collective enunciation.

Moving, then, from the caustic through the valorizing to the awkward assemblage. Guattari's journal entries for the period of October 1972 are a rich source of reflections on the implications of the process of writing *Anti-Oedipus*. Here we find Guattari's out-sider status – "a common psychoanalyst and an author" – on full display to the extent that his manner of working puts him at odds with the "systematic academic" approach mastered by Deleuze in the field of philosophy. Guattari asserts: "I don't really recognize myself in the A.O. [*Anti-Oedipus*]. I need to stop running behind the image of Gilles and the polishedness, the perfection that he brought to the most unlikely book. Dare to be an asshole. It's so hard being strapped onto Gilles! Be stupid in my own away."[10] Guattari iso-lates a residue of the process of writing with Deleuze: strapped onto Deleuze in a way that forms a contraption within a stereotypical hierarchy of the extra-academic (muddy and banal) and academic (pristine and polished) relationship. The contraption was a conse-quence of the success of *Anti-Oedipus*; it is a contraption rather than a desiring-machine because it is a tool-like projection imposed upon Guattari by the fallout of the book; it gets between him and his own practices, for instance, leading to a false distribution of mastery, to a second-rate identity, thus interrupting by deactivat-ing desire, also distorting his relationship with Deleuze. Guattari strapped onto Deleuze gives us a rattletrap. As Guattari once said in a joint interview: "we couldn't just hook a Freudian engine up to the Marxist-Leninist train" (*DI* 217). Not any old assemblage suffices to free desiring-production.

INTRODUCTION

It may be true that "Genosko has done the most to restore Guattari to his rightful place as equal collaborator" in his work with Deleuze, as Julian Bourg so generously put it,[11] but it is a task that requires constant attention and reinforcement. As Bifo suggests, what is called "DG thought" is a semiocompound of Guattarian molecular perturbations and Deleuzean ontology of events.[12] However, there is, he insists, a Deleuze without Guattari and a Guattari without Deleuze. But when they worked together, they set in motion a "rhi-zomatic machine" to whose functioning Guattari's contributions cannot be underestimated and, therefore, to treat this machine as a whole determined by Deleuze alone (and with Guattari strapped on) is not only to distort it but to suppress the collective assemblage of its functioning. Any denial of the two who are several who are also a crowd, the admission that begins *A Thousand Plateaus* (*ATP* 3), diminishes the assemblage's creativity and arrests the transversal movements of its components of passage. The insertion of a hierarchy into the rhizomatic machine in the form of an authorial contraption like the academic/militant re-identifies who is doing most of the writing. Deleuze has observed that he and Félix did not write a book in which one played the madman and the other the analyst; on the contrary, "we did write a book [*Anti-Oedipus*] in which you no longer know who is speaking" (*DI* 219). The goal was to avoid traditional dualities and not to have recourse to stereotypical hierarchies; any effort to secret a totality into a book of flows runs it aground on one bank.

It is useful to refer to specific academic straps-ons. The use of parentheses is commonplace. Take, for instance, Patricia Clough's quoting of *What is Philosophy?*, a book apparently by "Deleuze (and Guattari)."[13] Such is a simple qualification of Guattari's authority. And of course one winces at Slavoj Žižek's highly clichéd attempts to separate the "Deleuze proper" from the "guattarized" books.[14] Clearly, I have not done enough over time to discourage these practices. But some solace can be taken that acknowledgements of the problem are more and more often published, like Nicolas Bourriaud: "Guattari may still seem significantly under-estimated to us, and he is often reduced to the role of Deleuze's foil, yet it does today seem easier to acknowledge his specific contribution to the co-authored writings."[15] Easier, but no less treacherous.

Deleuze is perhaps one of the most insightful decoders of Guattari as an author and as a collaborator. Considering Guattari as a group schizo-subject consisting of an anti-Self, Deleuze figures his friend as a "catatonic stone" (when Félix is without his glasses) who also "lights up and seethes with multiple lives the moment he looks, acts, laughs, thinks or attacks" (*DI* 193). Pierre and Félix (Pierre-Félix Guattari): militant and psychoanalyst. It is useful to look at the figures to which Deleuze has recourse when describing how he worked with Guattari, for they are remarkably consonant with his characterization of Félix. Deleuze responds to Kuniichi Uno to this effect: he is the unmoving hill, with some internal movements, talking little; and Félix is the rolling sea, "sparkling with light." Deleuze then finds a sporting figure, which is rare in his writing (the exception is tennis), that suits them: "Together, Félix and I

would have made a good Sumo wrestler" (*TRM* 237). While enig-
matic, the principles Deleuze evokes with this figure are based on
size and strength – the wrestler's body type – and lightning-quick
reflexes and power exercised within a confined space – the circular ring. Traditionally, the Sumo wrestler belongs to a stable and
lives collectively – hence, he is a group subject. Deleuze continues
with a number of contrasts: Félix tinkers with diagrams; while he
prefers articulated concepts; their written letters to one another,
composed for *Anti-Oedipus*, were "disorderly" and the manner in
which each handled them put their rhythms of work at odds with
one another; Félix had "brainstorms" and Gilles was a "lightning
rod." What Deleuze emphasizes is the "accumulation of bifurcations" in a rhizomatic proliferation. To which he adds, during the
process of writing *A Thousand Plateaus*, "resonances" established
between disciplines in which they worked; and mutually fructu-
ous "guesses" about where they would go next. Deleuze even writes
about being "under Félix's spell" and in this state perceiving new
worlds. Deleuze's careful and imaginative figurations of his relationship with Guattari are consistently laudatory and insightful, yet
also seem to be resisting pressure – not from the cliché of Guattari's
erasure and the rise of the first author, full credit system – but from
the normative force of a pairing, sliding irrevocably into the couple,
which stills process and stalls proliferation. The couple has a bad
name in Deleuze and Guattari's thought. Every time the couple is
excoriated, there is whispering: Mommy–Daddy and their assigned
roles in the family drama. The couple crushes multiplicity: no exit.
To be coupled by others (doubled) is a difficult fate, but to find oneself acting like a couple (i.e. finishing each other's sentences) is even
worse. Coupling can be like a drug, Guattari thought, that people
take in order to protect themselves from greater dangers; coupledom
can be hell, and it can also be productive.[16]

Deleuze's brief remarks in "For Félix" are reserved for his friend's
creations, noting at the outset the "discovery and joy" of their collaborations, but the wish "not to talk about the books [they] wrote
together" after Félix's passing (*TRM* 382). Relief: not to yet again
explain their collaboration, but to focus on the singular creations
of Félix. Not to profess their mutual love, or find witness-readers to
it. But identify and problematize a symptomatic response to joint
publications read without love: referring to *Anti-Oedipus*, Deleuze

once commented that "I've wondered whether one general reason for some the hostility toward the book is simply the fact that there are two writers, because people want you to disagree about things, and take different positions. So they try to disentangle inseparable elements and identify who did what" (*N* 7). A partnership with problems is good for the business of criticism. Bickering satisfies the critics. Bile pollutes love.

COUPLING ISSUES

In *Anti-Oedipus* machines couple according to the productive, connective synthesis: and ... and then ... Constant coupling is the productive force of this synthesis that connects flows and partial objects, "continually producing production" (*AO* 7). When this rule is bent and broken a contraption results, the process stalls; but this is not an element of anti-production. It is the influencing machine of couplehood that persecutes partnerships (but without Victor Tausk's reduction of machines to genitalia). A coupled contraption doesn't simply break down; rather, a couple oozes self-destruction. Intimacy is toxic. According to Guattari in *The Anti-Oedipus Papers*:

The persistence of the oedipalized couple depends on the vertigo of reciprocal destruction, "low heat" self-destruction through the other one's fire. With couples, the desire for abolition makes its own laws and compromises. The conjugal couple is the elementary social structure, in a capitalist regime, for the exhaustion of the death drive. Its function is simultaneously to autonomize its existence and to delimit its rule. It's the minimum overcoding unit in a system based on decoded flow which, without it, would be too disorienting. It's how people find their status, the principle of their identity and their immanent legitimacy. The fraud of the person rests on that of the couple and that of the couple rests on the oedipal triad.[17]

There is a continuum between machinic coupling and a married heteronormative couple. Deleuze and Guattari create figures of their collaboration that deflect all efforts to push them toward the conjugal pole, whether it is by means of the critical need for knowing who wrote what (disentangle), or the creation of cartoon monsters (entangle). They resist this overcoding which infects the representation of all partnerships under capitalism. When Deleuze and Guattari retort they do so in the name of machinic couplings and assemblages; for Deleuze, the priority is given to nuptials rather than couples, exchanges, binaries (*D* 2). Many critics find this strategy disorienting and resort to interpolating themselves as the third party who completes the couple by expressing the truth of the relation, which is generally at the expense of Guattari and, secondarily, both authors. The question of how to distribute the weight of authorial input and authority correctly still bewitches readers of Deleuze and Guattari.

ACCORDING TO THE AMPERSAND

Any deviation from the intermezzo in favor of an average, or one or the other of authors, is a betrayal of the logic of the and. In this sense, then, Dosse's effort around how to explain the workings of the "duo" is not designed to sweep both away, "reciprocally implicated and transformed in a transversal cross-cutting."[18] Sweeping away the question of "who wrote what" (still, Dosse wants to attribute specific concepts to Guattari like the ritornello because he was a pianist) and restoring Guattari's "competence" through his "palpable marks" are laudable goals. But "both and" are never really swept up and away in this approach. The conjunction of the "duo" remains too exclusive, and departures are forfeited. According to the logic of the ampersand, then, the emphasis is placed on the and between Deleuze and Guattari. By the time we reach *A Thousand Plateaus*, the language of synthesis has been displaced by a linguistics in which a redundancy of ampersands "and ... and ... and [et]" gets the upper hand on "is" ["est"] to introduce continuous variation into language (*D* 98–99). 'And' – an "atypical expression" – works as a tensor: "it causes language to tend toward the limit of its elements ... the tensor effects a kind of transitivization of the phrase ... An expression as simple as AND ... can play the role of tensor for all language. In this sense AND is less a conjunction than the atypical expression of all of the possible conjunctions it places in continuous variation" (*D* 99). Deleuze takes such care in creating figures that describe his modus operandi vis-à-vis Guattari because in them he is uprooting restrictive configurations of the relation between the two authors, emphasizing variability and redistribution, and collective enunciations. Deleuze defines the conjunction AND: "neither a union, nor a juxtaposition, but the birth of a stammering, the outline of a broken line which always sets off at right angles, a sort of active and creative line of flight" (*D* 9–10). Stumbling over "and ... and ... and" is a way of creation for Deleuze.

For Parnet, AND is a multiplicity and, as such, it is never alone: "And, And, And – stammering. And even if there are only two terms, there is an AND between the two, which is neither the one nor the other, nor the one which becomes the other, but which constitutes the multiplicity" (*D* 34–35). The line – a "narrow stream" – between sweeps both away undoing dualisms from the inside (as they become about "successive choices" (*D* 19).[19] All the ANDs of a collaboration "would appear as so many distorted images in running water" (*D* 35).

ASIGNIFYING CREATIVITY

Another strap-on: "I'm strapped to this journal. Grunt. Heave. [Oct. 6, 1972]."[20] At this point in 1972, *Anti-Oedipus* had been out for about eight months; Guattari was supposed to be contributing to "volume 2" of *Capitalism and Schizophrenia*, keeping his journal had become a burden, and he was experiencing anxiety at reading the proofs for *Psychanalyse et transversalité*. He had become an author, publishing two books in one year, his first and second. Guattari engaged in a protracted self-analytic assessment of his strategy of writing during this period, and whenever the occasion arose thereafter. He expressed his worries about not producing and being accountable for Gilles; that he was just "fucking around"; yet that was how he worked because the energy was in the mess: mayhem, bad spelling, poor expression, arguments to hide behind; multiple beginnings. "I'm a sort of inveterate autodidact, a do-it-yourself guy, a sort of Jules Verne – *Journey to the Centre of the Earth*. In my own way I don't stop ... But you can't tell. It's the never ending work of reverie. Lots of ambitious plans. Everything in my head, nothing in the pocket."[21] Guattari's explanations are full of denials – "I'm not a philosopher" – and colorful characterizations and alignments. Around 1982, while in Brazil, Guattari explained how he worked in contrast to Deleuze: "I try out ploys, like people who try to rob banks – I venture into maneuvers of expression in a certain context, in a certain situation. Later, I abandon it all and go and do something else."[22] Guattari's reticence about producing meaning effects is worked though in his desire to diagram. The plan without the heist; the outline without the text. "I stole Félix, and I hope he did the same for me," Deleuze once said, invoking constructive thievery in the conceptual realm (D 17). Scrunched-up papers in a dustbin. Restlessness at his writing desk. These deterritorialized, machinic signs conjoin directly with other signs and objects and affects, but without the crutches of representation and signification and the anchor of an individuated subject. Guattari's diagrams operate whether or not anybody, including Deleuze, can make sense of them. They generate ideas and objects: little machines of invention that relate to one another by triggering interactions.

Taking a cue from Deleuze's description of how his book *Dialogues* with Claire Parnet "made a new point which made possible a new line-between" (D ix), in addition to which it fell between *Anti-Oedipus* and *A Thousand Plateaus* (not to mention *Kafka* in 1975), which were themselves between himself and Guattari, Guattari is a momentary point of subjectification, as an author with his name on a book contract, caught up in the semiotic and material flows that spirit him away in a plurality of articulations. He is also between *Anti-Oedipus* and *A Thousand Plateaus* by way of *Psychanalyse et transversalité*, intersected by his journal entries and letters to Deleuze. Muddled lines forming rhizomes between the points and carrying them away. Stammering, stumbling, drawing diagrams, unable to get down to writing the next text.

ETHOLOGICAL BECOMINGS

Ethology is the scientific study of processes of animal behavior, favoring field observation, and a subdiscipline of evolutionary biology. The ideas of its Austrian founders Nikolaas Tinbergen and Konrad Lorenz were influential in postwar anthropology and spread via Lévi-Strauss in France. In *The Machinic Unconscious*, Guattari approaches ethology in order to criticize its mechanistic behaviorist assumptions and hierarchical arborescent logics by means of the insertion of refrains (rhythms of temporization and territorialization and facility traits like silhouettes) that precipitate innovations (rhizomic mutations) in and between the semiospheres of animals, and animals and plants. Guattari further rethinks territory in nonhuman animals by describing the open assemblages of components, some of which become non-passively expressive and give consistency to social relations between the same and different species. Instead of explaining territory by means of innate mechanisms and the need to satisfy the big drives (hunger, sex, flight, aggression), Guattari turns to expressivity as surplus value of code (beyond the sum of genetic encoding, ecological adaptation, and social communication) as a source of innovation, that is, as art, which "perhaps begins with the animal, at least with the animal that carves out a territory and constructs a house ... The territory-house system transforms a number of organic functions – sexuality, procreation, aggression, feeding. But this transformation does not explain the appearance of the territory and house; rather, it is the other way around" (*WP* 183).

To the extent that Guattari's *The Machinic Unconscious* may be read as a workbook for *A Thousand Plateaus*, the emphasis on ethology plays a vital role as a "very privileged molar domain for demonstrating how the most varied components ... can crystallize in assemblages that respect neither the distinction between orders nor the hierarchy of forms. What holds all the components together are transversals, and the transversal itself is only a component that has taken upon itself the specialized vector of deterritorialization" (*ATP* 336).

Famously, the aparallel evolution of "the wasp AND the orchid" (*D* 7) has become for some a description of Deleuze and Guattari's work together.[23] Guattari writes:

It is known that the wasp, effectuating a simulated sex act with a morphological and olfactory lure constituted by the rostellum of the orchid, afterwards releases and attaches the pollen that it transports onto other plants ... The ensemble of the transcoding systems authorizing these round-trip tickets between the vegetable kingdom and the animal kingdom appears completely closed to any individual experimentation, training, or innovation ... Nothing would be gained by reducing a symbiosis like that of the wasp and the orchid to a simple "attachment" between two heterogeneous worlds. This encounter produces what I called elsewhere a "surplus-value of code" ... the new symbiotic assemblage actually functions like a mutant wasp-orchid species evolving on its own account and redistributing the genetic and semiotic components selected from both original species according to its own standards ... thus a new evolutionary line of flight is launched on the bio-ecological rhizome which is in other respects immediately masked by the genetic encodings which delimit it.[24]

Borrowing from studies of the wasp and the orchid, baboon-troop communication, and tool usage by various birds, Guattari interpolates freedom, in the form of semiotic expansion, into closed behavioral sequencing. Improvisation and individual initiative helps to deterritorialize a given assemblage (i.e. courtship rituals) and establish new transversal co-relations between the most and least deterministic components. Guattari wanted to expose ethology's "misunderstanding" of linear causality (higher to lower) and its binarisms (inhibitors–innate releasing mechanisms) through the non-transcendent entanglements of components of assemblage. Guattari's goal was to complexify ethological logic rather than simply reverse its priorities or substitute one hierarchy for another. He accomplishes this task in part by leveling the differences between animal and human desire and by injecting psychoanalytic, semiotic, and political concepts as explanatory principles into points of rupture.

The relationship between the wasp AND orchid does not adequately describe the work of Deleuze and Guattari. The selectively is far too exclusive. The emphasis is on the "and" hence on the new lines thrown out into the rhizome beyond the conjunction; on what "each becomes" and on "that which becomes," pace Deleuze; the bestiary required to account 'for the AND' is enormous. After all, Deleuze found many animals in Guattari: "In Guattari there has always been a sort of wild rodeo, in part directed against himself" (D 11). This is the menagerie that one encounters in conversation and collaboration: a wild rodeo, a happening, a growing solitude populated with animal becomings. Aparallel evolution, Deleuze (D 18) explains, happens between animals, between ideas, not between persons.

FLYING PAPERS

In a review of Guattari's *The Anti-Oedipus Papers*, philosopher Charles T. Wolfe remarked:

[W]hat exactly is in this book? Most notably, the "matrix" for one of the most unusual intellectual collaborations in the 20th century: *Anti-Oedipus*. Deleuze once described this collaboration, disarmingly, as follows: "If I told [Guattari] that at the centre of the earth there was redcurrant jelly, his role would be to find what might support such an idea (if it is an idea!). It's the opposite of a series or exchange of opinions" … And when Deleuze was asked in the same interview to describe the method of their collaboration, he answered: "It's a secret." So the texts in this volume shed light for the first time on the nature, not just of the "creative process" of the two-headed monster that produced *Anti-Oedipus*, but of the invention of a collective language.[25]

Enter the matrix: this non-book is a disparate collection of materials cobbled together by editor Stéphane Nadaud from archival materials and assembled around the process of composing *Anti-Oedipus* with Deleuze. These writings include annotated notes and clarifications written by Guattari to Deleuze and then corrected and revised; reminders to himself; autobiographical and theoretical journal entries (1971–72); a glossary of concepts. Meta-comments on letters between Guattari and Deleuze as well as the former's entreaties to the latter and his partner Fanny appear throughout. These papers provide scattered and suggestive insights into how Guattari and Deleuze worked together, apart, and lay bare some of the conceptual challenges faced by the authors in fine-tuning their investigations: how to read Marxism unconventionally by focusing on its conceptualization of capitalism; how to extract from psychoanalysis schizoanalytic principles; how to be done with representational semiotics. Guattari's conceptual and practical struggles are front and center; diverse theoretical skirmishes are punctuated by practical examples from Guattari's practice at La Borde and criticisms of bad psychoanalytic clinical habits. Guattari often responds to Deleuze's requests for clarification with intense explanations marked by exclamations, name-calling, and asides. Brief characterizations of how Guattari approached concepts punctuate explanations: surf their crests; make messy outlines. Guattari's journal entries provide insight into his self-analysis and how he thought about his relationship with Deleuze. When we look for answers and find sketches, the dynamic diagrammatic thought of Guattari is thrown into relief. The principles of affirmation, transformation, metamodeling (singular automodelization), and "mad drawings"[26] are affirmed in a wild diagram of still restless papers.

KAFKA EFFECT

If *Anti-Oedipus* "stands apart" in a number of ways from Deleuze and Guattari's other collaborations because "they themselves are made other in that work,"[27] what is the character of the alterity initiated by the Kafka book? Deleuze treads carefully and expresses concern in other-worldly terms, when describing how he and Félix approached Kafka: "My ideal, when I write about an author, would be to write nothing that could cause him sadness, or of he is dead, that might make him weep in his grave ... So many dead writers must have wept over what has been written about them" (D 119). Respect for the dead mingles with a double refusal of the familiar (identifying with him) and the object of scholarship. "I hope Kafka was pleased with the book that we did on him." Experimenting with Kafka through the concepts of rhizome, assemblage, missing people, and minor literature, Deleuze and Guattari proceed with respect and care so as not to disturb the rest of the great author. AND Kafka: for Guattari, finding new means of alterification to join the Kafka assemblage became a lifelong preoccupation. His first effort was to co-curate with Yasha David an exhibition at the Centre Pompidou ("Le siècle de Kafka," 1984) on the occasion of the Kafka centenary in 1983. Guattari collected Kafka's dreams; he organized performances around this theme; he even envisaged a film by as opposed to about Kafka during this period that could be shown on television in the form of a cultural series.[28] Despite Guattari's mistrust of television, it was in this instance a choice medium for forging a potential public and connecting it with independent Kafka affects, precipitating becomings-Kafka. The film would build highly abstract and lyrical sequences around molecular elements such as bowed heads; heads bursting through windows, doorways, even ceilings; and the wall that is at the heart of the project operates as a machine that both breaks up and connects movements of characters. It is a screen, a molecularized face, bearing geological strata, vegetal becomings (moss) and receptacle for men's urine. Guattari described a "Kafka effect" based on the appreciation of a richly processual "chronic precarity" that makes his work perfectly suited to the twentieth century.[29] Both Deleuze and Guattari were caught up in Kafka effects that fascinate, that bring about experimentation across media (books, essays, film, theater, curation) and both express tender constraints with regard to their favorite author. This movement is a multi-media stuttering. And it was already evident to some degree in Anti-Oedipus as examples borrowed from Kafka – machines, the eminent character of the state, and the law – are qualified as unequalled in relevance (AO 198, 212).

AND NEGRI

If we were to write "Deleuze and Guattari and" the connections based not so much on topics but on commitments to lines of thought and action would allow for a multiplication that is at once a complexification and pragmatic orientation. Invoking the theorist of new forms of dispersed subjectivity of labor beyond the mass industrial worker who is counted among the leaders of the Italian extra-parliamentary leftist groups *Potere Operaio* (Workers' Power) and *Autonomia* (Autonomy), AND Negri expands the Deleuze connections beyond the problem of how to represent collaborations by following ethico-political lines of force. Guattari defended his friend, then professor at University of Padua, in a series of appeals after Negri was named in an arrest warrant as a terrorist, pointing out that he and his fellow activist-intellectuals had nothing to do with the armed violence of the Red Brigades.[30] Guattari helped Negri while in Paris, until his arrest in 1979, as did Deleuze. Negri was held in prison for four years, during which time Guattari visited regularly and began collaboration on a book. Negri won his freedom in 1983 by means of winning a parliamentary seat and receiving immunity, which was shortly thereafter revoked. Again, he fled to Paris with Guattari's help. Two years later their collaboration on the reinvention of communism was completed, *Les nouveaux espaces de liberté*.[31] Both thinkers worked through their debts to Leninism and refocused theoretical attention on the political problem of subjectivity while labor was in the process of becoming more immaterial. Excerpts from Negri's prison journal (2000) from Rebibbia Penale, written in the late 1990s, concerning the plight of mentally ill inmates who find themselves in prison after being released from psychiatric hospitals, expressing support for the association that agitated for their re-education and resocialization, appeared in Guattari and Deleuze's journal *Chimères*.[32] Deleuze's short but stirring statements "Open Letter to Negri's Judges" and "This Book is Literal Proof of Innocence" address the "Negri Affair" in terms of its democratic deficits: logical inconsistency of the charges and the violations of a "basic legal identity" (*TRM* 170); the abuse of the evidence by an insistent and paranoid deployment of disjunction and exclusion as inclusion of contradictories; and culpability of the press in Europe which enshrine in their pages the "accumulation of falsehoods" (*TRM* 171). Further, Deleuze insisted on Negri's innocence through the evidence of what he presents in his books. The public and political character of these reflections on philosophy by Deleuze and Guattari is grounded in a concern with democratic institutions like the courts and the press. "AND Negri" contains limits not only to the proliferation of connections, but to the terms of engagement as a struggle for democracy against its abuse by Italian lawmakers. This "becoming democratic" contains explicit appeals to normative legal concepts and practices[33] and reinforcement of them defines Negri's own revolutionary becomings.

CONCLUSION

The many examples and details discussed in this chapter may be connected together by a number of ANDs in order to create the kind of rhizome with a particular logic discussed throughout, in addition to the limitations on connectivity in the defense of practical, juridical reason. The lines of connective alliances include the authorial collaborations of Deleuze and Guattari, which are themselves modified and expandable by other ANDs. The logic of AND is a war machine; not a contraption, a strap-on, a Marxo-Freudo remake. Yet the war machine has both positive and negative sides: affirmation and reaction.[34] The former is often integrated into the collaborative books themselves as a statement of how Deleuze and Guattari understood their collaborations (subjects do not enunciate; collective assemblages enunciate); at other times their explanations are reactive in the sense that they answer the questions of those looking for secrets, for evidence, for the statement that will make an interview, for the bare author-subject. There are some very ugly moments in the universe of reception that clog the collective assemblages, but also some remarkable creations as well (as we have seen, figures of the sumo, ocean waves, running water, thievery). Why is it important to continue considering the ways in which the relationship between Deleuze and Guattari have been characterized by the authors themselves and others? Simply put, because of the unresolvable tension between the name, signature, and identity, and the desire to escape authorial pairing, division, separation, and the erection of contrived (dis)unities. Recourse to a movement from the name as pseudonym for philosophical conceptual characters is no guarantee – there is no escape from the disaster of sales promotion (*WP* 10–12, 64). Performed successfully, this escape operation may give rise to new names, like the one suggested by Ronald Bogue for Deleuze: "Alice H. Challenger."[35] Some of these names are playful; others are raw, like Guattareuze, and still provocative, like writing Guattari and Deleuze and …

It would be an exaggeration to claim that the use of Guat[t]areuze to preface this discussion of figurations of Deleuze and Guattari constitutes a method in its own right. However, recourse to graphic art as an approach is not unknown, and may put me, in fact, in good company. After all, Charles Stivale takes a "relaxing" approach to the question of the folds of friendship by reading Martin tom Dieck and Jens Balzer's *bande dessinée, Salut, Deleuze!*[36] While "offbeat" Stivale qualifies his choice in terms of how the graphic artists engage both seriously and playfully, creatively doing philosophy while offering an *homage* to the late philosopher. Compared to the "gentle fun" of the scenario in which Deleuze is delivered by the boatman of the dead to the eagerly awaiting trio of friends Barthes, Foucault, and Lacan, a similar description for Lauzier's comic would not be possible to offer, as the humor is vicious. Nevertheless, recourse to the medium shows some promise as a new machine in the philosopher's cultural kit for connecting heterogeneous materials.

NOTES

1   François Dosse, *Gilles Deleuze and Félix Guattari: Intersecting Lives*, trans. Deborah Glassman (New York: Columbia University Press, 2010), pp. 10, 424.
2   *Ibid.*, p. 595, n.3.
3   Gérard Lauzier, "Enfin le cri," in *Tranches de vie*, vol. iv (Paris: Les Éditions Dargaud, 1978), p. 21.
4   Jean-Pierre Beauchard ("David B"), *Epileptic*, trans. Kim Thompson (New York: Pantheon, 2005), p. 13.
5   Dosse, *Gilles Deleuze and Félix Guattari*, pp. 333–34.
6   Félix Guattari, *The Guattari Reader*, ed. Gary Genosko (Oxford: Blackwell, 1996), p. 38.
7   Dosse, *Gilles Deleuze and Félix Guattari*, p. 342.
8   Nick Thoburn, *Deleuze, Marx and Politics* (London: Routledge, 2003), p. 134.

9   Collectif A/traverso, *Radio Alice, radio libre* (Paris: Laboratoire de Sociologie de la Connaissance, 1977), p. 71.

10 Félix Guattari, *The Anti-Oedipus Papers*, ed. Stéphane Nadaud, trans. Kélina Gotman (New York: Semiotext(e), 2006), p. 404.

11 Julian Bourg, *From Revolution to Ethics: May 1968 and Contemporary French Thought* (Kingston and Montreal: McGill-Queen's University Press, 2007), p. 36, n.1.

12 Franco Bifo Berardi, *Félix Guattari: Thought, Friendship, and Visionary Cartography*, trans. G. Mecchia and C. Stivale (Basingstoke: Palgrave Macmillan, 2008), p. 43.

13 Patricia T. Clough, "Introduction," in *The Affective Turn* (Durham, NC: Duke University Press, 2007), p. 14.

14 Slavoj Žižek, *Organs without Bodies: Deleuze and Consequences* (London: Routledge, 2004), p. 20.

15 Nicolas Bourriaud, *Relational Aesthetics*, trans. S. Pleasance and F. Woods (Dijon: Les Presses du Réel, 2002), p. 87.

16 Guattari, *The Anti-Oedipus Papers*, pp. 414–15.

17 *Ibid.*, pp. 318–19.

18 Barbara Godard, "Deleuze and Translation," *Parallax* 6:1 (2000), 56–81, p. 60. See also Dosse, *Gilles Deleuze and Félix Guattari*, pp. 192ff.

19 See also Rodrigo Nunes, "Politics in the Middle: For a Political Interpretation of the Dualism in Deleuze and Guattari," *Deleuze Studies*, 4 (Supplement) (2010), 104–26.

20 Guattari, *The Anti-Oedipus Papers*, p. 399.

21 *Ibid.*, p. 400.

22 Félix Guattari (with Suely Rolnick), *Molecular Revolution in Brazil*, trans. K. Clapshow and B. Holmes (Los Angeles: Semiotext(e), 2008), p. 449.

23 Dosse, *Gilles Deleuze and Félix Guattari*, p. 15.

24 Félix Guattari, *The Machinic Unconscious: Essays in Schizoanalysis*, trans. T. Adkins (Los Angeles: Semiotext(e), 2011), pp. 121–22.

25 Charles T. Wolfe, "Review of *The Anti-Oedipus Papers*," *Metapsychology Online Reviews*, 11:35 (August 28, 2007), http://metapsychology.mentalhelp.net/poc/view_doc.php?type=book&id=3790&cn=394.

26 Janell Watson, *Guattari's Diagrammatic Thought: Writing between Lacan and Deleuze* (London: Continuum, 2009), p. 6.

27 Fadi Abou-Rihan, *Deleuze and Guattari: A Psychoanalytic Itinerary* (London: Continuum, 2008), p. 37.

28 Gary Genosko, "Introduction to the English Translation of Félix Guattari's 'Project for a Film by Kafka'," *Deleuze Studies*, 3:2 (2009), 145–49.

29 Félix Guattari, *Les années d'hiver 1980–85* (Paris: Les Prairies Ordinaires, 2009), p. 271.

30 Félix Guattari, *La révolution moléculaire* (Paris: Union Générale d'Éditions 10/18, 1980), pp. 203–4.

31 Félix Guattari and Antonio Negri, *Les nouveaux espaces de liberté* (Paris: Dominique Bedou, 1985).

32 Antonio Negri, "Notes de prison et projet Ulysse," *Chimères* 39 (2000), 113–25.

33 Paul Patton, "Deleuze's Practical Philosophy," in Constantin V. Boundas (ed.), *Gilles Deleuze: The Intensive Reduction* (London: Continuum, 2009), pp. 186–203, pp. 198ff.

34 Eugene Holland, "Affirmative Nomadology and the War Machine," in Boundas (ed.), *Gilles Deleuze: The Intensive Reduction*, pp. 218–25, p. 219.

35 Ronald Bogue, *Deleuze's Wake: Tributes and Tributaries* (Albany, NY: SUNY Press, 2004), p. 26.

36 Charles Stivale, *Gilles Deleuze's ABCs: The Folds of Friendship* (Baltimore: Johns Hopkins University Press, 2008), pp. 7–9.

8 Nomadic ethics

INTRODUCTION

Deleuze's engagement with ethics – both his specific monographs on Spinoza's thought and the more extensive engagement with the ethical implications of affirmative nomadic ontology throughout his work – constitutes the core of his philosophy. This claim needs to be contextualized from the outset in two ways. Firstly, Deleuze's ethics of freedom and affirmation offers a robust reply to the *doxa*-driven belief that any attempt at challenging or decentering the traditional, universalistic view of the moral subject can only result in moral and cognitive relativism. This intellectually lazy position enjoys high popularity in the current global climate of political conservatism, which paradoxically rejoices in public display of interest in moral values and has branded new forms of bio-ethics, corporate ethics, media ethics, and so forth. This quantitative proliferation of ethical brands in the age of advanced capitalism leaves untouched the qualitative issue of what constitutes the core of an ethical subject. Against the common-sense belief that only steady identities resting on firm grounds of rational and moral universalism can guarantee basic human decency, moral and political agency, and ethical probity, Deleuze's philosophy proposes a post-humanistic but robust alternative through his nomadic vision of the subject. My argument in this essay is that such a vision can provide an alternative foundation for ethical subjectivity that respects the complexity of our times while avoiding the pitfalls of postmodern and other forms of relativism.

Secondly, there is a contextual consideration: Deleuze's innovative neo-Spinozist ethical stand strikes a distinctly affirmative note in relation to the rest of the poststructuralist generation. The following discursive alignments can be seen at present in poststructuralist ethical thought. To start with: the later Foucault has produced a form of residual Kantian thought that stresses the importance of bio-politics and bio-political citizenship as a form of moral account-ability. Nicholas Rose and Paul Rabinow, for instance, focus on the notion of "Life" as *bios*, that is to say, as an instance of governmen-tality that is as empowering ("potentia") as it is confining ("potes-tas") and functions as the circulation of power effects.[1] The ethical instance is located accordingly in the inter-rational accountability of a bio-ethical subject in process that aims at stylizing alternative practices of social and personal connection and intimacy.

Giorgio Agamben also takes off from Foucault's unfinished pro-ject and mixes it with Heidegger's work on finitude and Schmidt's antagonistic notion of the political to produce a scathing indictment of the moral grounds and the political practice of modernity.[2] In this strand, "Life" is quite central too, but it is defined as extreme onto-logical vulnerability: it is that which sovereign power harps upon in order to erect and sustain its necro-political governmentality. For, Agamben, "bare life," that is to say "zoe" – non-human or pre-indi-vidual Life – is contiguous with Thanatos or death. The vitality of the subject ("zoe") is identified with his perishability (the gender is not a coincidence) and with his propensity for homicidal extinction. Bio-power here means Thanatos-politics.

A third and ethically more hopeful coalition stems from the Levinas–Derrida tradition of ethics. This is centered on the relation-ship between the subject and Otherness – symbolized by the other's face.[3] It also stresses ontological connection and the indebtedness to the demands of others;[4] the non-negotiable nature of "justice" and "hospitality," as well as the permanence of mourning.[5] The emphasis falls on vulnerability as the defining feature of the human as the potential capacity to be wounded and hence to require the care, soli-darity, and love of others. Respect for vulnerability is therefore the basis of the ethical human relation. There is a clear political side to this, insofar as sovereign power has the right as well as the means to legislate on survival and extinction. Ethics consequently cuts two ways: on the public side it calls into question the foundational vio-lence of such a system and is thus intrinsically political. On the pri-vate side, it also inscribes issues of pain and cruelty at the core of the ethical interaction. I shall return to the question of pain below.

Deleuze's neo-Spinozist ethics, on the other hand, chooses a different emphasis, which rests on an active relational ontology. Deleuze's neo-vitalism refers to Nietzsche and Spinoza but updates them both to different contextual and conceptual concerns.[6] Otherness is approached as the expression of a productive limit, or generative threshold, which calls for an always already compromised set of negotiations. Nomadic theory prefers to look for the ways in which Otherness prompts, mobilizes, and allows for flows of affirmation of values and forces which are not yet sustained by the current conditions. Insofar as the conditions need to be brought about or actualized by collective efforts to induce qualitative transformations in our interactions, it requires the praxis of affirmative ethics.

Deleuze's life-oriented philosophy of becoming differs profoundly from Levinas' and Derrida's emphasis on the incommensurable presence of the Other. They inscribe the totality of the Self's reliance on the other as a structural necessity that transcends the "I" but remains internal to it. Deleuze's immanence, on the other hand, firmly locates the affirmation in the exteriority, the cruel, messy outside-ness of Life itself. Creative chaos is not chaotic – it is the virtual formation of all possible forms (LS). Life is not an a priori that gets individuated in single instances, but it is immanent to and thus coincides with its multiple material actualizations. The middle/milieu is always the site of birth and emergence of the new – life itself. I refer to this generative force as *zoe*, which is the opposite of Agamben's "bare life" in that it is a creative force that constructs possible futures.

To conclude this brief comparative survey: the bio-political and bio-power are only the starting points for an ethical reflection about the politics of life itself as a relentlessly generative and not exclusively human force. Contrary to the Heideggerians, the emphasis here is on generation, vital forces, and a culture of affirmation. Contrary to the Kantians, the ethical instance is not located within the confines of a self-regulating subject of moral agency, but rather in a set of interrelations with both human and inhuman forces. These forces can be rendered in terms of immanence and relationality (Spinoza), duration (Bergson), transmutation of the negative (Nietzsche), but are all indexed on the project of forging ethical sustainability.[7] The notion of the non-human, in-human, or post-human emerges therefore as the defining trait of nomadic ethical subjectivity. These concepts will constitute the backbone of the rest of my essay.

ETHICAL PREMISES

The point in common to all poststructuralist philosophies is that ethics is not confined to the realm of rights, distributive justice, or the law. It rather bears close links with the notions of political agency, freedom, and the management of power and power relations. Issues of responsibility are dealt with in terms of alterity or the relationship to others, as processes of intensive becoming. This implies accountability, situatedness, and the composition of common planes of active collaborative ethical conduct.[8] A Deleuzian position, therefore, far from thinking that a liberal individual definition of the subject is the necessary precondition for ethics, argues that liberalism at present hinders the development of new modes of ethical behavior.

In other words, for nomadic thought, the proper object of ethical enquiry is not the subject's universalistic or individual core – his/her moral intentionality, or rational consciousness – as much as the effects of truth and power that his/her actions are likely to have upon others in the world. This is a kind of ethical pragmatism, which defines ethics as the practice that cultivates affirmative modes of relation, active forces, and values. It is also conceptually linked to the notion of embodied materialism and to a non-unitary vision of the subject. Ethics is therefore the discourse about forces, desires, and values that act as empowering modes of becoming, whereas morality is the implementation of established protocols and sets of rules (*EPS*). Philosophical nomadism shares Nietzsche's distaste for morality as sets of negative, resentful emotions and life-denying reactive passions. Deleuze joins this up with Spinoza's ethics of affirmation to produce a very accountable and concrete ethical line about joyful affirmation.

The precondition for the constitution of an ethical subject is for nomadic theory the immanent, materially embedded and yet vitalist or dynamic structure of all entities – human and non-human. Deleuze does take "Life" as the point of reference, but this vital force is *zoe* defined as the non-human, generative, trans-individual and post-anthropocentric dimension of subjectivity. This results is an affirmative project that stresses positivity and not only vulnerability and in a very close link between ethics and an eco-philosophy or common ecologies of belonging.

This monistic ontology – inspired by Spinoza's notion of ontological desire or *conatus* – entails a horizontal organization of different categories of beings defined as actualizations of different forces, speeds, and materialities (bodies without organs). As a result, hierarchical levels and hegemonic differences are rejected and replaced by the renewed emphasis on the 'situated' nature of all entities – a common plane of immanence. This emphasis on the middle/ the milieu is the premise for the radical relationality of nomadic subjectivity. The middle is a point, any point, which by definition challenges the notion of a fixed center, a matrix of power or a hierarchical core. These vertical notions constitute the backbone of the traditional notion of the transcendent nature of power, which Deleuze – with Guattari – is committed to undoing. They replace it with a flat ontology of immanent relations of mutual constitution through a transversal, collective rhizomatic web of relations. These ensure mutual specification and are therefore post-individualistic in a productive manner. The emphasis on immanence also sets the threshold for the actualization of intensive or virtual becomings and for the composition of collective assemblages that sustain the project of actualizing them. This transformative, relational project lies at the core of Deleuze's ethics.

This is not to say that the issue of pain and vulnerability is not raised, but rather that it is not lifted to an ontological dimension. If it is indeed the case that radical immanence instills an open ecology of *zoe*-centered egalitarianism,[9] then vulnerability is another name for being-there and being-in-relation to others. Openness to others is an expression of the nomadic relational structure of the subject and a precondition for the creation of ethical bonds. The emphasis therefore falls not so much on vulnerability as on the immanent structure of a subject – an entity, or a body's – capacity to affect and be affected – in pleasure as in pain – and to express multiple forms of intensity. This implies the ability to cultivate, establish, and sustain empowering relations as well as the commitment to the production of the social conditions that are conducive to transform the negative instance, including hurt and pain, into affirmative and productive ethical relations. Nomadic theory embraces this ethical relation by proposing a materially embodied and embedded, but ontologically vital and self-organizing notion of matter. In the case of humans this immanent materiality gets actualized through a rhizomic expanse of interrelations which flow transversally across all entities, over and against the hierarchical forms of normativity and traditional modes of containment of the other supported by mainstream moral thought.

BEYOND INDIVIDUALISM

The ethical subject in a nomadic perspective lies at the intersections with external, relational forces: it is about assemblages. Encountering them requires a careful selection and composition of factors: the frame of orientation, the points of contact and entry into a relation, the constant unfolding of the relation to the multiple others that constitute our environment/milieu. In this field of transformative forces, sustainability is a very pragmatic ethical practice that provides some homeostatic stability to the subject's ethical compass. It actualizes the productive elements of the subject's intensive nature: affectivity is the propensity for changes or transformation that is directly proportional to the subject's ability to sustain the shifts without cracking. The border, the framing or containing practices are crucial to Deleuze's neo-Spinozist ethical project, one which aims at affirmative and not nihilistic processes of becoming, which means joyful-becoming as *potentia*, or a radical force of empowerment. Genevieve Lloyd, in her commentary on Spinoza, explains how such a vitalistic and positive vision of the subject is linked to an ethics of passion that aims at joy and not at destruction.[10] She carefully points out the difficulties involved in approaching Spinoza's concept of ethics as "the collective powers and affinities of bodies."[11] She stresses the advantages of approaching these potencies of embodied subjects in terms of the ethology proposed by Deleuze, insofar as it challenges the centrality of the notion of the individual and replaces it with an ethical commitment to social values conducive to a collectively well-functioning system.

Thus, selection is involved: the composition of the forces that propel the subject, the rhythm, speed, and sequencing of the relations and affects as well as the selection of the constitutive elements are the key criteria. This has nothing to do, however, with the argument for choice and individual free will. Quite on the contrary, it establishes collective and transversal relations as the core ethical agency. Moreover, stability is also involved: the actualization of affirmative ethical relations is the effect of adequate dosage, while it is also simultaneously the prerequisite for sustaining those same forces. The subject is an affective entity; *conatus* defined as a "striving" without an agent in control of it. The founding ethical desire of this subject is to be worthy of a life force that intersects with all that moves and exists. Far from being the case that the individual possesses or controls such a force, it is rather the case that being a subject consists in partaking in such a striving in a collaborative model of relation to others. In all these respects, the nomadic ethical subject defeats relativism at each step of its actualization.

The notion of the individual is enlarged to enclose a structural sense of interconnection between the singular self and the environment or totality in which it is embodied and embedded. Lloyd defines this interconnectiveness not as a synthesis, but rather as a series of "nested embeddings of individuals."[12] According to this enlarged sense of the individual, an inward-looking understanding of the individual self is not only an error, but also a cognitive and an ethical misjudgment. The inward-looking individual fails to see the interconnection as part and parcel of his/her nature, and is thus inhabited by an inadequate understanding of him/her-self. The truth of self lies in its interrelations to others in a rhizomic manner that defies dualistic modes of opposition. Reaching out for an adequate representation of oneself includes the process of clearing up the confusion concerning one's true nature as an affective, interconnected entity. Ultimately this implies understanding the bodily structure of the self. Because of this bodily nature, the process of self-consciousness is forever ongoing and therefore incomplete, or partial. This partiality is built into the nomadic understanding of the subject.

Bodily entities, in fact, are not passive, but rather dynamic and sensitive forces forever in motion which "form unities only through fragile synchronization of forces."[13] This fragility concerns mostly the pitch of the synchronization efforts; the lines of demarcation between the different bodily boundaries, the borders that are the

thresholds of encounter and connection with other forces, the standard term for which is: limits. Because of his monistic understanding of the subject, Spinoza sees bodily limits as the limits of our
awareness as well; this means that his theory of affectivity is connected to the physics of motion. Another word for Spinoza's *conatus*
is therefore self-preservation, not in the liberal individualistic sense
of the term, but rather as the actualization of one's essence, that is
to say of one's ontological drive to become. This is not an automatic,
nor an intrinsically harmonious process, insofar as it involves interconnection with other forces and consequently also conflicts and
clashes. Negotiations have to occur as stepping-stones to sustainable flows of becoming. The bodily self's interaction with his/her
environment can either increase or decrease that body's *conatus*
or *potentia*. The mind as a sensor that prompts understanding can
assist by helping to discern and choose those forces that increase its
power of acting and its activity in both physical and mental terms.
A higher form of self-knowledge by understanding the nature of
one's affectivity is the key to a Spinozist ethics of empowerment.
It includes a more adequate understanding of the interconnections
between the self and a multitude of other forces, and it thus undermines the liberal individual understanding of the subject. It also
implies, however, the body's ability to comprehend and to physically sustain a greater number of complex interconnections, and to
deal with complexity without being overburdened. Thus, only an
appreciation of complexity and of increasing degrees of complexity
can guarantee the freedom of the mind in the awareness of its true,
affective, and dynamic nature.

Thinking the unity of body and mind, sustainable ethics stresses
the power ("potentia") of affects ("affectus"). Starting from the
assumption that the property of substance is to express itself, the
term "expression" implies "dynamic articulation"[14] and not merely
passive reflection: "*Affectus* refers to the passage from one state to
another in the affected body – the increase or decrease in its powers of acting."[15] This "power of acting" – which is in fact a flow
of transpositions – is expressed by Spinoza in terms of achieving
freedom through an adequate understanding of our passions and
consequently of our bondage. Coming into possession of freedom requires the understanding of affects or passions by a mind
that is always already embodied. The desire to reach an adequate

understanding of one's *potentia* is the human being's fundamental desire or *conatus*. An error of judgment is a form of misunderstanding (of the true nature of the subject) that results in decreasing the power, positivity, and activity of the subject. By extension: reason is affective, embodied, dynamic – understanding the passions is our way of experiencing them – and making them work in our favor. In this respect Spinoza argues that desires arise from our passions. Because of this, they can never be excessive – given that affectivity is the power that activates our body and makes it want to act. The human being's inbuilt tendency is towards joy and self-expression, not towards implosion. This fundamental positivity is the key to Deleuze's attachment to Spinoza.

Clearly, this implies a very non-moralistic understanding of ethics which focuses on the subject's powers to act and to express their dynamic and positive essence. An ethology stresses the field of composition of forces and affects, speed and transformation. In this perspective, ethics is the pursuit of self-preservation, which paradoxically assumes the dissolution of the self: what is good is what increases our power of acting and that is what we must strive for. This results not in egotism, but in mutually embedded nests of shared interests. Lloyd calls this: "a collaborative morality."[16] Because the starting point for Spinoza is not the isolated individual, but complex and mutually depended co-realities, the self–other interaction also follows a different model. To be an individual means to be open to being affected by and through others, thus undergoing transformations in such a way as to be able to sustain them and make them work towards growth. The activity/passivity distinction is far more important than that between self and other, good and bad. What binds the two is the idea of interconnection and affectivity as the defining features of the subject. An ethical life pursues that which enhances and strengthens the subject without reference to transcendental values but rather in the awareness of one's interconnection with others.

This ethical project can be synthesized in the concept of a sustainable, non-unitary, perspectival self that aims at endurance. Endurance has a temporal dimension. It has to do with lasting in time; hence, duration and self-perpetuation (traces of Bergson here). But it also has a spatial side to do with the space of the body as an enfleshed field of actualization of passions or forces. It evolves affectivity and joy (traces of Spinoza), as in the capacity for being affected by these forces to the point of pain or extreme pleasure (which comes to the same). It may require putting up with and tolerating hardship and physical pain. It also entails the effort to move beyond it, to construct affirmative interaction. Apart from providing the key to an ethology of forces, endurance is also an ethical principle of affirmation of the positivity of the intensive subject, or in other words, its joyful affirmation as *potentia*. The subject is a spatio-temporal compound that frames the boundaries of processes of becoming. This works by transforming negative into positive passions through the power of an understanding that is no longer indexed upon a phallogocentric set of standards, but is rather relational and affective.

This turning of the tide of negativity is the transformative process of achieving freedom of understanding, through the awareness of our limits, of our bondage. This results in the freedom to affirm one's essence as joy, through encounters and mingling with other bodies, entities, beings, and forces. Ethics means faithfulness to this *potentia*, or the desire to become. Becoming is an intransitive process: it's not about becoming anything in particular, only what one is capable of and attracted to and capable of becoming. It's life on the edge, but not over it. It's not deprived of violence, but deeply compassionate. It's an ethical and political sensibility that begins with the recognition of one's limitations as the necessary counterpart of one's forces or intensive encounters with multiple others. It has to do with the adequacy of one's intensity to the modes and time of its enactment. It can only be empirically embodied and embedded, because it's interrelational and collective.

TRANSFORMATIVE ETHICS AND THE RELOCATION OF OTHERNESS

The core of Deleuze's ethical project therefore is a positive vision of the subject as a radically immanent, intensive body. That is, an assemblage of forces or flows, intensities, and passions that solidify in space and consolidate in time, within the singular configuration commonly known as a constituted entity or an "individual" self. This intensive and dynamic entity is rather a portion of forces that is stable enough to sustain and undergo constant though non-destructive fluxes of transformation – a "dividual" self. It is the body's degrees and levels of affectivity that determine the modes of differentiation. Joyful or positive passions and the transcendence of reactive affects are the desirable ethical relation. The emphasis on "immanence" and "becoming" implies a commitment to duration and, conversely, a rejection of self-destruction. Positivity is built into this program through the very idea of the immanence of matter and its self-organizing vitality. Life sets its own boundaries, or rather composes its ever-shifting folds of sustainable actualization of intensity.

Thus, an ethically empowering relation increases one's *potentia* or empowering force and creates joyful energy in the process. The conditions that encourage such a quest are not only historical; they concern processes of transformation or self-fashioning in the direction of affirming positivity. Because all subjects share in this common nature, there is a common ground – the middle or the milieu – on which to negotiate the interests and the eventual conflicts.

This fundamentally positive vision of the ethical subject does not deny conflicts, tension, or even violent disagreements between or within different subjects. The legacy of Hegel's critique of Spinoza is looming large here, notably the criticism that a Spinozist approach lacks a theory of negativity, which may adequately account for the complex logistics of interaction with others. This charge is moved against Deleuze today by the new theorists of the negative – notably Žižek and Badiou – whose residual Hegelianism is merely the prelude to nostalgic longings for neo-Leninist certainties. Against such micro-fascist discursive formations, Deleuzian ethics pleads simultaneously for an open ecology of immanence and the quest for actualization of the interactions that may sustain ethically affirmative relations.

It is simply not the case that the emphasis Deleuze places on the positivity of desire cancels or denies the tensions of conflicting interests. It merely displaces the grounds on which the negotiations take place from an individual to a transversal collectively constituted relational subject. The nomadic view of ethics takes place within a monistic ontology that sees subjects as modes of individuation within a common flow of *zoe*. Consequently there is no self–other distinction in the traditional mode, but variations of

intensities, assemblages set by affinities and complex synchronizations. This breaks the expectation of mutual reciprocity that is central to liberal individualism. Accepting the impossibility of mutual
recognition and replacing it with one of mutual specification and
mutual codependence is what is at stake in nomadic ethics of sustainability. This is against both the moral philosophy of rights and
the humanistic tradition of making the anthropocentric Other into
the privileged site and inescapable horizon of Otherness.

The Kantian imperative of not doing to others what you would
not want done to you is not rejected as much as enlarged. In terms
of the ethics of *conatus*, in fact, the harm that you do to others
is immediately reflected in the harm you do to yourself, in terms
of loss of *potentia*, positivity, self-awareness, and inner freedom.
Moreover, the "others" in question are not just constituted human
selves, but also non-anthropomorphic and planetary others. These
include external and non-human forces: the environment as a
whole – the earth – and hence also animals;[17] cells;[18] seeds;[19] viruses
and bacteria.[20] This post-human ethics rests on a multi-layered form
of relationality. It assumes as the point of reference not the individual, but the relation. This means openness to others, in the positive sense of affecting and being affected by others, through couples
and mutually dependent co-realities. Containment of the other – as
I suggested earlier – occurs through interrelational affectivity and
the construction of common planes of actualization of projects and
communities: it is a pragmatic praxis of immanent relations.

ENDURANCE AND NEGATIVE PASSIONS

The ethics of affirmation, with its emphasis on moving across the
pain and transforming it into activity, may seem counterintuitive.
In our culture people go to great lengths to ease all pain, but especially the pain of uncertainty about identity, origin, and belonging.
Great distress follows from not knowing or not being able to articulate the source of one's suffering, or from knowing it all too well, all
the time. People who have been confronted by the irreparable, the
unbearable, the insurmountable, the traumatic and inhuman event
will do anything to find solace, resolution, and also compensation.
The yearning for these measures – solace, closure, justice – is all too
understandable and worthy of respect.

What is positive in the ethics of affirmation is the belief that negative affects can be transformed. This implies a dynamic view of all affects, even those that freeze us in pain, horror, or mourning. Affirmative nomadic ethics puts the motion back into e-motion and the active back into activism, introducing movement, process, and becoming. This shift makes all the difference to the patterns of repetition of negative emotions. What is negative about negative affects is not a value judgment (any more than it is for the positivity of difference), nor is it a psychologically depressed state. It rather concerns the effect of arrest, blockage, and rigidification that comes as a result of an act of violence, betrayal, a trauma – or which can be self-perpetuated through practices that our culture chastises as self-destructive: all forms of mild and extreme addictions, differing degrees of abusive practices that mortify the body, from food and alcohol binging to bodily scarring. Abusive, addictive, or destructive practices do not merely destroy the self but harm the self's capacity to relate to others, both human and non-human others. Thus they harm the capacity to grow in and through others and become others. Negative passions diminish our capacity to express the high levels of interdependence, the vital reliance on others, which is the key to a non-unitary and dynamic vision of the subject. What is negated by negative passions is the power of life itself, as the dynamic force, vital flows of connections and becomings (the nomadic intensity of *zoe*). This is why they should not be encouraged, nor should we be rewarded for lingering around them too long. Negative passions are black holes.

An ethics of affirmation involves the transformation of negative into positive passions: resentment into affirmation, as Nietzsche put it. The practice of transforming negative into positive passions is the process of reintroducing time, movement, and transformation into a stifling enclosure saturated with unprocessed pain. It is a gesture of affirmation of hope in the sense of affirming the possibility of moving beyond the stultifying effects of the pain, the injury, the injustice. The displacement of the hurt is achieved through a sort of de-personalization of the event, which is the ultimate ethical challenge.

Moreover, the ethics of affirmation is about suspending the quest for claims and compensation, resisting the logic of retribution of rights and taking instead a different road. In order to understand this move it is important to de-psychologize the discussion of affirmation. Let's keep in mind that affectivity is intrinsically understood as positive: it is the force that aims at fulfilling the subject's capacity for interaction and freedom. It is Spinoza's *conatus*, or the notion of *potentia* as the affirmative aspect of power. It is joyful and pleasure-prone, and it is immanent in that it coincides with the terms and modes of its expression. This means concretely that ethical behavior confirms, facilitates, and enhances the subject's *potentia*, as the capacity to express his/her freedom. The positivity of this desire to express one's innermost and constitutive freedom (*conatus*, *potentia*, or becoming) is conducive to ethical behavior, however, only if the subject is capable of making it endure, thus allowing it to sustain its own impetus. Unethical behavior achieves the opposite: it denies, hinders, and diminishes that impetus or is unable to sustain it. Affirmation is therefore not naïve optimism or Candide-like unrealism. It is about endurance and transformation. Endurance is self-affirmation. It is also an ethical principle of affirmation of the positivity of the intensive subject – its joyful affirmation as *potentia*. The subject is a spatio-temporal compound which frames the boundaries of processes of becoming. This works by transforming negative into positive passions through the power of an understanding that is no longer indexed upon a phallogocentric set of standards, but is rather unhinged and therefore relational.

This sort of turning of the tide of negativity is the transformative process of achieving freedom of understanding through the awareness of our limits, of our bondage. This results in the freedom to affirm one's essence as joy, through encounters and mingling with other bodies, entities, beings, and forces. Ethics means faithfulness to this *potentia*, or the desire to become. Deleuze defines the latter with reference to Bergson's concept of "duration," thus proposing the notion of the subject as an entity that lasts, that endures sustainable changes and transformation and enacts them around him/ herself in a community or collectivity. Affirmative ethics rests on the idea of sustainability as a principle of containment and tolerable development of a subject's resources,[21] understood environmentally, socially and psychically, as argued by Félix Guattari in his analysis of the three fundamental ecologies of the post-humanist era.[22] A subject thus constituted inhabits a time that is the active tense of continuous "becoming." Endurance has therefore a temporal dimension: it has to do with lasting in time – hence duration and self-perpetuation. But it also has a spatial side to do with transversal relations and assemblages, as an enfleshed field of actualization of passions or forces. It evolves affectivity and joy, as in the capacity for being affected by these forces, to the point of pain or extreme pleasure.

The point, however, is that extreme pleasure or extreme pain – which may score the same on a Spinozist scale of ethology of affects – are of course not the same. On the reactive side of the equation, endurance points to the struggle to sustain the pain without being annihilated by it. It also introduces a temporal dimension about duration in time. This is linked to memory: intense pain, a wrong, a betrayal, a wound are hard to forget. The traumatic impact of painful events fixes them in a rigid, eternal present tense out of which it is difficult to emerge. This is the eternal return of that which precisely cannot be endured and returns in the mode of the unwanted, the untimely, the unassimilated or inappropriate/d. They are also, however, paradoxically difficult to remember, insofar as remembering will entail retrieval and repetition of the pain itself.

Psychoanalysis had shown the way through the notion of the return of the repressed as it is the key to the logic of unconscious remembrance.[23] It inscribed it, however, within a metaphysics of lack and within the knotted time span or spasm of the symptom, which is always indexed on a traumatic past whose negative legacy undermines the very thinkability of sustainable futures and hence also of an affirmative present. Kristeva's notion of the abject expresses clearly the circular temporality involved in psychoanalysis – by stressing the structural function played by the negative, the incomprehensible, the unthinkable, the other of understandable knowledge.[24] Deleuze, on the other hand, calls this alterity "Chaos," and defines it ontologically as the virtual formation of all possible form, whereas Lacan – and Derrida with him – defines Chaos epistemologically as that which precedes form, structure, and language. This makes for two radically divergent conceptions of time and negativity. That which is incomprehensible for Lacan, following Hegel, is the virtual for Deleuze, following Spinoza, Bergson, and Leibniz.

This produces a number of significant shifts: from negative to affirmative; from entropic to generative; from the incomprehensible, meaningless, or unrepresented to the virtual waiting to be actualized; from constitutive outsides to a geometry of affects that require mutual synchronization; from a melancholy and split to a productive and open-ended web-like subject; from the epistemological to the ontological turn in ethics.

It also introduces a temporal dimension into the discussion that leads to the very conditions of possibility of a sustainable future, to futurity as such. For an ethics of sustainability, the expression of positive affects is that which makes the subject last or endure. It is like a source of long-term energy at the affective core of subjectivity.[25] The eternal return in Nietzsche is the repetition, yet neither in the compulsive mode of neurosis nor in the negative erasure that marks the traumatic event. It is the eternal return of and as positivity.[26] This kind of ethics addresses the affective structure of pain and suffering but does not locate the ethical instance within it, be it in the mode of compassionate witnessing or empathic co-presence.[27] In a nomadic, Deleuzian–Nietzschean perspective, ethics is essentially about the transformation of negative into positive passions, that is, about moving beyond the pain. This does not mean denying the pain but rather activating it, working it through. Again, the positivity here is not supposed to indicate a facile optimism or a careless dismissal of human suffering.

Contrary to the traditional morality that follows a rationalist and legalistic model and interprets the wrongs one suffered within a logic of responsibility, claim, and compensation, affirmative ethics rests on the notion of the random access to the phenomena that cause pain (or pleasure). This is not fatalism, and even less resignation, but rather *amor fati*. The difference is crucial: we have to be worthy of what happens to us and rework it within an ethics of relation, without falling into negativity. Of course, repugnant and unbearable events do happen. Ethics consists, however, in reworking these events in the direction of positive relations. This is not carelessness or lack of compassion, but rather a form of lucidity that acknowledges the impossibility of finding an adequate answer to the question about the possible meaning of the ill fate, the painful event, and even of the violence suffered. Acknowledging the futility of even trying to answer that question is a starting point.

LIMITS AND THRESHOLDS

The dissolution of the hard-core self of liberal individualism is a foundational notion in poststructuralist philosophy. Foucault, for instance, rendered it through the idea of the "limit-experience" which breaks the frame of predictable subject positions. Deleuze pursues this line, influenced by Bataille, Blanchot, as well as Nietzsche. The point of dissolution of the subject is usually marked by confrontation with an extreme experience, which leads to de-subjectivation. The fragility and vulnerability of the human is revealed in this experience, which concerns both affect and cognition. As a limit-experience it marks the threshold of (un)sustainability, that is, it prompts the awareness of fragility and the recognition of contingency. It also propels the subject, however, to act according to this awareness. The result of the confrontation with the limit (the limit-experience) is the transformation of the subject's relation to knowledge and to itself as a knowing subject. The limit experience accounts for the conversion of the subject into something else. This is the ethical moment.

The later Foucault argues, contrary, for instance, to Deleuze, that the question of the limits of the philosophical subject, which is operationalized through Bataille, was already raised by Kant's critical thought. This is expressed in both *Preface to Transgression* and in Foucault's genealogy of the human and social sciences in *The Order of Discourse*. Through this reference, Foucault links the domain of ethics to knowledge and cognition in the sense of forces that activate a subject's capacity to act upon itself and others (*potentia*). This is self-styling or *auto-poiesis* as productive self-creation. Ethics as praxis.

Ethics is about freedom from the weight of negativity, freedom through the understanding of our bondage. A certain amount of pain, the knowledge about vulnerability and pain, is actually useful. It forces one to think about the actual material conditions of being interconnected and thus being in the world. It frees one from the stupidity of perfect health, and the full-blown sense of existential entitlement that comes with it.

What is ethics, then? Ethics is a thin barrier against the possibility of extinction. It is a mode of actualizing sustainable forms of transformation. This requires adequate assemblages or interaction:

one has to pursue or actively create the kind of encounters that are likely to favor an increase in active becomings and avoid those that diminish one's *potentia*. It is an intensive ethics, based on the shared capacity of humans to feel empathy for, develop affinity with, and hence enter in relation with other forces, entities, beings, waves of intensity. This requires dosage, rhythms, styles of repetition, and coordination or resonance. It is a matter of unfolding-out and enfolding-in the complex and multi-layered forces of *bios-zoe* as a deeply inhuman force.

In other words, *potentia*, in order to fulfill its inherent positivity, must be "formatted" in the direction of sustainability. Obviously, this means that it is impossible to set one standard that will suit all; a differential approach becomes necessary. What bodies are capable of doing or not is biologically, physically, psychically, historically, sexually, and emotionally specific: singular and hence partial. Consequently, the thresholds of sustainable becomings also mark their limits. In this respect "I can't take it anymore" is an ethical statement, not the assertion of defeat. It is the lyrical lament of a subject in process who is shot through with waves of intensity, like a set of fulgurations that illuminate his self-awareness, tearing open fields of self-knowledge in the encounter of and configuration with others. Learning to recognize threshold, borders, or limits is thus crucial to the work of the understanding and to the process of becoming. For Lacan limits are wounds or scars, marks of internal lacerations and irreplaceable losses, and for liberal thoughts limits are frontiers that cannot be trespassed without the required visas or permissions. For Deleuze, however, limits are simultaneously points of passage or thresholds and markers of sustainability.

Deleuze has an almost mathematical definition of the limit, as that which one never really reaches. In his *Abécédaire*, Deleuze discusses with Claire Parnet the question of the limit in terms of addiction. Reminiscing on his own early alcoholism, Deleuze notes that the limit or frame for the alterations induced by alcohol is to be set with reference not so much to the last glass, because that is the glass that is going to kill you. What matters instead is the "second-last" glass, the one that has already been and thus is going to allow you to survive, to last, to endure – and consequently also to go on drinking again. A true addict stops at the second-last glass, one removed from the fatal sip, or shot. A death-bound entity, however, usually shoots straight for the last one. That gesture prevents or denies the expression of the desire to start again tomorrow, that is to say to repeat that "second-last shot," and thus to endure. In fact, there is no sense of a possible tomorrow: time folds in upon itself and excavates a black hole into which the subject dissolves. No future.

THE ETHICS OF DE-PERSONALIZATION

Pain in our culture is associated to suffering by force of habit and tradition and is given negative connotations accordingly. Supposing we look a bit more critically into this associative link, however: what does pain, or suffering, tell us? That our subjectivity consists of affectivity, interrelationality, and forces. The core of the subject is affect and the capacity for interrelations to affect and to be affected. Let us agree to de-psychologize this discussion from this moment on, not in order to deny the pain, but rather to find ways of working through it.

This vision of ethics involves a radical repositioning or internal transformation on the part of subjects who want to become-minoritarian in a productive and affirmative manner. It is clear that this shift requires changes that are neither simple nor self-evident. They mobilize the affectivity of the subjects involved and can be seen as a process of transformation of negative into positive passions. Fear, anxiety, and nostalgia are clear examples of the negative emotions involved in the project of detaching ourselves from familiar and cherished forms of identity. To achieve a post-identity or non-unitary vision of the self requires the dis-identification from established references. Such an enterprise involves a sense of loss of cherished habits of thought and representation, and thus is not free of pain. No process of consciousness-raising ever is.

The beneficial side-effects of this process are unquestionable and in some way they compensate for the pain of loss. Thus, the feminist questioning and in some cases rejection of gender roles triggers a process of dis-identification with established forms of masculinity and femininity, which has fueled the political quest for alternative ways of inhabiting gender and embodying sexuality.[28] In race discourse, the awareness of the persistence of racial discrimination and of white privilege has led, on the one hand, to the critical reappraisal of blackness[29] and, on the other, to radical relocation of whiteness.[30]

In a Spinozist vein, these are transformative processes that not only rework the consciousness of social injustice and discrimination but also produce a more adequate cartography of our real-life condition, free of delusions of grandeur. It is an enriching and positive experience which, however, includes pain as an integral element. Migrants, exiles, refugees have firsthand experience of the extent to which the process of dis-identification from familiar identities is linked to the pain of loss and uprooting. Diasporic subjects of all kinds express the same sense of wound. Multi-locality is the affirmative translation of this negative sense of loss. Following Glissant, the becoming-nomadic marks the process of positive transformation of the pain of loss into the active production of multiple forms of belonging and complex allegiances.[31] What is lost in the sense of fixed origins is regained in an increased desire to belong, in a multiple rhizomic manner which transcends the classic bilateralism of binary identity formations.

The qualitative leap through pain, across the mournful landscapes of nostalgic yearning, is the gesture of active creation of affirmative ways of belonging. It is a fundamental reconfiguration of our way of being in the world, which acknowledges the pain of loss but moves further. This is the defining moment for the process of becoming-ethical: the move across and beyond pain, loss, and negative passions. Taking suffering into account is the starting point; the real aim of the process, however, is the quest for ways of overcoming the stultifying effects of passivity, brought about by pain. The internal disarray, fracture, and pain are the conditions of possibility for ethical transformation. Clearly, this is an antithesis of the Kantian moral imperative to avoid pain or to view pain as the obstacle to moral behavior. Nomadic ethics is not about the avoidance of pain; rather it is about transcending the resignation and passivity that ensue from being hurt, lost, and dispossessed. One has to become ethical, as opposed to applying moral rules and protocols as a form of self-protection. Transformations express the affirmative power of Life as the vitalism of *bios-zoe*.

The sobering experience – the humble and productive recognition of loss, limitations, and shortcomings – has to do with self-representations. Established mental habits, images, and terminology

railroad us back towards established ways of thinking about ourselves. Traditional modes of representation are legal forms of addiction. To change them is not unlike undertaking a disintoxication
cure. A great deal of courage and creativity is needed to develop
forms of representation that do justice to the complexities of the
kind of subjects we have already become. De-familiarization is an
essential component of this process. The point is that de-personalization is a necessary step on the road to the acquisition of ethical
subjectivity because it bypasses the spiral of negative passions and
the political economy of resentment which lies at the heart of the
ego. The necessity to undergo such a fundamental transformation of
our system of self-understanding as subject is also supported by contextual concerns. We already live and inhabit social reality in ways
that surpass tradition: we move about, in the flow of current social
transformations, in hybrid, multicultural, polyglot, post-identity
spaces of becoming.[32] We fail, however, to bring them into adequate
representation. There is a shortage on the part of our social imaginary, a deficit of representational power, which underscores the political timidity of our times.

BECOMING ETHICAL: ON SUSTAINABILITY

What is, then, the subject of ethical affirmation? It is a slice of living, sensible matter activated by a fundamental drive to life: a *potentia* (rather than *potestas*) – neither by the will of God, nor the secret
encryption of the genetic code – and yet this subject is embedded
in the corporeal materiality of the self. The enfleshed intensive or
nomadic subject is rather a transversal entity: a folding-in of external influences and a simultaneous unfolding-outwards of affects.
A mobile unit in space and time and therefore an enfleshed kind of
memory, this subject is not only in process, but is also capable of
lasting through sets of discontinuous variations, while remaining
extraordinarily faithful to itself.

This idea of the "faithfulness" of the subject is important and it
builds on the rejection of liberal individualism. This may appear
counterintuitive to the Anglo-American reader and require of them
an effort of the imagination. Allow me to plead for the short-term
benefits that will flow, however, from this stretching exercise, and
for the dividends it will return in terms of added understanding.

This "faithfulness to oneself," consequently, is not to be understood in the mode of the psychological or sentimental attachment to a personal "identity" that often is little more than a social security number and a set of photo albums. Nor is it the mark of authenticity of a self ("me, myself and I") that is a clearinghouse for narcissism and paranoia – the great pillars on which Western identity predicates itself. It is rather the faithfulness of mutual sets of interdependence and interconnections, that is to say, sets of relations and encounters. It is a play of complexity that encompasses all levels of one's multi-layered subjectivity, binding the cognitive to the emotional, the intellectual to the affective and connecting them all to a socially embedded ethics of sustainability. Thus, the faithfulness that is at stake in nomadic ethics coincides with the awareness of one's condition of interaction with others, that is to say, one's capacity to affect and to be affected. Translated into a temporal scale, this is the faithfulness of duration, the expression of one's continuing attachment to certain dynamic spatio-temporal coordinates.

In a philosophy of temporally inscribed radical immanence, subjects differ. But they differ along materially embedded coordinates, because they come in different mileage, temperatures, and beats. One can and does change gears and move across these coordinates, but cannot claim all of them, all of the time. The latitudinal and longitudinal forces that structure the subject have limits of sustainability. By latitudinal forces Deleuze means the affects a subject is capable of, following the degrees of intensity or potency: how intensely they run. By longitude is meant the span of extension: how far they can go. Sustainability is about how much of it a subject can take.

In other words, sustainable subjectivity reinscribes the singularity of the self, while challenging the anthropocentrism of Western philosophies' understanding of the subject, and of the attributes usually reserved for "agency." This sense of limits is extremely important to ensure productive synchronizations and prevent nihilistic self-destruction. To be active, intensive, or nomadic does not mean that one is limitless. That would be the kind of delirious expression of megalomania that you find in the new master narratives of the cyber-culture of today, ready and willing to: "dissolve the bodily self into the matrix." On the contrary, to make sense of this intensive, materially embedded vision of the subject we need a sustainability threshold or frame. The containment of the intensities or enfleshed passions so as to ensure their duration is a crucial prerequisite to allow them to do their job, which consists in shooting through the humanistic frame of the subject, exploding it outwards. The dosage of the threshold of intensity is both crucial and inherent to the process of becoming, insofar as the subject is embodied and hence set in a spatio-temporal frame.

What is this threshold of sustainability, then, and how does it get fixed? A radically immanent intensive body is an assemblage of forces, or flows, intensities, and passions that solidify in space, and consolidate in time, within the singular configuration commonly known as an "individual" self. This intensive and dynamic entity – it's worth stressing it again – does not coincide with the enumeration of inner rationalist laws, nor is it merely the unfolding of genetic data and information. It is rather a portion of forces that is stable enough to sustain and to undergo constant, though non-destructive, fluxes of transformation. D. W. Smith argues that there are three essential questions about immanent ethics: "How is a mode of existence determined? How are modes of existence to be evaluated? What are the conditions for the creation of new modes of existence?"[33] On all three scores, it is the body's degrees and levels of affectivity that determined the modes of differentiation. Joyful or positive passions and the transcendence of reactive affects are the desirable mode. The emphasis on "existence" implies a commitment to duration and conversely a rejection of self-destruction. Positivity is inbuilt into this program through the idea of thresholds of sustainability.

Thus, an ethically empowering option increases one's *potentia* and creates joyful energy in the process. The conditions which can encourage such a quest are not only historical; they all concern processes of self-transformation or self-fashioning in the direction of affirming positivity. Because all subjects share in this common nature, there is a common ground on which to negotiate the interests and the eventual conflicts. It is important to see in fact that this fundamentally positive vision of the ethical subject does not deny conflicts, tension, or even violent disagreements between different subjects. Again, the legacy of Hegel's critique of Spinoza is still looming large here. It is simply not the case that the positivity of desire cancels or denies the tensions of conflicting interests. It merely displaces the grounds on which the negotiations take place. The Kantian imperative of not doing to others what you would not want done to you is not rejected as much as enlarged. In terms of the ethics of *conatus*, in fact, the harm that you do to others is immediately reflected in the harm you do to yourself, in terms of loss of *potentia*, positivity, self-awareness, and inner freedom.

This move away from the Kantian vision of an ethics that obliges people, and especially women, natives, and others, to act morally in the name of a transcendent standard or a universal moral rule is not a simple one. I defend it as a forceful answer to the complexities of our historical situation: it is a move towards radical immanence against all Platonist and classical humanistic denials of embodiment, matter, and the flesh. Containing the other in the name of one's right to differ, or in the name of the vital powers of becoming. They stress that moral reasoning locates the constitution of subjectivity in the interrelation to others, which is a form of exposure, availability, and vulnerability. This recognition entails the necessity of containing the other, the suffering and the enjoyment of others in the expression of the intensity of our affective streams.

If the point of ethics is to explore how much a body can do, in the pursuit of active modes of empowerment through experimentation, how do we know when we have gone too far? How does one know if one has reached the threshold of sustainability? This is where the non-individualistic vision of the subject as embodied and hence affective and interrelational, but also fundamentally social, is of major consequence. Your body will thus tell you if and when you have reached a threshold or a limit. The warning can take the form of opposing resistance; falling ill, feeling nauseous; or it can take other somatic manifestations, like fear, anxiety, or a sense of insecurity. Whereas the semiotic-linguistic frame of psychoanalysis reduces these to symptoms awaiting interpretation, I see them as corporeal warning signals or boundary markers that express a clear message: "too much!" One of the reasons why Deleuze and Guattari are so interested in studying self-destructive or pathological modes of behaviors, such as schizophrenia, masochism, anorexia, various forms of addiction, and the black hole of murderous violence, is precisely in order to explore their function as markers of thresholds. This assumes a qualitative distinction between, on the one hand, the desire that propels the subject's expression of his/her *conatus*, which in a neo-Spinozist perspective is implicitly positive in that it expresses the essential best of the subject, and, on the other, the constraints imposed by society. The specific, contextually determined conditions are the forms in which the desire is actualized or actually expressed.

This is all the more salient if we consider that advanced capitalism is a system that tends to constantly stretch its limits and plays with the idea of over-reaching itself, moving towards "timeless time,"[34] How shall I put it? All planes are always overbooked, and this is a fitting metaphor for the political economy of profit and its saturation of our social space. Insofar as the subject is under constant pressure to function and find points of stability within the ever-shifting limits or boundaries, capitalism is a system that actively generates schizophrenia in the sense of enhancing the value of unfixed meanings: an unlimited semiosis without fixed referents.[35] This makes the question of negotiation thresholds of sustainability all the more urgent. If the boundaries are forever being stretched and hence blurred, however, perspectival shifts are necessary in order to keep up and account for the process and thus identify points of resistance. Schizophrenia is a molecular mode of undoing the molar aggregates of the commodification system, of inducing flows into them. This avoids the consolidation and the over-codification (constant control) that are characteristic of the Majority, but in return it runs the danger of fluidity to the point of self-destruction. How to find a point of balance is an ethical question.

CONCLUSION

A nomadic Deleuzian ethics prioritizes relation, praxis, and complexity as the key components and it accordingly promotes a triple shift. Firstly, it continues to emphasize a radical ethics of transformation in opposition to the moral protocols of Kantian universalism. Secondly, it shifts the focus from a unitary and rationality-driven consciousness to ontology of process, that is to say, a vision of subjectivity that is propelled by affects and relations. Thirdly, it disengages the emergence of the subject from the logic of negation and attaches subjectivity to affirmative Otherness – reciprocity as creation, not as the recognition of Sameness. This results in renewed emphasis on affirmation as the politics of life itself, as the generative intensive force of *zoe*.

In response to the charge of moral relativism, I have emphasized the central role of sustainability in nomadic ethics. Sustainable ethics allows us to contain the risks while pursuing the original project of transformation. This is a way to resist the dominant ethos of our conservative times that idolizes the new as a consumerist trend, while thundering against those who believe in social change. Cultivating the art of living intensely in the pursuit of change is a political act. In this regard, I have insisted on the importance of endurance – in the double sense of learning to last in time, but also to put up and live with pain and suffering. Again, it is a question of dosage and of balance. Thresholds of sustainability need to be mapped out, so that a rate and speed of change can be negotiated and set that will allow each subject to endure, to go on, to stop at the second-last smoke, shot, drink, and book. This implies a differential type of ethics, which clashes with dominant morality but contains criteria for the section of the ethical relation and a regard for the limits. These need to be set by experimentation with the collectively shared intensities of a community that longs for the activation of affirmative forces and hence require careful negotiations. The embodied structure of the subject is a limit in itself, though limits in Deleuze's philosophy are just the threshold of sustainable changes.

The key ideals of this ethics of freedom are, firstly, the focus on self-determination or self-styling through the very acts of resistance or transgression. This is in contrast to the juridical conception of freedom as a set of universal rights or entitlements. Secondly, this idea of freedom emphasizes critical analysis and constant questioning. This is linked to the notion of governmentality in the sense of a general organization of knowledge and of disciplinary apparati that produce modes of subjectivity.[36] The lesson of Spinoza about the structurally repressive function of the state in relation to the project of realizing the *conatus* is also relevant. This tradition of thought, to which Toni Negri also belongs, is wary of the institutions that govern us. Thus vigilance is the price of freedom; it is the task of the critical thinkers, as analysts of power, to assess the conditions that are conducive to social change, as opposed to the emphasis on unchangeable factors.

Thirdly, the issue of self-scrutiny cannot be separated from the social analysis of the conditions of domination. A micropolitics of resistance can be seen as a web of emancipatory practices. Localized and concrete ethical gestures and political activities matter more than grand overarching projects. In this respect, nomadic theory is a form of ethical pragmatism.

NOTES

1 See Nicholas Rose, "The Politics of Life Itself," *Theory, Culture and Society*, 18:6 (2001), 1–30, and Paul Rabinow, *Anthropos Today* (Princeton University Press, 2003).
2 Giorgio Agamben, *Homo Sacer. Sovereign Power and Bare Life* (Stanford University Press, 1998).
3 Emmanuel Levinas, *Alterity and Transcendence* (London: Athlone, 1999).
4 See Simon Critchley, *The Ethics of Deconstruction* (Edinburgh University Press, 1992), and Judith Butler, *Precarious Life* (London and New York: Verso, 2004).
5 Jacques Derrida, *The Work of Mourning* (University of Chicago Press, 2001).
6 Keith Ansell Pearson, *Viroid Life: Perspectives on Nietzsche and the Transhuman Condition* (New York: Routledge, 1997) and *Germinal Life: The Difference and Repetition of Deleuze* (London and New York: Routledge, 1999).
7 Rosi Braidotti, *Transpositions: On Nomadic Ethics* (Cambridge: Polity Press, 2006).
8 Genevieve Lloyd, *Part of Nature: Self-Knowledge in Spinoza's "Ethics"* (Ithaca, NY: Cornell University Press, 1994) and *Spinoza and the "Ethics"* (London and New York: Routledge, 1996).
9 Ansell Pearson, *Viroid Life*.
10 Lloyd, *Part of Nature* and *Spinoza and the "Ethics."*
11 Lloyd, *Spinoza and the "Ethics,"* p. 23.
12 Lloyd, *Part of Nature*, p. 12.
13 *Ibid.*, p. 23.
14 Lloyd, *Spinoza and the "Ethics,"* p. 31.
15 *Ibid.*, p. 72.
16 *Ibid.*, p. 74.
17 Donna Haraway, *The Companion Species Manifesto: Dogs, People, and Significant Otherness* (Chicago: Prickley Paradigm Press, 2003).
18 Sarah Franklin, Celia Lury, and Jackie Stacey, *Global Nature, Global Culture* (London: Sage, 2000).

19 Vandana Shiva, *Biopiracy. The Plunder of Nature and Knowledge* (Boston: South End Press, 1997).

20 Luciana Parisi, *Abstract Sex. Philosophy, Biotechnology, and the Mutations of Desire* (London: Continuum, 2004), and Lynn Margulis and Dorion Sagan, *What is Life?* (Berkeley: University of California Press, 1995).

21 Braidotti, *Transpositions.*

22 Félix Guattari, *The Three Ecologies* (London: Athlone, 2000).

23 Jean Laplanche, *Life and Death in Psychoanalysis* (Baltimore and London: Johns Hopkins University Press, 1976).

24 Julia Kristeva, *Pouvoirs de l'horreur* (Paris: Seuil, 1980).

25 Elizabeth Grosz, *The Nick of Time* (Durham, NC: Duke University Press, 2004).

26 Ansell Pearson, *Germinal Life.*

27 Zygmunt Bauman, *Postmodern Ethics* (Oxford: Blackwell, 1993) and *Globalization: The Human Consequences* (Cambridge: Polity Press, 1998).

28 Rosi Braidotti, *Metamorphoses: Towards a Materialist Theory of Becoming* (Cambridge: Polity Press, 2002) and *Transpositions.*

29 Paul Gilroy, *Against Race. Imagining Political Culture beyond the Colour Line* (Cambridge, MA: Harvard University Press, 2000), and Patricia Hill Collins, *Black Feminist Thought. Knowledge, Consciousness, and the Politics of Empowerment* (London and New York: Routledge, 1991).

30 Gabriele Griffin and Rosi Braidotti, *Thinking Differently. A Reader in European Women's Studies* (London: Zed Books, 2002).

31 Édouard Glissant, *Poétique de la relation* (Paris: Gallimard, 1990).

32 Braidotti, *Metamorphoses* and *Transpositions.*

33 D. W. Smith, "The Place of Ethics in Deleuze's Philosophy: Three Questions of Immanence," in Eleanor Kaufman and Kevin Heller (eds.), *Deleuze and Guattari: New Mappings in Politics and Philosophy* (Minneapolis: University of Minnesota Press, 1998), pp. 251–69, p. 259.

34 Manuel Castells, *The Rise of the Network Society* (Oxford: Blackwell, 1996).

35 Eugene Holland, *Deleuze and Guattari's "Anti-Oedipus": Introduction to Schizoanalysis* (London and New York: Routledge, 1999).

36 Thomas Dumm, *Michel Foucault and the Politics of Freedom* (London: Sage, 1996).

9 Deleuze's political philosophy

Much of Deleuze's work, especially the books co-authored with Guattari, has been read as political philosophy.[1] Deleuze clearly viewed their initial collaboration in this light. In a 1990 interview with Antonio Negri, "Control and Becoming," he remarked that "*Anti-Oedipus* was from beginning to end a work of political philosophy" (*N* 170). Their biographer, François Dosse, goes even further in suggesting that all of Deleuze's work, "from his first works on Hume to his final reflections on the virtual, is inscribed in the space of the political."[2] However, not everyone accepts this image of Deleuze as a thoroughly political thinker. Slavoj Žižek argues that "*not a single one* of Deleuze's own texts is in any way directly political; Deleuze 'in himself' is a highly elitist author, indifferent toward politics."[3]

Alain Badiou outlines several reasons for doubting whether Deleuze was first and foremost a political thinker and even whether there is such a thing as a Deleuzian politics.[4] A first difficulty is that Deleuze never identified the political as a specific object or domain of thought, in the same way that, in *What is Philosophy?*, he singled out art, science, and philosophy.[5] A second, more subjective difficulty is that Deleuze was never very interested in politics. In his solo writings, he never claimed that politics determined his philosophical activity. Unlike many of his contemporaries, such as Althusser, Derrida, Lyotard, or Nancy, he never argued that the primary purpose of philosophy was political. On the contrary, he

Earlier versions of this chapter were presented as talks at the University of Sydney in April 2011 and at a workshop at the China Foreign Affairs University in June 2011. I am grateful to the participants on both occasions for their comments, questions, and criticisms.

198

tended towards a more traditional view of philosophy as the creation of concepts and suggested in a 1985 interview that he was interested in "the relations between the arts, science and philosophy" (N 123).

A third difficulty concerns the content of Deleuze's political writings. Badiou suggests that there are two distinct objects of Deleuzian politics. The first is aligned with the virtual realm of becoming and pure events that is the ultimate source of creativity and the emergence of the new, while the second is aligned with the actual realm of embodied events, forms of society, and historical processes of contestation and change. In *Anti-Oedipus* and again in *A Thousand Plateaus* Deleuze and Guattari outline a theory of universal history involving at least three stages. In the short essay "Postscript on Control Societies," Deleuze outlines another historical series of types of society modeled on Foucault's analysis of the "diagram" of disciplinary society (N 177–82). However, as Badiou points out, none of this is really the work of a historian. On the contrary, Deleuze subscribes to a violent anti-historicism that leads him to insist more and more on the distinction between history and becoming:

The thing is, I became more and more aware of the possibility of distinguishing between becoming and history. It was Nietzsche who said that nothing important is ever free from a "nonhistorical cloud." This isn't to oppose eternal and historical, or contemplation and action: Nietzsche is talking about the way things happen, about events themselves or becoming. What history grasps in an event is the way it's actualized in particular historical circumstances; the event's becoming is beyond the scope of history. (N 170)[6]

For Deleuze, it is becomings that are the real object of philosophy. Philosophy as it is defined in *What is Philosophy?* creates concepts that express particular kinds of becoming or "pure events." In view of the priority that Deleuze assigns to becoming at the expense of history, Badiou argues that his politics remains divided between an ethics of creation and creativity and a mundane governmental politics that is bound up with history and the analysis of capitalism. Peter Hallward pursues this line of argument by outlining a reading of Deleuze as a theophantic thinker of unworldly creation, to the point of suggesting that Deleuze's ethics of creativity offers no basis for any determinate political activity whatsoever.[7] In common with another critic of Deleuze's politics, Philippe Mengue, Hallward wavers between denying that Deleuze is a political philosopher and asserting that he is the wrong kind of political philosopher. Jeremy Gilbert summarizes their respective conclusions in the following terms:

Deleuze is a mystic, a nostalgist for elitist modes of avant-gardism which have no purchase on the present, at best an implicit conservative whose romanticism leaves no scope for rational calculation or collective action.[8]

There is some truth to each of Badiou's claims about Deleuze's relation to politics.

It is also true, as Gilbert suggests, that his work encompasses both political and anti-political moments.[9] However, these must be understood in their context and especially in their relation to one another if we are to appreciate the character of Deleuze's political thought and his distinctive contribution to political philosophy. While he would undoubtedly not be regarded as a political philosopher by many professional philosophers and political scientists, there are no grounds for the suggestion that Deleuze's philosophy has nothing to offer in relation to politics. Before outlining some of the ways in which the content of his work with Guattari may be read as a contribution to specifically political philosophy, I begin with the subjective, biographical problem raised by Badiou. It is important to read Deleuze against the background of the developments in his thought and to take at face value his claim that it was only after the tumultuous events of May 1968 in France that he undertook his own "move into politics" (N 170).

In his 1990 interview with Negri, Deleuze admits that in his early years he was more interested in the creation of new social relations than in the manner in which these were represented. As such, he was "more interested in right than in politics" (N 169).[10] François Dosse takes Deleuze's interest in empiricists such as Hume and vitalists such as Bergson, in a period when French philosophy was dominated by Marxism and phenomenology, to be evidence not only of originality but also of a certain intellectual "dandyism" that took delight in embracing unfashionable and untimely thinkers.[11] It is true that he repeated this gesture with an essay on Sacher-Masoch in 1961, at the height of intellectual interest in Sade, and with a suggestion in

1993 that his next and last book would be called "The Importance of Marx" (*N* 51). In the same interview in 1993, in which he points out that he was never a member of the Communist Party and never underwent psychoanalysis, Deleuze admits that he did not become Marxist until he read Marx in the 1960s (*N* 51). Latecomer to politics that he may have been, he was nonetheless the only member of the philosophy department and one of the few professors at the University of Lyon in 1968 to publicly declare his support for the student movement and to take part in assemblies and demonstrations.[12] Only after this social and political upheaval, and a long period of ill-health and convalescence, did he become actively engaged in particular causes alongside people such as Guattari, Foucault, and Elie Sambar (*N* 170). From this point onwards, as Badiou admits, Deleuze wrote a great deal about politics and political issues, both alone and in collaboration with Guattari. Moreover, their final co-authored text, *What is Philosophy?*, does claim a political vocation for philosophy. Philosophy is a certain kind of criticism of the present that works through the creation of concepts. These express forms of absolute deterritorialization that can only be thought and can only produce effects in relation to existing forms of relative deterritorialization within a given society (*WP* 88). Deleuze and Guattari call this point of engagement between philosophy and its social milieu "utopia": "In each case it is with utopia that philosophy becomes political and takes the criticism of its own time to its highest point" (*WP* 99). This conception of philosophy as utopian engagement with the present raises a number of questions about the kind of political activity envisaged and the precise sense in which this is political philosophy.

MARXIST POLITICS OR ANTI-POLITICS?

In answer to the first set of questions about the kind of politics envisaged, we can begin by noting that, like many of their compatriots mobilized by the events of 1968, Deleuze and Guattari were heavily influenced by Marxist approaches to politics.[13] They focused on the conditions of revolutionary social change rather than the conditions of maintaining society as a fair system of cooperation among its members. In contrast to traditional Marxist politics, however, they were less interested in the capture of state power than in the qualitative changes in individual and collective identities that occur alongside or beneath the public political domain. In their view, all politics is simultaneously a *macropolitics* that involves social classes and the institutions of political government and a *micropolitics* that involves subterranean movements of sensibility, affect, and allegiance. However much they borrowed from Marx's analysis of history and capitalism, their own work focused on the individual and collective forms of desire that constitute the micropolitical dimension of social change. This focus on the politics of desire led them to abandon key tenets of Marxist social and political theory such as the concept of the party as a revolutionary vanguard and the philosophy of history that sustained Marxist class politics. They proposed a non-teleological conception of history along with a more nuanced appreciation of the deterritorializing as well as the reterritorializing aspects of capitalism. They insisted that the impetus for social change was provided by movements of deterritorialization and lines of flight rather than by class contradictions. Their rejection of the organizational and tactical forms of traditional Marxist politics is definitively expressed at the end of *Dialogues* when Deleuze and Parnet abandon the goal of revolutionary capture of state power in favor of the *revolutionary-becoming* of people throughout society: "why not think that *a new type of revolution is in the course of becoming possible*, and that all kinds of mutating living machines conduct wars, are combined and trace out a plane of consistence which undermines the plane of organization of the World and the States?" (*D* 147). This new concept of revolutionary-becoming sought to encompass the multitude of ways in which individuals and groups deviate from the majoritarian norms that ultimately determine the rights and duties of citizens.

The fact that Deleuze read Marx during the 1960s alongside Nietzsche perhaps explains some of the anti-political themes that occasionally manifest themselves in his work (*N* 51). There is no discussion of Nietzsche's views on politics and the state in *Nietzsche and Philosophy*, only comments on his theory of culture and, at the end of the book, on the implications of Nietzsche's theory for practice. However, if Deleuze had elaborated a Nietzschean politics on the basis of applying the theory of power outlined in *Nietzsche and Philosophy* to the social and political field, and supposed a simple axiological priority of the active over the reactive and the affirmative over the negative, the argument might run along the following lines. Power is fundamentally active and relational, appearing in the interaction between different kinds and degrees of force. In the state of nature, individual and collective bodies collide in the pursuit of their activities. However, purely chaotic interaction is not a state of social existence: at best, life under such conditions will be uncertain, at worst it will be brutish and short. Hence, it can be argued, the overriding aim of political government is the establishment and maintenance of relatively stable forms of interaction. Social relations require the stabilization and fixation of certain forms of interaction, including the institution of forms of government which enable stable and predictable forms of action upon the actions of others. In these terms, government is a form of action upon individual or social forces which seeks to limit or constrain their possibilities for action. From the perspective of the forces governed, the government of individual and collective bodies is essentially reactive. Deleuze and Guattari's account of the state as a process of capture operating upon the primary flows of matter and activity in the social field renders explicit this reactive character of the political apparatus. The state, they argue, captures flows of population, commodities, or money in order to extract from these flows a surplus which then becomes a means to maintain and enhance its own power. It is an institution whose primary mode of operation is one of limitation or constraint, a matter of separating active forces from what they can do. In these terms, the state is by definition always a secondary formation, and the political sphere is always reactive by nature. In this way, the argument sketched above would lead to a fundamentally anti-political orientation.

Elements of such an orientation may be found in *Difference and Repetition*, for example, in the form of Deleuze's defence of the singular against the general, the individual against the herd, and a resistance to forms of equality and equalization. This "anti-political" theme emerges from the conception of the social field (like every other) as a field of free differences and the rejection of representation: every time there is representation there is always "an unrepresented singularity" who does not recognize himself or herself in the representant. Hence the misfortune of speaking for others (*DR* 52). Elsewhere in *Difference and Repetition*, Deleuze points out that for every philosophy that begins from a subjective or implicit claim about what everybody is supposed to know there is another which denies this knowledge or fails to recognize what is claimed. Such philosophies rely not upon the common man but on a different persona: "Someone who neither allows himself to be represented nor wishes to represent anything" (DR 130).[14]

The theory of capitalist society outlined in *Anti-Oedipus* establishes a fundamental dualism within capitalist society between the deterritorializing tendency of capital and the necessary reterritorialization effected by the state and its agents. Moreover, Deleuze and Guattari suggest, the revolutionary path lies not in the attempt to set limits to market forces and the impetus of deterritorialization, but in the opposite direction, pursuing ever further the movement of decoding and deterritorialization (AO 239–40). Much of the analysis of capitalism in *Anti-Oedipus* supports such a reading. For example, the authors describe the capitalist axiomatic as a system of enslavement in which all are subject to the constraint of its axioms. By contrast with the form of slavery established by the Despotic state, which at least retained an apparatus of anti-production distinct from the sphere of production and a corresponding class of masters, capitalism installs "an unrivalled slavery, an unprecedented subjugation" in which "there are no longer even any masters, but only slaves commanding other slaves" (AO 254). Here, there is only one class, and bourgeois and proletarian alike are slaves of the social machine. In contrast, Deleuze and Guattari point to "the revolutionary potential of decoded flows" and suggest that the opposition to this machine which is relevant from the point of view of revolutionary politics is not that between capitalist and worker but that between "the decoded flows that enter into a class axiomatic on the full body of capital, and on the other hand, the decoded flows that free themselves from this axiomatic" (AO 255).

Other elements of Deleuze and Guattari's mature political philosophy disallow a simplistic anti-political point of view. The axioms of the capitalist social machine do not simply repress a natural state of free and undirected social existence. They are also constitutive of new social forces and forms of life. Deleuze and Guattari are not Romantic anarchists who believe in a realm of social being beyond the subjection to political power. It would be an error, they argue, "to take a disinterested stance toward struggle on the level of the axioms" (*ATP* 463). The reason is not simply that the conditions of people's lives are at stake in those axioms, but also that forcing changes at the level of the axiomatic is itself an indispensable mechanism of affecting the possibility of future changes. As we have seen, it is a fundamental feature of the axiomatic that it cannot reterritorialize existing flows without creating conditions that will generate new forms of deterritorialization.

MICROPOLITICS, FORMAL NORMATIVITY, AND DETERRITORIALIZATION

Deleuze and Guattari's political philosophy does not conform to the disciplinary norms of anglophone normative political philosophy or German Critical Theory. For the most part, the concepts developed in *Anti-Oedipus* and *A Thousand Plateaus* do not directly address the macropolitical public domain, much less the normative principles on which this should be based. They consider the different forms of modern government only from the Marxist perspective of their subordination to the axioms of capitalist production. From this point of view, authoritarian, socialist, and liberal democratic states are considered equivalent to one another insofar as they function as models of realization of the global axiomatic of capital. They allow that there are important differences among the various modern forms of state but provide little discussion of these differences. They affirm the importance of changes to regimes of public right that come about through struggles for civil and political rights, for equality of economic condition and opportunity, as well as for regional and national autonomy. However, they offer no normative theory of the basis of such rights, nor of the kinds and degrees of equality or regional autonomy that should prevail (*ATP* 470–71). They offer no justification for the establishment of basic civil and political rights, for the kinds of differential rights that might apply to cultural or national minorities, or for particular ways of distributing wealth and other goods produced by social cooperation.

Instead, they focus on the micropolitical sources of political change such as the minoritarian becomings that provide the affective impetus for political movements. On their view, the sources of political creativity must always be traced back to shifts in the formations of individual and group desire that in turn lead to changes in sensibility, allegiance, and belief. To the extent that such micro-political movements bring about changes in the majoritarian stand-ards themselves, along with new forms of right or different status for particular groups, they effectively bring about what Deleuze and Guattari refer to as "new earths and new peoples" (WP 99, 101). At the same time, the significance of such minoritarian becomings for public political right depends on their being translated into new forms of right and different statuses for individuals and groups: "Molecular escapes and movements would be nothing if they did not return to the molar organizations to reshuffle their segments, their binary distributions of sexes, classes and parties" (ATP 216–17). In this manner, even though they offer neither descriptive nor normative accounts of macropolitical institutions and procedures, Deleuze and Guattari do provide a supplement to liberal democratic conceptions of political order. They invent a language in which to describe micropolitical movements and infrapolitical processes that give rise to new forms of constitutional and legal order. They outline a social ontology of assemblages and processes that bears indirectly on the forms of public right. They invent concepts such as becoming-minor, nomadism, smooth space, and lines of flight or deterritorialization that are not meant as substitutes for exist-ing concepts of freedom, equality, or justice but that are intended to assist the emergence of another justice, new kinds of equality and freedom, as well as new kinds of political differentiation and constraint.[15]

Although this political ontology does not include normative polit-ical concepts of equality, freedom, and justice, it does include a kind of formal normativity. Moreover, there is a progression in Deleuze and Guattari's work from a focus on this formal normativity in the earlier work toward increasing engagement with explicitly political normativity in their later work. By "formal normativity" I mean the way in which Anti-Oedipus discusses political institutions only from the perspective of a universal theory of society and history. The specifically political organization of society plays no independ-ent role in this theory. Rather, it is treated as continuous with the co-ordination and control of flows of matter and desire in non-state societies governed by the Territorial machine with its systems of alliance and filiation.[16] Deleuze and Guattari present the state as a new mechanism of alliance rather than as the embodiment of any ideal treaty or contract on the part of its subjects (*AO* 195–96). They argue that the state form appeared in human history in the guise of the different kinds of Despotic machine, each with its own mechanisms of overcoding the flows of desire, before becoming subordinate to the "civilized machine" that is global capitalism. What they call the Territorial, Despotic, and Civilized social machines are treated only as different regimes of co-ordination and control of the local desiring-machines that constitute individual, familial, and social life. There is no discussion of the norms that regulate modern political life, only the normativity inherent in the typology of desiring machines as embodying either the paranoiac, reactionary, and fascistic pole of desire or the schizoid and revolutionary pole (*AO* 340). For this reason, their "schizoanalytic" theory and practice of desire proposes neither a political program nor a project for a future form of society.

A Thousand Plateaus broadens and generalizes Deleuze and Guattari's social ontology so that it becomes a general theory of assemblages and the manner in which these are expressed throughout human history. The last vestiges of Marxist teleology are removed from their universal history such that social formations are defined by processes or becomings and "all history does is to translate a coexistence of becomings into a succession" (*ATP* 430). The successive plateaus provide a series of new concepts and associated terminology with which to describe different kinds of assemblages. These include concepts designed to express social, linguistic, and affective assemblages, such as strata, content and expression, territories, lines of flight, or deterritorialization; the terminology employed to outline a micro- as opposed to macropolitics, along with concepts such as body without organs, intensities, molar and molecular segmentarities, and the different kinds of line of which we are composed; the terminology employed to describe capitalism as a nonterritorially based axiomatic of flows of materials, labor, and information as opposed to a territorial system of overcoding; and finally, they include a concept of the state as an apparatus of capture that, in the forms of its present actualization, is increasingly subordinated to the requirements of the capitalist axiomatic, along with a concept of abstract machines of metamorphosis, or nomadic war machines, that are the agents of social and political transformation.

This machinic theory of society is normative in a specific and formal sense, namely that the different kinds of assemblage amount to a world in which systematic priority is accorded to minoritarian becomings over majoritarian being, to planes of consistency over planes of organization, to nomadic machines of metamorphosis over apparatuses of capture, to smooth rather than striated space, and so on. Deleuze and Guattari's political ontology presents certain kinds of movement as primary: becoming-minor as a process of deviation from a majoritarian standard, lines of flight or deterritorialization rather than processes of reterritorialization or capture, and so on. In this sense, their ontology of assemblages is also an ethics or an ethology. This ethics might be characterized in the language of one or other of the plateaus as an ethics of becoming, of flows or lines of flight, or as an ethics and a politics of deterritorialization.[17] It is "political" only in the very broad sense that it enables us to conceptualize and describe transformative forces and movements as well as the forms of "capture" or blockage to which these are subject.

In order to appreciate the complexity of this ontology and the kind of description that it allows, consider Deleuze and Guattari's concepts of *deterritorialization* and *reterritorialization*. In the concluding statement of rules governing some of their most important concepts at the end of *A Thousand Plateaus*, deterritorialization is defined as the movement or process by which something escapes or departs from a given territory, where a territory can be a system of any kind: conceptual, linguistic, social, or affective (*ATP* 508). By contrast, reterritorialization refers to the ways in which deterritorialized elements recombine and enter into new relations in the constitution of a new assemblage or the modification of the old. Systems of any kind always include "vectors of deterritorialization," while deterritorialization is always "inseparable from correlative reterritorializations" (*ATP* 509). Deterritorialization can take either a negative or a positive form. It is negative when the deterritorialized element is subjected to reterritorialization that obstructs or limits its line of flight. It is positive when the line of flight prevails over the forms of reterritorialization and manages to connect with other deterritorialized elements in a manner that extends its trajectory or even leads to reterritorialization in an entirely new assemblage. As well as distinguishing between negative and positive deterritorialization, Deleuze and Guattari further distinguish between an absolute and a relative form of each of these processes. Absolute deterritorialization refers to the virtual realm of becoming and pure events, while relative deterritorialization concerns only movements within the actual realm of embodied, historical events and processes. In the terms of their ontology of assemblages, it is the virtual order of becoming that governs the fate of any actual assemblage.

Finally, in accordance with their method of specification of concepts by proliferating distinctions, they distinguish between the *connection* and *conjugation* of deterritorialized elements in the construction of a new assemblage. The effective transformation of a given element of social or political life requires the recombination of deterritorialized elements in mutually supportive and productive ways to form assemblages of connection rather than conjugation. Absolute and relative deterritorialization will both be positive when they involve the construction of *"revolutionary connections* in opposition to the *conjugations of the axiomatic"* (*ATP* 473). Under these conditions, absolute deterritorialization "connects lines of flight, raises them to the power of an abstract vital line or draws a plane of consistency" (*ATP* 510).

Deleuze and Guattari's concepts are normative in the sense that they provide a descriptive language within which to judge the character of particular events and processes. They enable us to pose questions such as: Is this negative or positive reterritorialization? Is this a genuine line of flight? Will it lead to a revolutionary new assemblage in which there is an increase of freedom, or will it lead to a new form of capture or worse (*D* 143–44)? In this sense, the judgments enabled by Deleuze and Guattari's ontology of assemblages and processes are entirely practical and pragmatic. They enable a form of reflective judgment, although one that is closer to Kant's aesthetic judgment than to his determinative judgments of practical or theoretical reason. Philosophy, Deleuze and Guattari suggest, "is not inspired by truth. Rather, it is categories like Interesting, Remarkable or Important that determine success or failure" (*WP* 82).

DELEUZE'S TURN TOWARDS POLITICAL NORMATIVITY

Deleuze and Guattari's machinic social and political ontology has a normative dimension insofar as it presents a world of interconnected machinic assemblages, the innermost tendency of which is toward the "deterritorialization" of existing assemblages and their "reterritorialization" in new forms. Nevertheless, their ontology remains formal in relation to actual societies and forms of political organization. Disagreements with Marxism aside, all of their political theoretical innovations were carried out within a broadly Marxist perspective that envisaged the emergence of new and better forms of social and political life. However, at no point did they address the normative principles that inform their critical perspective on the present, much less the question how these might be articulated with those principles that are supposed to govern political life in late capitalist societies. Nowhere did they engage directly with the political norms embedded in liberal democratic political institutions and ways of life, such as the equal moral worth of individuals, freedom of conscience, the rule of law, fairness in the distribution of material goods produced by social cooperation, and so on. The principled differences between liberal democratic, totalitarian, and fascist states were mentioned only in passing in the course of their analysis of capitalism and present-day politics as a process of axiomatization of the social and economic field.

Read in the context of Western Marxism during the 1960s and 1970s, Deleuze and Guattari's failure to engage directly with the political values and normative concepts that are supposed to inform the basic institutions of modern liberal democracies is not surprising. Their political philosophy predates widespread understanding and acceptance of the ways in which Marx's critique of capitalist society is bound up with concepts of distributive justice, as it does the efforts to identify the relevant principles of justice that occurred under the impact of so-called analytic Marxism in the course of the 1980s. Since then, there have been numerous attempts to combine Marxist social theory with the normative principles informing varieties of left-liberal political theory.[18] While these developments had little impact in France, there was a similar rediscovery of ethical and political normativity in French political thought during this period. This was expressed, for example, in a renewed interest in human rights, subjectivity, justice, equality, and freedom in the work of contemporaries such as Foucault and Derrida. Guattari became involved in electoral politics during the latter part of the 1980s, standing as Green candidate in 1992 regional elections.

Deleuze's writings and comments in interviews from the 1980s mark a significant shift in his thinking about such normative issues. For example, he responds to the renewed interest in human rights during this period by insisting on the importance of jurisprudence as the means to create new rights. While he criticizes the manner in which human rights are represented as "eternal values" and "new forms of transcendence," he makes it clear that he is not opposed to rights as such but only to the idea that there is a definitive and ahistorical list of supposed universal rights. He argues that rights are not the creation of codes or declarations but of jurisprudence, where this implies working with the "singularities" of a particular situation (*N* 153). He returns to the question of rights and jurisprudence in his *Abécédaire* interviews with Claire Parnet, recorded in 1988–89, where he affirms the importance of jurisprudence understood as the invention of new rights, along with his own fascination for the law.[19] In his 1990 interview with Negri, he reaffirms the importance of jurisprudence as a source of law with reference to the question what rights should be established in relation to new forms of biotechnology (*N* 169). Deleuze's endorsement of rights and jurisprudence clearly commits him to the existence of a rule of law and the kind of constitutional state that this implies. In the case of societies that seek to govern themselves in this manner, the concept of a right implies that certain kinds of action on the part of all citizens will be protected by law and, conversely, the enforcement of limits to the degree to which citizens can interfere with the actions of others.

Deleuze's political writings from the 1980s onward provide evidence not only of his commitment to the rule of law but also to democracy. His 1979 "Open Letter to Negri's Judges" already adopted the speaking position of a democrat committed to certain principles in relation to due process and the rule of law (*TRM* [2007 edition] 169). His concern with democracy becomes more pronounced in *What is Philosophy?*, where there is a series of highly critical remarks about actually existing democracies. Far from dismissing the democratic ideal, these comments imply that other actualizations of the concept or "pure event" of democracy are possible. *What is Philosophy?* offers no more direct account of principles that are supposed to govern modern democratic societies than *A Thousand Plateaus*. In this sense, it offers no theory of public right. Many of the elements of

Deleuze and Guattari's prior commitment to Marxism remain in the diagnosis of the present outlined in *What is Philosophy?* For example, the analysis of the isomorphic but heterogeneous character of all states with regard to the global capitalist axiomatic is reproduced in identical terms. From this perspective, there are political differences between different kinds of state but also complicity with an increasingly global system of exploitation. They suggest that even the most democratic states are compromised by their role in the production of human misery alongside great wealth (*WP* 107; *N* 173). They maintain their commitment to the revolutionary-becoming of people rather than the traditional Marxist concept of revolution, even as they point out that the concept of revolution is itself a philosophical concept par excellence, one that expresses "absolute deterritorialization even to the point where this calls for a new earth, a new people" (*WP* 101).

What is Philosophy? argues for the inherently political vocation of philosophy. Philosophy is defined as the creation of concepts where these serve an overtly utopian function: "*We lack resistance to the present*. The creation of concepts in itself calls for a future form, for a new earth and people that do not yet exist" (*WP* 108). In the present, the task of philosophy is aligned with the struggle against capitalism. Deleuze and Guattari suggest that philosophical concepts are critical of the present to the extent that they "connect up with what is real here and now in the struggle against capitalism" (*WP* 100). At this point, the outline of a new concept appears in their political philosophy. *What is Philosophy?* contrasts the actual universality of the market with the virtual universality of a global democratic state and describes philosophy as it is envisaged here as reterritorialized on a new earth and a people to come quite unlike those found in actually existing democracies. Deleuze and Guattari's neo-Marxist support for becoming-revolutionary as the path towards a new earth and a people to come is combined with a call for resistance to existing forms of democracy in the name of a "becoming-democratic that is not to be confused with present constitutional states" (*WP* 113). In contrast to the formal normativity of their earlier work, the political normativity of Deleuze and Guattari's later philosophy is defined by this relation between becoming-revolutionary and becoming-democratic. On this basis, in full recognition of their differences from liberal normative political philosophy, it nevertheless becomes possible to compare their later work with that of a left-liberal political philosopher such as John Rawls.[20]

IMMANENT UTOPIANISM AND BECOMING-DEMOCRATIC

In *Justice as Fairness: A Restatement*, Rawls identifies four purposes served by his kind of reconstructive liberal normative political philosophy: First, it can help to resolve deeply disputed questions by searching for common philosophical and moral ground between the protagonists. Second, it can serve the task of orientation that seeks to identify reasonable and rational ends, both individual and collective, and to show "how those ends can cohere within a well-articulated conception of a just and reasonable society."[21] Third, it can address the task of reconciliation by showing the limits of what can be achieved within a democratic society characterized by the existence of "profound and irreconcilable differences in citizen's reasonable comprehensive religious and philosophical conceptions of the world."[22] Finally, it serves the "realistically utopian" task of "probing the limits of practicable political possibility." It asks what a just and democratic society would be like, given the "circumstances of justice" that obtain in the actual historical world in which we live, but also what it would be like "under reasonably favourable but still possible historical conditions."[23] Rawls notes that the limits of the practicable are not simply given by the actual, because we can and do change existing social and political institutions. However, he does not pursue any further the question of what determines the limits of the practicable or how we might ascertain what these limits are.[24]

Deleuze's conception of philosophy is concerned above all to challenge the limits of our present social world. *What is Philosophy?* presents a conception of the political vocation of philosophy with far more radical ambitions than those acknowledged in Rawls' realistic utopianism. Of the four functions of political philosophy identified by Rawls, Deleuze's philosophy does not address those of resolution, orientation, or reconciliation. It does address the utopian function, although not by setting out normative principles against which we might evaluate the justice or fairness of social institutions. The sense in which Deleuze and Guattari's political philosophy is utopian must be understood in terms of the connection between the absolute deterritorialization pursued in philosophy and the relative deterritorializations at work in its social milieu: "There is always a way in which absolute deterritorialization takes over from a relative deterritorialization in a given field" (WP 88). The utopian vocation of philosophy can be achieved only when the concepts that it invents engage with existing forms of relative deterritorialization. This conception of philosophy therefore implies an immanent utopianism in the sense that it does not simply posit an ideal future but rather aims to connect with processes of relative deterritorialization that are present in but stifled by the present milieu, extending these and taking them to extremes. To the extent that these processes or "lines of flight" encompass resistant political forces *along with the ideals or opinions that motivate them*, this immanent utopianism cannot avoid drawing on elements of present political normativity to suggest ways in which the injustice or intolerability of existing institutional forms of social life might be removed. In this manner, because the concept of democracy ties together a number of the values at the heart of contemporary political thought, elements of that concept may be used to counteractualize certain forms of resistance to the present in public political culture. These elements in turn provide the components of the concept of "becoming-democratic" which serves the utopian task of political philosophy by probing the limits of democratic processes in contemporary society.

Deleuze offers no detailed account of "becoming-democratic." However, it is possible to fill out the concept with elements of his prior work with Guattari as well as occasional comments in interviews. For example, in his interview with Negri, he suggests that new rights in relation to the situations created by modern biology should be proposed by "user-groups" rather than "supposedly well-qualified wise men" (N 170). In effect, he invokes the principle that decisions ought to be taken in consultation with those most affected by them. This is one of the founding principles of modern democratic governance, and Deleuze is not the only theorist to recommend its extension and application to new contexts. This suggests that the opening-up of decision-making procedures throughout society might constitute a vector of "becoming-democratic."

Minoritarian becomings provide another vector of "becoming-democratic." These are defined as the variety of ways in which individuals and groups fail to conform to the majoritarian standard (*ATP* 105–6). They have given rise to a succession of measures to extend the scope of the standard and thereby broaden the subject of democracy: first, in purely quantitative terms by extending the vote to women and other minorities; second, in qualitative terms by changing the nature of political institutions and procedures to enable these newly enfranchised members to participate on equal terms. Efforts to change the nature of public institutions in ways that both acknowledge and accommodate many kinds of difference are ongoing, for example in relation to sexual preference and physical and mental abilities, as well as cultural and religious backgrounds. Deleuze and Guattari's support for minoritarian becomings affirms the importance of efforts to enlarge the character of the majority. By their nature, processes of minoritarian becoming will always exceed or escape from the confines of any given majority. Nevertheless, they embody the potential to transform the affects, beliefs, and political sensibilities of a population in ways that can lead to the advent of a new people. To the extent that a people is constituted as a political community, the transformations it undergoes will affect its conceptions of what is fair and just. In turn, these will affect the distribution of rights and duties as well as the presence of minority citizens in the public institutions and political functions of the society.

A third vector of "becoming-democratic" involves efforts to achieve a more just distribution of material social goods. Deleuze is often critical of the way that modern democratic states fail to live up to this aspect of their egalitarian promise (*WP* 106–7; *N* 172). However, his suggestion that democratic states are morally and politically compromised by their role in the perpetuation of this form of injustice implicitly raises the normative question: What principles of distribution should apply in a just democratic society? Should we advocate radically egalitarian principles that would treat any undeserved inequality of condition as unjust, or should we be satisfied with Rawls' difference principle, according to which social and economic inequalities are allowed but only when they are attached to positions open to all and when they are "to the greatest benefit of the least advantaged members of society"?[25] Should the principles of distributive justice apply globally or only within the borders of particular democratic states? Deleuze does not provide us with the means to answer these normative questions but they are inevitably raised by his criticisms of existing states of affairs.

CONCLUSION

Deleuzian philosophy as it is presented in *What is Philosophy?* is clearly political in the sense that it has an inherently political vocation. The creation of concepts serves the larger project of bringing about new earths and new peoples. Deleuze and Guattari propose a novel kind of utopian political thought that is neither Marxist nor liberal. They rely upon a political ontology of assemblages rather than individual subjects of interest and right. Their goal is the transformation of existing political norms and institutions rather than the reconstruction of the normative principles implicit in existing liberal democratic institutions into a coherent political theory. Despite the substantive differences that separate their approach from that of liberal normative political philosophy, there is at least a degree of convergence between them. Deleuze and Guattari's collaborative work moves from a formal to a more substantive engagement with the explicitly political concepts and norms that make up the public political culture of liberal democratic states. The concept of a "becoming-democratic" at the heart of their later political philosophy points to the role of elements of existing concepts of democracy in historical struggles to implement or expand democratic government.

NOTES

1   See, for example, Paul Patton, *Deleuze and the Political* (London and New York: Routledge, 2000); Ian Buchanan and Nicholas Thoburn (eds.), *Deleuze and Politics* (Edinburgh University Press, 2008); Jeremy Gilbert (ed.), in the special edition "Deleuzian Politics?," *New Formations*, 68 (2010).

2   François Dosse, *Gilles Deleuze and Félix Guattari: Intersecting Lives*, trans. Deborah Glassman (New York: Columbia University Press, 2010), p. 21.

3   Slavoj Žižek, *Organs without Bodies: Deleuze and Consequences* (New York and London: Routledge, 2004), p. 20.

4   Alain Badiou, "Existe-t-il quelque chose comme un politique deleuzienne?," *Cités*, 40 (*Deleuze Politique*), 2009, 15–20 (talk given in English at "Immanent Choreographies: Deleuze and Neo-Aesthetics," Tate Modern Public Programme, London, September 21–22, 2001).

5 Philippe Mengue also points out the absence of any place for specific-ally political thought in the tripartite division of thought described in *What is Philosophy?* See Mengue, *Deleuze et la question de la démocratie* (Paris: L'Harmattan, 2003), p. 52. See also Nicholas Thoburn, *Deleuze, Marx and Politics* (London and New York: Routledge, 2003), pp. 5–6.

6 On Deleuze's relation to history, see Jay Lampert, *Deleuze and Guattari's Philosophy of History* (London and New York: Continuum, 2009); Jeffrey Bell and Claire Colebrook (eds.), *Deleuze and History* (Edinburgh University Press, 2009); and Craig Lundy, *History and Becoming: Deleuze's Philosophy of Creativity* (Edinburgh University Press, 2012).

7 Peter Hallward, *Out of This World: Deleuze and the Philosophy of Creation* (London and New York: Verso, 2006), pp. 136–39. Hallward's book has been critically reviewed by a number of Deleuze scholars: see *inter alia* Gregory J. Seigworth, "Little Affect: Hallward's Deleuze," *Culture Machine* (Reviews 2007), www.culturemachine. net/index.php/cm/article/view/166/147; John Protevi, "Review of Peter Hallward," *Notre Dame Philosophical Reviews* (2007), http://ndpr. nd.edu/news/23058-out-of-this-world-deleuze-and-the-philosophy-of-creation/; and Erinn C. Gilson, "Review of Hallward, *Out of this world: Deleuze's Philosophy of Creation,*" *Continental Philosophy Review*, 42 (2009), 429–34.

8 Jeremy Gilbert, "Deleuzian Politics? A Survey and Some Suggestions," *New Formations*, 68 (2010), 10–33, p. 10.

9 *Ibid.*

10 The English text of *Negotiations* uses "law" here to translate "*droit,*" thereby obscuring a contrast in the original between "*loi*" and "*droit.*" For this and for other reasons, it is more appropriate to translate "*droit*" here as "right": see Paul Patton, "Immanence, Transcendence and the Creation of Rights," in Laurent de Sutter and Kyle McGee (eds.), *Deleuze and Law* (Edinburgh University Press, 2012).

11 Dosse, *Gilles Deleuze and Félix Guattari*, pp. 98, 109.

12 *Ibid.*, p. 177.

13 There is extensive discussion of Deleuze's relation to Marxism in the secondary literature on his and Guattari's work. See in particular Eugene Holland, *Deleuze and Guattari's "Anti-Oedipus": Introduction to Schizoanalysis* (London and New York: Routledge, 1999); Jason Read, *The Micro-Politics of Capital* (Albany, NY: SUNY Press, 2003); Thoburn, *Deleuze, Marx and Politics*; Isabelle Garo, "Deleuze, Marx and Revolution: What It Means to 'Remain Marxist',*"* in J. Bidet and S. Kouvelakis (eds.), *Critical Companion to Contemporary Marxism* (Leiden and Boston: Brill, 2007), pp. 605–24; the essays in *Deleuze*

Studies, 3 (2009), Issue Supplement: *Deleuze and Marx*, ed. Jain Dhruv; and Simon Choat, "Becoming Revolutionary: Marx through Deleuze," in *Marx through Postructuralism* (London and New York: Continuum, 2010).

14   In the "Intellectuals and Power" interview with Foucault, Deleuze suggests that it was Foucault who taught the intellectuals of his generation the indignity of speaking for others: "We laughed at representation, saying it was over, but we didn't follow this 'theoretical' conversion through – namely theory demanded that those involved finally have their say from a practical standpoint" (*DI* 208). This interview first appeared in the Deleuze issue of *L'Arc* (Paris, 1971). Another translation appears in Michel Foucault, *Language, Counter-Memory, Practice: Selected Essays and Interviews*, ed. Donald F. Bouchard, trans. Donald F. Bouchard and Sherry Simon (Ithaca, NY: Cornell University Press, 1977), pp. 205–17.

15   This is by no mean an exhaustive list of Deleuzian concepts which might be supposed relevant to political philosophy. Other concepts that have been taken up in this connection include Deleuze's concepts of "the missing people," the "event," "dramatization," and "nomadology." In relation to these concepts, see Alain Beaulieu, "Gilles Deleuze's Politics: From Marxism to the Missing People," in Constantin V. Boundas (ed.), *Gilles Deleuze: The Intensive Reduction* (London and New York: Continuum, 2009), pp. 204–17; Tom Lundborg, *Politics of the Event: Time, Movement, Becoming* (London and New York: Routledge, 2011); Iain Mackenzie and Robert Porter, *Dramatizing the Political: Deleuze and Guattari* (Basingstoke: Palgrave Macmillan, 2011); Eugene Holland, *Nomad Citizenship: Free-Market Communism and the Slow-Motion General Strike* (Minneapolis and London: University of Minnesota Press, 2011).

16   "In *Anti-Oedipus* ... every society, every form of social production is nothing but a specific organisation and articulation of desiring-production, assigning it specific goals and aims." Jason Read, "Fetish is Always Actual, Revolution is Always Virtual," *Deleuze Studies*, 3 (2009), Issue Supplement: *Deleuze and Marx*, ed. Jain Dhruv, 78–101, pp. 98–99.

17   Patton, *Deleuze and the Political*, pp. 9, 136.

18   For an example of one such attempt, see Rodney Peffer, *Marxism, Morality, and Social Justice* (Princeton University Press, 1990). For more general discussions of so-called "analytic Marxism," see G. A. Cohen, *Karl Marx's Theory of History* (Oxford University Press, 2000); Will Kymlicka, *Contemporary Political Philosophy* (Oxford University

Press, 2002), pp. 166–207; and Andrew Levine, *A Future for Marxism?* (London: Pluto Press 2003).

19 See *ABC*, *G comme Gauche*. On Deleuze's understanding of the invention of rights, see Patton, "Immanence, Transcendence and the Creation of Rights."

20 See Paul Patton, "Utopian Political Philosophy: Deleuze and Rawls," *Deleuze Studies*, 1:1 (2007), 41–59, *Deleuzian Concepts: Philosophy, Colonization, Politics* (Stanford University Press, 2010), pp. 185–210.

21 John Rawls, *Justice as Fairness: A Restatement* (Cambridge, MA: Harvard University Press, 2001), p. 3.

22 *Ibid.*

23 *Ibid.*, p. 4.

24 *Ibid.*, p. 5.

25 John Rawls, *Political Liberalism: Expanded Edition* (New York: Columbia University Press, 2005), p. 6.

10 Deleuze, mathematics, and realist ontology

REALISM IN HISTORY

Unlike most of his contemporaries, Deleuze was a realist philosopher. But his realist stance was deeply innovative and constituted a sharp break with the brand of realism that dominated Western thought for 2,500 years, the one created by Aristotle. As is well known, the Greek philosopher's world was populated by three categories of entities: *genus, species*, and *individual*. Entities belonging to the first two categories subsisted essentially, those belonging to the third one subsisted only accidentally.[1] The genus could be, for example, Animal, the species Human, and the individual this or that particular person characterized by contingent properties: being white, being musical, being just. A genus was linked to its various species (Horse, Human) by a series of logically necessary subdivisions. The genus Animal, for example, could be subdivided into two-footed and many-footed types; then subdivided into differences in extremities: hooves, as in horses, or feet, as in humans. When we reached a point at which any further distinctions were accidental, like a foot missing a toe, we arrived at the level of the species, the lowest ontological level at which we could speak of an essence or of the very nature of a thing.

Possession of these essential traits is what guaranteed the mind-independent identity of things in Aristotelian realism. It follows that any new brand of realism, if it is to be truly novel, must replace the categories of genus and species with something that does not imply an ontological commitment to transcendent entities (essences). This task is easier for species than for genera. The transcendent nature of species can be eliminated simply by transforming them into historical entities, like Darwin did. In evolutionary theory a biological

220

species is as singular, as unique, and as historically contingent as an individual organism: a species is born when its gene pool is closed to the flow of genetic materials from other reproductive communities – that is, it is born through *reproductive isolation* – and its dies through *extinction*. In other words, species like organisms are "subject to corruption and decay," as Aristotle would say.[2] And their defining properties are not logically necessary. Reproductive isolation is a contingent achievement that varies by degree, so nothing guarantees that the identity of a biological species will endure forever. Similarly, driving a species to extinction is like killing an individual organism: we destroy a unique historical creation that can never return again.

Thus, getting rid of essences at the level of species is simply a matter of introducing history (evolutionary history in this case) into a realist ontology. But essences at the genus level are an entirely different matter. What we need here is a means to conceptualize a "topological animal," an abstract animal that can become a human or a horse through a series of embryological operations: foldings, stretchings, invaginations, cellular migrations. This second replacement is the one that involves mathematics. More specifically, if species must be conceived as *individual singularities*, genera must be replaced by a topological diagram structured by *universal singularities*.[3] This can only be achieved by going beyond deductive logic, the source of the concepts of the general and the specific, and into mathematics: the differential calculus, group theory, non-metric geometry. To understand how mathematics must replace logic in a non-transcendent form of realism we must first give a simple description of how differential equations are used in science, because what we want to explore is not the ontology of mathematics itself (Platonist, Constructivist) but the ontological issues raised by the use of mathematics to model the real world.

THE ROLE OF MATHEMATICS

To create a mathematical model of an actual physical system one must first specify the relevant ways in which the system is free to change, that is, we must discover its "degrees of freedom." Because as the degrees of freedom of a system change its overall state changes, a model of the system must capture the different possible states in which it can exist. As the mathematician Henri Poincaré showed a century ago, this set of states may be represented as a *space of possibilities* with as many dimensions as the system has degrees of freedom. This space is referred to as "state space," the space of all possible states in which the system being modeled can exist. In this space each point represents one possible state for a physical system, the state it has at a given instant of time. As the states of a physical system change with time, that is, as the system goes through a temporal sequence of states, its representation in state space becomes a continuous sequence of points: a curve or a trajectory.[4] A set of different trajectories captures several possible histories for the system. Each point in this space, each possible state, can have different probabilities of existing. A space in which all the points are equally probable is a space without any structure, and it represents a physical system in which states change in a completely random way, the trajectories wandering around state space without settling down.

By the eighteenth century, however, mathematicians like Leonard Euler knew that the space of possible solutions for differential equations did have structure. In particular, he showed that some of the points that constituted this space were special or remarkable in that the states they represented were much more likely to occur than any other possible state. This implies that these special or singular points are like the long-term tendencies of a system, the states that would be realized if we just waited long enough. It does not matter where they begin, all the possible histories will tend to end at a singular point. Moreover, these singularities are universal in the sense that they can be shared by entirely different physical systems: gravitational, mechanical, optical, electrostatic. Indeed, the unification of all branches of Classical Mechanics in the nineteenth century was made possible by this universality. To return to our original example, the space of all possible animals must be conceived as structured by universal singularities determining the overall tendencies shaping evolutionary history. But replacing the genus Animal by such a topological diagram faces a major obstacle: unlike the spaces of classical physics we do not know the structure of the possibility spaces associated with animals. Nevertheless, many of the concepts that we would need to understand the "topological animal" can be developed starting with the simpler cases, the only ones explicitly discussed by Deleuze.

Deleuze is not, in fact, the only contemporary philosopher that has displayed an interest in state space and the universal singularities that structure it. In the analytical approach to philosophy of science there has recently been a move away from logic and towards the mathematics actually used by scientists, and it will prove useful to review these recent developments to frame our discussion of Deleuze's views in comparative terms. For many analytical philosophers abandoning the categories of the general and the particular is a difficult step because many of them were trained to believe that *all of mathematics had been reduced to logic* in the late nineteenth century: first the differential calculus was reduced to arithmetic – the concept of infinitesimals was replaced by the notion of limit and the latter reduced to that of number – and later on arithmetic was reduced to set theory. For those philosophers who believed that this reduction was in fact achieved, mathematics disappeared and deductive logic became the only formal discipline that needed to be mastered. It is not surprising, therefore, that realist analytical philosophers tend to speak like Aristotle, defining the identity of things by the necessary and sufficient conditions to belong to a general category. In other words, defining identity by the possession of an essence.

Moreover, those who accept the reduction of mathematics to logic take an *axiomatic approach* to scientific theories: the content of a theory is modeled by a set of axioms, or self-evident truths, and by all the theorems that may be derived from those axioms using deductive logic. This approach stresses the role of both logic and language. But the new school of thought, the *semantic approach*, views axiomatics as a false model. These other philosophers argue that it is through the use of tools like the differential calculus that scientists create models of physical phenomena, and it is these models, not any logical reconstruction of them, that should be the subject of philosophy of science. Among the leaders of this movement is Bas Van Fraassen, who has stated his position this way:

The semantic view of theories makes language largely irrelevant to the subject. Of course, to present a theory, we must present it in and by language. That is a trivial point ... In addition, both because of our own history – the history of philosophy of science which became intensely language-oriented during the first half of [the last] century – and because of its intrinsic importance, we cannot ignore the language of science. But in a discussion of the structure of theories it can largely be ignored.[5]

The reason for leaving language and logic behind and bringing back the differential calculus – and the geometric approach to its study, that is, state space diagrams – is that it is only by analyzing actual models that we can explore the relation between theories and the laboratory phenomena they are designed to explain. In other words, we want to know why these models actually work, why they manage to capture the regularities in the behavior of real systems, and the answer to these questions is not given by the logical structure of an axiomatic. Since it is their success in practice that makes mathematical models interesting for a realist ontology let's give a simple description of how models are matched to phenomena. Let's assume that we have a laboratory where we can manipulate real physical phenomena, that is, where we can restrict their degrees of freedom (by screening out other factors) and where we can place them in a given initial state and then let them run spontaneously through a sequence of states. Let's also assume that we can measure with some precision the values of the degrees of freedom (say, temperature, pressure, and volume) at each of those states. After several trials we generate data about the phenomenon starting it at different initial states. The data will consist, basically, of sequences of numbers giving the values of temperature, pressure, and volume that the phenomenon takes as it evolves from different initial conditions. We can then plot these number series on a piece of paper, turning them into a curve or trajectory.

We then run our mathematical model, giving it the same values for initial conditions as our laboratory runs, and generate a set of state space trajectories. Finally, we compare the two sets of curves. If the mathematical and experimental trajectories display geometrical similarity this will be evidence that the model actually works. As one analytical philosopher puts it:

[W]e can say that a dynamical theory is approximately true just if the modeling geometric structure approximates (in suitable respects) to the structure to be modeled: a basic case is where trajectories in the model closely *track trajectories* encoding physically real behaviors (or, at least, track them for long enough).[6]

It is only when mathematical models have the capacity to track the results of laboratory experiments that there is a philosophical justification to perform an ontological analysis of state space. This analysis is needed because the tracking ability of models must be given an explanation, unless we are prepared to accept it as a brute fact, or worse yet, as an unexplainable miracle.

MATHEMATICAL MODELS AND ONTOLOGICAL COMMITMENTS

Starting with different ontological commitments, however, we may arrive at very different explanations of the success of models. Some philosophers, for example, believe in the autonomous existence of objects of direct experience (pets, automobiles, buildings) but assume that entities like oxygen, electrons, or causal relations are mere theoretical constructs. Ontological commitments of this sort are associated with positivism and empiricism, though different philosophers draw the line between what is directly observable and what is not at different places. Van Fraassen, for instance, seems to believe that objects perceived through telescopes, but not microscopes, count as directly experienced.[7] Realist philosophers, on the other hand, reject the distinction between the observable and the unobservable, but they too differ on what they believe are the contents of the world. Deleuze is a realist philosopher, but one determined to populate an autonomous reality exclusively with immanent entities, and to exorcise from it any transcendent ones, like Aristotelian essences. Let's now discuss how these different ontological commitments lead to different assessments of the components of state space. The first candidates for ontological evaluation are the trajectories themselves. These, as I said, represent possible histories (possible temporal sequences of states). As is well known, empiricists are skeptical about possible entities. Quine, in particular, is fond of ridiculing them:

Take, for instance, the possible fat man in the doorway; and again, the possible bald man in the doorway. Are they the same possible man, or two possible men? How do we decide? How many possible men there are in that doorway? Are there more possible thin ones than fat ones? How many of them are alike? Or would their being alike make them one?[8]

What Quine is arguing here is that we do not possess the means to *individuate* possible entities, that is, to identify them in the midst of all the possible variations. The traditional approach to possible worlds, and the target of Quine's sarcasm, is *modal logic*. This branch of logic is concerned with the analysis of counterfactual sentences like "If J.F.K. had not been assassinated the Vietnam War would have ended sooner." In the case of counterfactuals we may agree with Quine that there is not enough structure in a *linguistically* specified possible world to know whether we are dealing with one or several entities as we modify the details. But as realist philosophers like Ronald Giere have argued, while Quine's skeptical remarks are valid for modal logic, the extra structure that state space possesses can overcome these limitations:

As Quine delights in pointing out, it is often difficult to individuate possibilities ... [But] many models in which the system laws are expressed as differential equations provide an unambiguous criterion to individuate the possible histories of the model. They are the trajectories in state space corresponding to all possible initial conditions. Threatened ambiguities in the set of possible initial conditions can be eliminated by explicitly restricting the set in the definition of the theoretical model.[9]

The extra structure that state space brings to the determination of possible histories, however, is not enough to satisfy an empiricist. Van Fraassen, for example, can still deny the need to be ontologically committed to possible histories given that for him the goal of science is not to capture unobservable traits of reality but merely to achieve *empirical adequacy*, that is, to increase our ability to make predictions and to control outcomes in the laboratory. For this limited purpose all that matters is that we generate a single trajectory for a given initial condition and match it to a series of measurements of *actual states* obtained in the laboratory. The rest of the population of trajectories is merely a useful fiction. Giere refers to this ontological stance towards modalities as "actualism."[10] But actualism misses the fact that the population of possible trajectories displays regularities that play a role in shaping any one particular actual history. In the terms used above the space of possibilities has structure, and this structure is not displayed by any one single trajectory. Understanding a system, argues Giere, is not just knowing how it actually behaves in this or that specific situation, but knowing *how it would behave* in conditions that may not in fact occur. Thus, an ontological assessment of the structure of possibility spaces is what is needed.

The significance of Deleuze's realist approach is precisely that it supplies us with such an assessment. Deleuze is not an actualist but he is not a realist about traditional modalities, either. He would not agree, for example, that the possibilities that constitute the points of state space exist independently of our minds. It is only the structure of possibility spaces that demands a realist commitment. We must therefore introduce a new form of physical modality, *virtuality*, to account for both the regularities in the models and the immanent patterns of becoming in nature. Something virtual is *something that is real but not actual.*[11] Thus Deleuze would disagree with Van Fraassen in being committed only to actual entities but also with Giere's commitments to possible ones. Only the virtual structure of state space needs to be considered mind-independent. A rigorous formal analysis of this structure involves considering a different component of state space: *the velocity vector field.*

When the study of the behavior of differential equations was given a geometric form, the abstract spaces used were differential manifolds, not metric Euclidean spaces. While a metric space is a set of points defined by global coordinates, in a differential manifold the component points are defined using only local information: the instantaneous rate of change of curvature at a point. To put this differently, while the points in a metric space are defined by a set X, Y, and Z values, presupposing a set of Cartesian coordinates and a transcendent global space in which the space being studied is inscribed, a differential manifold is *a field of rapidities and slownesses*, the rapidity or slowness with which curvature changes at each point. In a differential manifold, in fact, every point is not only a speed but a velocity, since a direction may be assigned to it. Because a velocity can be represented by a vector, state spaces possess in addition to points (representing possible states) a field of velocity vectors. The importance of this is that the distribution of universal singularities that constitutes the structure of state space is not given by the trajectories (or integral curves) but by the vector field itself. More precisely, while the nature of a singularity must be established through the use of nearby trajectories – whether a point singularity is a focus or a node, for example, must be determined by observing how the integral curves in its vicinity approach it, spirally or on a straight line – the *existence and distribution* of the singularities does not need any trajectories to be established. As Deleuze writes:

Already Leibniz had shown that the calculus ... expressed problems which could not hitherto be solved or, indeed, even posed ... One thinks in particular of the role of the regular and the singular points which enter into the complete determination of the species of a curve. No doubt the specification of the singular points (for example, dips, nodes, focal points, centers) is undertaken by means of the form of integral curves, which refers back to the solutions of the differential equations. There is nevertheless a complete determination with respect to the existence and distribution of these points which depends upon a completely different instance, namely, the field of vectors defined by the equation itself ... Moreover, if the specification of the points already shows the necessary immanence of the problem in the solution, its involvement in the solution which covers it, along with the existence and distribution of points, testifies to the transcendence of the problem and its directive role in relation to the organization of the solutions themselves. (DR 177)

PROBLEMS AND THE STRUCTURE OF POSSIBILITY SPACES

For Deleuze the mathematical distinction between a vector field and its singularities, on the one hand, and the trajectories or curves, on the other, becomes the philosophical distinction between *the defining conditions of a problem* and *its many possible solutions*. This must be understood both epistemologically and ontologically. In the first sense an epistemological problem is posed by *giving a distribution of the significant and the insignificant*, that is, by discovering the important ways in which a phenomenon is free to change and eliminating all the trivial ways. The problem can then be given a spatial form (by turning the degrees of freedom into the dimensions of a non-metric space) and its structure determined via the vector field. Finally, we can find numerical solutions to the equations and generate trajectories, each representing a series of states that we can compare with a series of actual states of a laboratory phenomenon. Clearly, the crucial moment in this epistemological sequence is the first step: discovering what makes a difference and what does not make a difference in the behavior of a phenomenon. The solutions

we obtain at the end are only as good as the problem they are supposed to solve: if we included trivial degrees of freedom in the original specification of the problem its solutions may also be trivial
or misleading. Moreover, the concrete distribution of the significant
and the insignificant that defines the problem retains its virtual
existence even as we solve it, since it guides the generation of all
individual solutions.

And similarly for the laboratory phenomena that are the target
of the mathematical model. A state space structured by a single
singularity defining an optimum value (a minimum of energy, for
example) captures a real *optimization problem* to which a whole
variety of actual entities (soap bubbles, crystals, light rays) are concrete solutions. But the optimization problem subsists once it is
given a physical solution, ready to be posed again the next time a
flat piece of soap film must wrap itself into a sphere, or a set of
molecules must conform itself to the geometrical shape of a crystal. To return to our original example, the structured space of all
possible animals with which we must replace the genus Animal
must be thought as an objective ontological problem, a problem to
which every species and organism are concrete adaptive solutions.
As Deleuze writes: "An organism is nothing but the solution to a
problem, as are each of its differentiated organs, such as the eye
which solves a light problem" (*DR* 211).

This implies that problems are not only independent of their
solutions, they have a genetic relationship with them: *a problem
engenders its own solutions as its conditions become progressively
better specified*. Deleuze's discussion of this point uses a different
branch of mathematics, group theory, and its application to the solutions of algebraic, not differential, equations, so we first need to give
the historical background of this other field. There are two kinds
of solutions to equations, numerical and analytical. A numerical
solution is given by numbers that, when used to replace an equation's unknowns, make the equation come out true. For example, an
algebraic equation like $x^2 + 2x - 8 = 0$ has as its numerical solution
$x = 2$. An analytical or exact solution, on the other hand, does not
yield any specific value or set of values but rather the global pattern
of all values, a pattern expressed by another equation or formula.
Or in the terms used before, an analytical solution gives us the

structure of the space of all possible solutions. The above example, which may be rewritten without numerical constants as:

$$ax^2 + bx + c = 0$$

has the analytic solution:

$$x = \frac{-b \pm \sqrt{b^2 - 4ac}}{2a},$$

By the sixteenth century mathematicians knew the exact solutions to algebraic equations where the unknown variable was raised up to the fourth power (that is, those including x^2, x^3, and x^4). But then a crisis ensued. Equations raised to the fifth power refused to yield to the previously successful method. The breakthrough came two centuries later when it was noticed that there was a pattern to the solutions of the first four cases, a pattern that might hold the key to understanding the recalcitrance of the fifth, known as *the quintic*. The mathematicians Niels Abel and Évariste Galois found a way to approach the study of this pattern using resources that today we recognize as belonging to group theory.[12] The term "group" refers to a set of mathematical entities (numbers, operations on numbers) and a rule of combination for those entities. The set must possess closure, which means that when we use the rule to combine any two entities in the set, the result is also an entity in the set. For our purposes here the most important type of entities are *transformations*, and the rule a consecutive application of those transformations. For example, the set consisting of rotations by 90 degrees (that is a set containing rotations by 90, 180, 270, and 360 degrees) forms a group, since any two consecutive rotations produce a rotation also in the group. A group, in turn, can be used to determine the properties of a mathematical entity that remain *invariant* under transformations and that are therefore its most significant properties. A cube, for example, remains unaltered (as far as its optical behavior is concerned) under the above group of rotations, so the group captures an important aspect of its identity.

To understand how a group of transformations can be used to establish the conditions of a problem, that is, to generate a distribution of the significant and the insignificant, let's give a concrete example: the use of groups of transformations to study the invariants of physical laws. For the laws of classical physics, the group includes displacements in space and time, as well as rotations and other transformations. Let's imagine a physical phenomenon that can be reliably produced in a laboratory. If we displace it in space – by reproducing the phenomenon in another, far away laboratory – we will leave all its properties invariant. Similarly, if we simply change the time at which we begin an experiment, we can expect this time displacement to be irrelevant as far as the regularity of the phenomenon is concerned. It is only the difference in time between the first and final states of the experiment that matters, not the absolute time at which the first state occurs. Thus, via transformations applied to the equations expressing laws we can discover those types of change to which *the law is indifferent*, that is, the type of changes that do not make a difference to it, allowing us to correctly conclude that using absolute time or absolute position as inputs to the equation expressing a law is irrelevant.

In a similar way, Galois used certain transformations (*substitutions* or *permutations* of an equation's solutions) that, as a group, revealed the invariances in the relations between solutions. More specifically, when a permutation of one solution by another left the equation valid, the two solutions became *indistinguishable* as far as their validity was concerned. The group of an equation is crucial to its solvability, because it expresses the degree of indistinguishability of the solutions.[13] Or as Deleuze would put it, the group reveals not what we know about the solutions, but *the objectivity of what we do not know about them*, that is, the objectivity of the problem itself (*DR* 162). And he goes on to argue that, besides demonstrating the autonomy of problems from solutions, the group-theoretic approach shows that the solutions to the equation are produced as the original group gives rise to subgroups that successively limit the substitutions that leave relations invariant. That is, the problem gives birth to its solutions as its own conditions become progressively better defined. As he writes:

We cannot suppose that, from a technical point of view, differential calculus is the only mathematical expression of problems as such … More recently other procedures have fulfilled this role better. Recall the circle in which the theory of problems was caught: a problem is solvable only to the extent that it is "true" but we always tend to define the truth of a problem by its solvability … The mathematician Abel was perhaps the first to break this circle: he elaborated a whole method according to which solvability must follow from the form of a problem. Instead of seeking to find out by trial and error whether a given equation is solvable in general we must determine the conditions of the problem which progressively specify the fields of solvability in such a way that the statement contains the seed of the solution. This is a radical reversal of the problem–solution relation, a more considerable revolution than the Copernican ... The same judgement is confirmed in relation to the work of Galois: starting from a basic "field" (R), successive adjunctions to this field (R', R'', R''' ...) allow a progressively more precise distinction between the roots of an equation by the progressive limitation of possible substitutions. There is thus a succession of "partial resolvents" or an "embedding of groups," which make the solutions follow from the very conditions of the problem. (DR 179–80)

PROBLEMS AND ACTUALIZATION OF THE VIRTUAL

To link this genetic concept of problems to a realist ontology we need to combine the resources of group theory with those of dynamical systems theory, as the geometrical approach to the study of differential equations is known. In state space the relevant transformations are mathematical events, known as *bifurcations*, that can change one distribution of universal singularities into another. These mathematical events result from operations applied to the vector field of a state space: a small vector field is added to the main one to perturb it, and when the perturbation reaches a critical threshold, a bifurcation results.[14] In some cases it is only the number of singularities that changes, but in other cases their type may also be transformed. So far we have considered only point singularities, defining the tendency of a physical system to reach a steady-state. But there are also line singularities, shaped into a loop, that define tendencies to oscillate in a stable way. These are called "periodic attractors" or "limit cycles." More recently a third variety of universal singularity has been found, the result of repeatedly stretching and folding a closed loop. These are referred to as chaotic or strange attractors. The transformations that convert one of these types of singularity into another are also well known: the *Hopf bifurcation* changes a point singularity into a periodic one, and the *Feigenbaum bifurcation* changes a periodic singularity into a chaotic one. A sequence of bifurcations has a similar group theoretic structure as the series of permutations used by Galois to generate the solutions to the quintic equation: as the bifurcations transform one singularity (or set of singularities) into another, all the solutions to the problem posed by the differential equations progressively unfold: steady-state solutions, periodic solutions, chaotic solutions.

These regular sequences can be found not only in mathematical models but also in objective phenomena, such as the phenomena studied by fluid mechanics. Moving fluids are presented with a problem as their speed increases, and they solve this problem by adopting a variety of regimes of flow adapted to each range of speeds. At a slow speed the solution to the problem is simple: stick to steady-state or uniform flow. But after a critical threshold of speed that solution becomes insufficient and the moving fluid must switch to a convective or wavy flow. Finally, after crossing yet another critical threshold, the faster speeds present the flow with a problem that it cannot solve by moving rhythmically and it is forced to become turbulent, distributing its energy into a structure of vortices within vortices.[15] As these different manners of moving unfold one after another, they display all the solutions to the problem of flow. Moreover, the isomorphism between the behavior of the mathematical model and the fluid mechanical phenomena shows that they may be considered as *different actual solutions to the same virtual problem*. In other words, to explain the success of a mathematical model all we need to do is to consider it an actualization of the same virtual problem that the phenomenon being modeled solves. There is no correspondence between models and reality but a relation of *co-actualization*.[16]

The fact that Deleuze compared the achievements of Abel and Galois to the revolutionary impact of astronomy's switch to heliocentrism clearly shows that he thought these ideas represented a radical departure from the past. But, as he adds elsewhere, the gains from group theory can only be realized philosophically if we blend its insights with those of non-metric geometries to create a theory of problems:

Solvability must depend upon an internal characteristic: it must be determined by the conditions of the problem, engendered in and by the problem along with the real solutions. Without this reversal, the famous Copernican revolution amounts to nothing. Moreover, there is no revolution so long as we remain tied to Euclidean geometry: we must move to a geometry of sufficient reason, a Riemannian-like differential geometry *which tends to give rise to discontinuity on the basis of continuity*, or to ground solutions in the conditions of the problem. (*DR* 162)

When I described the nature of state space above I remarked that, unlike the points that compose a metric space, defined by their relation to a set of global coordinates, a point of state space is individuated by the instantaneous rate of change of curvature at that point. This entirely new way of conceptualizing space was the achievement of two great nineteenth-century mathematicians, Carl Friedrich Gauss and Bernhard Riemann. Another giant of nineteenth-century mathematics, Felix Klein, gave us the way to link this achievement with the resources of group theory. Klein realized that the different geometries known to him (Euclidean geometry, affine geometry, projective geometry) could be associated with groups of transformations that left their basic features invariant. Thus, the space of Euclidean geometry remains invariant by a group containing all displacements, rotations, and mirror-imagings, that is, transformations that leave rigid features like lengths, areas, and volumes unchanged. In projective geometry, on the other hand, lengths and other rigid features do not remain unchanged – they are distorted or changed in size depending on the type of projection used – but other more abstract features do remain invariant. As one historian of mathematics puts it:

> [I]t was evident from the work of Von Staudt that projective geometry is logically prior to Euclidian geometry because it deals with qualitative and descriptive properties that enter into the very formation of geometrical figures and does not use the measures of line segments and angles. This fact suggested that Euclidian geometry might be some specialization of projective geometry. With the non-Euclidean [metric] geometries now at hand the possibility arose that those ... might also be specializations of projective geometry.[17]

When differential geometry and topology were added to the growing list of non-metric geometries Klein's followers specified their transformation groups and realized that they were more abstract than, and hence logically prior to, projective geometry. A mathematical entity possessing invariant properties under a larger group of transformations is said to have more symmetry than one with a smaller group. The achievement of Klein and his followers was to realize that all the geometries were related to one another by a *symmetry-breaking cascade*: starting with the least "metric" of all geometries, topology, we can break its symmetry (by reducing the number of transformations in its group) and generate differential geometry. Similarly, differential geometry becomes projective geometry as it loses symmetry, projective becomes affine, and affine becomes Euclidean. Although mathematicians do not draw ontological conclusions from this fact, it is not too difficult to discern in this cascade the same genetic relation that Deleuze establishes between problems and solutions: through a series of broken symmetries topology gives rise to Euclidean geometry, or to phrase it like Deleuze, *continuous spaces give birth to discontinuous ones.*

Moreover, the sequence of geometries also illustrates another Deleuzian concept: *progressive differentiation.* While in topology all closed figures (a circle, an ellipse, a square, a triangle) are identical, in projective geometry only those that are conic sections (circles, ellipses, parabolas) are identical. In affine geometry these figures become different from each other, but the same figure in different sizes is still the same. And finally, in Euclidean geometry all figures of different sizes are distinct from one another.[18] In other words, the more continuous and flexible spaces have the least degree of differentiation (the smallest number of distinct figures), while the most discontinuous and rigid have the largest number of differentiated figures. It is this progressive differentiation that links epistemological and ontological problems: solutions in both mathematics and laboratory phenomena are engendered as the problem itself progressively differentiates.

Although Deleuze never mentions the work of Felix Klein, it seems clear that Klein supplies precisely what Deleuze is asking for when he says that there is no revolution in the theory of problems unless we link group-theoretic ideas and non-metric spaces. Moreover, the progressive differentiation of the geometries that transforms unsegmented spaces into fully segmented ones supplies us with a powerful image to contrast the Deleuzian and Aristotelian approaches to realist ontology. For Aristotle the world is already pre-segmented by general and specific categories that are eternal, that is, not subject to corruption and decay. For Deleuze, on the other hand, the world of segmented entities (rocks, plants, animals) emerges as solutions to ontological problems that are defined by conditions that do not presuppose segmentation of any kind. The ontological problems are defined by *topological invariants*: the number of dimensions of a space of possibilities, its connectivity, and its universal singularities. As these ontological problems undergo a process of actualization they become progressively differentiated into a multiplicity of actual solutions. This differentiation proceeds in a fully historical way, and may only reveal a portion of the possibility space at a time. Thus, when reptiles dominated the world of vertebrate animals, they exhibited a large degree of differentiation into species that occupied most available ecological niches. Mammals, on the other hand, were at that time undifferentiated nocturnal creatures constituting a small component of ecosystems. But with the mass extinction of dinosaurs, the empty ecological niches left behind presented mammals with the opportunity to differentiate and explode into the multiplicity of species that we can observe today.[19]

To conclude this essay we may return to the world of mathematics and ask ourselves whether we have not introduced transcendent entities through the back door when we speak of "invariants," topological or otherwise? If the term "invariant" were used by itself, it would certainly carry implications of an eternally unchanging essence. But in its technical meaning it is always used *relative to a transformation*: rotations, displacements, projections, stretchings, foldings. These transformations involve both the *capacities to affect* of mathematical operators, as well as the *capacity to be affected* of the numbers, figures, or equations that these operators affect. The application of an operator to its target, the addition of a small vector field to the main one causing a bifurcation to occur, for example, is always an event. And events, unlike essences, are not necessary but contingent. Unlike what happens in an axiomatic approach, in a problematic conception of geometry

figures are considered only from the view point of the affections that befall them: sections, ablations, adjunctions, projections. One does not go by specific differences from a genus to its species, or by deduction from a stable essence to the properties deriving from it, but rather from a problem to the accidents that condition it and resolve it. This involves all kinds of deformations, transmutations, passages to the limit, operations in which each figure designates an "event" much more than an essence; the square no longer exists independently from a quadrature, the cube from a cubature, the straight line from a rectification. Whereas the theorem belongs to the rational order, the problem is affective and is inseparable from the metamorphoses, generations, and creations within science itself. (*ATP* 362; see also *DR* 187–89)

NOTES

1 Aristotle, *The Metaphysics* (New York: Prometheus Books, 1991), p. 100.

2 *Ibid.*, p. 160.

3 This terminology derives from my reconstruction of Deleuzian ontology. The terms "individual singularity" and "universal singularity" do not appear in Deleuze's work. He uses the terms "haecceity" and "singularity" respectively. Moreover, these two terms are not explicitly offered as replacements for "genus" and "species" in Deleuze's work. The comparison is mine but I believe it captures Deleuze's ontological approach.

4 Ralph Abraham and Christopher Shaw, *Dynamics: The Geometry of Behavior* (Santa Cruz, CA: Aerial Press, 1985), vol. I, pp. 20–21.

5 Bas Van Fraassen, *Laws and Symmetry* (Oxford: Clarendon Press, 1989), p. 222.

6 Peter Smith, *Explaining Chaos* (Cambridge University Press, 1998), p. 72 (my italics).

7 Bas Van Fraasen, *The Scientific Image* (Oxford: Clarendon Press, 1980), p. 16.

8 Willard Van Orman Quine, quoted in Nicholas Rescher, "The Ontology of the Possible," in Michael J. Loux (ed.), *The Possible and the Actual* (Ithaca, NY: Cornell University Press, 1979), p. 177.

9 Ronald N. Giere, "Constructive Realism," in Paul M. Churchland and Clifford A. Hooker (eds.), *Images of Science* (University of Chicago Press, 1985), pp. 83–84.

10 *Ibid.*, p. 44.

11 Cf. *B* 96–97. Deleuze takes the concept of virtuality, and its distinction from other modalities like possibility, from Henri Bergson.

12 Ian Stewart and Martin Golubitsky, *Fearful Symmetry* (Oxford: Blackwell, 1992), p. 42 (italics in the original).

13 Morris Kline, *Mathematical Thought from Ancient to Modern Times* (New York: Oxford University Press, 1972), vol. II, p. 759.

14 Abraham and Shaw, *Dynamics*, vol. III, pp. 37–41.

15 Stewart and Golubitsky, *Fearful Symmetry*, pp. 108–10.

16 This is also part of my reconstruction of Deleuze. The term "coactualization" does not occur in his work, nor does he offer anywhere an explanation for the success of mathematical models. For further elaboration of this point see Manuel DeLanda, *Intensive Science and Virtual Philosophy* (New York: Continuum, 2002), chapter 4.

17 Kline, *Mathematical Thought*, vol. III, p. 904.

18 David A. Brannan, Matthew F. Esplen, and Jeremy J. Gray, *Geometry* (Cambridge University Press, 1999), p. 364.

19   The relation between topological diagrams and the evolution of animals and plants is in fact more complex that this. In particular, it is not enough that vertebrates be topologically transformable into one another (by virtue of sharing a basic body plan), these transformations must also be inheritable so they can be part of an evolutionary process. In other words, we must also consider the role of the space of possible genes. I attempt to give an account of this in Manuel DeLanda, "Materialist Metaphysics," in *Deleuze: History and Science* (Dresden: Atropos, 2010), pp. 96–102.

11   Deleuze and life

"Life" was a major theme for Deleuze, so much so that he would say at one point: "Everything I've written is vitalistic, at least I hope it is" (N 143). But before we get out the pitchforks at this uttering of a forbidden word, we should remember Deleuze's love of provocation, and read the beginning of the passage to see his idiosyncratic notion of vitalism: "There's a profound link between signs, life, and vitalism: the power of nonorganic life that can be found in a line that's drawn, a line of writing, a line of music. It's organisms that die, not life. Any work of art points a way through for life, finds a way through the cracks" (N 143).

In this chapter we will skirt the relation of life and art,[1] however, and instead focus upon Deleuze's writings that are aimed at life as it is understood in the biological register.[2] We'll begin with a guide to some key biophilosophical investigations in Deleuze's single-authored masterpiece, *Difference and Repetition*: chapter 2 on organic syntheses and organic time, and chapter 5 on embryogenesis.[3] Then, in the second part of the chapter, we will consider several biophilosophical themes in Deleuze and Guattari's *Anti-Oedipus* and *A Thousand Plateaus*, addressing "vitalism," "life," "nature," "content and expression," "evolution and involution," "milieus, codes, territories," "non-organic life," "body without organs," and "organism."

DIFFERENCE AND REPETITION

Deleuze's overall aim in *Difference and Repetition* is to provide a "philosophy of difference," in which individuals are seen as produced by the integration of a differential field, or the solution of a "problem" (*DR* 211); a paradigm case would be lightning produced from a field of electrical potential differences between cloud and ground (*DR* 119). The philosophy of difference counters what we might call identitarian philosophy in which individuals are seen as produced by a prior individual. A paradigm case for identitarian philosophy would be a parent giving birth to a child: there is always a horizon of identity (the family lineage) within which differences can be located. Following Gilbert Simondon,[4] Deleuze certainly notes differences between physical and living individuation: physical individuation occurs all at once, at a boundary that advances; biological individuation occurs via "successive waves of singularities" triggering qualitative changes that affect the entire internal milieu of an organism (*DR* 255). But Deleuze will show that a philosophy of difference (individuation from a field of difference) is not restricted to physical events like the lightning case, but can also account for living individuation, so that children are also integrations of a differential field (of epigenetic and genetic factors). In fact, the philosophy of difference maps form and content such that its basic model (individuation as integration of a differential field) is itself divided into (or "differenciated," to use a technical Deleuzian term we will explain shortly) its physical and biological models without compromising its universality. In this way, the physical and biological models can apply to either register without reducing the difference between the registers. Thus children, like all other individuals, are lightning flashes ("every phenomenon flashes [*fulgure*] in a signal-sign system" [*DR* 222]), just as clouds, like all other differential fields, are "eggs" ("the world is an egg" [*DR* 251]).

Organic time and organic syntheses

Deleuze provides two genetic accounts in *Difference and Repetition*, static and dynamic; in terms we will explain later, the static moves from virtual Idea to actual individual, while the dynamic moves from immediate object of intuition to Idea.[5] Chapter 2 of *Difference and Repetition* is part of Deleuze's dynamic genesis moving from intuition to Idea; in this section he will establish the form of organic time as, literally, a "living present."[6] Deleuze drives down to the most basic syntheses; he shows how beneath active syntheses (thought) are passive syntheses (perception) and beneath passive perceptual syntheses are passive organic syntheses (metabolism).⁷ The challenge is to describe passive syntheses in differential terms, so as to avoid the "tracing" of empirical identities back to transcendental identities; avoiding such "tracing" is a basic principle of Deleuze's thought. In other words, passive syntheses are genetic or constitutive of the identities that arise within their series; there is no perceiving subject prior to the series of perceptions nor is there a living subject prior to the series of metabolic "contractions." Perceptual and metabolic syntheses are not grounded but are grounding.

Deleuze will distinguish the organic and perceptual syntheses by showing that organic syntheses "perform a contraction" or induce a habit in their own, material, register. For Hume and Bergson, as Deleuze reads them, the psychological imagination moves from past particulars to future generalities, so that from a series of particulars we come to expect another of the same kind. Deleuze will abstract the process of "drawing a difference from repetition" as the essence of contraction or habit and show that it occurs at the organic level as well as on the level of the passive perceptual imagination (*DR* 73).⁸ Perceptual syntheses thus refer back to "organic syntheses," which are "a primary sensibility that we *are*" (*DR* 73, emphasis in original). Such syntheses of the elements of "water, earth, light and air" are not merely prior to the active synthesis that would recognize or represent them, but are also "prior to their being sensed." So each organism, not only in its receptivity and perception, but also in its "viscera" (that is, its metabolism), is a "sum of contractions, of retentions and expectations" (*DR* 73). Here we see the form of organic time, the level of what is literally the "living present" of retention and expectation. Organic retention is the "cellular heritage" of the organic history of life and organic expectation is the "faith" that things will repeat in the ways to which we are accustomed. So Deleuze has isolated a "primary vital sensibility" in which we have past and future synthesized in a "living present." At this level, the future appears as need, as "the organic form of expectation," and the retained past appears as "cellular heredity" (*DR* 73).

Now we must distinguish two genres of contraction in Deleuze's treatment: (1) contraction as activity in series as opposed to relaxation or dilation, and (2) contraction as fusion of succession of elements. With the second form of contraction, we come upon the notion of a "contemplative soul." Deleuze knows that the notion of an organic "contemplative soul" might strike his readers as a "mystical or barbarous hypothesis," but he pushes on: passive organic synthesis is our "habit of life," our expectation that life will continue. So we must attribute a "contemplative soul" to the heart, the muscles, the nerves, the cells, whose role is to contract habits. This is just extending to "habit" its full generality: habit in the organic syntheses that we are (DR 74).[9] Organic syntheses operate in series, and each series has a rhythm; organisms are polyrhythmic: "the duration of an organism's present, or of its various presents, will vary according to the natural contractile range of its contemplative souls" (DR 77). The rhythm of organic syntheses can be seen from two perspectives, "need" and "satiety" (or "fatigue" in the sense of being tired of something, fed up with something). Deleuze writes: "need marks the limits of the variable present. The present extends between two eruptions of need, and coincides with the duration of a contemplation" (DR 77). "Fatigue," then, is being fed up, being overfull, when "the soul can no longer contemplate what it contracts" (DR 77). There are thousands of such rhythmic periods between need and fatigue, periods that compose the organic being of humans: from the long periods of childhood, puberty, adulthood, and menopause to monthly hormonal cycles to daily cycles (circadian rhythms) to heartbeats, breathing cycles, all the way down to neural firing patterns. Everything organic, each "contemplative soul," has a period of repetition, everything is a habit, and each one of these repetitions forms a living present that synthesizes the retention of the past and the anticipation of the future as need.

Organic individuation

To appreciate fully Deleuze's treatment of individuation in chapter 5 of *Difference and Repetition*, we must make a brief foray into Deleuze's metaphysics, where we find a tripartite ontological scheme, positing three interdependent registers: the virtual, the intensive, and the actual. For Deleuze, in all realms of being (1) intensive morphogenetic processes follow the structures inherent in (2) differential virtual multiplicities to produce (3) localized and individuated actual substances with extensive properties and differenciated qualities that, in the biological realm, can be used in classification schemes that distinguish species from each other and distinguish the organs of an organism from each other. Simply put, the actualization of the virtual, that is, the production of the actual things of the world, proceeds by way of intensive processes.

In a fuller picture of Deleuze's ontology, we see that the virtual field is composed of "Ideas" or "multiplicities," which are constituted by the progressive determination of differential elements, differential relations, and singularities; what are related are precisely intensive processes, thought as linked rates of change (*DR* 182–91). Beneath the actual (any one state of a system), we find "impersonal individuations" or intensive morphogenetic processes that produce system states, and beneath these we find "pre-individual singularities" (that is, the key elements in virtual fields, marking system thresholds that structure the intensive morphogenetic processes). We thus have to distinguish the intense "impersonal" field of individuation and its processes from the virtual "pre-individual" field of differential relations and singularities that make up an Idea or multiplicity. But it's even more complex than just three modes or registers, for we have to distinguish "individuation" as the field of individuation (called variously "the egg" or the "metastable field"), from "dramatization" as the process of individuation (embryogenesis or "spatio-temporal dynamisms"). Deleuze has thus a fourfold "order of reasons: differentiation-individuation-dramatization-differenciation (organic and specific)" (*DR* 251, translation modified). Differentiation is the mark of the virtual, the "pre-individual," while differenciation is the mark of the actual, the fully individuated end product. So both "individuation" and "dramatization" are intensive and impersonal; they are the field and the process of individuation.

A simple example distinguishing field and process of individuation can be found in the meteorological register, where the *field* of individuation is composed of the cloud–ground system with its electrical potential differences, while lightning is the process of individuation, the production of an event. On a slower temporal scale, the field of individuation of a weather system would be bands of different temperature and pressure in air and water which exist prior to and allow for the morphogenesis of wind currents or storms, which are the spatio-temporal dynamisms, the *process* of individuation of a singular event, sometimes worthy of its own name, as with hurricanes. In the biological register, an example of the field of individuation is the egg, while the process of individuation is embryogenesis; to save Deleuze from tracing empirical individuation back to a transcendental identity qua "genetic program" we must see the biological virtual as the differential Idea of genetic *and* epigenetic factors, as does the contemporary school of thought known as Developmental Systems Theory or DST.[10]

A very important point for Deleuze in his account of the biological model for ontogenesis is the priority of individuation to differenciation. In other words, singular differences in the genesis of individuals must precede the categories into which they are put; creative novelty must precede classification. As Deleuze puts it: "Individuation precedes differenciation in principle ... every differenciation presupposes a prior intense field of individuation. It is because of the action of the field of individuation that such and such differential relations and such and such distinctive points (pre-individual fields) are actualized" (*DR* 247). Individuation is thus the answer to the dramatic question "who?" not the essentialist "what is?" Individuals are singular events before they are members of species or genera; a species is a construct, an abstraction from a varying population of singulars. Deleuze is insistent here: we have to beware the "tendency to believe individuation is a continuation of the determination of species" (*DR* 247). Deleuze puts it very strongly: "any reduction of individuation to a limit or complication of differenciation compromises the whole of the philosophy of difference. This would be to commit an error, this time in the actual, analogous to that made in confusing the virtual with the possible" (*DR* 247). The key point is that "individuation does not presuppose any differenciation; it provokes it" (*DR* 247, translation modified). In other words, Deleuze must distinguish between any comparable difference between individuals – difference within a horizon of resemblance (i.e., representation), which can be classed in genus and species – and divergent difference or "individual difference," the difference thought by Darwin, the "differenciation of difference," that which does not track genus and species but produces it via natural selection as a stabilizing procedure. Making species turn around individual and diverging difference is Darwin's "Copernican Revolution" (*DR* 247–49; see also *ATP* 48).

In seeking a concrete example of the precedence of individuation, Deleuze now turns to embryos, where he must finesse what looks to be a contradiction to his insistence on the priority of individuation to differenciation. Commenting on von Baër, Deleuze admits that embryonic life goes from more to less general.[11] However, this generality "has nothing to do with an abstract taxonomic concept" (that is, it is not produced by differenciation as conditioning the comparison of the properties of finished products in a classification scheme), but is *"lived* by the embryo" in the process of individuation-dramatization (*DR* 249, emphasis in original). Thus the "experience" of the embryo (dramatization as "spatio-temporal dynamism" or morphogenetic process, the third element in the order of reasons) points "backwards" as it were to the first two elements of the order of reasons (differentiation and "individuation" as field), rather than "forward" to the fourth element (differenciation). The experience of the embryo points to differential relations or virtuality "prior to the actualization of the species" and it points to "first movements" or the "condition" of actualization, that is, to individuation as it "finds its field of constitution in the egg" (*DR* 249). This means that the lived generality of the embryo points "beyond species and genus" to the individual (that is, to the field of individuation and that process of individuation) and to pre-individual singularities, rather than toward "impersonal abstraction" (*DR* 249). So even though the specific form of the embryo appears early, this is due to the "speed and relative acceleration" of the elements of the individuation process, that is, to the "influence exercised by individuation upon actualization or the determination of the species." Thus a species is an "illusion – inevitable and well founded to be sure – in relation to the play of the individual and individuation" (*DR* 249–50).

At this point, Deleuze provides a fascinating critique of genetic determinism. First, we are reminded again of the primacy of individuation over differenciation, and that the "embryo is the individual as such caught up in field of its individuation" (*DR* 250). After the famous phrase "the world is an egg" (*DR* 251) we read that "the nucleus and the genes designate only the differentiated matter – in other words, the differential relations which constitute the pre-individual field to be actualized; but their actualization is determined only by the cytoplasm, with its gradients and its fields of individuation" (*DR* 251). Again, the virtual is "pre-individual," while the intensive is "impersonal." By showing how the genetic expression in ontogenesis is determined by cytoplasmic conditions Deleuze is thus prefiguring a move in contemporary biology, known collect-ively as "Developmental Systems Theory," away from a self-identical and transcendent genetic program to a differential network of gen-etic and epigenetic factors controlling development. This move to a differential virtual structuring organic individuation matches the Deleuzian principle of critique, the outlawing of the tracing relation between transcendental/virtual and empirical/actual, a principle that commands a non-resemblance of actualized species and parts to virtual differential relations and singularities. Deleuzian critique also commands the non-resemblance of both virtual multiplicity and actual adult individual to the intensive processes of morpho-genesis or to what Deleuze calls the lived experience of the embryo. The twists and folds of embryogenesis do not resemble either the virtual network of relations among DNA strings and epigenetic fac-tors or the actual structures and qualitatively different cell types of the adult organism.

To conclude this all-too-brief sketch of organic individuation in *Difference and Repetition*, we see that, for Deleuze, the "principal difficulty" of embryology is posing the field of individuation for-mally and generally (*DR* 252). Eggs thus seem to depend upon the species. But this reverses the order in which individuation precedes differenciation. So we must conceive individuating difference as individual difference: no two eggs are identical (*DR* 252). Organic individuation, field and process together, is a singular event preced-ing differenciation. Once we've seen that, we've traced the order of reasons from (1) virtual differentiation through (2) the impersonal and intensive field of individuation to (3) spatio-temporal dynamisms as the process of individuation or dramatization to (4) differencia-tion as the formation of species and "parts," that is, qualitatively different cell types and functions which can then be classified in taxonomic schemes.

ANTI-OEDIPUS AND A THOUSAND PLATEAUS

Difference and Repetition is different in both form and content from *A Thousand Plateaus*. While *Difference and Repetition* has the clas-sical form of a *thèse d'état* – and *Anti-Oedipus* still has something of the same linear argument – *A Thousand Plateaus* is written as a "rhizome," a non-centered "open system," with many occasions for reading "transversally" across its chapters or "plateaus" (*ATP* 3–25). We will thus present our reading of *Anti-Oedipus* and *A Thousand Plateaus* thematically, rather than attempting to construct a narrative. In terms of content, we find a shift as well. *Difference and Repetition* focuses on how individuation determines the actualization of virtuality, whereas in *A Thousand Plateaus* the focus is on the intermeshing of different rhythms of intensive processes. *Difference and Repetition* is thus somewhat "vertically" oriented (from virtual to actual and back), whereas *A Thousand Plateaus* is more "transversal" (the meshing or clashing of intensive processes). These relative emphases should not be hardened into theses, however, especially as the terms "plane of consistency" and "abstract machine" in *A Thousand Plateaus* do seem to have an ontological status a reader of *Difference and Repetition* would see as "virtual."

With these preliminary remarks, let us turn to our treatment of biophilosophical themes in *AO* and *ATP*.

Vitalism

We began this chapter with one of Deleuze's provocations, in which he proclaimed his writings "vitalistic" (*épater les bourgeois* is an old French philosophical gesture), but Deleuze is not vitalistic in any technical sense of espousing a non-material intelligent guiding force, a "vital principle" or "life force" or "entelechy."[12] He proclaims himself a monist and materialist in many passages; Deleuze and Guattari go so far as to call fascism "a problem of pure matter, a phenomenon of physical, biological, psychic, social, or cosmic matter" (*ATP* 165). But, as we will explain below, Deleuze is a machinic materialist, not a mechanist, and it is only as a reaction to mechanism that classical vitalism makes sense. It is the impoverished sense of matter in mechanism, as chaotic or passive, that creates the temptation to classical vitalism of the "entelechy" type. Seeing matter as chaotic or passive creates the need for a hylomorphic rescue in which a transcendent organizing force swoops down to instill a form that organizes the matter. But Deleuze learned from Gilbert Simondon to mistrust hylomorphism, as much for its social origins in command relations as for its metaphysical assumptions (*ATP* 408–10). What we need to look for in Deleuze's notion of vitalism is the "life" that encompasses both organisms and "non-organic life."

This life concerns the capacity for novel emergent properties in the self-organization of material systems, a conception that bypasses the dichotomy that would oppose a vital life force or entelechy to mechanistic biochemistry and physics.

Life

For Deleuze and Guattari, "life" has a double sense, reflecting both stratification and destratification. It means both "organisms" as a certain set of stratified beings and also the creativity of complex systems, their capacity to produce new emergent properties, new behavior patterns, by destratifying and deterritorializing. Organisms are "a particularly complex system of stratification" (*ATP* 336), while life qua creativity is "a surplus value of *destratification* ... an aggregate of consistency that disrupts orders, forms, and substances" (*ATP* 336, italics in original). In the second, creative sense, one example of which is speciation, the creation of novel "orders, forms, and substances," then, life is not limited to the organism form: "the organism is that which life sets against itself in order to limit itself" (*ATP* 503). This notion of life as creativity gives rise to "the prodigious idea of *Nonorganic Life*" (*ATP* 411, italics in original), which we gloss as creative self-organization of material systems in registers other than the "organismic." As we will shortly see, by "organism" Deleuze and Guattari mean both homeostatic or autopoietic conservation of a living entity, and organ patterning useful to social machines.

Nature

By various terms built around the word "machine," Deleuze and Guattari offer a conceptual scheme that allows us to treat inorganic, organic, and social being with the same concepts. They thus strive for an ontological naturalism, a stance that would refuse to see humans as separate from nature. This sort of naturalism is apparent in the beginning of *Anti-Oedipus*, where a schizophrenic's stroll shows "a time before the man-nature dichotomy ... He [the schizophrenic] does not live nature as nature [i.e., as separate from man], but as a process of production" (*AO* 2). The schizophrenic's being in contact with nature as "process of production" allows us to see man as "the being who is in intimate contact with the profound life of all forms or all types of beings, who is responsible for even the stars and animal life" (*AO* 4).

The term used for the "profound life" of nature's process in *Anti-Oedipus* is "desiring-production." Crisscrossing Marx and Freud, Deleuze and Guattari use "desiring-production" to put desire in the eco-social realm of production and production in the unconscious realm of desire. Desiring-production is a "universal primary production" (*AO* 5) underlying the seemingly separate natural (earthly and biological) and human (psycho-social) realms. Desiring-production is not anthropocentric; it is the very heart of the world; all natural processes, even those well beyond the human, are processes of machinic desiring-production: "everything is a machine. Celestial machines, the stars or rainbows in the sky, alpine machines ... nature as process of production" (*AO* 2). Universal in scope, desiring-production is also immanent and non-subjective – there is no subject that lies behind the production, that performs the production – and purely positive – the desire in desiring-production is not oriented to making up a lack (*AO* 25). Desiring-production is immanent, autonomous, self-constituting, and creative: it is the *natura naturans* of Spinoza or the will to power of Nietzsche.

The machinic naturalism of *Anti-Oedipus* should not be confused with "mechanism," that is, the law-bound repetition of physical events with creativity shuffled off from dead matter into some spiritual realm. For Deleuze and Guattari, nature as desiring-production or process of production is the linking together of "desiring-machines" (*AO* 5). A desiring-machine is formed in the breaking of a material flow produced by one machine by another machine: "there is always a flow-producing machine, and another machine connected to it that interrupts or draws off part of this flow (the breast – the mouth)" (*AO* 5). Although these machinic connections are for the most part patterned repetitions under the sway of a geological process, a biological species, or a social machine, there is always the chance for novel connections to be formed. For example, human desiring-machines are often patterned by the social machines into which they fit, but not always; there's always a slippage, a derailment that would allow for novel connections, often made by artists (*AO* 31).

In *A Thousand Plateaus*, "desire" drops out of the description of nature, which is described in terms of "abstract machines" and "machinic assemblages." Again, as in *Anti-Oedipus*, "machinism," the term for creative self-organization of material systems, is not mechanism, or deadened, routinized, repetition. In fact, we could say, mechanism is a residue of machinism: creativity comes first, then routinization. In *A Thousand Plateaus'* terminology, "strata" (forms which induce mechanical repetition) are ontologically secondary to "lines of flight" (which provide the occasion of creative novelty by disrupting – "destratifying" and "deterritorializing" – stratified, mechanical, processes). Deleuze and Guattari write: "what is primary is an absolute deterritorialization, an absolute line of flight ... it is the strata that are always residues ... The question is not how something manages to leave the strata but how things get into them in the first place" (*ATP* 56). As we will see in more detail below, "organism" is one of three strata "binding" humans to patterned repetitions (*ATP* 159).

Despite the ontological priority of lines of flight, stratification is chronologically "simultaneous" with destratification and is a "very important, inevitable phenomenon that is beneficial in many respects and unfortunate in many others" (*ATP* 40). Nature as process, *natura naturans*, is thus bivalent, constituting an "abstract machine" of stratification – a tendency to hierarchically ordered, mechanically repetitive systems – and destratification – a tendency to experimental, creative processes or "lines of flight." Nature as stratification is called "the judgment of God" (*ATP* 40), while destratification allowing creative novelty is called "life" (*ATP* 336, 503, 507); as we will see, such life can be "non-organic."

While stratification produces a body composed of homogenous layers, destratification allows the construction of "consistencies" or "assemblages," functional wholes that preserve the heterogeneity of their component parts and enable further non-hierarchical or "rhizomatic" connections (*ATP* 505). The "abstract" part of the term "abstract machine" simply means that the processes of stratification and destratification occur in many material registers, from the geological through the neural, the biological through the social. An "abstract machine" is thus the diagram for processes that form functional wholes in different registers (*ATP* 510–14). In sum, nature is the construction and destruction of strata, freeing parts to form connections with heterogeneous others in consistencies or assemblages.

Content and expression

In one of their most bewildering slogans, Deleuze and Guattari tell us in the "Geology of Morals" chapter of *A Thousand Plateaus* that "God is a Lobster" (*ATP* 40). The term is meant to indicate the "double articulation" of the stratification process. To explain double articulation, they develop a specialized terminology of "form-substance" and "content-expression" which can be read with regard to organisms (*ATP* 40–45).

Content is that which is put to work in a stratum or assemblage, while expression is the takeover of content, putting it to work in a "functional structure." As the first articulation of stratification, content is composed of bodies whose recruitment from a substratum retrospectively qualifies them as matter for that stratum. Stratified content has both form and substance. The "substance of content" is homogenized matter selected out from a heterogeneous source or exterior milieu. The "form of content" is the ordering of those selected elements by a code which is in turn overcoded by the "form of expression" to produce an emergent functional structure or "substance of expression" (*ATP* 41). In the double articulation characteristic of stratification, content is relative to its expression, so that what is content for one expression can itself be the expression of another content.

In strata (actualized systems, to use the terms of *Difference and Repetition*), expression takes part in a double articulation, and ultimately results in a new substance, with new emergent, albeit fixed, properties, while in assemblages (intensive fields and processes of individuation), expression results in new affects, new capacities to form further assemblages (in the best case). Within the system of the strata, expression takes different forms. Following Simondon, Deleuze and Guattari write that in the inorganic strata, expression is the molarization of molecular content, that is, the carrying forth to the macroscopic scale of the "implicit forms" of molecular interactions (*ATP* 57).[13] On the organic stratum, expression becomes autonomous in the linear genetic code, which results in greater deterritorialization (greater behavioral flexibility) of organisms due to "transductions" (*ATP* 59–60). In some parts of the "alloplastic" (niche constructing) stratum, expression becomes "linguistic rather than genetic," that is, achieves a "superlinear" or temporal form allowing "translation" (*ATP* 60).

On the organic stratum, content and expression must be specified at many different scales: genes and proteins, cells, tissues, organs, systems, organism, reproductive community, species, biosphere. In Deleuze and Guattari's discussion of genes and proteins the substance of content, the materials drawn from the "pre-biotic soup" as substratum, are amino acids, and the form of content or coding of these acids are amino acid sequences or proteins (*ATP* 42, 59). Expression, as we recall, is the putting of content to work, so the form of expression at this scale is composed of nucleotide base sequences, which specify amino acids, while the substance of expression, the emergent functional unit, is the gene, which determines protein shape and function.[14] Skipping over several scales (cell, tissue, organ) for simplicity's sake, we arrive at the level of organic systems (e.g., the nervous, endocrine, and digestive systems), where the substance of content is composed of organs and the form of content is coding or regulation of flows within the body and between the body and the outside. The form of expression at this level is homeostatic regulation (overcoding of the regulation of flows provided by organs), while the substance of expression, the highest level emergent unifying effect, is the organism, conceived as a process binding the functions of a body into a whole through co-ordination of multiple systems of homeostatic regulation.

Evolution and involution

Deleuze and Guattari have a strong and a weak sense of the creative transformation involved in the production of biological novelty. The strong sense is novelty that does not produce substantial filiation (i.e., does not produce an organism with descendants); this can be connected to the notions of "niche construction" and "life cycle" in DST.[15] The weak sense is novelty that does produce substantial filiation (an organism with descendants); this can be connected to the notions of "serial endosymbiosis" in the work of Lynn Margulis[16] and "developmental plasticity" in the work of Mary Jane West-Eberhard.[17]

The strong sense, which excludes substantial filiation, is expressed in the following passage from the "Becoming-Intense" plateau of *A Thousand Plateaus*:

Finally, becoming is not an evolution, at least not an evolution by descent and filiation ... It concerns alliance. If evolution includes any veritable becomings, it is in the domain of *symbioses* that bring into play beings of totally different scales and kingdoms, with no possible filiations. There is a block of becoming that snaps up the wasp and the orchid, but from which no wasp-orchid can ever descend. (*ATP* 238, emphasis in original)

We can connect this to the thoughts of "niche construction" and "life cycle" in DST. Here, "niche construction" looks to the way organisms actively shape the environment and thus the evolutionary selection pressures for themselves and their offspring. Thus evolution should be seen as the change in organism-environment systems, that is, the organism in its constructed niche. It's the "becoming" of the organism-in-its-niche that needs to be thought as the unit of evolution (e.g., the "wasp-orchid"). In generalizing and radicalizing the thought of niche construction, DST thinkers propose the "life cycle" as the widest possible extension of developmental resources that are reliably present (or better, re-created) across generations. DST thinkers thus extend the notion of inheritance beyond the genetic to the cytoplasmic environment of the egg (an extension many mainstream biologists have come to accept) and beyond to intra-organismic and even (most controversially) to extra-somatic factors, that is, to the relevant, constructed, features of the physical (for example, termite colonies),[18] biological (inherited symbionts), and social environments (for example, normal brain development in humans needs positive corporeal affect and language exposure in critical sensitive windows). This notion of "life cycle" as the unit of evolution encompassing intranuclear, cytoplasmic, organic, and extra-somatic elements comes close to what Deleuze and Guattari refer to above as "symbioses that bring into play beings of totally different scales and kingdoms."

The weak sense of biological novelty is that which does result in a substantial filiation, that is, organisms with descendants. There is still the emphasis on heterogenous elements entering a symbiosis, but the result has organismic form. The foremost connection here is with the work of Lynn Margulis, who posits that symbiosis, rather than mutation, is the most important source of variation upon which natural selection works. Her most famous example is mitochondrial capture at the origin of eukaryotic cells. Margulis holds that mitochondria were previously independent aerobic bacteria engulfed by anaerobic (proto-nucleated) bacteria; eukaryotic cells thus formed produce the lineage for all multicellular organisms. Serial endosymbiosis thus short-circuits the strict neo-Darwinist doctrine of mutation as origin of variation upon which we find selection of slight adaptations. Although there is organismic filiation here, Margulis' notion of evolution via the symbiosis of different organisms seems at least in line with the spirit of what Deleuze and Guattari call "involution" (*ATP* 238–39). (We will discuss the relation of Deleuze and Guattari's work to that of Mary Jane West-Eberhard in the next section.)

Milieus, codes, and territories

As we note above, the discussion of evolution in *A Thousand Plateaus* emphasizes what is now called "niche construction" or the action of an organism on its environment such that the selection pressure for future generations are changed.[19] Here the discussion deploys the terms of milieus, codes, and territories. We begin with "milieu," which is a vibratory, rhythmic, and coded material field for bodies (strata) and territories (assemblages). Heterogeneous milieus are "drawn" by rhythms from chaos, while territories form between ever-shifting milieus. Now milieus are coded – the "code" is the repetition of elements such that milieus are a "block of space-time constituted by the periodic repetition of the component" (*ATP* 313). But there is always "transcoding" or change of pace so that "rhythm" is the difference between one code and another: "there is rhythm whenever there is a transcoded passage from one milieu to another, a communication of milieus, coordination between heterogeneous space-times" (*ATP* 313). The notion of rhythm here is differential or intensive; it is to be distinguished from metered or extensive cadence: "rhythm is critical; it ties together critical moments" (*ATP* 313). "Critical" here means a threshold in a differential relation, a singularity in the linked rates of change of a living system in its ecological niche.

Milieus and rhythms are thus interrelated. Milieus are coded and repetitive – but the rhythm is always shifting in "transcoding" (313). Every living being has four milieus:

1. the exterior milieu, materials furnished by substratum (*ATP* 49);
2. the interior milieu, the domain of homeostasis for the composing elements and composed substances (*ATP* 50);
3. the intermediary milieu or set of membranes (*ATP* 51) which establish the possibility of "epistrata" as stable states determined by homeostatic set points;
4. the annexed or associated milieu (*ATP* 51), the ecological niche or "parastrata," in turn composed of (a) sources of energy different from food (respiration); (b) the discernment of materials (perception); and (c) the fabrication of compounds (response/reaction).

Rhythm is the difference between one code and another, so rhythm and the milieu are relational: "A milieu does in fact exist by virtue of a periodic repetition [i.e., a code], but one whose only effect is to produce a difference by which the milieu passes into another milieu" (*ATP* 314). Codes are that which determines order (in a milieu, or as forming a body in content-expression). Every code has a "margin of decoding" (*ATP* 53, 322) from two factors: supplements (unexpressed genetic variation, that is, non-coding DNA) and transcoding or "surplus value of code" (transverse communication or serial endosymbiosis) (*ATP* 314).

Territorialization affects multiple milieus and rhythms. Territories themselves have exterior, interior, intermediary, and annexed milieus (as do bodies) (*ATP* 314). With territories, milieu components are no longer directional but now dimensional, that is, they are no longer merely functional, but now expressive (*ATP* 315). There are thus now qualities as matters of expression. For example, color in birds or fishes is functional when tied to an action (when it indicates readiness for physiological function: feeding, fighting, fleeing, mating), but it is expressive when it marks a territory. The difference is temporal: functional color shifts are transitory and tied to the action, while expressive color has a "temporal constancy and a spatial range" (*ATP* 315). Territories depend on decoding: The key is the disjunction of code and territory (*ATP* 322): "the territory arises in a free margin of the code," that is, while in milieus there is transcoding, territories are associated with decoding.

When they note that there is non-coding DNA as a "free matter for variation," Deleuze and Guattari add that in their view the simple presence of non-coding DNA is not enough for creative speciation, as "it is very unlikely that this kind of matter could create new species independently of mutations" (*ATP* 322; see also 53). On the other hand, in the views of some recent biologists, mutation is not the only means of providing variation for selection; such free DNA can serve as "unexpressed genetic variation" allowing "environmental induction" of novel phenotypic traits leading to evolutionary change in specific circumstances.[20] Deleuze and Guattari's text resonates with this notion when they note that there are "events of another order [i.e., other than mutation] capable of multiplying the interactions of the organism with its milieus" (*ATP* 322). This other factor is territorialization, which has both spatial and intensification effects. Spatially, it spreads organisms out, making them keep their distance from each other. It also intensifies the relation of the organism and its milieus; it speeds up evolution from having to wait for mutation: "Territorialization is precisely such a factor that lodges on the margins of the code of a single species and give the separate representatives of that species the possibility of differenciating [translation modified from "differentiating"]" (*ATP* 322). Remembering the principle of the priority of individuation we saw in *Difference and Repetition*, we should read "differenciating" here as tracking the concrete process of creating singular differences in individuation processes; we can connect this notion of singular, creative, and concrete organic individuation with that of "developmental plasticity" in relation to shifting milieus as they are territorialized in "niche construction."[21]

Consistency/non-organic life

Non-organic life or the establishment of "consistency" is the linking together of heterogeneous elements to produce emergent properties in functional structures in a variety of registers beyond the organismic (*ATP* 507). Consistency is not achieved by imposing a form on matter, but by "elaborating an increasingly rich and consistent material, the better to tap increasingly intense forces" (*ATP* 329); such assemblages are creative in their self-ordering, that is, their makeup lends itself to novel becomings. However, consistency is not "restricted to complex life forms, [but] pertains fully even to the most elementary atoms and particles" (*ATP* 335). Thus "aggregates" (*ensembles*) can achieve consistency when "very heterogeneous elements" mesh together to achieve emergent effects, thus forming a "machinic phylum" (*ATP* 335).

Because of this extension of consistency and its creative emergence beyond complex life forms we find "non-organic life" in technological assemblages crossing the organic and the inorganic as in the "man-horse-bow assemblage" (*ATP* 391, 406, 411). Non-organic life is creativity outside the organism form, occurring in the physical, the evolutionary-biological, and the technological-artistic registers. Such creativity in the latter register is often named a "war machine," or a horizontal, rhizomatic social formation always exterior to the stratifying, homogenizing, social formation of the "State": "Could it be that it is at the moment that the war machine ceases to exist, conquered by the State, that it displays its irreducibility, that it scatters into thinking, loving, dying, or creating machines that have at their disposal vital or revolutionary powers capable of challenging the conquering State?" (*ATP* 356).

Body without organs or BwO

To reach the plane of consistency – to be open to new orderings and new potentials – an organism must be dis-ordered, it must reach its "body without organs." This term is responsible for much confusion; it would have been better to call it by the more accurate but less elegant term, a "non-organismically ordered body."[22] Deleuze and Guattari write: "the BwO is not at all the opposite of the organs. The organs are not its enemies. The enemy is the organism" (*ATP* 158). A BwO retains its organs, but they are released from the habitual patterns they assume in its organism form; insofar as the organism is a stratum (a centralized, hierarchical, and strongly patterned body), a BwO is a destratified (decentralized, dehabituated) body. Adding to the potential confusion is a significant change in the term "full BwO" from *Anti-Oedipus* to *A Thousand Plateaus*. In *Anti-Oedipus*, the BwO is "full" when it is catatonic, a moment of anti-production, a mere surface across which desiring-machines are splayed (*AO* 8). In *A Thousand Plateaus*, however, the full BwO is positively valued; it is the "empty" BwO that must be avoided. The full BwO allows for connection with other destratified bodies, while the empty BwO is a black hole for subjectivity, where nothing happens (*ATP* 150).

A BwO is not a regression to a natural state, despite the impression given by this remark, in which the BwO is described as "what remains after you take everything away" (*ATP* 151). Rather, it is an object of construction, a practice needing cautious experimentation to reach a "plane of consistency," a region in which one is now open to a field of new connections, creative and novel becomings that will give one new patterns and triggers of behavior. In dynamic systems terms, the BwO is the organism moved from equilibrium, out of a stable state or comfort zone (a certain functioning set of homeostatic mechanisms and regulated habits), to an state in which it is capable of producing new – and continually changeable – habits.

A BwO is not reached by regression, for a BwO is not the infantile body of our past, but the realm of potentials for different body organization precluded by the organism form. Thus it is reached by a systematic practice of disturbing the organism's patterns, which are arranged in "exclusive disjunctions" (specifying which organs can ever meet and outlawing other possible connections). In this way a body of purely distributed, rather than centralized and hierarchized, organs can be reached, sitting upon its underlying matter-energy flow. In other words, a BwO is purely immanently arranged production; matter-energy flowing without regard to a central point that drains off the extra work, the surplus value of the organs for an emergent organic subject in a "supplementary dimension" (*ATP* 265) to those of the organs (*ATP* 159). Since all actual bodies must make choices, the key ethical move is to construct a body in which patterning is flexible, that is, to stay in a sustainable intensive "crisis" situation, where any one exclusive disjunction can be undone and an alternate patterning accessed.

As an object of practice reached starting from the organism, the BwO needs to be cautiously constructed by experimentation with body practices: "staying stratified – organized, signified, subjected – is not the worst that can happen" (*ATP* 159). Nor is the BwO an individualist achievement: "For the BwO is necessarily ... a Collectivity [*un Collectif*] (assembling [*agençant*] elements, things, plants, animals, tools, people, powers [*pusissances*], and fragments of all of these; for it is not 'my' body without organs, instead the 'me' [*moi*] is on it, or what remains of me, unalterable and changing in form, crossing thresholds)" (*ATP* 161).

Organism

We will conclude this tour of biophilosophical themes with the notion of organism, a notion whose centrality for other biophilosophies Deleuze and Guattari challenge. For Deleuze and Guattari, an organism is type of body; it is a centralized, hierarchized, self-directed body. A body is a system considered in terms of appropriation and regulation of matter-energy flows; in Spinozist terms, it is a material system with a characteristic "longitude" or "relation" of the "speeds and slowness" among its constituent parts (*ATP* 260). (Bodies also have "latitude" or "the sum total of the intensive affects it is capable of at a given power or degree of potential" [*ATP* 260].) At a lower level of analysis, a body is an assemblage of organs; at higher levels, a body may itself be an organ in a social body. A body is thus a node in a production network that is plugged into a network of other flows, slowing some down, speeding others up. A stratum is composed of homogenized bodies put to work by an over-coding agent, while a consistency is an assemblage that retains the heterogeneity of the bodies composing it.

The organism is an emergent effect of organizing organs in a particular way, a "One" added to the multiplicity of organs in a "supplementary dimension" (*ATP* 21; 265). As we have seen in discussing *Anti-Oedipus*, an organ is a "desiring-machine," that is, an emitter and breaker of flows, of which part is siphoned off to flow in the economy of the body. Organs are a body's way of negotiating with the exterior milieu, appropriating and regulating a bit of matter-energy flow. The organism is the unifying emergent effect of interlocking homeostatic mechanisms that quickly compensate for any non-average fluctuations below certain thresholds to return a body to its statistically normal condition. The organism is "a phenomenon of accumulation, coagulation, and sedimentation that, in order to extract useful labor from the BwO, imposes upon it forms, functions, bonds, dominant and hierarchized organizations, organized transcendences" (*ATP* 159). The organism is hence a construction, a certain selection from the range of what a body can be, and hence a constraint, an imposition, a limitation: "The BwO howls: 'They've made me an organism! They've wrongfully folded me! They've stolen my body!'" (*ATP* 159). While all bodies are "ordered," that is, contain some probability structure to the passage of flows among their organs, the organism is "organized," that is, its habitual connections are centralized and hierarchical. The organs of an organism are patterned by "exclusive disjunctions" which preclude the actualization of other, alternative, patterns (*AO* 75–76).

There is also a political sense of "organism" we should discuss. "Organism" refers to body patterns being centralized so that "useful labor is extracted from the BwO" (*ATP* 159). We see that "organism" is a term for a particular type of political useful body when we realize that for Deleuze and Guattari the opposite of the organism is not death, but "depravity": "You will be an organism ... otherwise you're just depraved" (*ATP* 159). That is, being an "organism" today in Western capitalism means that your organs are Oedipally patterned for hetero-marriage and work. Getting outside the organism does not mean getting outside homeostasis guaranteed by a certain organic form so much as getting outside Oedipus into what Oedipal society calls "depravity." So we have to think the body as socially patterned, and the experimentation Deleuze and Guattari call for is not so much with somatic body limits (although that is part of it) but with bio-social-technical body relations in what Deleuze and Guattari will call a "consistency" or even a "war machine": "every creation is brought about by a war machine" (*ATP* 229–30, 356, 360).

CONCLUSION

We have provided a brief overview of some biophilosophical themes in *Difference and Repetition*, *Anti-Oedipus*, and *A Thousand Plateaus*. Researchers are working on exploring the relations between Deleuze's works and that of the biologists he reads (see note 3); further work is needed there as well as in using Deleuze's conceptual scheme(s) to discuss contemporary biophilosophical concepts such as developmental plasticity;[23] autopoiesis;[24] "process structuralism";[25] serial endosymbiosis theory;[26] and Developmental

Systems Theory (see note 10). Such "extended synthesis" models provide for multi-level, interlocking, distributed systems for cell, organ, organism, and life cycle development and function in an evolutionary perspective. Deleuze provides a philosophical context for this endeavor, one that provides a vocabulary and ontological scheme for interlocking processes of the formation, deformation, and transformation of self-organizing physical-biological-political systems.

NOTES

1   Treated ably in Ronald Bogue, *Deleuze on Music, Painting and the Arts* (New York: Routledge, 2003); Anne Sauvagnargues, "De l'animal à l'art," in *La philosophie de Deleuze* (Paris: Presses Universitaires de France, 2004) and *Deleuze et l'art* (Paris: Presses Universitaires de France, 2005); and Elizabeth Grosz, *Chaos, Territory, Art: Deleuze and the Framing of the Earth* (New York: Columbia University Press, 2008).

2   The founding work in examining Deleuze's biophilosophy is Keith Ansell Pearson, *Germinal Life: The Difference and Repetition of Deleuze* (London: Routledge, 1999). Also of interest are, in addition to the works cited in note 1: Howard Caygill, "The Topology of Selection: The Limits of Deleuze's Biophilosophy," in Keith Ansell Pearson (ed.), *Deleuze and Philosophy: The Difference Engineer* (London: Routledge, 1997), pp. 149–62; Mark Hansen, "Becoming as Creative Involution? Contextualizing Deleuze and Guattari's Biophilosophy," *Postmodern Culture*, 11:1 (2000), http://pmc.iath. virginia.edu/text-only/issue.900/11.1hansen.txt; Manuel DeLanda, *A Thousand Years of Nonlinear History* (New York: Zone Books, 1997) and *Intensive Science and Virtual Philosophy* (London: Continuum 2002); Luciana Parisi, *Abstract Sex. Philosophy, Biotechnology and the Mutations of Desire* (London and New York, Continuum Press, 2004); Rosi Braidotti, *Metamorphoses: Towards a Materialist Theory of Becoming* (Cambridge: Polity Press, 2002) and *Transpositions: On Nomadic Ethics* (Cambridge: Polity Press, 2006); Alberto Toscano, *The Theatre of Production: Philosophy and Individuation between Kant and Deleuze* (Basingstoke: Palgrave Macmillan, 2006); Steven Shaviro, "Interstitial Life: Remarks on Causality and Purpose in Biology," in Peter Gaffney (ed.), *The Force of the Virtual: Deleuze, Science, and Philosophy* (Minneapolis: University of Minnesota Press, 2010),

pp. 133–46; and Claire Colebrook, *Deleuze and the Meaning of Life* (Basingstoke: Palgrave Macmillan, 2010).

3   We will, regrettably, not be able to discuss Deleuze's relation to the biological thinkers whom he cites – an important field of research already well underway See Ansell Pearson, *Germinal Life*, on Darwin; Bogue, *Deleuze on Music, Painting and the Arts*, on Raymond Ruyer; Sauvagnargues, "De l'animal à l'art," *Deleuze et l'art*, and *Deleuze: l'empirisme transcendantal* (Paris: Presses Universitaires de France, 2009), on Gilbert Simondon, Georges Canguilhem, and Geoffroy Saint-Hilaire; and Todd May, *Gilles Deleuze: An Introduction* (Cambridge University Press, 2005) and John Marks, "Molecular Biology in the Work of Deleuze and Guattari," *Paragraph: A Journal of Modern Critical Theory*, 29:2 (July 2006), 81–97, on François Jacob and Jacques Monod.

4   Gilbert Simondon, *L'individu et sa genèse physico-biologique* (Grenoble: Millon, 1995); see also Sauvagnargues, "De l'animal à l'art" and *Deleuze: l'empirisme transcendantal*.

5   Joe Hughes, *Deleuze and the Genesis of Representation* (New York and London: Continuum, 2008) and *Deleuze's "Difference and Repetition": A Reader's Guide* (New York and London: Continuum, 2009).

6   We should note that organic time, the synthesis of habit producing the living present, is only the "foundation" of time. Deleuze's full treatment of time in *Difference and Repetition* posits a second synthesis of memory producing the pure past as the "ground" of time, while the third synthesis, producing the future as eternal return of difference, we might say unfounds and ungrounds time.

7   Many of the major commentators on *Difference and Repetition* – Hughes, *Deleuze's "Difference and Repetition"*; Levi R. Bryant, *Difference and Givenness: Deleuze's Transcendental Empiricism and the Ontology of Immanence* (Evanston: Northwestern University Press, 2008); Miguel de Beistegui, *Truth and Genesis: Philosophy as Differential Ontology* (Bloomington: Indiana University Press, 2004); James Williams, *Gilles Deleuze's "Difference and Repetition": A Critical Introduction and Guide* (Edinburgh University Press, 2003) – do not isolate the level of organic synthesis. The exceptions are Ansell Pearson, *Germinal Life* and DeLanda, *Intensive Science and Virtual Philosophy*.

8   Deleuze cannot go directly to his key notion of organic synthesis because he must first free a notion of habit from the illusions of psychology, which fetishizes activity. For Deleuze, psychology, through fear of introspection, misses the element of passive "contemplation." Indeed, current work in philosophical psychology says the self cannot

contemplate itself due to fear of an infinite regress of active constituting selves (Dan Zahavi, *Subjectivity and Selfhood: Investigating the First-Person Perspective* [Cambridge, MA: MIT Press, 2005]).

9 I pursue the theme of organic subjectivity inherent in Deleuze's notion of "contemplative soul" in John Protevi, "Larval Subjects, Enaction, and *E. coli* Chemotaxis," in Laura Guillaume and Joe Hughes (eds.), *Deleuze and the Body* (Edinburgh University Press, 2011) and "Mind in Life, Mind in Process: Toward a New Transcendental Aesthetic and a New Question of Panpsychism," *Journal of Consciousness Studies*, 18:5–6 (2011), 94–116.

10 The school of thought questioning the genetic program notion in favor of a notion of a distributed and differential field of interacting genetic and epigenetic factors is often called "Developmental Systems Theory." The main works here are Susan Oyama, *The Ontogeny of Information: Developmental Systems and Evolution* (Durham, NC: Duke University Press, 2000); Richard Lewontin, *The Triple Helix: Gene, Organism, and Environment* (Cambridge, MA: Harvard University Press, 2000); and Susan Oyama, Paul Griffiths, and Russell Gray (eds.), *Cycles of Contingency: Developmental Systems and Evolution* (Cambridge, MA: MIT Press, 2001). DST themes are also treated in Massimo Pigliucci and Gerd Müller (eds.), *Evolution: The Extended Synthesis* (Cambridge, MA: MIT Press, 2010).

11 Although it does not appear in the bibliography of *Difference and Repetition*, Deleuze and Guattari do refer to the original version of this work: Georges Canguilhem, Georges Lapassade, Jacques Piquemal, and Jacques Ulmann, *Du développement à l'évolution au XIXe siècle* (Paris: Presses Universitaires de France, 2003 [1962]) in *A Thousand Plateaus* (p. 522, n.9). It might be the source for the discussion of von Baër in *Difference and Repetition*.

12 On the notion of entelechy developed by Hans Driesch, see Klaus Sander, "Hans Driesch's 'Philosophy Really *ab ovo*' or Why to Be a Vitalist," *Development Genes and Evolution*, 202:1 (1992), 1–3, and "Entelechy and the Ontogenetic Machine – Work and Views of Hans Driesch from 1895 to 1910," *Development Genes and Evolution*, 202:2 (1993), 67–69.

13 Simondon, *L'individu et sa genèse physico-biologique*.

14 Note that in this treatment we are overlooking the DNA/RNA relation, the dependence of genes on cellular metabolism, and the role of genes in intervening in the self-organizing processes of morphogenesis.

15 See note 10.

16 Lynn Margulis, *Symbiotic Planet: A New Look at Evolution* (New York: Basic Books, 1998).

17 Mary Jane West-Eberhard, *Developmental Plasticity and Evolution* (New York: Oxford University Press, 2003).

18 J. Scott Turner, *The Extended Organism: The Physiology of Animal-Built Structures* (Cambridge, MA: Harvard University Press, 2000).

19 See Pigliucci and Müller, *Evolution: The Extended Synthesis*, for a discussion of niche construction.

20 West-Eberhard, *Developmental Plasticity and Evolution*, pp. 145, 499ff.

21 *Ibid.*

22 The term first appears in Deleuze's writings, in a Lacanian-psychoanalytic idiom, in the latter part of *Logic of Sense* in the "dynamic genesis" of sense from corporeal forces. The collaboration with Guattari in *Anti-Oedipus* produced the occasion for Deleuze's "escape" from psychoanalysis.

23 West-Eberhard, *Developmental Plasticity and Evolution*.

24 Humberto Maturana and Francisco J. Varela, *Autopoiesis and Cognition: The Realization of the Living* (Boston: Riedel, 1980).

25 Brian Goodwin, *How the Leopard Changed Its Spots: The Evolution of Complexity* (New York: Charles Scribner's Sons, 1994) and Stuart Kauffman, *The Origins of Order: Self-Organization and Selection in Evolution* (New York: Oxford University Press, 1993).

26 Margulis, *Symbiotic Planet*.

12 Deleuze's aesthetics of sensation

THE WRENCHING DUALITY OF AESTHETICS

From a certain point of view, it appears to be quite possible to characterize every aspect of Deleuze's work as aesthetics or as in some manner grounded in aesthetics. This possibility arises as a function of the "wrenching duality" characterizing aesthetics, which Deleuze cites in *The Logic of Sense* (*LS* 260). This characterization arises in a discussion of the Platonic distinction between well-founded copies that resemble the Idea and copies called simulacra, which exist as a perversion of or deviation from the Platonic notion of the Idea (*LS* 256–58). What is significant in this account is the claim that Platonism founds the philosophical domain of representation realized through copies-icons that are understood to be the product of an *intrinsic* relation to the model that serves as their foundation (*LS* 257). We may venture to say, then, that Deleuze is interested in this intrinsic relation and in the distinction between representations or true copies and simulacra, which are distorted or false copies. As we will see, the distortion of figuration pushed by the simulacra will be central to Deleuze's aesthetic thinking. It is, he says, the critical edge of modernity, destroying both models and their true copies (representations) in order to institute the creative chaos (*LS* 264, 266).

The development of this theme and of the structure supporting it appears to have continued throughout Deleuze's work, thus its introduction sets the stage for Deleuze's notion of philosophy in general. Referring to the wrenching duality, Deleuze states that aesthetics designates, first, a theory of sensibility, insofar as sensibility is assumed to be the *form of any possible experience*. As the form of any possible experience, aesthetics is clearly situated as an aspect of thought. As a form, it will be a calculus, *a formal structure of well-defined rules that make the system governing experience consistent*, so that it is not subject to interpretation. A formal system for aesthetics can be thought in relation to sensation as it arises in relation to Nature, or in relation to sensation produced by a specific work of art, but is always without a specific reference to the external events or entities that it governs. Formal systems, insofar as they are consistent, do not lend themselves to contradiction or to the search for meaning outside of the system. This, it seems, is the general purpose of *The Logic of Sense*, to articulate the system consisting of series that produce sense. This is also why Deleuze calls it the *logic* of sense. It articulates the formal system of well-defined rules according to which sense arises on an abstract surface in between forms of thought and the physical world, eschewing reference and the concomitant problems reference entails.[1]

In addition to its formal systematic character, Deleuze elsewhere calls aesthetics a theory of art, a reflection of real experience that may include "an aesthetic of the spectator, as in the theory of the judgment of taste; sometimes an aesthetic, or rather a meta-aesthetic, of the creator, as in the theory of genius. Sometimes an aesthetic of the beautiful in Nature; sometimes an aesthetic of the beautiful in art."[2] However, this second formulation of aesthetics does not simply stop here. Deleuze follows it with the proposal that if the conditions of experience in general do, in fact, become the conditions of real experience, then art may proceed as a series of experiments, as experimentation. This implies that aesthetics is also a theory of experimentation with reality.

Each of these characteristics appears to have at least been suggested by the philosophy that inspires the wrenching duality, that of Immanuel Kant. Kant proposed, in the *Critique of Judgment*, that in the free play of the faculties, the so-called aesthetic judgment is freed from the domination of both the faculty of Understanding (determining empirical knowledge) and the faculty of Reason (determining practical interests).[3] Freed from both faculties, aesthetic form is a nearly perfect model of disengagement. Emerging in free play, it is indifferent to the *existence* of the objects of its reflection as well as to their sensible matter. Aesthetic form, the formalized structure of any possible aesthetic experience, has a difficult task to perform. It must remain within the limits of the formal system and at the same time manage to be a theory of art, in order to be an aesthetic theory in both senses of the term. For Kant, this task remains well within the parameters of his overall philosophical system. Just as Understanding yields concepts for experience and Reason uses the transcendental Ideas as regulative principles for action, so too Imagination, the faculty of presentation, performs its task, which is not to yield to concepts, but to yield only to the faculty of concepts, the Understanding.

Adhering to the subjective but formal conditions of a judgment in general, the judgment of taste – resting on merely the sensation of the reciprocal interaction of a free Imagination and an Understanding conforming to law – yields the feeling of harmony in the play of mental powers, as those powers are felt in *sensation*.[4] Aesthetical judgment yields no knowledge of objects, nor does it give us practical principles for action. Aesthetical judgment is, however, itself both object and law, where our own feeling of pleasure in the harmony of the faculties is the object of the judgment, *and* it is also the law, the form of the judgment, since our pleasure arises in the mere act of judging, and thus lies only in the fact that we can and do make judgments.[5] As Deleuze points out, this is not just aesthetic judgment but *judgment in general*. The importance of this is that, as judgment in general, the aesthetical judgment grounds every determinate accord between Understanding, Reason and Imagination, even though the faculty of Imagination subjects no objects, and so subjects nothing, to its law, nothing at all.[6]

The aesthetic sensation is only the reflection on the *form* of an object by the Imagination, indifferent to the existence of objects as much as to their material constituents such as color or sound.[7] As Deleuze emphasizes, there must thereby be a clear distinction between the intuited form of sensibility, which includes colors and sounds, and the reflection on form carried out by Imagination alone. Only the latter introduces the free harmony of all the faculties and their contingent accord with sensible objects.[8] For only the latter exhibits a limited materiality that is not firmly established or "ensconced in our senses."[9] Of course, that Imagination reflects only on form requires the existence of an ability to reflect merely the *form of the object* so as to be free of immersion in sensibility. This ability distinguishes those possessing the original faculty of "taste" from those lacking it, insofar as only some are capable, it appears, of feeling the sensation that is the harmony of the faculties. For aesthetic sensation, as for knowledge and practical action, all three faculties must be in play.

This view of aesthetics persists in Deleuze's work, for in the case of the aesthetic form specifically, aesthetic "common sense" is said to keep the other two faculties in play so as to bring to life a proper aesthetic form.[10] Kant insists that the aesthetical judgment of taste is a legitimate common sense. Taste is communal, pleasure is communicable. In principle everyone is capable of forming such a judgment. Everyone possesses the faculties of Imagination and Understanding. All that is required is the ability to think for oneself, to put ourselves in another's place and to think consistently.[11] However, in reality, it appears that only certain individuals truly accomplish this. As will become clear, this is particularly the role of genius.

REASON'S IDEA

How an aesthetical judgment comes about for Kant is a matter of some importance as it provides Deleuze with the Idea organizing his own logic of sensation, his account of the manner in which the aesthetic Idea, the theory of sensibility with which we began, provides the *form* of any possible experience. How then does one arrive at the aesthetical common sense necessary for free Imagination and undetermined Understanding? The answer is that it requires a shock, which comes from elsewhere, from the one faculty not yet involved, which is Reason. Initially, Reason, the faculty of transcendental Ideas, played no role in aesthetic sensation, but it will be of the greatest importance because it situates the faculties with respect to Nature's physical forces. The judgment of the sublime, unlike that of the beautiful, takes place in relation to formlessness, to boundlessness.[12] And unlike the judgment of beauty, a judgment that is compatible with the play of Imagination, the judgment of the sublime stops us cold. We encounter Nature in its formless chaos, at its wildest and most irregular, in disorder and desolation, where it is only size beyond measure, or power beyond comprehension.

Nevertheless, the apprehension of the most fundamental unit utilized by mathematics is also aesthetic, as is the mere apprehension of any magnitude. Utilizing mathematics, we may, in principle, that is, at least from a theoretical point of view, count to infinity, but our aesthetic intuition is limited; it encounters its own maximum when confronted by Reason's Idea of the sublime.[13] Thus our successive apprehension of one unit following another is always countered by our simultaneous but necessarily limited conceptual comprehension of the totality.[14] For the Understanding, the logical estimation of magnitude is unperturbed by the count to infinity. But then, beware the voice of Reason! It desires comprehension in a single intuition; it demands that the infinite be thought as entirely given, as a totality.[15] But intuition fails at this, for only the faculty of supersensible Reason can manage it. Deleuze takes the failure of intuition very seriously. Imagination cannot comprehend the infinite in a single intuition. Therefore, Deleuze's aesthetics will abandon the intuition of the totality and turn to the Idea of Reason, the supersensible Ideas governing immanence.

For Kant, intuitions giving rise to judgments of the sublime are located exclusively in "rude Nature," since the empirical experience of infinite magnitude can only be found in Nature's apparently unlimited or formless regions. Simultaneously, however, the judgment reveals that the mind feels itself elevated by Reason when it finds Imagination inadequate to its Ideas.[16] It is only in Nature's immensity that we find our own limitations. It brings us to our knees as we recognize our physical impotence, the weakness and inadequacy of our sensation when confronted by unmediated Nature. But there is a positive aspect to this experience, for the Idea of the supersensible is brought to life by the object that is "Nature" as it exists in space and time.[17] In other words, Nature is to us the object of an intuition that informs us of the limits of our sensibility but expands our aesthetic reach when it provokes the feeling of the sublime, by means of which it is at least in accord with our faculties. Imagination is first crushed then freed from its own bounds, then welcomed into the realm of Reason. "At the very moment the Imagination believes it has lost its freedom, through the violence of Reason, it is freed from all the constraints of the Understanding, it enters into accord with Reason."[18]

Insofar as Deleuze turns away from the possibility of an *experience* of the sublime in Nature, he will reformulate it as a formal event, an event occurring in three-dimensional abstract space rather than the space of experience. Such an event, as we will see, has a formal, mathematical name. In that context, it may be called a *catastrophe* (*FB* 100). Mathematically, on a surface, the fixed point governing the system's behavior shifts from being a stable attractor with smooth transitions to a temporarily unstable one with discontinuous transitions.[19] However, "the change of stability forces the system to move abruptly to the region of a new stable fixed point."[20] Transposed by Deleuze into the Kantian framework, catastrophe describes what happens when Imagination moves from the harmony of free play to the violence of inadequacy, and finally to the stability of its suprasensible destination. It does so, as Deleuze emphasizes, by first approaching its limit, then experiencing a radical break, a discontinuous transition, finally restabilizing beyond the sensible, in an accord with Reason, as it awakens Reason to the rational Idea.[21]

These procedures are crucial to the development of Deleuze's aesthetics, for they set the stage for the arrival of the creator-genius who appears out of necessity, as an effect of formal rules and physical forces. This requires the ability to think formally. As Deleuze points out, the uneducated man does not rise up to the feeling of the sublime, but remains mired in sensible discord, miserable and distressed.[22] Something that happens when the individual undergoes the catastrophic transformation associated with the sublime is crucial to aesthetic sensibility. The implication is that the aesthetic judgment of the sublime is necessary, and not because it is the cause of our judgment – it is not. Nature follows its own laws, mechanical laws govern Nature, and it is pure *chance* that Nature conforms to judgment's order.[23] The laws governing Nature determine its course and those governing our faculties likewise determine what our faculties can do – that the two realms are in accord is mere contingency. In spite of this, we can say that the aesthetic judgment of the sublime is necessary because by means of Reason's violence, Imagination encounters its own limits. This, as we will see, makes it possible for those unique individuals, those with taste and those with artistic genius, to emerge from the general mass of humankind. Quite possibly, without this shock, this contradiction between Imagination's role, which is to reflect on form, and its inability to do so in the face of Nature, which gives rise to a new accord beyond the sensible, taste and genius would never find their place.

THE JUDGMENT OF THE BEAUTIFUL

Of equal importance is the role of the aesthetical judgment of the beautiful. Although the judgment is indifferent to the existence of objects, nevertheless, it proves that Nature is capable of producing objects that are formally reflected in the Imagination. There is an accord between Nature and us because our faculties make this possible.[24] Elsewhere, Deleuze has expressed a certain amount of discontent over Kant's interpretation of the free play of faculties as yet another common sense which is both an object and a law (*DR* 137). It seems that Deleuze is not sanguine about Kant's appeal to common sense as something arising from the communal feeling everyone ought to have for judgments of taste.[25] For even though everyone ought to have this feeling, certainly many do not.

In spite of this, aspects of this account, Kant's and his own, will continue to goad Deleuze, and are not truly resolved prior to his encounter with the paintings of Francis Bacon in *The Logic of Sensation*. The supersensible Idea of the sublime will give rise to the productions of the creator-genius capable of thinking the supersensible Idea in order to produce an exemplary work of art. Given the scarcity of exemplary works of art, so-called aesthetical common sense may, in the end, turn out to be less communal and more disjunctive than it originally appears. This is perhaps why Deleuze continues to think about the consequences of Kant's declaration that "beautiful arts must necessarily be considered as arts of *genius*."[26] The artistic work of genius is not common but exemplary. And beautiful art does not result from a concept applied to an object; this would be mere mechanism, meaning, it merely yields knowledge of Nature, which follows mechanical laws. It does not produce beauty. But Deleuze, along with Kant, remains interested in the production of beautiful works of art, which are themselves ideal or exemplary productions.

Tellingly, Deleuze will agree with Kant when he insists that there must be something original about the judgment of beauty, something exemplary, something that gives a rule but only to art.[27] Of course we must acknowledge and accept that "there is no beautiful art in which there is not a mechanical element."[28] This means that there is something in even beautiful art that can be understood according to some rules and as serving some purpose, without which it would be mere chance and not art. But natural beauty, concerned only with form, is *not the beautiful representation of a thing*, while art must be, although only in a particular sense.[29]

Artists must have talent cultivated in schools, but also genius, such that beautiful art may even present ugly things as beautiful! This sort of transformation occurs insofar as the work of art is not distinguishable from the object *in our* sensation, and so relies on allegory or pleasing attributes.[30] The work of art is the product of spirit, the animating principle of the mind, the faculty of *aesthetical Ideas*, and the counterpart of *rational Ideas*.[31] Aesthetical Ideas are the product of Imagination, which operates analogically, and for which no concept is adequate. Analogically, Imagination creates another Nature when experience is too *commonplace* and what we *feel* is our freedom from the law of association ([p.(q.r]] = [(p.q).r]], at least when association makes possible the empirical use of Imagination.[32]

The means by which genius accomplishes this is to generate an Idea associated with a concept but bound up with a multiplicity of partial representations such that no single definite concept is implicated and the association of empirical representations is defeated. Imagination thereby provides Understanding with abundant new material to quicken and possibly challenge cognitive powers.[33] This is also the point of Deleuze's aesthetics. It is a logic of sensation bound up with a multiplicity of partial representations for which no single concept is adequate. In this way, the aesthetic Idea, counterpart of rational Ideas, is the product of genius that quickens and challenges the cognitive powers.

By what means, then, does this come about? Deleuze takes particular note of Kant's claim that Reason is *interested* in the objective reality of its Ideas.[34] In other words, the *accord* between Nature and our human faculties interests Reason. Aesthetic judgments must be disinterested; they must be without interest in the existence of the object because they are purely formal judgments. Nonetheless, we experience a rational interest in the accord of Nature's beautiful products with human disinterested pleasure. Reason is interested in the "accord" between Nature and our faculties. It is interested that Nature itself contains some ground for the agreement, so that our pleasure is not merely the formal product of our faculties but has a basis in Nature, which would be in its colors or sounds. These two natural charms are "blended with beautiful forms" so that Reason may more readily reflect on the forms. This is called the language by which Nature speaks to us. We are immediately drawn to Nature's charms but we reflect on its forms, and by analogy we arrive at Reason's highest Ideas, which are moral Ideas.[35] Aesthetical judgments judge beautiful forms without concepts, but the satisfaction in the form of judgment is meant to be a rule for everyone. They are thus, by analogy, like moral judgments of Reason, whose a priori satisfaction in the forms of practical maxims is likewise a law for everyone. So we should not be surprised that natural beauties like white lilies awaken the idea of innocence, red suggests sublimity, and the song of birds suggests contentment and gladness.[36] But this is Nature, it is not yet art, and aesthetics must also determine how Reason proceeds from Nature to art.

FROM NATURE TO ART

Art is defined as production through freedom, indicating that a will with Reason lies at the basis of free actions.[37] In its design, the beautiful work of art must be like Nature, free from constraint with respect to our faculties, in other words, no concepts can determine it. This how we have aesthetical judgment; it is due to Imagination's free play of faculties, when Understanding remains undetermined and does not judge according to a concept. Reason's interest in the accord between objective reality and our subjective judgment leads to the realization that Nature produces beautiful, natural things. Nature provides a rule for beauty. Therefore, beautiful art must look like Nature, but since it cannot be merely the effect of mechanical laws as is Nature, art cannot be the product of Nature's laws. For this Reason the creation of art requires something beyond mere Nature and mechanical laws – it requires genius, for "genius is the innate mental disposition through which Nature gives the rule to Art."[38]

Nature, which is mechanical, gives a rule, but genius interprets it. Why? If a work of art is beautiful, it may not be determined by any concept, but a rule of some kind must determine that beautiful artifice is at least possible and indeed this occurs, but it is beautiful art only as long as the rule remains indefinite. Only the genius can produce a beautiful work of art that is not the product of any definite ideal. This is the meaning of *originality*. The work of art produced by the genius is original insofar as no determinate rule is given for it. Additionally, it is *exemplary*. It is a model that sets a standard, which is a rule for other works of art that will necessarily be less original and therefore less exemplary. And finally, since they do not arise from a determinate rule of Nature, no one, not even the genius knows where her ideas come from, that is, how they take on determinate form.[39]

Although Nature gives the genius the indeterminate rule which the genius then utilizes to produce original and exemplary works of art, we may still ask what makes it possible for an artist to be a genius. The quality of being an artistic genius and of producing beautiful works of art seems to be connected to the artist's daring and overwhelming experience of the sublime. What the genius possesses is *spirit*, the animating principle of the mind that puts the mental powers into play without a definite concept.[40] Reason seeks to comprehend infinite magnitude in a single intuition, but Imagination, the faculty of aesthetic intuition is inadequate to this command, it cannot intuit infinite magnitude or number in a single intuition. And so, it feels the pain of its encounter with Nature's sublime phenomena. It suffers astonishment bordering on terror, dread, holy awe. It undergoes melancholy meditations.[41] But the initial shock subsides, and in its place arises a state of joy.[42] How is this possible? It is possible because the artist of genius recognizes that she is ultimately secure, that far from being impotent she is actually superior in the face of Nature. Of course, what makes any of us superior to Nature is that we have the capacity to think the infinite without falling into sensible contradiction. We think infinity without sensible contradiction because our supersensible faculty of Reason allows us to think the sublime as an Idea of Reason rather than relying on the limited powers of Imagination.[43]

In this way, genius is born. First, there is the encounter with rude Nature, then the shock of submission, and finally, the joy of realizing our supersensible Nature, all made possible, of course, only through the encounter with Nature. Our mind feels elevated, abandoning itself to Imagination's freedom from limits, which comes only thanks to the Ideas of Reason. Imagination's greatest effort, which is to refer to something absolutely great, arises only by reference to the laws of Reason, a correspondence with Rational Laws.

As such, the mind is moved, vibrating between attraction and repulsion, disharmonious through their contrast. In this manner the two poles of vibration might be said to form a disjunctive synthesis, a *disharmony* of the faculties. This is how Imagination and Reason generate the subjective purposiveness of our mental powers; they do it by means of *conflict*.[44]

THE DISJUNCTION OF THE FACULTIES

The conflict of the faculties, their lack of harmony, Deleuze maintains, is the necessary prerequisite for works of genius. While Kant focuses on the harmony between aesthetical and moral feeling, between Nature and Reason's Ideas, Deleuze emphasizes their disjunction from the faculty of the Understanding. In what follows, we shall show how the account we have just given is incorporated into Deleuze's aesthetic theory, a theory which, we have noted, accounts for the creation of original and exemplary works of art, but which also provides a formal as well as a meta-aesthetical account. For Kant, that meta-aesthetical account lies primarily in the immediate interest in Nature's beauty, insofar as this is an interest in form alone which we judge to be beautiful for everyone. This implies, for Kant, that aesthetic judgments are analogous to practical maxims since both judge forms, forms without concepts (the aesthetic), and forms of practical maximums (the moral). What connects them is that, as forms, each is capable of universal application through the logical law of distribution. But Deleuze's meta-aesthetic analysis is aimed primarily at the other aspect of Kant's account. Indeed, aesthetical and moral judgments complement one another and Reason is *interested* in the agreement of its maxims with Nature. In other words, Reason has a moral interest in Nature's aesthetical agreement with its own Ideas such that Nature can symbolize Ideas, as the white lily symbolizes innocence.[45]

One final consideration emerges. We note that Deleuze makes a seemingly small but crucial addition to his analysis. He notes that in the disinterested judgment of beautiful art, Imagination not only reflects form but also color and sound. Color and sound are "blended" with beautiful form and implicated with our reflection on form, yielding some sort of higher sense.[46] Deleuze associates this with what Kant later calls free or fluid matter. This will be important insofar as it provides a link to the consideration of color in works of art that are the free products of genius. It also provides an insight into the role of sensation in Deleuze's account of aesthetics as a logic of sensation insofar as color and sound act directly on the nervous system and thereby bypass the "brain," which is the source of representation and figuration.

Given that beautiful Nature brings Understanding and Imagination into play, how is it that beautiful art is identified with freedom? Having undergone the crushing encounter with Nature's infinity, followed by the joyful thought of the Idea of Reason, the genius epitomizes freedom from Imagination's limitations, freedom from any constraint of arbitrary rules, the feeling of freedom in the play of our cognitive faculties, universally communicable but without determinate concepts.[47] In this sense, genius comes from Nature. Nevertheless, it would not be surprising if we were to wonder how the "closed and artificial" world of Francis Bacon could possibly reveal the same vital movement as that of the painter Paul Cézanne, whose "Nature" Deleuze takes to be in some way analogous (FB 43). The answer to this lies in the notion that Bacon's painting and Cézanne's painting are of the same temperament, that both are figural and both optimistic. To make sense of this, we have to continue articulating what we take to be Deleuze's transposition of Kant's aesthetics, with its wrenching duality, into his own logic of sensation. Although the latter seems to be much less an aesthetic of the beautiful object than an aesthetic of Nature's physical forces acting on the nervous system directly and violently, still, the echoes of Kant are everywhere.

FIGURATIVE NARRATION OR ASIGNIFYING FIGURES

In *The Logic of Sensation*, Deleuze begins by distinguishing different sorts of artworks. Figurative work is illustrative and narrative as well as signifying. Classical painting, especially single-point perspective painting, seems to be the target here. When works of art "escape" the Classical Figurative work of art, they do so either by veering into pure form through abstraction as so much modern art does, or into what Deleuze calls the purely figural, achieved through isolation, in which the painting is an isolated reality and the Figure is isolated in the painting in a way that prevents any sort of narrative from developing because in the image no associations are made (*FB* 2). Iconic images of this type are most often associated with medieval sacred art, but portraits by the Spanish artist El Greco (1541–1614) also appear to isolate the figure in the painting in a similar manner. So, it is perhaps not surprising when Deleuze maintains that the work of Francis Bacon is not abstract like the artworks of abstract expressionism or minimalism. It does not engage with pure form, either on the level of Understanding (narrative and illustrative) or on the level of Reason (it is not formless, not an image of the sublime) (*FB* 2, 103). It is something different, an isolated system on a single plane, a closed space where the flat wash grounds the Figure on that single plane, which is painted as if viewed from close range (*FB* 5). So close, that the Figure appears to try to overwhelm and eliminate the spectator, subjecting the spectator to the overwhelming power of the sublime through the dynamism of physical forces inhabiting the Figure (*FB* 13–14). This is why it is important for Deleuze, like Kant, that works of art have a relationship to Nature. The figure in Bacon's paintings is an effect of Nature's physical forces according the laws governing vector fields.

Deleuze states, with respect to his own work, that Nature is structured like mathematical vector space, so it is crucial for us to realize that in mathematics, the laws governing vector space are identical to the Kantian categories of relation (*DR* 1994). These laws of association, commutation, and distribution are carried out by means of what are also the Kantian categories of substance and accidents, cause and effect, and reciprocity between agent and patient. When translated into logical terms, the categories of relation represent the categorical relation (All S are P), the hypothetical (If S then P), and the disjunctive relation (Either S or P).[48] Of all the categories that unite our representations under a single concept and so yield knowledge, only the categories of relation are derived exclusively from logic. As such, the categories of relation have no need of sensible intuitions but immediately become cognitions.[49] The lack of the requirement for sensible intuitions allows Reason to extend the categories of relation beyond experience, beyond sensible intuitions to supersensible Ideas. Reason thus produces the supersensible Ideas – Self (substance), World (the chain of causal events), God (the capacity to join and disjoin) – which Reason is driven to extend to infinity thereby creating supersensible Ideas, Ideas for which we have no sensible intuitions.[50] In this way, they surpass our finite capacity to apply concepts to intuitions. We certainly cannot have an intuition of infinite supersensible Ideas, nor can we utilize them for knowledge, since in both cases, they exceed our finite human faculties. We have no knowledge of an immortal soul (Self), or of an infinite chain of causes (World), or of an all-powerful first cause (God).

What supersensible Ideas can do is constitute what Deleuze refers to as the Event. Nature's physical forces following the laws of supersensible Reason produce the Event. The Event consists of real, physical, and effective sensations that bypass Imagination and Understanding, and directly affect the nervous system, no intuitions or thought needed (*FB* 15).

The paintings of Francis Bacon constitute Events for Deleuze. Before the painter begins, the canvas consists of equally probable any spaces whatever – a canvas state space, the ideal space of Events (*FB* 93).[51] Nevertheless, as a material projection of ideal space, the specific canvas has three dimensions, a center, and boundaries. And then there is the painter with the mysterious *something in his head* (*FB* 86). This is not to say that the painter thinks about the Figures he paints, rather, everything in his head is already on the canvas. All he needs to do is clear it out by sweeping, dilating, contracting, flattening, elongating. The sensation of manual effort is particularly violent when the deformations concern the face and the face is cleared out so as to become a head that screams, capturing the invisible and insensible forces, sensations beyond mere pain and feeling (*FB* 93–98)

This then, is the work of Baconian genius. Clearing out what is already present is the original and exemplary act of genius. Manually subordinating eye to hand, the painter begins by destroying narrative figuration with the use of chance brush marks delivered by "the hand of the painter" onto the canvas (*FB* 106). These chance marks are not probabilities as the latter concern only statistical averages (*FB* 94). Chance marks are said to be irrational, involuntary, accidental, free, random, non-representative, non-narrative, neither significant nor signifiers. They enact the Kantian free play of Imagination and Reason that gives rise to the beautiful (*FB* 100). And yet, they appear on the canvas through the hand of the painter. As such, they are the contingent accord of Nature's laws and pure sensation in the aesthetical Idea. In Bacon's art, almost as much as in Cézanne's, geometry is the frame but color is the sensation, producing an immediate, felt, aesthetic analogue that is non-figurative, non-digital, and without a primary resemblance. It is not, then, the homogeneous and binary code of abstraction, which lies behind the organization of minimalism into grids (FB 117).

The clearing away of figurative givens, of narrative and representation, is the effect of what we have earlier called the catastrophe, those parameter values of a surface where the fixed point governing the system's behavior shifts from being a stable to an unstable attractor.[52] In Kant, this describes the encounter with the sublime. In engineering, such an event may result in support beams that buckle and collapse. In societies, it describes political upheaval.[53] In a Bacon painting, catastrophe is characterized by a mouth that is elongated and stretched, a head swiped with a brush, broom, sponge, or rag, bodies that are off-balance, planes that collide, and contour that is eliminated (FB 100, 118). The catastrophe, Deleuze claims, "liberates" the planes of the painting along with its color and bodies. In place of perspective, the logical forms of connection/conjunction/disjunction (this and that, this or that) randomly connect figurations (FB 118). In place of color value, the effect of light and dark, saturated or rarefied tone, there will be relations of modulation, tonality, the spectrum of warm or cool colors, haptic (tactile) rather than optical relations of color "within" sight (FB 132–33). Modulation is haptic; it is the spatializing energy of color on a surface where there is nothing to narrate because nothing is left of the body to narrate (FB 134). In place of figure/ground and body, there will be a body without organs, subject to laws of force ripping it apart (FB 118).

These dynamically sublime liberations, sublime because they exceed Understanding's ability to represent them in an Intuition, produce an immediate and violent sensation. Beginning with the flat wash, fields of motionless and uniform color, the movement of the paintings goes from this material structure to the Figure, contouring around it, enveloping and imprisoning it (FB 14). Likewise, the Figure moves toward the material structure, the motionless flat wash, as if to escape from narration, escaping also from Nature's laws, the physical forces that constitute it, and falling back into the material structure. In its escape, the Figure is deformed. It screams because the body escaping through the mouth forces the mouth wide open in another catastrophic deformation of the body. And there is a shadow because some of the body has leaked out, escaped through a point in the contour (*FB* 16). The structure of laws shaping physical forces cannot result in a molar figuration, a narrative, or representation, nor are they abstract, nor are they formless. Rather, what is revealed is the molecular becoming of suffering humanity.

The second law of thermodynamics states that in a closed system where no new matter or energy enters, there will be far more disordered states, mixtures of particles in more different thus less well-ordered states. At equilibrium, everything is homogeneous.[54] It is perhaps, then, this sensation, the sensation of the sublime catastrophic event, that ends with the transition from an organized molar body to a less-organized molecular body without organs, which Bacon's paintings capture … forever. Deleuze states that when the Figure tries to return to the material structure but has not yet dissolved into it, it is not yet become molecular. The becoming molecular of a human being reveals a body that is no longer supported by bones and flesh (*FB* 27). It is a body that looks like meat, a state that can be common to man and animal. When bodies are stripped of flesh and bone, all that is left is meat. This is what happens to animals when they are butchered, so Bacon's Figures are the very figure of the becoming animal (meat) of man. The Figure is a body for which the becoming animal of man occurs when the human figure assumes an animal head and the animal becomes the physical spirit of man, that is, the animal becomes the head of the man (*FB* 22).

Deleuze declares that the lived body of phenomenology is paltry compared with the almost unlivable Power of the body without organs (*FB* 44). Indeed, who can doubt this? Rather than senses, the body is left only with thresholds, the minimum intensity or value of a signal that will provoke a response (*FB* 45). When qualitative sensation is extended into space as intensity, it is possible to measure the amplitude of its molecular movements.[55] But Henri Bergson warns us that we tend to confuse different types of intensities. Some are connected with force exerted upon the body externally. But others, such as the sensible awareness of an obscure desire that becomes a deep emotion, or the image of an object that alters the shade of a thousand perceptions or memories, these correspond only to qualitative changes. These are the intensities of ontological memory.[56] What belongs to memory is heterogeneous but indivisible, but what belongs to the intensities of external forces can be broken up in *any way* whatever.[57] It is the intensities of external forces that Deleuze describes, so powerfully, and which he thinks clear away the other form of intensity, that of the qualitative changes of sensibility and ontological memory.

FRANCIS BACON, GENIUS

Like Kant's genius, this is where Deleuze's genius starts. Spirit, the animating principle of the mind, puts the faculties into play.[58] Imagination creates another Nature out of the material that actual Nature gives it. We are freed from the commonplace law of association; we remold matter; the deformations commence. "The poet ventures to realize, to sense rational Ideas of invisible beings, the kingdom of the blessed, hell, eternity, creation ... he tries ... to go beyond the limits of experience and to present them to Sense."[59] This is how it comes about that the intensive body is traversed by a wave tracing its thresholds, varying its amplitudes in accordance with them, acting on the body which screams and breathes, releasing the hysteria of painting. This autoscopia is feeling oneself inside a head, in a body, in the naked body, capturing forces and rendering them visible (*FB* 44–55). The sensation, Deleuze claims, is like Kant's, lively and full of spirit. Not entropy, but the clinamen, atoms falling in the void, but still according to rules! "In the void, the velocity of the atom is equal to its movement in a unique direction in a minimum of continuous time" (*LS* 269). Perhaps Deleuze thinks that atoms can escape the second law of thermodynamics through the catastrophe. But every Baconian triptych is unified by the law of distribution, the unity of light and color distributed across the canvases, and Deleuze admits that in these paintings, time is a monochromatic *eternity* (*FB* 85). Nothing more entropic in the universe.

How does one become capable of painting in this way? Bacon's act of painting consists of random marks, scrubbing, sweeping, and wiping the canvas, removing the figurative and narrative givens of painting, doing away with perspective and representation. It is, says Deleuze, as if a catastrophe has overcome the canvas. Catastrophe theory belongs, at least in part, to the physics of structurally stable systems where patterns repeat themselves in generally regular manners. But discontinuities appear, and catastrophe theory is an attempt to provide a mathematical framework for describing these processes.[60] If we take up Kant's harmony of the faculties, the manner in which concepts of the Understanding provide concepts for Imagination's intuitions, all under the influence of Reason, which seeks to unify consciousness, then we can assume that Reason is a fixed-point attractor in an abstract space. Every time a concept is applied to an intuition, it can be said to occur as a point in the abstract state space of the faculties, ultimately producing an entire surface of experience. Normally, shifts in intuition are minimal.

But what if Reason demands, as we saw it does, that Imagination attend to an infinitely large or powerful Intuition that exceeds its finite capacity? The result, we said, is that Imagination is crushed and must shift to an entirely new region of its faculties. It must shift in a discontinuous manner from Understanding to Reason. The point where this discontinuity occurs is called a catastrophe point.[61] Recall, however, what we said above. When the artist undergoes the encounter with the sublime, the feeling is one of joy over being freed from the limits of Imagination and Understanding. The freedom is prerequisite to the original and exemplary beautiful works of art of genius. Imagination "emulates the play of Reason in its quest after a maximum, to go beyond the limits of experience and to present them to Sense with a completeness of which there is no example in Nature."[62] Following the catastrophic break with Understanding, Imagination is free to approximate Reason's Ideas, but this means, also, a destabilization. These presentations do not "*represent* what lies in our concepts of the sublimity and majesty of creation," rather Imagination spreads itself over numerous kindred representations, arousing more thought than can be expressed in a concept to furnish an *aesthetical Idea*.[63] In this way, the kindred representations enliven the mind and stimulate the Imagination, but no single concept gives a rule for those representations.

Perhaps we can say that the paintings of Francis Bacon capture the sensation of the sublime, the catastrophe. Perhaps we can also say that sensation in Bacon's paintings is the effect of the action of invisible forces on the body producing, not feelings nor representations of violent feelings, but affects. And the movement of such affects is movement in place, spasms, contraction, dilation in contact with Nature's physical forces, what Deleuze calls here its vital power, violent and catastrophic. In this sense, for Deleuze, Bacon's paintings, regardless of the screaming, disintegrating heads, express optimism and belief in life, where life means the physical forces acting on bodies. And perhaps this is analogous to Cézanne's Nature, to the extent that Cézanne gives feeling to geometry, so that we feel the presence of the image as much as we see it (*FB* 112). From Deleuze's point of view, this is surely the case.

All this adds support to the idea, which we proposed at the beginning of this essay, that all of Deleuze's philosophy may be encountered from the point of view of aesthetics. It is a philosophy that takes its orientation from the wrenching duality that Deleuze says characterizes aesthetics. First, the theory of sensibility as the *form* of possible experience that takes us out of figuration and brings us to the reality of body, lines, and colors freed of organic representation, freed of the material reality of bodies (*FB* 55). And second, it is a theory of art, not merely as a reflection on art, but as a reflection on this new sort of real experience that unlocks areas of sensation that are neither representation nor the "mess," the confused sensation of abstract expressionism, nor the pure abstraction of minimalism (*FB* 102–3). What this aesthetic advocates is nothing other than the *hysteria of the senses*. One begins with categories of the Understanding, their representational and narrative organization, then one clears them away in what, for Deleuze, is the sublime work of genius: isolation, deformation, dissipation, melting, but, ultimately, eternal time (*FB* 63–64).

NOTES

1   For an account of some of the problems reference and non-reference entail see Dorothea Olkowski, "After Alice: Alice and the Dry Tail," *Deleuze Studies*, 2 (2008), 107–22.
2   Gilles Deleuze, "The Idea of Genesis in Kant's Aesthetics," trans. Daniel W. Smith, *Angelaki: Journal of Theoretical Humanities*, 5:3 (December 2000), 57–70, 59.
3   *Ibid.*, p. 60.
4   Immanuel Kant, *Critique of Judgment*, trans. J. H. Bernard, 2nd rev. edn. (London: Macmillan, 1914), section 35, p. 133.
5   *Ibid.*, section 36, p. 134; section 37, p. 135.
6   Deleuze, "The Idea of Genesis," p. 60.

7   Kant, *Critique of Judgment*, section 38, p. 137; Deleuze, "The Idea of Genesis," p. 61.

8   Deleuze, "The Idea of Genesis," p. 61.

9   *Ibid.*

10 *Ibid.*, p. 64; *DR* 137.

11 Kant, *Critique of Judgment*, section 37, p. 139.

12 *Ibid.*, section 23, p. 102; Deleuze, "The Idea of Genesis," p. 63.

13 Kant, *Critique of Judgment*, section 26, p. 111.

14 *Ibid.*, section 26, p. 111; Deleuze, "The Idea of Genesis," p. 63.

15 Kant, *Critique of Judgment*, section 26, p. 115.

16 *Ibid.*, section 26, p. 118.

17 *Ibid.*, section 29, pp. 124–25, 135.

18 Deleuze, "The Idea of Genesis," p. 63.

19 John Casti, *Complexification: Explaining a Paradoxical World through the Science of Surprise* (New York: HarperCollins, 1994), p. 53.

20 *Ibid.*, p. 55.

21 Deleuze, "The Idea of Genesis," p. 63.

22 *Ibid.*

23 *Ibid.*, p. 64.

24 *Ibid.*

25 Kant, *Critique of Judgment*, section 22, p. 95.

26 *Ibid.*, section 46, p. 152.

27 *Ibid.*

28 *Ibid.*, section 47, p. 154.

29 *Ibid.*, section 48, p. 155.

30 *Ibid.*, section 48, pp. 155–56.

31 *Ibid.*, section 49, p. 157.

32 *Ibid.*

33 *Ibid.*, section 49, p. 159.

34 *Ibid.*, section 42, p. 144; Deleuze, "The Idea of Genesis," p. 65.

35 Kant, *Critique of Judgment*, section 42, p. 145; Deleuze, "The Idea of Genesis," p. 65.

36 Kant, *Critique of Judgment*, section 42, p. 145.

37 *Ibid.*, section 43, p. 147.

38 *Ibid.*, section 46, p. 152.

39 *Ibid.*

40 *Ibid.*, section 49, p. 157.

41 *Ibid.*, section 29, p. 136.

42 *Ibid.*, section 28, p. 124.

43 *Ibid.*, section 26, p. 116.

44 *Ibid.*, section 27, pp. 120–21.

45 *Ibid.*, section 42, p. 145; Deleuze, "The Idea of Genesis," p. 66.

46   Kant, *Critique of Judgment*, section 42, p. 145; Deleuze, "The Idea of Genesis," p. 65.

47   Kant, *Critique of Judgment*, section 49, p. 160.

48   Immanuel Kant, *Critique of Pure Reason*, trans. Norman Kemp Smith (London: Macmillan, 1929), A80/B106, A70/B95, and Keith Devlin, *Mathematics: The Science of Patterns. The Search for Order in Life, Mind, and the Universe* (New York: Scientific American Library, 1994), p. 44.

49   Immanuel Kant, *Critique of Practical Reason*, trans. Lewis White Beck (New York: Liberal Arts Press, 1956), p. 68.

50   Kant, *Critique of Pure Reason*, A333–39/B390–97. For an extended discussion of Kant's categories of relation, why and how they become Transcendental Ideas, see Dorothea Olkowski, *The Universal (In the Realm of the Sensible)* (New York: Columbia University Press; Edinburgh University Press, 2007), chapter 2.

51   In mathematics, state space is a geometrical model posited for a set of idealized states of a phenomenon. Changes in position are represented by points, which, when connected, form curved lines called trajectories (Olkowski, *The Universal*, p. 208).

52   Casti, *Complexification*, p. 53.

53   *Ibid.*, pp. 55–56.

54   Devlin, *Mathematics*, p. 79.

55   Henri Bergson, *Time and Free Will: An Essay on the Immediate Data of Consciousness*, trans. F. L. Pogson (New York: Macmillan, 1959), p. 6.

56   *Ibid.*, pp. 7–11.

57   *Ibid.*, pp. 83, 85.

58   Kant, *Critique of Judgment*, section 49, p. 157.

59   *Ibid.*, section 49, pp. 157–58.

60   Casti, *Complexification*, p. 45.

61   *Ibid.*, p. 46.

62   Kant, *Critique of Judgment*, section 49, p. 158.

63   *Ibid.*

13   Deleuze and literature

In *Cinema 1* and *Cinema 2* Deleuze offered a relatively comprehensive philosophical approach to film. Unfortunately, he produced no comparable work on literature, despite having shown a deep and lasting interest in the art. Besides producing monographs on Marcel Proust (1964; 2nd aug. edn. 1970; 3rd aug. edn. 1976), Leopold von Sacher-Masoch (1967), and Franz Kafka (1975), he wrote long essays on Pierre Klossowski (1965), Michel Tournier (1967), Émile Zola (1967), Carmelo Bene (1979), Herman Melville (1989), and Samuel Beckett (1992), and in *The Logic of Sense* (1969) used Lewis Carroll's works as a leitmotif throughout the book. Indeed, allusions to writers are so abundant that Dominique Drouet's index of Deleuze's literary references runs to 279 entries.[1] In a 1988 interview, Raymond Bellour and François Ewald noted the absence of a literary counterpart to the cinema books, even though literature "is everywhere present in your work, running parallel, almost, to the philosophy," and asked if literature were too close to philosophy for him to undertake such a work. Deleuze answered that literature posed no special difficulty for him, and that in fact he had "dreamed about bringing together a series of studies under the general title 'Essays Critical and Clinical,' [but] it's just that I haven't had the chance to do the book I'd like to have done about literature" (*N* 142–43). Deleuze's last book, of course, bore the title *Essays Critical and Clinical* (1993), but its heterogeneous studies of writers and philosophers hardly lays out a general and detailed philosophy of literature.

Nonetheless, *Essays Critical and Clinical*'s brief opening essay, "Literature and Life," does bring together themes introduced at various points in Deleuze's career, and if the essay is not the micro-*Summa* of a single poetics unifying all his literary studies, it still preserves traces of Deleuze's journey through literature while offering an example of his genius for selectively gathering, synthesizing, and transforming elements of his earlier thought within intriguingly new configurations. The essay's few pages abound with dicta about writing and literature. "Writing is a question of becoming" (*ECC* 1); "Literature then appears as an enterprise of health" (*ECC* 3); "Health, as literature, as writing, consists in inventing a people who are missing" (*ECC* 4); "Literature is delirium" (*ECC* 54); "The ultimate aim of literature is to set free, in the delirium, this creation of health or this invention of a people, that is, a possibility of life" (*ECC* 4); literature "opens up a kind of foreign language within language" (*ECC* 6); "a foreign language cannot be hollowed out in one language without language as a whole in turn being toppled or pushed to a limit, to an outside or reverse side that consists of Visions and Auditions that no longer belong to any language" (*ECC* 5); "To write is also to become something other than a writer" (*ECC* 6). Becoming, health, inventing a people, delirium, possibility of life, foreign language within language, Visions and Auditions – save for Visions and Auditions, all of these themes appear in works preceding *Essays Critical and Clinical*, yet their synthesis in this essay grants them renewed intensity as components of a decades-long, open-ended thought-in-movement about literature, whose genealogy is worth tracing.

Deleuze's writings on literature fall into two principal groups, pre- and post-Guattari (the two met in mid 1970), the first focusing on psychoanalytic themes and the interpretation of signs, the second on sociopolitical dynamics and the deterritorialization of language. Deleuze introduces several new concepts in his essays on literature in the 1980s and 1990s, including fabulation, possibilities of life, and Visions and Auditions, while combining them with reconfigured versions of some motifs from his pre-Guattari writings (critical and clinical, the event), but I see these late essays as further elaborations on the fundamental concerns inaugurated in his initial collaboration with Guattari.

EARLY DELEUZE

The two central texts in Deleuze's early thought about literature are *Proust and Signs* (1964) and *Masochism: Coldness and Cruelty*

(1967). It is tempting to seek a developmental movement from the Proust book to the monograph on Sacher-Masoch, but in fact the basic outline of the latter study appeared in a 1961 article, and hence, if anything, the relationship should be reversed.[2] But it is safest simply to assert that the two projects coexisted during that decade, especially since the broad psychoanalytic preoccupations of *Masochism* continue in *The Logic of Sense* (1969). It is in *Masochism* that the terms "critical" and "clinical" (*critique* and *clinique*) first appear, and though the critical/clinical distinction is not explicitly enunciated in the 1961 article, it is implicit throughout the argument. Thus, if there is a single motif present in the earliest and the latest of Deleuze's literary writings, it is that of the critical and the clinical.

Like most of Deleuze's literary commentaries, *Masochism* advances a provocative thesis – in this instance, that sadism and masochism have little to do with one another, and that Sade and Masoch were great clinicians whose works disclose the psychodynamics of widely divergent universes. Sadomasochism is a false syndrome, Deleuze argues, a mistaken grouping of symptoms that obfuscates a clear understanding of sadism and masochism alike. To rethink this false syndrome, Deleuze proposes a literary approach, "since it is from literature that stem the original definitions of sadism and masochism." He suggests that "the critical (in the literary sense) and the clinical (in the medical) sense ... enter into a new relationship of mutual learning," because "symptomatology is always a question of art," and in this case, "the clinical specificities of sadism and masochism are not separable from the literary values peculiar to Sade and Masoch" (*M* 14).

Sade posits the existence of two natures: a secondary nature of procreation and death, and a primary nature of pure negation, "an original delirium, a primordial chaos solely composed of furious and lacerating molecules." Secondary nature alone exists in the real world; primary nature, by contrast, is an Idea, delirious no doubt, but "a delirium proper to reason" (*M* 27, translation modified). The sadist enacts such a primary nature through an apathetic, rational demonstration of this delirium, in repetitive scenes of violence supervised by the father and directed against the procreative mother. Masoch also posits two natures, but of an entirely different sort: a secondary nature of sensuality and disorder inducing a constant war between men and women, and a primary nature of cool suprasensuality and strict order. The presiding figure in this primary nature is the oral mother, "cold, maternal and severe" (*M* 51). In the masochistic fantasy, the son forms an alliance with the oral mother, and it is the father she punishes when she whips the son, at the same time that she purifies the son and makes possible the parthenogenesis of a new man, freed from the sensuality and disorder of secondary nature. If the sadist stands above the law in open defiance, the masochist mocks the law by parodically obeying it, drawing up elaborate contracts with the dominatrix in order to turn legal prohibitions of desire into sources of pleasure. Rather than reiterate a rational delirium of constant motion and destruction, the masochist fashions motionless tableaux of suspended desire. The fetish plays a special role for the masochist, since it is an object of Freudian disavowal, something that enables a simultaneous acceptance and denial of reality (specifically, according to Freud, the reality of the mother's lack of a penis), and thereby allows the real to pass into fantasy. Hence, "disavowal, suspense, waiting, fetishism and fantasy together make up the specific constellation of masochism" (*M* 71). Delirious reason is not the masochist's presiding faculty, but perverse imagination, whose goal is not to impose a violent Idea on the real, but "to neutralize the real and suspend the ideal within the pure interiority of the fantasy itself" (*M* 72, translation modified).

Both Sade and Masoch start with a personal obsession, but unlike ordinary sadists or masochists, they convert their obsessions into materials for artistic creation. In their fiction, each fashions a double of the world, a counter-real that distils the structures and practices of specific forms of erotic violence, a counterworld that clarifies the phenomena of sadism and masochism, and thereby serves as a diagnosis of these illnesses of civilization. And both suggest new possibilities beyond these illnesses, Sade, through ironic exaggeration, and Masoch, via humorous parody. Sade and Masoch are not pornographers, but "pornologists," whose aim is to confront "language with its own limits, with what is in a sense a 'nonlanguage' (violence that does not speak, eroticism that remains unspoken)" (*M* 22). They create a double of the world, but they also "form in language a sort of double of language, capable of acting directly on the senses" (*M* 37, translation modified).

In his 1988 interview with Bellour and Ewald, Deleuze links Masoch and Proust as "civilization's doctors," calling Masoch "a great symptomatologist" and labeling Proust's *À la recherche du temps perdu* "a general semiology, a symptomatology of different worlds" (*N* 142–43). But in the initial 1964 edition of *Proust and Signs*, Deleuze puts little stress on the notion of signs as symptoms, and nowhere does he describe Proust as a physician of civilization. Deleuze's focus is on signs in a broader sense, albeit one that owes nothing to Saussure. Signs in Proust's *Recherche* are like the moon, with a bright and a perpetually dark side. They are hieroglyphs, enigmas that elicit interpretation. Each sign enfolds, or implicates (Latin *plicare*, to fold), something hidden, and requires unfolding, or explication, to be grasped. The *Recherche* is the record of the narrator's apprenticeship in signs, one that leads Marcel from worldly signs, through the signs of love and signs of involuntary memory, to the signs of art. Each of these four groups of signs has its own temporality: "time wasted, time lost, time rediscovered, and time regained" (*PS* 87). Worldly signs are vapid, empty indices of fashion, status, and the ephemeral preoccupations of salons, coteries, and cliques. The signs of love are somewhat more substantial, yet deceptive and disappointing, revealed not through reciprocated love but through jealousy and the lover's exclusion from the hidden worlds enfolded in the loved one. Ultimately, these signs reveal a bifurcation in sexuality, such that all sexuality is homosexuality, even heterosexual men and women loving their respective male or female counterparts within their lovers. The signs of involuntary memory, such as the well-known madeleine that evokes a distant Combray, unlike worldly signs and the signs of love, do not represent wasted or lost time, but instead a rediscovery of what Proust calls "a morsel of time, in the pure state," or in Deleuze's words, "the localized essence of time" (*PS* 61). The madeleine enfolds an essence of Combray, a pure past that has never been actually present. In a Proustian phrase Deleuze cites frequently in his writings, essences are "real without being present, ideal without being abstract" (*PS* 61). Yet the signs of involuntary memory are contingent, revealed solely in haphazard circumstances, and only partially separable from their material embodiment. The signs of art alone reveal essences directly and fully, and though they are cloaked in the materials of paint, sounds, or words, they are "immaterial and no longer have anything opaque about them," for in art, "substances are spiritualized, media dematerialized" (*PS* 50).

Proustian essences, however, are not Platonic ideas. They do not belong to some separate, ideal world, but are immanent within the real. They are virtual rather than actual. An essence, as revealed in an artwork, "is a difference, the absolute and ultimate Difference" (*PS* 41). It is a generative, self-differentiating difference that constantly repeats itself. A virtual essence guides and informs the individuation of the substance in which it is embodied, this process of actualization of the virtual being one of "expression," as Deleuze calls it, a material unfolding of enfolded difference in which the actual is the expression of the virtual. Each essence is like a Leibnizian monad, which expresses the entire world, but only from its own perspective, revealing the world clearly in its proper region, obscurely outside that area. The essence of an artwork likewise perspectivally expresses an entire world, but that world itself, when grasped fully rather than locally, resembles a Neoplatonic *complicatio*, "which envelops the many in the One and affirms the unity of the multiple" (*PS* 45). In Proust, however, the One is self-differentiating difference, not self-same identity. Essences, then, prove to be not merely artistic but cosmic, and artistic creation is simply a particular instance of the world's ubiquitous actualization of the virtual, the universal unfolding of incessantly repeated difference.

Marcel's apprenticeship in signs leads him to the revelation of essences and to his vocation as a writer, yet if the *Recherche* is an apprenticeship in the signs of art, Proust's thought about signs is as much philosophical as artistic – or at least, Deleuze makes use of the *Recherche* as both an artwork and a work of philosophy. In *Proust and Sign*'s final chapter, "The Image of Thought," Deleuze credits Proust with "setting up an image of thought in opposition to that of philosophy" (*PS* 94), one in which truth is not disclosed through the good will of friends consciously deciding to seek it, but through a violence to thought. What Proust shows is that "the truth is not revealed, it is betrayed; it is not communicated, it is interpreted; it is not willed, it is involuntary" (*PS* 95). Those familiar with Deleuze's *Difference and Repetition* (1968) will recognize in this commentary on Proust a rough *précis* of Deleuze's own argument in *Difference and Repetition*'s third chapter (also titled "The Image of Thought"), just as they will find expanded counterparts of

Proust and Signs's discussions of difference, repetition and expression in *Difference and Repetition* (as well as in Deleuze's lengthy 1968 study of Spinoza, *Expressionism in Philosophy – Spinoza*).

In *The Logic of Sense* (1969), this intimate relationship between literature and philosophy continues, as does the close association of literature and psychoanalysis found in *Masochism*. A "logical and psychoanalytic novel" (*LS* xiv, translation modified), *The Logic of Sense* isolates in Lewis Carroll's nonsense works "a series of paradoxes which form the theory of sense" (*LS* xiii), a theory Deleuze develops through meditations on diverse philosophical arguments, including, among many others, those of the Stoics, Leibniz, Nietzsche, Frege, Meinong, and Husserl. Deleuze grants the Stoics pride of place because they lay the foundation for a theory of sense via their concept of the *lekton*, or "expressible." For the Stoics, bodies alone have true existence, but other entities, called "incorporeals," have a quasi-existence, insisting, or subsisting, if not genuinely existing. Bodies are causes of themselves, incorporeals mere surface effects of bodies. The *lekton* is one such incorporeal. When foreigners overhear an unknown language, they perceive the same sonic bodies as the native speakers, but for those native speakers, something is added to the sonic bodies – *lekta*, expressibles, incorporeal surface effects of meaning, or sense. Via this unusual differentiation of bodies, causes, and being from incorporeals, effects, and quasi-being, Deleuze formulates a broad theory of sense as an incorporeal surface at the interface of language and things, a transcendental, metaphysical surface of events, with their own floating time and paradoxical logic.

In the last third of *The Logic of Sense*, Deleuze turns from a philosophical account of sense to a psychoanalytic explanation of its psychosexual emergence along the surfaces of the body. Preliminary to this psychoanalytic analysis, however, is a crucial chapter ("Thirteenth Series of the Schizophrenic and the Little Girl") dedicated to Carroll's "Jabberwocky" and Antonin Artaud's "translation" of the poem. Carroll's nonsense poem has sense, just not good sense, its portmanteau words fusing ordinary words in recognizable combinations (such as "slithy," which, as Humpty Dumpty explains, combines "lithe" and "slimy"). Artaud's rendering of the poem, by contrast, fashions sonic blocks devoid of sense, good or bad, "breath-words [*mots-souffles*] and howl-words [*mots-*

cris]" (*LS* 88) without grammar or syntax. What these sonic blocks reveal is a domain in which words, affects, and things are indistinguishable, a primal depths of the unconscious from which the surface of language and sense emerges, and into which schizophrenics sink.

This differentiation of surface sense and the depths of sonic blocks provides the framework for Deleuze's psychoanalytic account of the psychic development of language. Using Melanie Klein's theory of part-objects, Deleuze posits a prelinguistic infant unconscious containing passion-words and action-words, the passion-words being part-objects that lacerate and destroy, the action-words countering such hostile part-objects by forming a fusional "organism without parts" (*LS* 188), what Artaud calls a "body without organs." From this unconscious of body-affect-words the psychic agencies of the ego and superego gradually take shape, and with them emerge the separate domains of language and the body, and eventually the surface of sense.

The literary texts of Carroll and Artaud, then, contribute to Deleuze's psychoanalytic thought, and Carroll's nonsense is central to both the philosophical and the psychoanalytic arguments of *The Logic of Sense*. In this regard, the dominant uses of literature evident in *Masochism* and *Proust and Signs* come together in *The Logic of Sense*. But this particular combination of literary, psychoanalytic, and philosophical analysis is short-lived, giving way to a very different mode of thought the year following *The Logic of Sense*'s publication, when Deleuze begins interacting with Guattari. The earliest indications of Guattari's influence appear in the second edition of *Proust and Signs* (1970), which includes the 1964 text, followed by a new section comparable in length to the first. The new Part Two focuses on the production of signs rather than their interpretation, and that production is framed in terms of "machines," a concept Guattari had been developing since 1961. In the concept of the machine, Deleuze finds a means of approaching literature from the vantage of function rather than meaning, and thereby adopting a mode of reading antithetical to any conventional hermeneutics. "Why a machine?" Deleuze asks. "Because the art work so understood is essentially productive." The modern work of art "is a machine and functions as such ... [it] has no problem of meaning, it has only a problem of use" (*PS* 145–46). This concept of the literary work as a functional entity, like a machine, prevails for the remainder of Deleuze's career.

DELEUZE AND GUATTARI

Anti-Oedipus (1972) marks an end to Deleuze's utilization of conventional psychoanalysis, as well as his abandonment of the language of depths and surfaces. Artaud's notion of the body without organs takes on a new function, designating no longer the primal corporeal depths but instead the entire domain of desiring-production that is immanent in the real. In *Anti-Oedipus*, one might say, the depths rise to the surface and form what in *A Thousand Plateaus* Deleuze and Guattari will call a "plane of immanence" of *n* dimensions. As *n*-dimensional plane, the newly conceived body without organs defies assimilation within all conventional spatial categories, including those of depths and surfaces.

Literary references abound in *Anti-Oedipus*, but it is in *Kafka: Toward a Minor Literature* (1975) that Deleuze and Guattari first engage in extended literary analysis. Their thesis is that Kafka is neither a melancholy neurotic nor a tormented mystic, but a joyous, humorous political writer, whose works are exemplary of what Deleuze and Guattari call "minor literature." They develop the concept of minor literature from a diary entry of Kafka's devoted to "small literatures" ("kleine Litteraturen"; in the French translation, "littératures mineures"), such as Czech and Yiddish literature. Minor literature has three characteristics. First, it is not written in a minor language per se, but makes a minor usage of language by inducing within it instabilities – grammatical, syntactic, or semantic anomalies, unexpected intensities of stress or cadence, neologisms, proliferations of images, ascetic iterations of a deliberately impoverished vocabulary, and so on – all of which undo linguistic conventions and thereby "deterritorialize" language, detaching it from its native soil, as it were. Second, in minor literatures, "everything ... is political." In a major literature, the writer addresses individual concerns within a quotidian social milieu, whereas the minor writer's world "forces each individual intrigue to connect immediately to politics." And third, in minor literature "everything takes on a social value." Not only do minor writers address social and political concerns, but they also speak as a collective voice. Minor writers sense the absence of a national or community consciousness, and as a result "literature finds itself positively charged with the role and function of collective, and even revolutionary, enunciation ... and if the writer is in the margins or completely outside his or her fragile community, this situation allows the writer all the more the possibility to express another possible community" (*K* 17). In Deleuze and Guattari's terms, minor writers engage a "collective assemblage of enunciation" (*K* 18) via this thoroughly social usage of language.

Implicit in this characterization of minor literature is a conception of language that Deleuze and Guattari delineate most fully in *A Thousand Plateaus* (1980). In plateau 4, "Postulates of Linguistics," they argue against the assumptions that language is a homogeneous system of invariables or universals; that linguistics as a science must be based on a standard language separated from its social context; and that language's function is to facilitate communication or transmit information. Language's function, they assert, is to enforce power relations by issuing "order-words," which convey social obligations; all language is language-action, and hence linguistics proper is only an artificially delineated subset of a general pragmatics; and there are only variables in a language, which is in effect a heterogeneous collection of multiple languages. (The notions of invariants, standard usage, and homogeneity are simply markers of power whereby a dominant order valorizes its own norms and devalues deviations from the norm.) Phonemic constants, or pertinent differences, are actually idealized abstractions derived from virtual "lines of continuous variation" that are immanent within a language. A line of continuous variation passes through all possible enunciations of a phoneme, just as all possible syntactic permutations are manifestations of virtual lines of continuous variation, and all standard pronunciations, grammatical and syntactic regularities, are merely isolated, extracted, and rigidified segments of such oscillating, constantly moving lines of variation.

Even a language's semantic components are permeated by lines of continuous variation. Using certain elements of speech-act theory, Deleuze and Guattari assert that the same words enunciated in different contexts have a separate semantic function in each situation (and conversely, different sets of words in a given context can fulfill a single semantic function). The pertinent semantic unit is the statement ("énoncé"), which resembles to some extent Austin's "speech act." The example Deleuze and Guattari provide is that of the statement "I swear!," which "is a different statement depending on whether it is said by a child to his or her father, by a man in love to his loved one, or by a witness before the court." If "I swear!" appears in Kafka's "Letter to the Father," in a hotel meeting with his fiancée's family (which Kafka described as a veritable trial), or in *The Trial*, it functions as three different statements. A line of continuous variation passes through the three statements of "I swear!," such that "all of the statements are present in the effectuation of one among them." What Kafka does as a minor writer is "to place the statement in continuous variation" and "send it through all the prosodic, semantic, syntactical, and phonological variables that can affect it" and thereby build "the *continuum* of 'I swear!' with the corresponding transformations" (*ATP* 94). To deterritorialize language is to place its elements in continuous variation.

Deleuze and Guattari identify the underlying function of statements as that of effecting "incorporeal transformations" (*ATP* 86) (a term derived from the Stoic opposition of incorporeals and bodies Deleuze first discussed in *The Logic of Sense*). When the priest says "I thee wed," or the judge "Guilty!," an incorporeal transformation takes place – two individuals become a married couple, the accused becomes the condemned. These are but overt instances of a universal process of incorporeal transformation involving discursive and non-discursive elements in a single pragmatics. Discursive and non-discursive elements are never isolated units but always components of what Deleuze and Guattari call "assemblages," complexes of heterogeneous entities – bodies, buildings, institutions, words, dreams, animals, plants, what have you – that function together while remaining open-ended, changing multiplicities. Language, then, as general pragmatics, involves two basic assemblages: "a *machinic assemblage* of bodies, of actions and passions, an intermingling of bodies reacting to one another," and "a *collective assemblage of enunciation*, of acts and statements, of incorporeal transformations attributed to bodies" (*ATP* 88). Incorporeal transformations effect power relations, and hence the characterization of language's function as the transmission of "order-words." "The only possible definition of language," Deleuze and Guattari conclude, "is the set of all order-words, implicit presuppositions, or speech acts current in a language at a given moment," or more precisely, "the set of all *incorporeal transformations* current in a given society and *attributed* to the bodies of that society" (*ATP* 79–80).

One can see, then, that the three characteristics of minor literature – "the deterritorialization of language, the connection of the individual to a political immediacy, and the collective assemblage of enunciation" (*K* 18) – issue from a single conception of language and its usages. For Deleuze and Guattari, Kafka is an exemplary minor writer, whose works are informed by a general pragmatics of political language-action. Kafka's writings are to be understood not in terms of their hidden meaning but their function, which is to deterritorialize language and thereby destabilize political power relations and activate a collective assemblage of enunciation. As a functional entity, Kafka's corpus is a writing machine, whose three "machinic" components are the letters, the short stories, and the novels (the diaries serving as an immanent milieu, like the sea, within which Kafka, like a swimming fish, constructs his machine). Given Deleuze and Guattari's conception of language as a general sociopolitical pragmatics, there can be no separation of Kafka's diaries and letters from his fiction, any more than a separation of his life as a whole from his writings, since language-actions of all kinds are inextricable from the world and its open-ended web of power relations. "That's why it is so awful, so grotesque, to oppose life and writing in Kafka, to suppose that he took refuge in writing out of some sort of lack, weakness, impotence, in front of life … [L]iving and writing, art and life, are opposed only from the point of view of a major literature" (*K* 41).

Deleuze and Guattari's aim is to map Kafka's writing machine and describe how it functions. Kafka's basic problem is to construct machines that do not close in upon themselves, but instead remain open, forming assemblages with the rest of the world. The letters are a machine for warding off conjugality, for keeping Kafka's fiancée and the dead end of familial relations at a distance, in perpetual postponement. The familial trap, however, constantly impedes the function of the letter machine. The short story machine constructs various means of escape (what Deleuze and Guattari call "lines of flight"), primarily through a process of "becoming-animal." An obvious instance of this process is Gregor Samsa's becoming-insect in "The Metamorphosis." Deleuze and Guattari insist that Gregor's transformation is not a metaphor or an allegory, but a literal becoming-other, a process in which Gregor as human fashions a zone of indiscernibility with an insect and engages in a metamorphic undoing of human and animal identities and thereby constructs a line of flight. But the story also maps the failure of such a machinic becoming-animal. The insect-Gregor tries three times to escape the family prison of his bedroom, and each time he is driven back until he dies from the wound inflicted by his father. Deleuze and Guattari argue that in all the short stories, lines of flight are eventually blocked and the writing machine stops functioning. Only in the novels does the writing machine remain open, each novel's machine constructing assemblages that form unending circuits connected to various machines in the sociopolitical world.

Paradigmatic of the novel machine is *The Trial*, which is not so much an unfinished project as a perpetually self-constructing machine that by design cannot and should not be completed. (Deleuze and Guattari argue that the unnumbered section in which Josef K. dies is a dream sequence and not the projected conclusion of the novel.) Kafka's novel serves as an analysis and critique of the law, but not in the ordinary sense of the terms "analysis" and "critique." Kafka's law is a parodic version of Kant's conception of law as "a pure form on which the good such as it is depends," a form in which "the good is that which the law expresses when it expresses itself" (*K* 43). Kafka's analysis and critique of the law as pure form proceeds not through abstract argument, but through a dissection of the mechanisms of a massive law machine and an experimentation on that machine. Josef K. is less a traditional character than a function, at once a component of the machine, its operator, and its constructor, whose movements activate and disclose the operation of the law as a machinic assemblage of interconnected, limitless parts.

The law represents itself as an ascending hierarchy of transcendent, omnipotent power, but the law machine K. discloses is a horizontal, acentered, entangled network, a "rhizome" (*K* 3) of topologically intercommunicating passageways and spaces. Everyone and everything belong to the law in one way or another, even though the law itself is always next door, somewhere else. Three clerks from K.'s bank accompany the arresting officers, K.'s uncle already knows about his case, the lawyer's maid is on intimate terms with defendants, lawyers, and judges, the artist Titorelli is the court painter, the cathedral priest is also the prison chaplain. Everywhere K. goes the law is eroticized and shown to be a machine of desire, whose "two coexisting states of desire are the two states of the law: on the one hand, *the transcendent paranoiac Law* that never ceases to agitate a finite segment, to make it a complete object, to crystallize this or that; on the other hand, *the immanent schiz-law*, which functions like a justice, an antilaw, a 'procedure' that dismantles the paranoiac Law in all its assemblages" (*K* 59, translation modified).

The Trial succeeds as a writing machine because it produces assemblages interconnected with proliferating assemblages along an open line of flight, such that the writing machine in principle could continue operating indefinitely. Rather than accept conventional representations of the law and all its institutions and then use the novel to promote some form of sociological, economic, or political critique, as might the stereotypical *écrivain engagé*, "Kafka attempts to extract from social representations assemblages of enunciation and machinic assemblages and to dismantle these assemblages" (*K* 46). For Kafka, writing has "a double function: to transcribe into assemblages, to dismantle the assemblages," and through this practice of transcription and dismantling, Kafka makes "the world and its representation … take flight" (*K* 47, translation modified). *The Trial*'s law machine is at once a transcription and dismantling of the world around him, and hence an experimentation on the real institutions, practices, and discourse of the law in Prague and the Austro-Hungarian Empire. Through that experimentation Kafka discloses not only the operative assemblages of his milieu but also the tendencies and trajectories of the assemblages' movement, a virtual line of flight that forecasts *"diabolical powers that are knocking at the door"* (*K* 41), possible mutations of the bureaucratic machinery of the Austro-Hungarian Empire – which Deleuze and Guattari see manifested in the bureaucracies of Nazi Germany, Stalinist Russia, and capitalist America. Yet the trajectories Kafka traces are also lines of flight with the potential for transformation and revolutionary change. By transcribing the real into assemblages, setting them in motion, and dismantling them, Kafka opens lines of potential metamorphosis, whose ultimate outcome cannot be predicted, even now. What future assemblage will issue from this line of flight: "fascist? revolutionary? socialist? capitalist? Or even all of these at the same time, connected in the most repugnant or diabolical way? We don't know, but we have ideas about these – Kafka taught us to have them" (*K* 85).

The Trial, then, is not an oneiric fantasy or a religious allegory. Nor is it a symptom of Oedipal neurosis or a lament of existential dread. It is an experimentation on the real. The machinic assemblages and assemblages of collective enunciation that Kafka transcribes from conventional representations and discourse actually exist and function in the world around him. The pragmatic language-action of the novel is directly plugged into the sociopolitical power circuits of the Austro-Hungarian Empire's legal machinery. Kafka's dismantling of these transcribed assemblages is itself a deterritorialization of language, in the sense that *The Trial* is simply a large-scale version of the minor usage of the statement "I swear!," which deterritorializes this semantic unit of language-action and thereby builds "the *continuum* of 'I swear!' with the corresponding transformations" (*ATP* 94). In disassembling *The Trial*'s assemblages Kafka reveals immanent, virtual lines of flight, tendencies within the assemblages toward the diabolical powers of the future, but also trajectories of possible transformation and revolution. Ultimately, Kafka's art is not one of gloom, dread, angst, and death, but one filled with humor – dark to be sure – and vitality, which resists closure, stasis, repression, and death and affirms life as the animating force of process, becoming, metamorphosis, and open possibilities of change.

In the aesthetics of minor literature, then, Deleuze and Guattari attempt a new means of bringing together the concerns of *littérature engagée* and the practices of modernist and avant-garde formal experimentation. Throughout his works, Deleuze shows a predilection for modernism, but in the post-Guattari writings he brings to the fore the sociopolitical dimension of literature, a dimension that, while not absent in the pre-Guattari corpus, is subordinated to other concerns, chiefly those of psychoanalysis, traditional philosophy, and the means of moving beyond their assumptions.

LATE DELEUZE

The term "minor literature" all but disappears in writings after *Kafka*, although the concept of the "minor" does play a role in analyses of language and science in *A Thousand Plateaus* (1980).

Rather, after 1975 Deleuze speaks not of "minor literature" but of "literature" and "writing" in general when treating literary works. Yet much of what he says about literature and writing echoes and elaborates on elements central to the "minor literature" of *Kafka*, as one may see by examining the primary characteristics of literature that Deleuze outlines in the 1993 essay "Literature and Life" – those of becoming, fabulating, stuttering, and creating Visions and Auditions.

In this brief text, Deleuze focuses first on writing as "inseparable from becoming: in writing, one becomes-woman, becomes-animal or vegetable, becomes-molecule to the point of becoming-imperceptible" (*ECC* 1). In *Kafka*, becoming plays a restricted role, limited to the "becoming-animal" of the short stories, but Deleuze soon recognizes the potential of this concept, stating in 1977 that "To write is to become" (*D* 43) and that such becoming takes the form of becoming-woman, becoming-black, becoming-animal, becoming-imperceptible (*D* 45). In plateau 10 of *A Thousand Plateaus*, Deleuze and Guattari explore at length the process of becoming-other, incorporating in their analyses a number of literary references (to Proust, Melville, Kafka, Kleist, Woolf, Faulkner, Hardy, James, among others), and in Deleuze's literary essays in the 1980s and 1990s becoming remains a constant preoccupation. As Deleuze repeatedly stresses, becomings are not metaphors or processes of imitation. Just as Gregor's becoming-insect does not involve imitating an insect but instead creating a zone of indiscernibility between the human and the animal, so all becomings create zones of indiscernibility that undo such binary power oppositions as man–woman, adult–child, human–animal, and eventually open up becomings that venture into the molecular and the imperceptible. In all these processes, the aim is to find a line of flight that leads beyond writing and into life.

Besides engendering lines of flight through becomings, Deleuze says that writing "consists in inventing a people who are missing" (*ECC* 4), a people to come. In *Kafka*, Deleuze and Guattari characterize minor literature as immediately political and state that for Kafka writing is "a concern of the people," but always a "collectivity that is not yet constituted." Such an unconstituted collectivity is a "virtual community" with which the actual Kafka engages, and the actual writer and "virtual community – both of them real – are the components of a collective assemblage" (*K* 84). This motif of a virtual community is only briefly touched on in *Kafka*, but Deleuze takes up the idea again in *Cinema* 2 (1985) during his analyses of the documentaries of Pierre Perrault and Jean Rouch. In their films, both directors try to facilitate "the invention of a people" (*TI* 150) via a process Deleuze identifies as "fabulation," a concept he borrows from Bergson's *The Two Sources of Morality and Religion* (1932) and then reconfigures for his own ends. Bergson's fabulation (rendered as "myth-making" by Bergson's English translators) is a fundamental human tendency in service of a social instinct whereby humans personify and deify natural forces, eventually projecting images of the gods into the real. Deleuze proposes to give Bergson's concept "a political meaning" and view fabulation as an activity "which a people and art both share" (*N* 174). In Perrault's and Rouch's documentaries, the subjects participate with the directors in shaping the films, and in so doing the subjects join with the directors in fabulating, "legending *in flagrante delicto*" (*TI* 150, translation modified), initiating the process of inventing a new collectivity, a people to come. Writers also fabulate, though without direct collaboration with social groups. They engage a virtual collectivity in order "to invent a people ... a people to come ... a minor people, taken up in a becoming-revolutionary ... This is the *becoming* of the writer. Kafka (for central Europe) and Melville (for America) present literature as the collective enunciation of a minor people ... who find their expression only in and through the writer" (*ECC* 4). The ultimate aim of fabulation and literature is to set free "the creation of a health or this invention of a people, that is, a possibility of life" (*ECC* 4).

Literature, then, is both becoming and fabulation, the prolongation of lines of flight and the invention of a people, through which possibilities of life are set free and health is restored. (Clearly, by including "life" and "health" in this characterization, Deleuze is incorporating the early concepts of the critical and clinical and the artist as civilization's physician within this final formulation of literature and its function.) But literature is also stuttering, "a becoming-other of language, a minorization of this major language ... the invention of a new language within language" (*ECC* 5). In this third characteristic of literature, of course, one sees a continued stress on the concepts of linguistic deterritorialization and minor usage introduced in *Kafka* and *A Thousand Plateaus*. Yet in "Literature and Life" stuttering takes on an added dimension, that of creating Visions and Auditions, which may be seen as a fourth characteristic of literature.

The concept of Visions and Auditions only emerges explicitly in *Essays Critical and Clinical*. In making language stutter, writers create a foreign language within their own language, but "a foreign language cannot be hollowed out without language as a whole in turn being toppled or pushed to a limit, to an outside or reverse side that consists of Visions and Auditions that no longer belong to any language." Such Visions and Auditions "are not outside language, but the outside of language" (*ECC* 5). They are "not of language, but which language alone makes possible … a painting and a music characteristic of writing, like the effects of colors and sonorities that rise up above words" (*ECC* lv). They are not fantasies, "but veritable Ideas that the writer sees and hears in the interstices of language, in its intervals" (*ECC* 5).

Nowhere does Deleuze specify much further the theoretical underpinnings of the concept of Visions and Auditions (although in other essays from *Essays Critical and Clinical* he does speak briefly of Visions in Roussel, Beckett, T. E. Lawrence, Melville, and Whitman).[3] But the notion of pushing language to its limits is a pre-occupation that runs throughout Deleuze's work, from *Masochism*'s reference to pornologists who confront "language with its own limits" (*M* 22), through the surface of sense and events in *The Logic of Sense*, modern cinema's exploration of the limits of sound and the visual in *Cinema 2* (see especially *TI* 260–61), the disjunction of speaking and seeing as the two reach their limits in *Foucault* (*F* 116–17), to Beckett's efforts to bore holes in language and create a pure image in "The Exhausted." As Jean-Jacques Lecercle has rightly observed, Deleuze, like Beckett, is both obsessed and impatient with language, constantly seeking means of thinking outside of and yet through words (perhaps one motive for the proliferation of neologisms in Deleuze's work).[4] Deleuze does not take modern philosophy's "linguistic turn," but instead stresses the differences between language and non-language and the need to subordinate language to a general semiotics (an emphasis particularly marked in *A Thousand Plateaus* and the cinema books). In *What is Philosophy?*, he and Guattari say that philosophers create concepts and artists create sensations, but concepts and sensations have no essential relation to language. Writers may use words as their medium, just as painters use paint, but only as a means to create sensations, for sensations "are *beings* whose validity lies in themselves," and "the work of art is a being of sensation and nothing else: it exists in itself" (*WP* 164).

In interviews Deleuze repeatedly states that whatever the subject matter of his analyses – politics, anthropology, cinema, painting, literature, and so on – he is always doing philosophy. If he engages in what looks like literary criticism, it is only to think alongside literary works, to create philosophical concepts through interaction with something outside philosophy. For Deleuze, philosophy, art, and science "enter into relations of mutual resonance and exchange," and for that reason "we really have to see philosophy, art and science as sorts of melodic lines that are foreign to one another and that constantly interfere with one another." Without such interferences, nothing moves in philosophy, but when it does, interferences function as "intercessors." "Intercessors are fundamental. Creation is all about intercessors" (*N* 125, translation modified). Despite their mutual interference and intercession, however, philosophy, art, and science remain autonomous domains. In *What is Philosophy?*, Deleuze and Guattari emphasize the divide between the three domains, asserting that philosophers create concepts whereas artists create sensations (which they define as "percepts" and "affects"). Even figures such as Kierkegaard and Nietzsche, who appear to be both philosophers and writers, "do not present a synthesis of art and philosophy ... They are hybrid geniuses who neither erase nor cover over differences in kind, but, on the contrary, use all the resources of their 'athleticism' to install themselves within this very difference, like acrobats torn apart in a perpetual show of strength" (*WP* 67).

Yet in Deleuze's thought this division between philosophy and literature ultimately seems porous and provisional. In a short text on Spinoza written in 1989, two years before *What is Philosophy?*, Deleuze says that "style in philosophy strains toward three different poles: concepts, or new ways of thinking; percepts, or new ways of seeing and construing; and affects, or new ways of feeling. They're the philosophical trinity, philosophy as opera: you need all three to *get things moving*" (*N* 164–65). And in "Spinoza and the Three

'Ethics'" from *Essays Critical and Clinical*, published two years after *What is Philosophy?*, Deleuze says that Spinoza's *Ethics* is actually three books: a "river-book" of "definitions, axioms and postulates, demonstrations and corollaries" that flows through Books I–IV; a volcano book of interspersed scholia; and Book V, which is "an aerial book of light" (*ECC* 151). And the three books' forms of content and expression are respectively "Notions or concepts," "Signs or affects" and "Essences or percepts" (*ECC* 138). (In the 1989 text on Spinoza, Deleuze says that in Book V Spinoza ceases "speaking from the viewpoint of concepts" and begins to "speak directly and intuitively in pure percepts" [*N* 165].)

Deleuze claims that the basic problem faced by artists does not "take a different form in literature than in the other arts" (*N* 143) and that literature's proximity to philosophy poses no special difficulties for him. Yet there is an important difference between literature and the other arts. When working as a philosopher, Deleuze is not a painter or a composer, but he is a writer, and much of what he says about writing applies equally well to his own linguistic practice and to that of the authors he admires. In *A Thousand Plateaus*, when he and Guattari describe the book as "a little machine" with its own "body without organs" (*ATP* 4), they offer Kleist and Kafka as examples, yet they are clearly characterizing their own book when they talk about the books of these authors. Deleuze bridles at the assertion that philosophers, unlike creative writers, have no style, countering that "great philosophers are also great stylists." Style in philosophy involves the invention or redefinition of words, but also syntax, "which is a sort of straining toward something that isn't syntactic, nor even linguistic (something outside language)" (*N* 164). Clearly, philosophers and literary authors who create Visions and Auditions are both stylists who strain toward something outside language. When asked whether *A Thousand Plateaus* was a work of literature, Deleuze responded that it was "philosophy, nothing but philosophy, in the traditional sense of the word" (*TRM* 176, translation modified), and it would be foolish not to take him at his word. But it does seem that philosophy and literature share a broader zone of indiscernibility than those between philosophy and the other arts – the zone of language and writing, a zone that grants literature a special place in Deleuze's work and makes literature one of the most powerful "intercessors" in his thought.

NOTES

1   Dominique Drouet, "Index des références littéraires dans l'œuvre de Gilles Deleuze," in Bruno Gelas and Hervé Micolet (eds.), *Deleuze et les écrivains: littérature et philosophie* (Nantes: Cécile Defaut, 2007), pp. 551–81. (All of the contributions to this collective volume are outstanding and well worth consulting.)

2   Gilles Deleuze, "De Sacher Masoch au masochisme," *Arguments*, 21 (1961), 40–46.

3   For further commentary on Visions and Auditions, see Ronald Bogue, *Deleuze on Literature* (New York: Routledge, 2003), pp. 162–76.

4   Jean-Jacques Lecercle, *Deleuze and Language* (Basingstoke: Palgrave Macmillan, 2002), pp. 1–2. Lecercle argues that language is an unresolved – and hence fruitful – problem in Deleuze, and that Deleuze actually holds two different views of language, which converge in his concept of style. See also Lecercle's equally provocative and insightful study *Badiou and Deleuze Read Literature* (Edinburgh University Press, 2010).

14 Deleuze and psychoanalysis

What happens when psychoanalysis encounters Deleuze? Ultimately, the result is its transformation into schizoanalysis, of course, thanks in large part to the collaboration with Guattari. But Deleuze brings to the encounter a whole set of conceptual resources derived from Spinoza, Leibniz, Kant, Nietzsche, Bergson, and Jung, just as Guattari brings to the collaboration invaluable resources derived from Marx, Hjelmslev, and Lacan.[1] Perhaps most important: Deleuze had developed a distinctive philosophical understanding of the unconscious before addressing psychoanalysis itself in works such as *Logic of Sense* and *Anti-Oedipus*. So it is critical to examine the sense of unconsciousness that emerges from Deleuze's readings of Nietzsche, Kant, Bergson, and Jung as necessary context for explaining what happens to psychoanalysis when it becomes schizoanalysis through Deleuze's collaboration with Guattari.[2]

BEFORE PSYCHOANALYSIS: A PHILOSOPHICAL UNCONSCIOUS

We start with Nietzsche for a number of reasons: first of all, because Nietzsche is the most important of the three great materialists (including Freud) on whom Deleuze will draw in *Anti-Oedipus*, and because it is he who provides the most capacious sense of unconsciousness. For Nietzsche, human being expresses will to power, and will to power is mostly unconscious; consciousness is strictly epiphenomenal. Moreover, what consciousness there is for Nietzsche is transitory and unreliable: the psyche is a battleground for warring forces or perspectives, and consciousness represents merely the momentary victory of one partial perspective over others – or indeed its disguise, as something other than conquering force. Most importantly, though: Nietzsche provides important correctives to Kant, one of Deleuze's most favored and influential philosophical precursors, despite his idealism.

Where Nietzsche (arguably in response to Kant himself) fractured the psyche, Kant sought to unify the psyche and harmonize its faculties, and to systematize knowledge by bringing the intuitions of sensibility into consistent correspondence with the concepts of understanding under the supervision of the regulative Ideas of Reason (Self, World, and God). Even where Kant recognizes that sensible experience can have no corresponding concept – as in the case of the sublime – he subjects intuition to Reason (and the Idea of infinity). Following Nietzsche, Deleuze will dissect, disaggregate, and disorganize the Kantian psyche, yet without dismissing some of its parts altogether. Using the sublime as a kind of wedge, Deleuze refutes Kant's three regulative Ideas of reason as well as the Transcendental Unity of Apperception that would add a unified subject ("I think") to all experience: as a general rule rather than the exception, experience defies subsumption by the understanding and becomes Problematic; not only is God long since dead, but the Self is not self-identical (it is composed of partial and competing larval selves, instead) and the World is not completely or even predominantly knowable (it is instead composed of ephemeral islands of Being all but submerged in chaos and indeterminacy).[3] The very forms of space and time that our experience takes are not the product of conscious intention; the syntheses of the imagination, meanwhile, will continue to produce experience, but no longer under the aegis of Reason and understanding: consciousness is not the subject **of** but rather subject **to** the syntheses – which Deleuze will insist on calling "passive" syntheses for this very reason. Even the third synthesis of recognition in *Anti-Oedipus*, when conscious awareness finally supervenes ("So that's what that was!"),[4] occurs **to** the subject rather than being under its conscious control (as Wittgenstein aptly illustrates with the composite figure of the duck-rabbit which we alternately "see as" as one or the other, more or less involuntarily).[5] Without the premise of a unified sovereign subject governed by Reason, much of the productive activity of the Kantian psyche turns out to be unconscious, and we become conscious of it – if we ever do – only *ex post facto*.

Bergson's sense of unconsciousness, like Nietzsche's, relates it more directly to action than to experience and cognition, and situates it in a broadly ethological rather than a narrower psychological context.[6] For Bergson, consciousness represents the interruption of an otherwise automatic or autonomic "sensory-motor schema" that ordinarily relates a specific response-behavior to a perceptual trigger in the environment. Behavior that is completely determined by instinct – Deleuze is fond of citing the tick's "drop!" response to the trigger-scent of the chemicals in mammalian sweat – leaves no room for conscious thought, or what Bergson calls intelligence. But actual human behavior, not being completely determined instinctually, alternates or is supplemented with intelligent contemplation, reflection, and recollection. Rather than trigger an immediate behavioral response, a perceived image may inspire reverie, or may recall images from the past. Whereas in Freud's analysis of neurosis, repression of a specific traumatic past deforms action in the present, for Bergson conscious human action in the present requires repression of the past as a whole, or at least repression of most of the past, except when specific elements of the past are brought to bear on a situation requiring action in the present. So for Bergson, most of the past remains unconscious most of the time, except when hesitation to act in the present calls some portion of the past to consciousness in order to help perform an action, or when completely free from any demands for present action we contemplate the past for its own sake. As Deleuze insists in an early essay, the past in itself "is the unconscious, or more precisely, as Bergson says, the *virtual*" (DI 29). So for Bergson and Deleuze, a philosophical unconscious – the virtual past as a coexisting whole – emerges out and because of the gap in non-instinctually determined human being between perception and action.

And yet humans are by no means purely contemplative beings: they act; and they act to some degree in accord with instinct and to a large degree in response to perceptions. So what bridges the gap between perception and action in human being? For Bergson, the bridge depends on the interplay of instinct and intelligence. And it is significant in this regard that just before devoting an entire essay to Bergson and just after publishing his first book, on Hume, Deleuze wrote a short introductory essay on "Instincts and Institutions", for the essay adopts the Bergsonian framework of instinct and intelligence, albeit without mentioning Bergson by name, and adopts the focus on institutions characteristic of Hume.[7] Instincts and institutions are the two forms mobilized to solve the Problem of satisfying what Deleuze prudently calls "tendencies." Instinctually, satisfaction is direct and determinate: the tick drops and must obtain mammalian blood, or die. In institutions, satisfaction is indirect and under-determined: the various means or objects of satisfaction never correspond intrinsically to the tendency. "The same sexual needs will never explain the multiple possible forms of marriage ... Tendencies are satisfied by means that do not depend on them ... [and] no tendency exists which is not at the same time constrained or harassed, and thus transformed, sublimated – to such an extent that neurosis is possible" (*DI* 20). Instincts and institutions form a continuum: the more perfect and exclusive the match between tendency and object, the greater the role of an instinct common to the entire species; the more variable the objects of satisfaction, the greater the role of intelligence rooted in historically and/or geographically specific tools and institutions (or of neurosis in a particular individual). Deleuze thus takes Bergson one step further, or provides greater clarity: even when the sensory-motor gap is bridged by a reflective determination of what appears "useful," any such sense of utility for human being is defined socially and institutionally:

[H]uman utility is always something other than mere utility. The institution refers us back to a social activity that is constitutive of models of which we are not conscious, and which are not explained either by tendencies or by utility, since the latter, as human utility, presupposes tendencies in the first place. (*DI* 20, translation modified)

So institutions provide socio-historically specific behavioral models for matching a wide range of objects to tendencies, and these contingent models (which Hume would call habits) may be as unconscious as those provided by instinct.

We end with Jung, not only because he developed a notion of unconsciousness in direct contradistinction to Freud's, but also because he derived that notion explicitly from Kant and Bergson. Jung's differences with Freud are well known; three are particularly important to Deleuze. First of all, and most generally, whereas Freud's understanding of psychodynamics was based squarely on neurosis, and therefore could accommodate psychosis only cursorily and with great difficulty, Jung's perspective centers on processes of dissociation, of which neurosis and psychosis are milder and severer versions. This is related to a second, more basic difference, regarding the very definition of psychic energy or libido. Freud defined libido exclusively as sexual energy, whereas Jung defined libido as psychic energy in general, of which sexualized psychic energy is a subset arising with the sexual instinct in puberty and preceded by other, pre-sexual libidinal forms. Jung can thus agree with Freud that many neuroses arise from difficulties with sexuality; but whereas for Freud psychosis, too, must arise as a reaction to sexual anxiety (usually a reaction against homosexuality), for Jung psychoses can involve regression to pre-sexual libidinal stages where magical thinking dissociated from reality-testing by the ego prevails.

Finally, and most important, is the disagreement over instincts and their relation to the unconscious. Despite retaining a theory of instinct throughout his career, Freud fairly quickly came to distinguish categorically between the unconscious proper, conceived of as the result of repression, and an older concept of the "id" conceived of as a reservoir of instinctual or biological urges. (Lacan will maintain this distinction even more strenuously than Freud.) His view of instinct, meanwhile, was always a dual or dialectical one, involving Eros and Thanatos late in his career, self-preservation and sexual reproduction earlier in his career. While Jung's theory of instinct resembles Freud's earlier theory, it is not dialectical but evolutionary and developmental: instincts evolve in each human being from a concern for preservation of the organism itself to a concern for the perpetuation of the species. Moreover, Jung's theory is not dualistic but multiple: there are many instincts (not just two), and for Jung they take the form of archetypes; it is here that he draws most directly on Bergson and Kant.[8]

In relation to Bergson, instincts are understood as dispositions to act in order to satisfy urges, yet these dispositions are always socio-historically contingent and specific; they combine instinctual intuition and institutional intelligence to varying degrees, and are therefore always to some extent unconscious. But for human beings, instincts affect more than action itself, according to Jung:

Just as we have been compelled to postulate the concept of an instinct determining or regulating conscious behavior, so, in order to account for the uniformity and regularity of our perceptions, we must have recourse to the correlated concept of a factor determining the mode of apprehension. It is this factor I call the archetype ... [which] might suitably be described as the *instinct's perception of itself.*[9]

In relation to Kant, archetypes are Ideas that shape experience through intuition rather than understanding. Archetypal Ideas are understood not as transcendent, stabilizing, and totalizing solutions to problematic experience (the Identical Self, the Wholly Knowable World, an Omni-Causal God), but as immanent expressions of the many and multifarious Problems experienced in and as human being. What's more, archetypes are accessible to intuition only through archetypal images, which are (just like Bergsonian tools and institutions) always historically contingent and specific, and represent more or less conscious solutions to unconscious Problems. In exactly the same vein, Deleuze will argue that Problems are unconscious and virtual, knowable only through actual cases of solution (in specific historical institutions and conjunctures), and will conclude that "one of the most important points of Jung's theory [is] to be found here: the force of 'questioning' in the unconscious, the conception of the unconscious as an unconscious of 'problems'" (*DR* 317, n.17). So it is not just human experience that is problematic (as for Kant): human instincts are equally problematic (as in Jung). It could thus be said (channeling Heidegger and Marx, as it were, along with Bergson and Jung) that the human animal is the animal whose instinctual species-being is a Problem – or rather, is composed of an open-ended multitude of Problems.

So where do such Problems come from? Do they arise (in Kantian fashion) from without, from problematic experience that defies subsumption by understanding and the Regulative Ideas of Reason? Or do they arise (in Jungian fashion) from within, from instinctual archetypes which in the human animal are never completely determining but always and only appear transformed or sublimated in human institutions? For Deleuze, ultimately, **these are only apparently different sources**; each is in fact a fold of the other: we have on one hand the differenciating and transformative **unfolding** of instinct in and through institutions, and on the other we have the internalizing **infolding** or imprinting of social representations and institutions onto the psyche.[10] Problems arise at the juncture (*au* *milieu*) between archetypal instinct and institutional intelligence. And inasmuch as "Nature = Industry = History" (as Deleuze and Guattari will put it in *Anti-Oedipus* [*AO* 25]), it makes no sense to try to assign Problems exclusively to one source or the other.

One final element of Jungian theory will prove crucial to the transformation of psychoanalysis into schizoanalysis: given that unconscious archetypes become accessible to consciousness only through their expression in and translation into historically contingent images, behaviors, rituals, and institutions, it is impossible to infer the true nature of an instinct from any actual representation of it – including, most notably, from any laws or taboos supposedly repressing or prohibiting it, such as the Oedipus Complex. Deleuze and Guattari, it is true, will prefer to formulate this crucial insight in terms of high-structuralism's "critique of representation" (for reasons and with additional benefits that will become clear below), but already in Jung it meant that an unconscious defined strictly as the result of repression is an impossibility. This is not to say that repressed materials don't become unconscious, for they certainly do. But an unconscious understood only in terms of repressed material would be completely unreliable, and would offer only a distorted image of the unconscious itself, falsified by the inevitably partial and contingent representations of it available to consciousness.

AFTER PSYCHOANALYSIS: SCHIZOANALYSIS

We can start with the critique of the psychoanalytic Oedipus Complex that gives the first volume of *Capitalism and Schizophrenia* its name. It will become clear that Deleuze and Guattari do not simply reject psychoanalysis (any more than Deleuze simply rejected Kant): important aspects of psychoanalysis are retained, even as others for good reason get pared away. Jung had already concluded, as we have just seen, that it is impossible to infer the true nature of instinct from its instantiation in social institutions and images. Immediately following one of the rare references in *Anti-Oedipus* that Deleuze and Guattari make to Jung by name, they say this:

The law tells us: You shall not marry your mother, and you shall not kill your father. And we docile subjects say to ourselves: so *that's* what I wanted! Will it ever be suspected that the law discredits – and has an interest in discrediting and disgracing – the person it presumes to be guilty, the person the law wants to be made to feel guilty? One acts as if it were possible to conclude directly from psychic repression the nature of the repressed, and from the prohibition the nature of what is prohibited. (*AO* 114, translation modified)

Now from a Jungian perspective, let us suppose that the developmental biology, neurophysiology and psychology of human being make the issue of attachment to and separation from the Mother an archetypal Problem: we would expect that Problem to express itself differently in different socio-historically specific institutions and representations. Deleuze and Guattari's comparison of capitalism with despotism in *Anti-Oedipus* demonstrates precisely that: under capitalism, separation from the Mother is achieved by means of a negative taboo proscribing sexual relations with other members of the nuclear family; but under despotism, separation is achieved by means of a positive dispensation prescribing incest among members of the royal family as a privilege only they may enjoy (*AO* 200–2). In one case, the archetypal Problem is "solved" with a negative proscription bearing exclusively on family relations, while in the other, the same Problem is "solved" with a positive though invidious prescription bearing inclusively on caste relations in society as a whole that differentiate royalty from everyone else. There is a lot more to such a comparison and the contextualizing procedure underlying it than this, but one thing they suggest is that the existence of the psychoanalytic Oedipus Complex depends entirely on the historically contingent institution of the nuclear family, and that it is critical to understand the nuclear family in turn as a strictly capitalist institution. It is crucial to note that this does **not** mean that the Oedipus Complex doesn't exist, or that psychoanalysis somehow got it wrong: on the contrary, the Oedipus Complex is in an important sense all **too** real, and the problem with psychoanalysis is that it got it right but does nothing to free us from it; instead, it ends up actually reinforcing our subjection to ultimately capitalist social and familial relations under the guise of promoting personal psychic health.

Now what makes the Oedipal-nuclear family a strictly capitalist institution is this: at the same time that the accumulation of wealth is privatized in the economy, the reproduction of subjectivity is privatized in the family. So it is not simply that the nuclear family is smaller in scope or scale than all other "extended" family forms throughout history (although this result is crucial): it is also that the relations of reproduction in the family are increasingly segregated from the relations of production in the economy (which themselves become increasingly segregated from politics and everyday life). Under capitalism, economic production takes place exclusively outside the family, with the family relegated to being a locus of consumption and reproduction. It is for this reason that Deleuze and Guattari say that of all the modes of production, capitalism fosters the greatest "difference in regime" between social production and what they call "desiring-production," whereas in all other social formations, production relations and "extended" family relations coincide more or less and interconnect.[11] The complex relations between social production and desiring-production are key to Deleuze and Guattari's transformation of psychoanalysis, and bear closer examination.

Most important, the distinction between desiring-production and social production does **not** correspond to the distinction between fantasy and reality: desiring-production and social production are equally real, and they are both equally informed, invested, and motivated by fantasy. They are (to revert to the term Deleuze deploys later, in his work on Leibniz and Foucault, and that we used a moment ago) precisely **folds** of one another. While it is true that they belong to "different regimes," and that the degree of difference between them varies historically, ultimately, like instincts and institutions, they are utterly interdependent and "identical in nature," as Deleuze and Guattari put it, comprising the two sides of a single, universal process of production:

There is only one kind of production, the production of the real. And doubtless we can express this identity in two different ways ... We can say that social production, under determinate conditions, derives primarily from desiring-production: which is to say that *Homo natura* comes first. But we must also say, more accurately, that desiring-production is first and foremost social in nature, and tends to free itself only at the end [of history]: which is to say that *Homo historia* comes first. (*AO* 32–33)

Paradoxically, the identical nature of desiring and social production only becomes apparent toward the end of history, under capitalism, where the difference in regime is the greatest. To understand how this is so, we can as a kind of first approximation think of desiring-production as libido and of social production as labor power. They are both expressions of a single energy source which, as a second approximation, we can consider to be actually akin to and conceptually derived from Nietzschean will to power and Bergsonian *élan vital*. But under capitalism, this single form of energy is divided in two so radically by the wholesale segregation of the relations of reproduction (in the nuclear family) from the relations of production (in the economy) that libido appears to be the proper object and discovery of psychoanalysis and labor power the proper object and discovery of political economy. And, in a limited sense, they are indeed discrete objects or concepts. But schizoanalysis will insist on breaking through the limitations of the disciplinary effects of institutionalized segregation (proclaiming that "Nature = Industry = History" [AO 25]), in order to grasp production as a universal and thereby restore its full critical force, beyond both psychoanalysis and political economy.

One measure of the critical force unleashed by the schizoanalytic axiom that desiring-production and social production are ultimately identical in nature despite their difference in regime is the insight it affords into the capitalist "solution" to the archetypal Problem of the Mother, alluded to above. Imagine an abstract machine or institution composed of three parts, where one's access to a life-giving source is prevented by the intermediation of a domineering third party. Now note that these are simultaneously the structural dynamics of **both** the nuclear family **and** the capitalist economy: just as capital separates the worker from the means of life (from "Mother Nature") through **primitive accumulation** and defers the satisfactions of consumption (*consommation* in French) until after work, after pay-day, and after retirement, so does the father separate the child from the nurturing Mother (its means of life) through **castration** and defers the satisfactions of sexual consummation (also *consommation* in French) until maturity and the founding of a new family: "Father, mother, and child thus become the simulacrum of the images of capital ('"Mister Capital, Madame Earth," and their child the Worker')," Deleuze and Guattari pointedly suggest, adapting a quotation from Marx (AO 264). (It should go without saying that there are myriad other ways of imagining, representing, and institutionalizing solutions to the archetypal Problem of separation.) But the point is that this is more than a mere structural homology: the Oedipal-nuclear family provides the perfect training ground in subservience and asceticism (or subservience and other-directed consumerism, when the economy requires it) for the production of "docile" capitalist subjects. Ultimately, not only is the nuclear family a strictly capitalist institution, but psychoanalysis is, too – in that it sanctions, perpetrates, and reinforces the Oedipal psycho-dynamics of castration, obedience, self-denial, and deferral so perfectly suited to the socio-dynamics of capital accumulation.

This diagnosis of the nuclear family and Oedipal psychoanalysis as capitalist institutions does not exhaust the power of schizo-analytic critique, however. The importance of historical variation in the relations between desiring-production and social production, initially prompted by Bergson and Jung perhaps, becomes all the greater in *Anti-Oedipus* with the application of the structuralist and post-structuralist critique of representation. As we have just seen, Deleuze and Guattari argue that it is impossible to conclude directly from a prohibitive law the true nature of what is prohibited, or from psychic repression the true nature what is repressed. By drawing on semiotics, however, they insist on the importance of distinguishing not just between two terms – repression and the repressed – but among three: first of all, the repressing representation (the signifier); second, the distorted image of desire produced by the representation (its signified); and finally, the referent, the desire that actually gets repressed (*AO* 115 and *passim*). Two critical points follow immediately from this semiotic analysis. The first is that we don't necessarily learn about the contents of the unconscious from the process of representation: the referent is not the same as the signified. The second is that representation itself is the basis of repression, so that unconsciousness is assigned (following Kant and somewhat in line with Lacan) to those forms of experience that defy or are denied representation. A third critical point then follows from the mobilization of the tripartite critique of representation for a genealogy or archaeology of the Oedipus Complex itself.

For even though they insist that the Oedipus gets actualized as a lived complex only within the nuclear family under capitalism, Deleuze and Guattari also recognize that incest is an archetypal Problem for human beings, so that the figure of Oedipal incest can appear as a kind of spectral universal haunting all types of social formation. But in each type (analyzed by Deleuze and Guattari in the form of three distinct modes of desiring- and social production), it follows a specific distribution among the three terms of repressive representation. In the savage mode of production, the incest taboo as a negative prohibition is the distorted image of desire (the signified) produced by the real social imperative, which is a positive requirement (the signifier) to knit productive social relations by marrying outside the clan; the real desired referent, meanwhile, is direct access to life (the reproductive power of women). In the despotic mode of production (examined briefly above), incest occupies both the position of the repressing representation (the signifier) and of the distorted image of desire (the signified): in the former position, incest within the ruling family appears as a royal prerogative, while for everyone else in a caste society it is taboo; the real desired referent, meanwhile, is rebellion against the despot and re-distribution of his accumulated wealth and privilege. In the capitalist mode of production, and only there, incest occupies all three positions: the taboo against incest is at the same time the repressing representation (the signifier: "Thou shalt not ..."), the distorted image of desire (the signified: "So **that**'s what I wanted!"), and the real referent of desire – for within the confines of the nuclear family, the only objects of desire left are all actually taboo: the Oedipus is now a complex. Social production has captured desiring-production in a distinctive institution (the nuclear family) and deployed corresponding representations (chief among them psychoanalysis itself) that together end up straitjacketing desire and producing Oedipalized subjects ideally suited for enduring or even enjoying or craving the rigors and blandishments of capitalism. In the worst light, Oedipal psychoanalysis thus appears as a technology for reproducing and reinforcing capitalist subjectivity. But of course there is much more to psychoanalysis than the Oedipus Complex, and psychoanalysis remains a particularly important reference for Deleuze and Guattari in their definition of desiring-production, to which we now turn.

As a first approximation, we compared the schizoanalytic concept of desiring-production to psychoanalytic libido, and this is indeed the primary basis for the concept. Deleuze and Guattari credit Freud with having discovered the "abstract subjective essence" of desire: "His greatness lies in having determined the essence or nature of desire, no longer in relation to objects, aims, or even sources ... but as an abstract subjective essence – libido or sexuality [in general]" (*AO* 270). Freud is therefore hailed as "the Luther and the Adam Smith of psychiatry" (*AO* 270), but with an identical drawback: just as they discovered free labor power as the abstract subjective essence of wealth only to re-alienate it onto capital as an illegitimate external determination, Freud defines free libido as abstract subjective essence but then re-alienates it onto the illegitimate external determination of Oedipus. This twin alienation will establish the dual project of schizoanalysis as revolutionary materialist psychiatry: free labor power from capital; free libido from Oedipus.

There may be another limitation to Freud's contribution to the concept of desiring-production, suggested by the hesitation in the passage quoted above between "libido" and "sexuality." If libido is indeed an abstract subjective essence, then how can it be defined in terms of a fixed aim such as specifically sexual gratification? In this respect, Deleuze and Guattari would appear to side with Jung in his disagreement with Freud over the definition of libido, for Jung defined it as an energy of passion in general rather than a specifically sexual energy. Yet Deleuze and Guattari also express concern about Jung's possible betrayal of materialism through an idealism of archetypes construed as fixed images in a collective unconscious, rather than as Problems.[12] To avoid fruitless polemics over the semantics of "sexuality" while retaining the claim of schizoanalysis to be a "materialist psychiatry," we can say that desiring-production is powered by the pleasure principle, with whatever degree or quality of sexuality pleasure entails.

Desiring-production also has important Kantian components, although here once again Kant is corrected by Nietzsche, as well as supplemented by Marx and Bergson. Unlike the terms intuition, imagination, and understanding which dominate the first critique (of pure reason), desire plays an important role in the second and third critiques (of practical reason and judgment). Whereas pure reason concerns knowledge, practical reason "is concerned not with objects in order to know them, but with its own capacity to make them real (which does require knowledge of them)," and desire is defined – surprisingly – as "the faculty which by means of its representations is the cause of the actuality of the objects of those representations."[13] How could desire possibly be understood to "cause the actuality" of its objects by means of representations? For Kant, this is explained by distinguishing between two kinds of "actuality," only one of which involves the exercise of reason. Without a grounding in reason, desire causes the actuality of its objects only in the "pathological" form of hallucinations, not in reality; only when informed by reason does desire become will, and thus become able to cause the actuality of its objects in reality: "will ... is a causal agent so far as reason contains its determining ground."[14] In order to convert desire into a will that has rational causal agency in reality, however, Kant must rely on his three transcendent Ideas of Reason (Self, World, and God), and as we have seen, this is where, with help from Nietzsche, Deleuze parts company with Kant. For Nietzsche in effect refuses Kant's distinction between irrational-pathological desire and rational will: they become indistinguishable aspects of will to power. In stark contrast to the nihilism of modern science and the cult of knowledge for its own sake, Nietzsche's noble artist or overman does not require rational knowledge in order to be a causal agent: he creates his own reality, along with whatever knowledge of it he may require. In a similar vein, but from a very different perspective, Marx highlights the ability of human beings to picture objects in the mind and then produce them in reality, instead of producing them instinctually, as most other species do (Marx cites bees and spiders). Bergson, too, highlights the human propensity to interrupt instinctual motor responses to sensory stimuli in order to generate virtual images of Problems before producing actual solutions to them. Basing their concept of desiring-production mainly on these sources, Deleuze and Guattari will insist that "desire produces, [and] its product is real ... [and that] the objective being of desire is the Real in and of itself" (AO 26–27). With this refusal or "loss of reality" attendant on the Nietzschean demotion of the conventional reality principle in favor of a principle of real creativity, schizoanalysis in a certain sense favors the perspective of the psychotic over that of the neurotic.

The final and perhaps most basic component of desiring-production drawn from Kant is the notion that the mind functions via syntheses. For Kant, experience is not only ordered according to the a prioris of space and time, but also processed by a set of three mental operations he calls the syntheses of apprehension, reproduction, and recognition. These syntheses form the basis of all possible knowledge, and understanding how they operate is thus crucial to determining which forms of knowledge are legitimate and which are not. While there are no doubt resemblances between Kant's syntheses and those formulated by Deleuze and Guattari, one difference is key: Kant's syntheses are organized by a unified rational thinking subject in order to produce stable knowledge of a fixed reality, whereas the syntheses of desiring-production are largely unconscious, and operate in order to produce reality itself (in connection with social production) as well as our experience of it. And since the syntheses of desiring-production are largely unconscious, it is not surprising that Deleuze and Guattari should draw on psychoanalysis for their formulation of them.

The connective synthesis of production connects libidinal drives with objects of satisfaction, both physically and perceptually; it incorporates or replaces the Freudian concept of "cathexis." Crucially, the objects of the connective synthesis are always "partial objects" (following the perspective of Melanie Klein here, more than that of Freud), in two senses of the term: they are parts of wholes that have yet to be constituted (pertaining to what she called the "paranoid-schizoid" stage of development preceding the emergence of a unified ego), and the drives are partial to them because they are invested with erotic value.[15] In line with Freud's dual-instinct model, Klein reduces such value to "good" and "bad"; more in line with Nietzsche and Jung, Deleuze and Guattari consider the potential value of any partial object to be as multiple as the drives themselves (and the many Problems they give rise and respond to). But in any case, whole objects only appear later as representations of a unified ego and as an effect of the conjunctive synthesis of recognition ("Oh! – so **that**'s what that was."). The syntax of the connective synthesis is therefore "and ... and ... and ...": drives cathect partial-objects continuously and in a sense indiscriminately, depending on which drive or perspective predominates in the unconscious at a given moment.

The disjunctive synthesis of recording is far more complicated, incorporating and rewriting a number of important Freudian concepts, but also including many created by Deleuze and Guattari themselves. Its syntax can be expressed as "or ... or ... or ... or ..." with multiple "or"s rather than just one ("this or that"), because the disjunction of this synthesis is inclusive rather than exclusive: it is never merely a choice between one thing and another (e.g., good vs. bad), but a momentary selection among a multitude of possibilities that never permanently rules the others out. Taken together with the connective synthesis, the disjunctive synthesis thus maps what Freud referred to as the "polymorphous perversity" of the infantile (pre-ego) unconscious: anything goes; before being fixated on specific organs, erogenous zones, or activities, pleasure can be found or taken almost anywhere; it is not instinctually determined.

Even more important, though, are the psychodynamics of the disjunctive synthesis: for it brings about a suspension or interruption of the connective synthesis of production. The productive energy of connection is matched and counter-acted by a disjunctive energy Deleuze and Guattari call "anti-production" – a concept that effectively incorporates and replaces the Freudian categories of repression, anti-cathexis, and the death instinct.[16] But there are three degrees or modes of anti-production in desiring-production, and much of the critical force of schizoanalysis depends on the relations and distinctions among them.[17] First degree: an infant's mouth (partial object) is connected to "a" nipple (not "the Mother's breast": just "a" partial object); some valuable energy flow is produced (its value is simultaneously and indistinguishably nutritional and erotic); then satiation is achieved, the sucking stops, and the connection is dropped: the nipple is expelled from the mouth; a product has been produced, the intensity of the pleasure taken in the productive process vanishes to zero: production succumbs to anti-production, but not without the latter recording the image of the nipple as an object of satisfaction on a recording surface that Deleuze and Guattari (borrowing from Antonin Artaud) call the Body-without-Organs (henceforth the "BwO").[18] Second degree: a mouth is connected to a nipple, producing a valued energy flow; then, some distraction (rather than satiation) supervenes: this sucking stops; the mouth–nipple connection is dropped in favor of an eye–face connection, or a mouth–finger connection, or a mouth–penis connection, or a cigarette, or ... or ... Anti-production is the energy of inclusive disjunction that enables what is already a multitude of instinctually under-determined drives to find satisfaction and take pleasure in an even greater multitude of objects and modes of satisfaction – polymorphous perversity – and that records them on the BwO for future reference, as it were. Although the term is borrowed from Artaud, the concept of the BwO is rather Bergsonian in inspiration: the fact that the connection between sensory stimulus and motor response is not instinctually determined but can be suspended or interrupted in human beings opens access to the virtual past, which contains (among many other things) a vast data bank of recorded images of previous modes of satisfaction or frustration. The anti-productive disconnection from any single instinctually or habitually determined mode of satisfaction ultimately gives human beings the freedom to reflect on, choose among, and indeed create multiple modes of satisfaction.

Of course, Freud has his own version of this whole process: the repetition compulsion grounded in the death instinct induces humans to seek for the same objects of satisfaction that match the memory traces of previous objects of satisfaction; since Freud assumes that the instincts are "innately conservative," human beings are governed by a compulsion to repeat that always entails repetition of the same.[19] For Deleuze, by contrast, the cosmos as a whole – but also and especially the human being – is governed by the repetition of difference rather than identity; thus instinctual repetition in humans, far from being innately conservative, opens onto the practically limitless variety of modes of satisfaction afforded by intelligence and institutions operating with but beyond instinct. What potential would exist for the institution of culinary or erotic arts, for instance, if humans remained exclusively fixated on the breast for nourishment, or for oral gratification? The disjunctive synthesis usually works in tandem with the connective synthesis in a continuous process of attraction, differentiation, and repulsion of drive–partial object relations to produce the staggering variety of human experience. At one extreme – connection without disjunction – you would have total fixation on an instinctually or habitually predetermined object: obsessive-compulsive disorder or neurosis; at the other – disjunction without connection – you would have total withdrawal from contact with reality: catatonia or psychosis.

Third degree: multifarious modes of satisfaction – produced by the anti-productive force of inclusive disjunction in the opening in human being between instincts and institutions, and registered on the BwO – get **qualified** in and by social representations as good or bad; as taboo, permitted, or required. Anti-production here arises not from satiation or distraction, but from repression proper – what

Deleuze and Guattari call specifically "social repression" – and it therefore entails not inclusive but exclusive disjunction: no longer "this or that, or … whatever" but "this and not that!" This is the form of repression that for Freud (and Lacan) creates "the" unconscious. But for schizoanalysis, the operations of both the connective and the disjunctive syntheses are themselves already unconscious, regardless of whether they suffer social repression – unless and until their results get recognized through the third synthesis, the conjunctive synthesis of consumption–consummation. Hence the tremendous importance of the BwO – and especially of the **ambivalent** makeup of the BwO – as recording apparatus and site or scene of "the" unconscious for Deleuze & Guattari: desiring-production registers multifarious images of objects of satisfaction on the BwO as reminders of potential future satisfaction, but some of them then get captured in and by censorious social representations and are thereby repressed. This two-stage process of registration-representation on the BwO corresponds approximately to Freud's notions of primal repression and proper repression – yet places unconsciousness in schizoanalysis on a footing very different from that of psychoanalysis: one that, in line with structuralism and post-structuralism, mobilizes the critique of representation to understand repression and the unconscious. One important by-product of this critique: social representation of **any** kind – positive or negative, prescriptive or proscriptive – constitutes a form of repression, and conversely, desiring-production would be completely free only if it could escape from the codes of social representation entirely: at the limit, this is the decoded form of desire Deleuze and Guattari call "schizophrenia."

In the conjunctive synthesis, finally, a sense of self and conscious awareness emerges; importantly, the consciousness and self-consciousness of the third synthesis arise retrospectively and epiphenomenally relative to the operations of the first two syntheses: "So that's what that was!" "That's me! That's mine!" When the syntheses of production and anti-production conflict systematically, two specific forms of subjectivity result which are noteworthy in part because Freud had already identified them as corollaries of one another: the neurotic and the pervert.[20] In the neurotic, the forces of anti-production prevail: desiring-production is denied one or more of its own connections by social representations and is constrained to fix on a relatively ungratifying substitute connection (the neurotic symptom), instead. In the pervert, the forces of production prevail: an unorthodox organ–object connection is maintained despite (or in some cases because of, as in transgression according to Bataille) the social sanctions promulgated to forbid and repress it. As in the prioritization of psychosis over neurosis mentioned above, here, too, schizoanalysis favors the perspective of the pervert over that of the neurotic, and the forces of production over the forces of anti-production.

Beyond their symmetrical relation with one another, however, the subjects of neurosis and perversion are noteworthy because they illustrate in dramatic form the position of the third synthesis relative to the interplay of production and anti-production comprising the first two: the subject emerges **only as an after-effect** of the selections made by desire among various disjunctive and connective syntheses, **not as the agent** of selection. Neurotics and perverts are not so by voluntary, conscious choice; they are not the agents but the **results** of involuntary connections and disjunctions made on the BwO by the interplay of forces of production and anti-production that constitute them as subjects. "Normal" adults, meanwhile, typically indulge in the illusion (of sovereign subjectivity) whereby they choose their pleasures and desires, rather than being "chosen," that is to say constituted, by them; Deleuze and Guattari draw directly on Nietzsche to dispel this illusion and insist that the productions and anti-productions of desire, like "will to power," always come first, and the appearance of the subject afterward. This reversal of the relation between process and product, which is crucial to such misrecognition on the part of the subject and conducive to the illusion of sovereign subjectivity, is made possible by the earlier process–product reversal of the disjunctive synthesis, whereby only results of the **suspension** of the process of connective synthesis register on the BwO, as images of "finished" products. The process of connective synthesis is not just continual: this and then that, and then this, and so on; it is also for that very reason equally evanescent. Desiring-production thus registers permanently in the psyche (gets stored in memory) only when it is attracted by, and its results get recorded on, the BwO. From this point on, what is merely a recording surface henceforth appears to be the **source** of what gets recognized in the constitution of the subject in conjunctive syntheses. Finally, the subject in turn claims mastery or ownership of the BwO – or of its products: consummate experience, intensities – when it is in fact a mere derivative of them. The subject as product appropriates and obscures (represses) the very process that constitutes it as subject.

Indeed, even to speak of "the" subject in the singular is in a sense to have already succumbed to the product–process reversal and the illusions of sovereign subjectivity, for even the last of the syntheses produces a subject always different from itself. Just as much as the productive synthesis continually connects (and ... and ... and ...) and the disjunctive synthesis continually differentiates (or ... or ... or ...), the conjunctive synthesis in turn generates, from the vast networks of relations among organs–machines on the BwO, an indefinite series of constellations or states of intense experience, each of which gets recognized and consummated *ex post facto* by a subject of that experience: "Thus the subject consumes and consummates each of the states [on the BwO] through which it passes, and is born of each of them anew" (*AO* 41, translation modified). When the forces of production and anti-production interact in less rigid ways, forms of subjectivity emerge that remain closer to the continual, open-ended, indefinite nature of the syntheses and therefore enjoy or suffer experience with that much greater intensity. Foremost among them, for Deleuze and Guattari, is the schizo, the protagonist of *Anti-Oedipus*, who affirms the forces of both attraction and repulsion, and takes them to the limit: the connective syntheses, instead of being repelled or merely having their finished products registered, are continually brought back into play on a BwO whose disjunctive syntheses multiply their ramifications indefinitely, thereby fueling the consummation of a perpetually renewed, "nomadic" subject always different from itself – a kind of "permanent revolution" of psychic life.

Having proposed this schizoanalytic model of the psyche as an alternative to Freud's (and, by implication, Kant's), Deleuze and Guattari are able to formulate a vehement and detailed critique of Oedipal psychoanalysis by enumerating what they call (again echoing Kant) the five "paralogisms" (fallacies) of psychoanalysis, three of which arise from illegitimate use of the syntheses of experience we have just examined.[21] This, too, echoes a Kantian operation: speaking from the perspective of unified reason, knowledge, and morality,

Kant had asserted that the conscious mind utilizes a specific set of processes (the syntheses of apprehension, reproduction, and recognition) to arrive at knowledge, and had insisted furthermore that knowledge would have to conform to these processes or else stand condemned as metaphysical.[22] Of critical importance for Kant was the idea that, since these processes were **constitutive** of conscious thought, they provided **immanent** criteria for judging knowledge as valid or metaphysical, depending on whether it was based on legitimate or illegitimate use of the three syntheses. In a similar way, but speaking not from the perspective of reason but from that of desire and especially schizophrenic desire, Deleuze and Guattari insist that the unconscious operates according to a specific set of syntheses to process or constitute experience, and that psychoanalysis must either be shown to conform to the immanent criteria provided by these processes or else stand condemned as metaphysical.[23] With respect to all five paralogisms, the fundamentally ambivalent makeup of the BwO and the product–process reversal it fosters play a critical role: images of organ–machine connections register on the BwO only when anti-production transforms the process of desiring-production into a finished, arrested, or repressed product, which has the disastrous consequence that fixed properties of the finished product are misattributed to the differential process that produced it, obscuring its genesis entirely; differences succumb to identity. And the disaster is this: genetic processes always harbor some potential to actualize differently, and to thereby produce different end products. But the paralogisms of Oedipal psychoanalysis end up crushing whatever critical political force (of counter-actualization) psychoanalysis may have contained, by replacing the productive indeterminacy of process with the fixed being of what is (and the nihilism of the reality principle).

We start with the paralogism of disfiguration or displacement, which we have already discussed in terms of the post-structuralist critique of representation: disfiguration amounts to mistaking the distorted image of desire (the signified) promulgated by a prohibition (the repressing signifier) for the referent that image displaces: the actual desire getting repressed. Repression on this view is an effect of representation – a view schizoanalysis shares with Lacanian psychoanalysis, which similarly defines repression in terms of desire that is unable to traverse the "defiles of signification." Deleuze and

Guattari will also agree with Lacan that the unconscious is structured – but not like a language: as an open-ended set of Problematic Ideas, instead (in the wake of Kant, Bergson, and Jung, as we have seen). For Lacan, that the unconscious is structured like a language means that an unbreachable bar separates bodily drives, which are substantial, from the universe of signification, which is differential: there is therefore an irreparable and tragic loss of any direct contact between consciousness and drives. But for Deleuze and Guattari, there is no such loss, and for two complementary reasons. First of all, the structure of the unconscious is semiotic without being strictly linguistic: the chains of this semiotic system are a-signifying, and are said to "resemble ... a succession of characters from different alphabets in which an ideogram, a pictogram, a tiny image of an elephant passing by, or a rising sun may suddenly make its appearance" (AO 39); a semiotic system containing pictograms and images of elephants cannot be purely differential in the way a (phonetic) linguistic system is. Conversely, bodily drives for Deleuze and Guattari are not purely substantial (as they are for Lacan): drives repeatedly differentiate themselves under the impetus of institutions and intelligence and the Problems they give rise and respond to, well beneath the level of representation, solutions, and conscious awareness. What's more, immanent criteria exist to evaluate solutions and representations according to their use or abuse of the syntheses of experience, and it is to them that we now return.

Illegitimate use of the connective synthesis (the paralogism of extrapolation) is global and specific instead of partial and non-specific – Kleinian, in a word, rather than Nietzschean. Klein was on the right track, according to Deleuze and Guattari, in her elucidation of partial objects, but went astray in considering them merely a temporary "pre-Oedipal" stage en route to the integration of instincts and drives under the aegis of a unified, sovereign ego. For Nietzsche and schizoanalysis, the unified ego is an illusion and an epiphenomenon, and objects remain partial in correlation with the partiality of the unconscious forces warring for temporary dominance in the psyche. In this respect, a specific (illegitimate) use of the connective synthesis involves selecting one element of a connective a-signifying chain – the phallus, say, or reason or money – and elevating it permanently to a place or role of privilege over and above all the other elements. Finally, the other thing to be said about the abuse of the connective synthesis is that it usually occurs as an effect of (or at the very least in tandem with) the illegitimate use of the disjunctive synthesis.

Abuse of the disjunctive synthesis (the paralogism of the double bind) is exclusive and restrictive rather than inclusive and non-restrictive. This difference underlies the crucial **ambivalence** of the BwO, which as we have seen allows for the differentiation of drives beyond instinct and habit but also their capture in social repression and neurosis. Inclusive disjunction generates an indiscriminate plurality of modes of satisfaction for the multifarious drives it thereby differentiates, whereas exclusive disjunction restricts the range and form of possible satisfactions to binary pairs and then forces an either–or choice between the paired terms: one must identify as man or woman, gay or straight, and so on. While there is much to be said (practically, everything to be said) in favor of full civil rights for gays, lesbians, bisexuals, the transgendered, and queers in general, each of these legitimate categories of civil representation can become reductive and repressive as an instance of illegitimate molar representation of fixed identities vis-à-vis the differentiating drives of the molecular unconscious.

Illegitimate use of the conjunctive synthesis (the paralogism of application), meanwhile, bears primarily on the constitution and recognition of identity, and is segregative and bi-univocal rather than nomadic and polyvocal. The segregative use involves defining the fixed identity of an individual, a family, a clan, race, tribe, nation, etc. in terms of its superiority to others, whereas schizophrenic or nomadic subjectivity, as we have seen, defies identification by remaining constantly in flux, and identifies temporarily (if it does so at all) always with the inferior or subaltern other: "I am of a race inferior for all eternity … I am a beast, a Negro" (*AO* 105, quoting Arthur Rimbaud). Related to the attribution of a unitary fixed self-identity to what is in fact a process of plural and nomadic subjectivity is the attribution of a single fixed meaning to experience that is in fact polysemous or polyvocal. The retrospective "So that's what that was" gets applied outside the therapeutic context to the psychoanalytic interpretation of socio-historical phenomena and translated into "So that's what that means" – so that (Oedipus) is what that (everything) means. This is what Deleuze and Guattari refer to as "bi-univocalization": the reduction of the real complexity of the unconscious to an expressive relation between a tenor that is held constant, on one hand – the Oedipus – and on the other hand a vehicle – comprising all the socio-historical material – that varies substantially but for psychoanalysis enjoys no explanatory power whatsoever. Hence the tiresome, mechanically repetitive quality of most psychoanalytic studies of culture and society: everything amounts to the Oedipus (for Freudians); to lack, castration, or the phallus (for Lacanians); or to some "kernel of surplus-enjoyment" (for Žižek).

The fifth paralogism seems in a sense to compensate for the abuse of bi-univocalization; Deleuze and Guattari call it the paralogism of the afterward. Here, the importance of real social and historical factors in psychic life is granted, but only insofar as they are understood to come **after** the familial factors, which form Oedipal subjectivity during childhood first. Real social relations are then construed merely as so many "sublimations" of Oedipal relations, which are supposed to be primary, and therefore universal as well: "the child is father to the man," as the saying goes. But for schizoanalysis, it is not the child but the **boss** who is father to the man, so to speak, and only then is the man father to the child.[24] Oedipal relations are neither primary – inasmuch as they derive, by delegation to the institution of the nuclear family, from the structure and dynamics of capital accumulation – nor universal – inasmuch as the nuclear family is a historically contingent, specifically capitalist institution.

Oedipal psychoanalysis embodies all five of the paralogisms diagnosed by Deleuze and Guattari. It presupposes that the productive synthesis makes specific whole-object connections to global persons in the family alone instead of general partial object connections to the natural and social environment at large; that the conjunctive synthesis first constructs subjects within a segregated field of restricted identifications instead of from the entire field of social relations; and that the disjunctive synthesis, positing a closed either–or alternative, effectively excludes society from the enclosure of the nuclear family altogether. But the family is not separate, not an autonomous and self-contained microcosm; the family is a social institution, and the nuclear family is in fact a capitalist institution.[25] And it is **delegated** the function of reproduction under capitalism as an apparently separate institution so that social production can proceed to develop and continually revolutionize itself without regard for the reproduction of subjects and the direct management of their desire.

Such delegation explains why the family can appear to be a microcosm, when it really is not; why familially constructed subjects often seem on one hand so ill-suited to the specific content-requirements of social production at any given moment of its development; why on the other hand the family's degree of abstraction as an apparently separate reproductive institution produces subjects perfectly suited formally to a system of social production in constant flux. For what they learn in the nuclear family is simply to submit as good, docile subjects to prohibitive authority – the father, the boss, capital in general – and relinquish until later, as good ascetic subjects, their access to the objects of desire and their objective being – the mother, the goods they produce, the natural environment as a whole. Far from being autonomous, much less originary, fundamental, or universal, the Oedipus Complex of the nuclear family appears as though it had been "fabricated to meet the requirements of … [the capitalist] social formation" (AO 101), from which it in fact derives by delegation.[26] And from the psychoanalytic perspective, to challenge or rebel against Oedipally constituted authority would amount to … committing incest!

Hence the importance of the critique of representation to the schizoanalytic critique of Oedipal psychoanalysis: in delegating the formation of desire to the nuclear family as system of reproduction–representation, capitalism manages to trap desiring-production in a deceptive and misleading image of itself whose familial content is mostly irrelevant, even while the form of that desiring-production ultimately echoes and reinforces precisely the kind of repression exercised by capitalist social production itself:

It is in one and the same movement that the repressive social production is replaced by the repressing family, and that the latter offers a displaced image of desiring-production that represents the repressed as incestuous familial drives. (AO 119, italics in original)

Desiring-production and social production are thus, in a **descriptive** sense, one and the same process, inasmuch as schizoanalysis sees no need and no room to posit any independent, universal formation of desire such as Oedipus intervening between one and the other: *"social-production is purely and simply desiring-production itself under determinate conditions"* (*AO* 29, italics in original).

Yet in another, **critical** sense, desiring-production and social production **are** different, inasmuch as schizoanalysis enables and expects us to judge any historical organization of social production according to the immanent criteria provided by desiring-production itself, and thereby expose "the repression that the social machine exercises on desiring-machines" (*AO* 54):

From the very beginning of this study, we have maintained both that social-production and desiring-production are one and the same, and that they have differing regimes, with the result that a social form of production exercises an essential repression of desiring-production, and also that desiring-production – "real" desire – is potentially capable of demolishing the social form. (*AO* 116)

Such a distinction is made possible by the constitutive ambivalence of the disjunctive synthesis of recording on the BwO, as Deleuze and Guattari construe it. Desire registers its satisfactions and frustrations as images on the BwO, as we saw, when primary repression caused by anti-production suspends the activity of the connective synthesis. As a result, desire is free to diversify through the disjunctive networks of images, but it can also become trapped in fixed representations deriving from and propagating social repression proper.

Delegation of social repression under capitalism to the nuclear family thus makes it appear as if there were an autonomous "psychic" repression originating in the Oedipus complex, which would only **afterward** get extended to "social repression" in society at large, through processes of sublimation and transference. But here is where the political implications of the Oedipal (mis)representation of desire become clear, for "if psychic repression did bear on incestuous desires," Deleuze and Guattari explain, "it would gain a certain independence and primacy … in relation to social repression" (*AO* 113). And, as they go on to say, accepting this primacy would constitute a "justification for psychic repression – a justification that makes psychic repression move into the foreground and no longer considers the problem of social repression anything more than secondary" (*AO* 117). If psychic repression did truly target incestuous desires, it would be justified by the natural necessity of the incest taboo, and social repression could be seen as a mere extension or "sublimation" of that natural necessity for the sake of higher civilization (as Freud claims). But such is not the case. Hence the importance of analyzing representation with three terms rather than two, to foil the ruses of representation and refute the Oedipal apology for repression. Psychoanalysis considered psychic repression in the Oedipus Complex to be primary and universal, and social repression to be secondary and inevitable. Schizoanalysis, by contrast, ascribes the potential for both psychic and social repression to the registration of desire on the BwO in the first place, due to the primary repression occasioned by anti-production.[27] It is thus able to reverse the causal order proposed by psychoanalysis and show that "psychic repression is a means in the service of social repression" (*AO* 119), thereby delegitimating social repression and making it a target for change.

This all-important reversal is in a sense a reversal of a reversal, inasmuch as the paralogisms of psychoanalysis all arose to begin with, as we saw, with a product–process reversal that confused the fixed properties of the finished product with the differential processes that produced it, obscuring its genesis entirely. Hence the critical importance of discovering criteria immanent to the operations of the unconscious: once we can discriminate between legitimate and illegitimate uses of the syntheses of experience, psychoanalysis must either conform to the criteria or be condemned as metaphysical and repressive – and the Oedipus complex proved on this count to be precisely the metaphysics of psychoanalysis. But schizoanalysis claims to be not just critical in this (Kantian) respect, but revolutionary. The critique of Oedipal psychoanalysis is good as far as it goes, but psychoanalysis serves merely as a discursive reinforcement and representative of the institution of the nuclear family, and the family serves in turn as an institutional delegate of capital for the production of a flexible but abstemious and deferential form of subjectivity. In this light, not just psychoanalysis but society as a whole, its modes of production and reproduction alike, will have to conform to the immanent criteria of the unconscious or else stand condemned as metaphysical and oppressive: in the light of schizoanalysis, it does stand condemned, with the point being ultimately not just to condemn the world, but to change it.

NOTES

1   For the sake of brevity and focus, I here leave the contributions of Spinoza and Leibniz to Deleuze's perspective out of consideration, and don't specifically identify or thematize the contributions of Guattari, either. It is clear that the collaboration between Guattari and Deleuze shifted the latter's focus away from an earlier, much broader conception of the unconscious and toward a more concerted engagement with Freud and Lacan.

2   For fuller accounts of Deleuze's early relations to Nietzsche, Kant, Bergson, and Jung, see Daniel W. Smith, "Deleuze and the Question of Desire: Toward an Immanent Theory of Ethics," *Parrhesia: A Journal of Critical Philosophy*, 2 (2007), 66–78; Christian Kerslake, *Deleuze and the Unconscious* (London: Continuum, 2007); and my essay on "Desire," in Charles J. Stivale (ed.), *Gilles Deleuze: Key Concepts* (Montreal and Kingston: McGill-Queen's University Press, 2005), pp. 53–62. For more on Deleuze and Guattari's relations to Freud, Marx, and Nietzsche, see my *Deleuze and Guattari's "Anti-Oedipus": Introduction to Schizoanalysis* (London: Routledge, 1999), on which some of the second part of this essay is based.

3   It is clear in *DR* and especially in *FLB* that Deleuze reworks rather than simply rejects Kant's regulative ideas.

4   As Deleuze and Guattari explain, "the subject is produced as a mere residuum alongside the desiring-machines ... he confuses himself with this third [synthesis] and the residual reconciliation that it brings about: a conjunctive synthesis of consummation in the form of a wonderstruck 'So *that's* what that was!'" (*AO* 17–18).

5   Ludwig Wittgenstein, *Philosophical Investigations* (New York: Macmillan, 1958).

6   In addition to Henri Bergson, *Matter and Memory*, trans. Nancy Margaret Paul and W. Scott Palmer (Mineola, NY: Dover Publications, 2004) and *Creative Evolution*, trans. Arthur Mitchell (London: Macmillan, 1914), see Deleuze's *Bergsonism*, "Bergson" (*DI* 22–31) and "Bergson's Conception of Difference" (*DI* 32–51).

7   Deleuze, "Instincts and Institutions" (*DI* 19–21).

8   Carl Jung, "Instinct and the Unconscious," in *Collected Works*, vol. VIII, trans. R. F. C. Hull (Princeton University Press, 1953), pp. 129–38, and *The Archetypes and the Collective Unconscious: Collected Works*, Vol. IX (London: Routledge, 1968). See also Kerslake, *Deleuze and the Unconscious*, especially pp. 86–99.

9   Jung, "Instincts and the Unconscious," p. 136. In his essay "Mind and Earth" (*Collected Works*, vol. X), Jung says that "Archetypes are

systems of readiness for action and at the same time emotions and ideas."

10 As we will see below, in *Anti-Oedipus* the "body-without-organs" is the site of such double-folding.

11 On the identity of nature but difference in regime of desiring-production and social production, see *AO* especially pp. 31–32, 54, 99, 119–20, 184, and 336–37, and my *Deleuze and Guattari's "Anti-Oedipus,"* especially pp. 18–24 and chapter 4.

12 For Deleuze and Guattari's discussion of the disagreements, but also the in some ways more important areas of agreement between Freud and Jung, see *AO* 46, 57–58, 114, 128, 276, 289, 300, 331, and 354.

13 The first quotation is from Kant's *Critique of Practical Reason*, trans. Werner S. Pluhar (Indianapolis: Hackett, 2002), p. 114; the second is from his *Critique of Judgment*, trans. J. C. Meredith (Oxford: Clarendon Press, 1991), p. 16.

14 Kant, *Critique of Practical Reason*, p. 114.

15 For Deleuze's first extended discussion of Klein's partial objects, see the "Twenty-Seventh Series of Orality" in *LS*, especially pp. 187–93. Her perspective is also discussed in *AO*, especially pp. 44–47 and 72.

16 Much the way desiring-production and social production in *AO* combine the concept of libido with labor power from Marx, anti-production combines the concepts of anti-cathexis and the death instinct from Freud with that of expenditure from Bataille. See my *Deleuze and Guattari's "Anti-Oedipus,"* especially pp. 28–34, 61–76.

17 Not only are there three degrees of anti-production on the BwO, but what I am calling the "third degree" is directly related to historically variable forces of anti-production on the socius. The important schizoanalytic critique of the psychoanalytic death instinct is beyond the scope of this essay, but see my "Infinite Subjective Representation and the Perversion of Death," *Angelaki: Journal of the Theoretical Humanities*, 5:2 (2000), 85–91.

18 On the body-without-organs, see *LS* 189–99; *AO* 9–21; *ATP* 149–66 (Plateau 6: "How Do You Make Yourself a Body without Organs?"); and my *Deleuze and Guattari's "Anti-Oedipus,"* especially pp. 27–33, 36–39, 61, 93–97, and 120–23.

19 On the schizoanalytic view, death becomes an instinct only under capitalism, because anti-production as expenditure is repressed by the imperative to accumulate capital (in Foucault, biopower replaces sovereign power); private capital accumulation deprives the public in general of means of expenditure, so that their ability to differentiate satisfactions is curtailed, and habit and neurosis prevail.

20   Freud mentions on several occasions that "neurosis is, as it were, the
       negative of perversion"; see "Three Essays on Sexuality" (*Standard
       Edition of the Complete Psychological Works of Sigmund Freud*
       [London: Hogarth Press, 1953–74], vol. VII, pp. 130–243), pp. 165 and 231,
       and "Fragment of an Analysis of a Case of Hysteria" (Dora) (*Standard
       Edition*, vol. VII, pp. 7–122), p. 50.

21   The five paralogisms of psychoanalysis are analyzed in the second
       chapter of *AO*, especially pp. 73–130.

22   The three syntheses are discussed in chapter II, section II of Book I
       of the "Transcendental Analytic" in Kant's *Critique of Pure Reason*,
       trans. Norman Kemp Smith (London: Macmillan, 1929).

23   Deleuze and Guattari explain their recourse to Kant this way: "In
       what he termed the critical revolution, Kant intended to discover cri-
       teria immanent to understanding so as to distinguish the legitimate
       and illegitimate uses of the syntheses of consciousness. In the name
       of *transcendental* philosophy (immanence of criteria), he therefore
       denounced the transcendent use of syntheses such as appeared in met-
       aphysics. In like fashion we are compelled to say that psychoanalysis
       has its metaphysics – its name is Oedipus. And that a revolution – this
       time materialist – can proceed only by way of a critique of Oedipus, by
       denouncing the illegitimate use of the syntheses of the unconscious
       as found in Oedipal psychoanalysis, so as to rediscover a transcenden-
       tal unconscious defined by the immanence of its criteria, and a cor-
       responding practice we call schizoanalysis" (*AO* 75).

24   See *AO* 275–76: "From the point of view of regression … it is the father
       who is first in relation to the child. The paranoiac father Oedipalizes
       the son. Guilt is an idea projected by the father before it is an inner
       feeling experienced by the son. The first error of psychoanalysis is in
       acting as if things began with the child … The father is first in relation
       to the child, but only because what is first is the social investment in
       relation to the familial investment, the investment of the social field
       in which the father, the child, and the family as a subaggregate are at
       one and the same time immersed."

25   On the determination of family relations by social production and
       desiring-production, see *AO* 99.

26   Deleuze and Guattari are categorical: "Oedipus is always and solely
       an aggregate of destination fabricated to meet the requirements of an
       aggregate of departure constituted by a social formation" (*AO* 101).

27   On the delegation of repression to the family, see especially *AO*
       120–21.

15 Deleuze's philosophical heritage: unity, difference, and onto-theology

INTRODUCTION

In this chapter, I want to look at Deleuze's philosophical heritage in two different senses. In the first part, I explore his relationship to perhaps the most influential philosopher of the twentieth century, Martin Heidegger. Heidegger plays a central role in Deleuze's early philosophy, and even when in his later collaborations with Guattari their explicit references to Heidegger are dismissive, Heidegger's influence can clearly be detected, particularly in their critiques of other philosophers. In the second part, I look at Deleuze's own contribution to philosophy, and to see how this contribution has been assessed by one of the most influential contemporary French philosophers, Alain Badiou. For Heidegger, Deleuze, and Badiou, perhaps the central problem for philosophy emerges from thinking about totality. For all three, the traditional metaphysical view of totality, derived from Aristotle's concept of paronymy, occludes rather than solves the problem of how we characterize our most general concepts. As we shall see, Heidegger's diagnosis of metaphysics, as constituted by what he calls onto-theology, is shared by all three philosophers, while their responses to this diagnosis differ. Deleuze and Badiou both reject Heidegger's poetics of being in favor of the language of mathematics, but the question I want to explore in the final part of the chapter is, which mathematics? The mathematics of the continuous, or the mathematics of the discrete?

I would like to thank Pete Wolfendale for his comments on an earlier draft of this chapter.

DEFINITION AND THE UNITY OF ANALOGY

For Aristotle, when we want to determine the nature of something, we do so by asking the question, "what is it?"[1] This question calls for an answer in terms of the kind of thing an object is, and an answer in terms of its *essential* properties. We are not concerned with whether Socrates is standing or sitting, for instance, as these characteristics are not essential, and can alter without Socrates ceasing to be Socrates. We might, therefore, say that, essentially, Socrates is a man. In order to explicate this definition, however, we need to ask what the meaning of the term "man" is. Aristotle's answer to this question, which seems a reasonable first approximation, is that the definition of man is a "rational animal," that is, he defines man by saying that he is an animal with a particular kind of property.[2] Likewise, we might say that an animal is a kind of living being with a particular property. When we say that "man" is a "rational animal," man is the species that Socrates belongs to. This species is itself a member of a larger class of things, known as a genus (in this case, "animal"). Now, in order to specify which species of the genus man is, we need to be able to distinguish it from other entities, that is, to say what it is not (to say that it is x, not y). The property that we use to define what something is is a property that divides entities in a wider class into two different kinds (rational and non-rational animals). Aristotle calls this a *difference*. Now if this difference were just an arbitrary difference between any two objects, then while it might allow us to tell one from another, it wouldn't allow us to advance in our definition of a thing. To know that a man is not a horse only gives us a minimal advance in our understanding of what man is. Rather, differences are differences in the kind of thing something is. Thus, for instance, rational and non-rational are both *kinds* of animals. Furthermore, all animals are either rational or non-rational (there is no third class they could belong to). The kind of difference used in definition is therefore essentially an opposition between two kinds (rational and non-rational) that share an underlying identity (animal) in order to allow us to create a taxonomy of species that doesn't allow undefined cases to slip through our system of definition.

Here we come to the problem which I want to explore in this chapter. If each term in the definition is defined by dividing a prior identity, then we have a hierarchy of terms, moving from the most general to the most specific. If we progress back from the most specific term in the hierarchy, however, then we find that we have a problem when we reach the most general term, being. If each term is to be defined in terms of a higher identity, then how can we define the highest identity in the hierarchy? To posit an identity higher than being would just lead to us reiterating the problem at a higher level. To give up on the concept of being seems to be equally problematic, as this would leave us unable to think the world as a totality, or to develop something like a science of metaphysics that is able to deal with any being, or a science of being qua being. Furthermore, as each term in the hierarchy is dependent on a higher term for its definition, then any failure to define the highest term in our hierarchy of terms will affect all of the terms in the hierarchy.

The importance of this question of the highest genus, and of the standard metaphysical answer to this question, cannot be overstated when we are looking at Deleuze's relationship to his predecessors and successors. At root is Heidegger's claim that metaphysics since the Greeks has been a history of *Seinsvergessenheit* (forgetfulness of being). To see why this is so, we need to briefly turn to Aristotle's own solution to the problem of the highest genus. Aristotle recognizes the problem of the highest genus in the *Metaphysics* as follows:

It is not possible that either unity or being should be a single genus of things; for the differentiae of any genus must each of them have both being and be one, but it is not possible for the genus taken apart from its species (any more than for the species of the genus) to be predicated of its proper differentiae; so that if either unity or being is a genus, no differentiae will either have being or be one.[3]

The essential point that Aristotle is making here is that a difference cannot be the same kind of thing as what it differentiates. If it were, then the question would arise of how we differentiate the difference itself from the class of things it is a difference of. This becomes a serious problem when we turn to the genus, being, itself. If we were to understand being as a genus, then, since differences cannot be of the same type as the genera they differentiate, then differences could not themselves have being or unity. "Remember the reason why Being itself is not a genus: it is, Aristotle says, because differences are" (*DR* 32). Being, the highest genus, therefore turns out not to be a genus at all. Instead, Aristotle posits ten "categories," or types of being. These are not related to one another as species to a genus, but are rather related to one another by way of what came to be called analogy.[4] To see how this works, we can turn to a more everyday example of analogy, or, more correctly, paronymy, that Aristotle uses:

> Just as that which is healthy all has reference to health – either because it preserves health, or because it produces it, or because it is a sign of health, or because it is capable of receiving health ... so too that which *is* is said in several ways, but all with reference to a single principle.[5]

Here, we can see that there are various ways of something being healthy, for example, a diet may be healthy, or a drug may restore health. In each of these cases, the use of the word "healthy" differs, but all of these uses are related to a central usage, or focal meaning. Thus, each of the terms is dependent on the meaning of health as, perhaps, the proper functioning of the organism. We can use the same kind of structure with the concept of being. Here, the focal meaning will be being as *ousia*, commonly, though somewhat problematically, translated as "substance." Other possible ways of saying that something is, for example, quantity, place, or quality, are all ways of being that essentially take the form of properties, or predicables, and as such are related to this primary sense of being.[6] We can draw out two related claims that will be central to the development of philosophical thought from Heidegger through to Deleuze and beyond. First, the problem of the highest genus emerges as a result of viewing the relation between concepts as being a subsumptive one. That is, concepts are related to one another through relations of predication (as rationality is predicated of animal, for instance). It therefore appears that any hierarchical model of organization structured according to subsumption will run into similar difficulties. Second, the highest genus problem appears to push us away from any knowledge of the nature of being itself, as this now falls outside of the hierarchy. Both these points will be taken up by Deleuze, but before looking as Deleuze's reading of these problems, I want to turn to Heidegger's account of the question of being.

HEIDEGGER AND THE QUESTION OF BEING

Heidegger opens *Being and Time* with a reference to the question of being: "This question has been forgotten – although our time considers itself progressive in again affirming 'metaphysics.'"[7] Furthermore, the reason why the question of the meaning of being has been forgotten can be traced directly to the analysis of being given by Aristotle: "On the foundation of the Greek point of departure for the interpretation of being a dogma has taken shape which not only declares that the question of the meaning of being is superfluous but sanctions its neglect."[8] While there is a certain ambivalence in Heidegger's own work as to whether Aristotle is fully prey to the difficulties he is responsible for, it is nevertheless the case that the question of being has not been raised in subsequent metaphysics. Heidegger gives three reasons why the question of being has not been raised. First, being is the most universal concept. So much so that, as we have seen, "the 'universality' of being surpasses the 'universality' of genus."[9] As Heidegger points out, while analogy does indeed allow being a form of universality, being by no means therefore becomes an empty term. Rather, the relation between the different terms brought into analogy with one another now becomes problematic. Second, and once again with reference to the problem of the highest genus, Heidegger notes that the question of being has not been asked, because being escapes definition: "Being cannot be derived from higher concepts by way of definition and cannot be represented by lower ones."[10] While this fact may be interpreted as ruling out an analysis of being, Heidegger draws a different conclusion, namely, that being cannot be considered to have the same subject–predicate structure that definition presupposes: "'being' is not something like a being."[11] Finally, being is seen to be a self-evident concept, and so not in need of clarification. Even the question, "what is being?" presupposes an understanding of being, insofar as it contains the word, "is." Rather than seeing this as a reason not to enquire into being, Heidegger instead takes the frequency with which this concept is encountered in our thinking to be the grounds for the pressing need for an enquiry into its meaning. At the heart of Heidegger's philosophy is therefore the claim that being cannot be understood according to the terms we use to understand beings. Rather, there is an *ontological difference* between them:

As the fundamental theme of philosophy being is not a genus of beings; yet it pertains to every being. Its "universality" must be sought in a higher sphere. Being and its structure transcend every being and every possible existent determination of a being. *Being is the transcendens pure and simple.*[12]

I do not want to explore Heidegger's own enquiry into the meaning of being, except to note that by focusing on our everyday involvement with the world, the ready to hand, Heidegger escapes the kind of subject–predicate understanding of the world that Aristotle's account of definition presupposes. In the process, Heidegger opens up the possibility of a relation to being that does not have to resort to the unity of analogy, at least in the sense that we find it in metaphysics subsequent to Aristotle.[13] This project is contrasted with that of traditional metaphysics, which is governed by the "forgetfulness of the difference [between being and beings]."[14] Rather than focusing on the question, "what is being?," metaphysics concerns itself with a categorial understanding of the principles and grounds of beings. It is concerned with being insofar as it is understood as having a predicable structure ("what is the thingliness of things?"). As such, it is concerned with first principles. This might either be in terms of that which all entities share in common (ontology), or the most exemplary entity that gives a ground to other entities (theology).[15] This mode of forgetfulness is, for Heidegger, constitutive of the entire tradition of metaphysics from Aristotle to the modern technological age.[16] It is labeled by Heidegger "onto-theology":

Because Being appears as ground, beings are what is grounded; the highest being, however, is what accounts for giving the sense of giving the first cause. When metaphysics thinks of beings with respect to the ground that is common to all beings as such, then it is logic as onto-logic. When metaphysics thinks of beings as such as a whole, that is, with respect to the highest being which accounts for everything, then it is logic as theo-logic.[17]

Before moving on to Deleuze and Badiou, I want to briefly return to the question of analogy. Given the structure of onto-theology, and the difficulties we have looked at with its conception of the highest genus, it should be clear that there is an immanent difficulty with the kind of conception we have been dealing with when it comes to the question of being. We could say that analogy represents the solution to the limitations of definition, in that it allows the incorporation of being into categorial thought. For Heidegger, however, the fact that it covers over the question of being instead marks it out as a signal of the failure of onto-theology:

The analogy of being – this designation is not a solution to the being question, indeed not even an actual posing of the question, but the title for the most stringent aporia, the impasse in which ancient philosophy, and along with it all subsequent philosophy right up to today, is enmeshed.[18]

DELEUZE AND ONTO-THEOLOGY

All philosophy presents constraints on our thinking as well as opportunities, and the constraints on thinking brought out in Heidegger's analysis of the history of metaphysics are definitive of twentieth-century French philosophy. The uptake of the Heideggerian critique of onto-theology constitutes one of the major fissures separating the twentieth-century analytic and continental traditions. In this respect, it is also a major influence on Gilles Deleuze's philosophy. Deleuze opens *Difference and Repetition* by noting that its subject is "manifestly in the air" with "Heidegger's more and more pronounced orientation towards a philosophy of ontological Difference" (*DR* xix). While Deleuze's question is not the question of being, but the question of difference, Deleuze begins his systematic exposition of this question with a critique of Aristotle's account of difference. As Deleuze notes, for Aristotle, difference can be understood "only in relation to the supposed identity of the concept" (*DR* 31). We have already seen that for Aristotle, difference between species can only be understood in relation to an overarching identity. In this sense, difference is understood in terms of its "predicative power" (*DR* 32) as something that is said of the genus. If difference is understood as the difference within a genus, however, we are once again returned to the problem of the highest genus. As we have seen in the previous couple of sections we cannot form a determinate concept of the highest genus. Without such a concept, any notion of difference which relies on an overarching identity breaks down at this point. Now, this failure of the predicative conception of difference *could* lead us to an

ontology of difference, with something like a Heideggerian distinction between fundamental and regional ontology:

It is as though there were two "Logoi," differing in nature but intermingled
with one another: the logos of Species, the logos of what we think and say,
which rests upon the condition of the identity or univocity of concepts
in general taken as genera; and the logos of Genera, the logos of what is
thought and said through us, which is free of that condition and operates
both in the equivocity of Being and in the diversity of the most general
concepts. (DR 32–33)

This possibility is closed off by the introduction of analogy, however, which allows us to relate the categories to one another, and
so to preserve the predicative model. "Difference is crucified" on
the "quadripartite fetters" (DR 138) of identity, analogy, opposition,
and resemblance. In this sense, the question of difference mirrors
the question of being, in that both questions are forestalled by the
understanding of being as predicative that constitutes onto-theological metaphysics.

   In spite of the similarities in the motivations behind the question of being and the question of difference, there are some fundamental differences in the way Heidegger and Deleuze go about
answering these questions. For Heidegger, the claim that metaphysics is onto-theology implies that "the origin of the difference
[between Being and beings] can no longer be thought of within the
scope of metaphysics."[19] "The time of 'systems' is over."[20] In contrast to these claims, Deleuze explicitly maintains a relationship to
the philosophical tradition, and with it, to the ideal of systematic
philosophy. In doing so, he does not reject Heidegger's analysis of
onto-theology, but rather Heidegger's equation of metaphysics with
onto-theology: "I believe in philosophy as system. The notion of
system which I find unpleasant is one whose coordinates are the
Identical, the Similar, and the Analogous" (TRM 361). Implicit in
Deleuze's claim is a richer conception of the history of metaphysics that includes moments where a genuine thinking of difference
was possible. That is, Deleuze recognizes that there are moments
in the history of metaphysics where the unity of analogy has been
rejected, and on this basis, a line of flight from the aporias of onto-
theology has been constituted. For instance, as Tonner notes, central to Heidegger's critique of Descartes is that he preserves an
analogical conception of being, understanding finite substance by

analogy with infinite substance, God.[21] As such, Descartes would represent an archetypal example of an onto-theological constitution of metaphysics. Deleuze follows Heidegger in his analysis of Descartes,[22] but argues that Spinoza's philosophy breaks with this analogical conception with his claim that the attributes are predicated of both substances and modes univocally, that is, in the same sense. Concomitant with this claim is the claim that being cannot be understood as *a* being, as only modes are numerically distinct. Being is therefore singular.[23] Spinoza, a figure hardly discussed by Heidegger, therefore breaks with the analogical conception of being, and hence develops an account that comes close to escaping the difficulties of onto-theology: "I believe that Spinoza's philosophy remains in part unintelligible if one does not see in it a constant struggle against the three notions of equivocation, eminence and analogy" (*EPS* 48–49).[24] While Heidegger condemns the metaphysical tradition as a whole, Deleuze recognizes a "distaff" tradition that, by rejecting the unity of analogy, at least holds the possibility of escaping from the shackles of onto-theology. Heidegger is, therefore, one in a series of thinkers to escape analogy, rather than the sole instigator of a new mode of thinking:

[F]rom Parmenides to Heidegger it is the same voice which is taken up, in an echo which itself forms the whole deployment of the univocal. A single voice raises the clamour of being. (*DR* 35)

The failure to see the possibility of an alternative tradition of metaphysics is at the root of Deleuze's critique of Heidegger. Thus, the reduction of metaphysics to onto-theology obscures the possibility that there may be other questions to ask which move beyond a predicative model of thinking besides the question of being, and in fact, the singularity of Heidegger's question risks reinstating an overarching identity (*DR* 66):

From the outset, however, what are these fiery imperatives, these questions which are the beginning of the world? The fact is that every thing has its beginning in a question, but one cannot say that the question itself begins. Might the question, along with the imperative which it expresses, have no other origin than repetition? Great authors of our time (Heidegger, Blanchot) have exploited this most profound relation between the question and repetition. Not that it is sufficient, however, to repeat a single question which would remain intact at the end, even if this question is "What is being?" ["Qu'en est-il de l'être?"] (*DR* 200)

Thus, a philosophy of the question of being is solely one instance of what is more fundamental: a philosophy of the question itself. Turning to Deleuze's own positive philosophy, we can say that in both his early work and his collaborations with Guattari, Deleuze aims to operate within the constraints of Heidegger's critique of onto-theology. The emphasis on univocity in the early work and immanence in the later work both present alternative ways of thinking difference that avoid any reliance on analogy.[25] In *Difference and Repetition*, Deleuze presents a transcendental philosophy governed by a distinction between two modes of organization, the actual and the virtual. We can equate this distinction loosely with the distinction between beings and being, the ontological difference at the heart of Heidegger's philosophy. Actuality is the domain of things, capable of being represented as predicable substances. The structure of the actual is governed by transcendental conditions. Whereas for Kant, these transcendental conditions are understood as conditions of possibility and related to a transcendental unity of apperception (a central identity, if not a thing), Deleuze wishes to avoid both of these structures. The transcendental unity of apperception plays the same role for Kant as God plays for other onto-theologies: "Finite synthetic Self or divine analytic substance: it amounts to the same thing. That is why the Man-God permutations are so disappointing, and do not advance matters one step" (*DR* 58). Similarly, the conditions given by the transcendental cannot be conditions of possibility. Possibility once again operates according to analogy in that we understand a possible derivatively in the same terms as actual substances, merely lacking existence:

> Every time we pose the question in terms of possible and real, we are forced to conceive of existence as a brute eruption, a pure act or leap which always occurs behind our backs and is subject to a law of all or nothing. What difference can there be between the existent and the non-existent if the non-existent is already possible, already included in the concept and having all the characteristics that the concept confers upon it as a possibility? (*DR* 211)

As such, possibility provides grounds (in Heidegger's terms) or hypotheses (in Deleuze's terms) that install a being as the highest principle in our metaphysical system. In order to accomplish what Deleuze calls an "ungrounding," he does not follow Heidegger in moving from the language of metaphysics to the language of poetry. Rather, he replaces the ground of a principle of sufficient reason with the unground of a "geometry of sufficient reason" (*DR* 162). This reference to geometry is significant, and points to an alternative to the later poetics of being instituted by Heidegger.[26] We have already seen how Deleuze argues that Heidegger is correct to emphasize the importance of the question in the development of his philosophy. In the realm of metaphysics, the impossibility of reducing the question to the structure of predicable being means that each philosopher poses a different question. For Deleuze, this structure is also discovered in mathematics, in the form of a distinction between problems and solutions.[27] The paradigmatic example of the relation between problems and solutions is the differential calculus. Deleuze argues that Leibniz's calculus allows the expression of "problems which could not hitherto be solved or, indeed, even posed (transcendent problems)" (*DR* 177). It allows us to talk about the rates of change of characteristics of bodies in the world, for instance, in a rigorous way simply not possible before its institution. While it therefore generates a wholly new field of solutions, it does so on the basis of foundations that were themselves aporetic, and incapable of being coherently expressed within the mathematical language of the solution. There is thus a difference in kind between the problematic of the calculus, which is non-representable, and the solutions, which are representable, which mirrors the ontological difference between being and beings. In this respect, modern mathematical interpretations that give consistency to the foundations of the calculus do so only at the cost of covering over the problematic nature of its foundations:

In a different manner, modern mathematics also leaves us in a state of antinomy, since the strict finite interpretation that it gives of the calculus nevertheless presupposes an axiom of infinity in the set theoretical foundation, even though this axiom finds no illustration in calculus. What is still missing is the extra-propositional or sub-representative element expressed in the Idea by the differential, precisely in the form of a problem. (*DR* 178)

Modern set-theoretic mathematics is, therefore, for Deleuze, subject to a "natural illusion," whereby the representational and predicable nature of solutions are extended to the problematic itself, in effect once again reducing being to beings.

BADIOU AND ONTO-THEOLOGY

This trend to attempt to escape from onto-theology through mathematics continues in the work of one of Deleuze's most significant critics to date: Alain Badiou. For Badiou, the central problem of the metaphysical tradition, "that in which philosophy is born and buried, phoenix of its own philosophical consumption,"[28] is the problem of the one and the many. Badiou's attempt to provide a novel solution to this dilemma once again rests on advances in mathematics, and is also thoroughly intertwined with the problem of onto-theology. I began this chapter with a discussion of Aristotle's account of definition, but for Badiou, it is certain aporias discovered in set theory that provide the motivation for his philosophy. In (naïve) set theory, class can be defined as a collection of entities that can be defined either enumeratively (by listing its members) or, more normally, in terms of a property that all of its members share. A class is therefore something like a species, albeit without the explicit claim that when we define a class we are defining the essence of the entities it contains. Now, the entities that a class ranges over are arbitrary, so there is no reason why we cannot have a class of classes. In fact, at the beginning of the twentieth century, it was believed that with sufficient ingenuity, the foundations of mathematics could be reduced solely to relations between classes, thus giving mathematics the same intuitive consistency that was thought to be found in set theory. Bertrand Russell, however, showed that by relying purely on this basic conception of what a class is, it was possible to generate an antinomy:

A class will be called "normal" if, and only if, it does not contain itself as a member; otherwise it will be called "non-normal." An example of a normal class is the class of mathematicians, for patently the class itself is not a mathematician and is therefore not a member of itself. An example of a non-normal class is the class of all thinkable things; for the class of all thinkable things is itself thinkable and is therefore a member of itself. Let "N" by definition stand for the class of *all* normal classes. We ask whether N itself is a normal class. If N is normal, it is a member of itself (for by definition N contains all normal classes); but, in that case, N is non-normal, because by definition a class that contains itself as a member is non-normal. On the other hand, if N is non-normal, it is a member of itself (by definition of "non-normal"); but, in that case, N is normal, because by definition the members of N are normal classes. In short, N is normal if, and only if, N is non-normal. It follows that the statement "N is normal" is both true and false.[29]

The significance of this paradox is that if we allow classes to contain themselves, an antinomy can be formulated within set theory. The obvious solution to this problem was to introduce rules to set theory preventing sets from referring to themselves, and Russell himself developed what he called a theory of types which specified a hierarchy of sets with each set only able to refer to sets below it in the hierarchy. Here, however, we find a parallel with Aristotle's problem of definition, as we can no longer formulate a proposition that refers to all classes (as, at minimum, the class making the assertion must be excluded). The most we can do is make assertions about all classes at a particular level of the hierarchy of types. Moreover, Russell's solution to the problem of universal assertions also mirrors Aristotle's solution to the problem of the highest genus. While Aristotle introduced the notion of analogy, Russell introduces a concept he calls systematic ambiguity:

It will be seen that, according to the above hierarchy no statement can be made significantly about "all a functions" where a is some given object … In some cases, we can see that some statement will hold of "all n-th order properties of a," whatever value n may have. In such cases, no practical harm results from regarding the statement as about "all properties of a," provided we remember that it is really a number of statements, and not a single statement which could be regarded as assigning another property to a, over and above all properties. Such cases will always involve some systematic ambiguity, such as that involved in the meaning of the word "truth," as explained above.[30]

In modern set theory we once again have a situation where the failure to formulate a concept of totality forces a different kind of organization of the most general concepts. Once again, this organization involves seeing a variety of concepts as systematically related to one another in an analogous or paronymous fashion.

For Badiou, in order to escape from the difficulties of positing an underlying unity we simply need to affirm that "the one is not."[31] That is, being is pure multiplicity. Badiou's claim is that while being is only encountered within a situation, being in its pure state is an "inconsistent multiplicity" which cannot be thought as a unity (understood as a class). That is, what makes it possible for being to be presented to us is an operation performed on being that "counts as one" the multiplicity, unifying it under central concepts. For Badiou, therefore, ontological enquiry involves meeting two conditions:

1. The multiple from which ontology makes up its situation is composed solely of multiplicities. There is no one. In other words, every multiple is a multiple of multiples.
2. The count-as-one is no more than a system of conditions through which the multiple can be recognized as multiple.[32]

The unity of the many emerges as a result of the operation of counting as one that is necessary to present being in a situation. Thus, it only appears that the object is composed of two moments: the unity of substance and the multiplicity of its properties. Badiou's claim is that in reality there is no contradiction between unity and multiplicity, because they are different in kind – while the multiple has genuine ontological status, unity is not a *kind* of being, but rather an *operation* performed on the multiple. In order for Badiou's approach to be coherent, therefore, it is necessary to provide an account of the multiple which does not present it in terms of unity. The idea of the multiple cannot simply be a form of nominalism of particulars devoid of universals, as in such a case, we still have the notion of unity, in the form of the elements that make it up. As Badiou notes, the impossibility of constructing a set of all sets without contradiction shows the limitation of the operation of "count as one." Such a set is "'too large' to be counted as a set in the same way as the others."[33] Badiou labels Cantor's attempt to think such sets a form of "onto-theology,"[34] since to do so implies that the same kind of structure that applies to sets that are presented to us as unities applies to the multiple as such. If we were to do so, the multiple would be understood in the same terms as beings, thus once again occluding the ontological difference between them. If we are to understand the multiple without counting "it" as one, we need a conception of multiplicity that is not "a multiple of this or that."[35] In order to develop a theory of the multiple that cannot be totalized into an ultimate unity, nor analyzed into its fundamental elements, Badiou draws on the resources of a particular branch of set theory, Zermelo–Fraenkel (ZF) set theory. ZF set theory both proscribes the formulation of a set of all possible sets (totalization), and the positing of atomic elements from which sets are constructed (it deals solely with the relations between different sets). Badiou takes it to be the singular achievement of modern set theory to give us a consistent account of this kind of pure multiple, thus allowing philosophy to proceed beyond the aporias of classical thinking. Thus, by relying on set theory, Badiou is able to avoid reference to unity at the top of his hierarchy of terms. Furthermore, rather than defining the multiple, which, as Aristotle showed, involves the subordination of a multiplicity to a central unity, set theory merely implies the definition of a multiplicity by specifying the conditions under which it can be constructed. As such, "the theory indicates, without definition, that it does not speak of the one, and that all that it presents, in the implicitness of its rules, is multiple."[36] For Badiou, therefore, axiomatics provides a real alternative to definition, with its reliance on unity. The axioms of set theory provide a model for the constitution of a hierarchy of sets without explicitly providing a definition of sets. By doing so, Badiou avoids the aporia that led to Aristotle's introduction of analogy. Baidou's solution to the problem is therefore in a sense an augmented Kantianism. Unity is a condition of presentation, or of thinking the multiple, but it is not a condition of the multiple itself. We can, nonetheless, specify the multiple using procedures that go beyond presentation. This is the root of his claim that "mathematics is ontology."[37]

CONCLUSION: TWO REGIMES OF MATHEMATICS

Badiou believes that his emphasis on the radically multiple nature of being allows him to escape the kind of onto-theology encountered both in the metaphysical tradition and in apologist interpretations of set theory itself. In presenting a metaphysics of the multiple, Badiou takes on a number of characteristics of Deleuze's own philosophy. First, Badiou accepts the need to think beyond the kind of onto-theology that dominates the metaphysical tradition.[38] Thus for Badiou as well as Deleuze, Heidegger is a major influence, or at least constraint, on how metaphysics can be conducted. Second, both argue that the aporetic nature of classical metaphysics does not necessarily lead us to a rejection of metaphysics in its entirety, but rather to a reformulation of how metaphysics is conducted. Both share what Badiou calls an "active indifference"[39] to the end of philosophy. Finally, both move to a philosophy of mathematics in order to develop an alternative to the predicative model of definition, and hence an alternative to analogy. It is on the basis of these shared values that Badiou criticizes Deleuze's approach to philosophy. Highlighting Deleuze's indebtedness to Heidegger, Badiou claims that "the question posed by Deleuze is the question of Being. From beginning to end, and under the constraint of innumerable and fortuitous cases, his work is concerned with thinking thought (its act, its movement) on the basis of a precomprehension of Being as One."[40] Badiou's fundamental complaint against Deleuze can be seen as the assertion that in spite of Deleuze's apparent rejection of onto-theology, the central notion of the problem still retains the structure of unity, capable of giving rise to a multiplicity of distinct solutions. As such, Deleuze's ontology preserves a fundamental feature of the onto-theological legacy that can only be expurgated by a move to the kind of radical multiplicity put forward by Badiou.[41] This leads Deleuze to privilege the virtual, as unity, at the expense of the actual, as multiplicity, generating a philosophy of dissolution into the One-All. We can see that this claim rests on two assumptions that misrepresent Deleuze's philosophical intentions, however. First, that in the equation, being/beings, Deleuze is only interested in the former of these two terms. In fact, as we have seen, Deleuze is concerned with ontological difference: the *relationship* between being and beings. As such, a reduction of beings to being would efface difference itself. Second, Badiou implicitly assumes that all unity is of the problematic kind that we discover in onto-theology. In fact, what is problematic about this form of unity is its nature as a highest substance, as predicable. Deleuze's concern with the notion of a problematic is precisely that it is not structured in such a way that it can be understood as supporting properties.[42] Once we relate Deleuze's metaphysics of the question to the Heideggerian constraints that both Badiou and Deleuze operate under, we can see that any claim to the reduction of beings to being is unwarranted.

While Badiou only began to gain influence as a philosopher towards the end of Deleuze's life, in his work with Guattari, *What is Philosophy?*, Deleuze provides the beginnings of a response to Badiou, claiming that "even mathematics has had enough of set-theoreticism" (*WP* 152). Badiou's solution, in Deleuze's terms, is still caught in the problematic of onto-theology to the extent that it fails to realize a true difference in kind between the structures of states of affairs and the structure of that which gives rise to states of affairs:

By starting from a neutralized base, the set, which indicates any multiplicity whatever, Badiou draws up a line that is single, although it may be very complex, on which [logical] functions and [philosophical] concepts will be spaced out. (*WP* 152)

Ultimately for Deleuze, Badiou's reduction of ontology to axiomatic mathematics repeats the kind of error discovered in classical metaphysics. Despite the sophistication of Badiou's metaphysics, being is understood purely according to one category: the set. As such, Badiou forestalls the possibility of any enquiry into the nature of ontological difference.

NOTES

1 See Aristotle, *Posterior Analytics*, in Jonathan Barnes (ed.), *The Complete Works of Aristotle* (Princeton University Press, 1991), 93b29.
2 See *ibid.*, where a definition is itself defined as "an account of what a thing is" (93b29).
3 Aristotle, *Metaphysics*, in Barnes (ed.), *Complete Works*, 998b.
4 Strictly speaking, the relationship here is one of paronymy, but will become an analogical relationship when taken up by the scholastic tradition.
5 Aristotle, *Metaphysics*, 1003a.
6 "Of things said without any combination, each signifies either substance or quantity or qualification or a relative or where or when or being-in-a-position or having or doing or being-affected." Aristotle, *Categories*, in Barnes (ed.), *Complete Works*, 1b25.
7 Martin Heidegger, *Being and Time*, trans. Joan Stambaugh (Albany, NY: SUNY Press, 1996), p. 1.
8 *Ibid.*, p. 1.
9 *Ibid.*, p. 2.
10 *Ibid.*, p. 3.
11 *Ibid.*
12 *Ibid.*, pp. 33–34.
13 I am here following Philip Tonner, *Heidegger, Metaphysics and the Univocity of Being* (London: Continuum, 2010), in claiming that while

analogy plays a role in Heidegger's conception of being, it is nonetheless fundamentally univocal.

14   Martin Heidegger, *Identity and Difference*, trans. Joan Stambaugh (University of Chicago Press, 2002), p. 50, translation modified.

15   "One might indeed raise the question whether first philosophy is universal, or deals with one genus, i.e. some one kind of being; for not even the mathematical sciences are all alike in this respect, – geometry and astronomy deal with a certain particular kind of thing, while universal mathematics applies alike to all. We answer that if there is no substance other than those which are formed by nature, natural science will be the first science; but if there is an immovable substance, the science of this must be prior and must be first philosophy, and universal in this way, because it is first. And it will belong to this to consider being *qua* being – both what it is and the attributes which belong to it *qua* being." Aristotle, *Metaphysics*, 1026a28–33.

16   On the historical development of onto-theology, see Iain Thomson, *Heidegger on Ontotheology: Technology and the Politics of Education* (Cambridge University Press, 2005), particularly chapters 1 and 2.

17   Heidegger, *Identity and Difference*, pp. 70–71.

18   Martin Heidegger, *Aristotle's* Metaphysics Θ *1–3*, trans. Walter Brogan and Peter Warnek (Bloomington: Indiana University Press, 1995), p. 38.

19   Heidegger, *Identity and Difference*, p. 71.

20   Martin Heidegger, *Contributions to Philosophy (From Enowning)*, trans. Parvis Emad and Kenneth Maly (Bloomington: Indiana University Press, 1999), p. 4.

21   Tonner, *Heidegger, Metaphysics and the Univocity of Being*, pp. 87–88.

22   "We will see how eminence, analogy, even a certain equivocation remain almost as spontaneous categories of Cartesian thought" (*EPS* 62).

23   For the role of real and numerical distinctions in Spinoza, see Michael Hardt, *Gilles Deleuze: An Apprenticeship in Philosophy* (Minneapolis: University of Minnesota Press, 1993), pp. 59–63.

24   See *DR* 50 for Deleuze's criticism of Spinoza.

25   In Deleuze's early work, univocity takes the place of analogy. That is, while being is not a genus, it is nevertheless said of all beings in the same sense (in one voice). As Daniel W. Smith notes in "The Doctrine of Univocity: Deleuze's Ontology of Immanence," in Mary Bryden (ed.), *Deleuze and Religion* (London: Routledge, 2001), pp. 167–83, pp. 179–80, the language of univocity is not present in Deleuze's collaborations with Guattari. In this later work, immanence is nonetheless understood in fundamentally non-analogical terms. In this regard,

Deleuze's later critique of the notion of "immanence to" in Husserl (*WP* 44–49) presents an important continuation of Deleuze's engagement with Heidegger, as can be seen by comparison with Heidegger's critique of an implicit moment of analogical thinking in Husserl (for an exposition of this critique, see Tonner, *Heidegger, Metaphysics and the Univocity of Being*, pp. 85–93).

26   As Constantin Boundas notes in "Heidegger," in Graham Jones and Jon Roffe (eds.), *Deleuze's Philosophical Lineage* (Edinburgh University Press, 2009), p. 329, the title *Difference and Repetition* mirrors *Being and Time*, with difference taking the place of being (and thereby removing the last vestiges of identity thinking), and repetition taking the place of time (through the retrieval of Nietzsche's doctrine of the eternal return).

27   For a more detailed account of Deleuze and Badiou's conceptions of mathematics, see Daniel W. Smith, "Mathematics and the Theory of Multiplicities: Badiou and Deleuze Revisited," *Southern Journal of Philosophy*, 41:3 (2003), 411–49. Simon Duffy (ed.), *Virtual Mathematics: The Logic of Difference* (Manchester: Clinamen Press, 2006) provides an excellent collection of essays on Deleuze's engagements with mathematics.

28   Alain Badiou, *Being and Event*, trans. Oliver Feltham (London: Continuum, 2005), p. 23.

29   Ernst Nagel and James R. Newman, *Gödel's Proof* (New York University Press, 2001), pp. 23–24.

30   Alfred North Whitehead and Bertrand Russell, *Principia Mathematica*, vol. 1 (Cambridge University Press, 1910), p. 58, quoted in I. M. Bochenski, *A History of Formal Logic*, trans. Ivo Thomas (University of Notre Dame Press, 1961), p. 397.

31   Badiou, *Being and Event*, p. 23.

32   *Ibid.*, p. 29.

33   *Ibid.*, p. 41.

34   *Ibid.*, p. 42.

35   *Ibid.*, p. 29.

36   *Ibid.*, p. 45.

37   *Ibid.*, p. 4.

38   "Along with Heidegger, it will be maintained that philosophy as such can only be re-assigned on the basis of the ontological question," *ibid.*

39   Alain Badiou, *Deleuze: The Clamor of Being*, trans. Louise Burchill (Minneapolis: University of Minnesota Press, 2000), p. 5.

40   *Ibid.*, p. 20.

41   Peter Hallward, *Out of This World: Deleuze and the Philosophy of Creation* (London: Verso, 2006), p. 103, follows Badiou in this claim,

arguing, for instance, that "The earth has never been more deterrito-
rialised nor its inhabitants more 'molecularised' (*ATP* 345), and this
is the result of a specific historical process. Deleuze and Guattari are
the first to admit that they have little to add to Marx's description of
this actual sequence. What they add is a new eschatology. The absolute
limit to the de-coding of all values, the evacuation of every territory
is a value or event beyond any conceivable presentation. The subject
that may survive the dissolution of every presentable or actual subject
will be an exclusively virtual or supra-historical subject – a nomadic
or schizophrenic subject, one worthy of the end of history or the end
of actuality. It's in this sense that, beyond capital's limit, schizophrenia is 'the end of history' (*AO* 130). By striving to reach the 'furthest
limit of deterritorialisation', Deleuze and Guattari's as-yet-unseen
schizophrenic 'seeks out the very limit of capitalism: he is its inherent tendency brought to fulfilment', and thereby incarnates the very
'becoming of reality' itself (*AO* 35)."

42 In this respect, Deleuze's critique of Kant's Ideas is indicative of
    Deleuze's opposition to predicative unity. While Kant's Ideas of God,
    self, and world are problematic, insofar as they are outside of experi-
    ence, yet presupposed by Reason's task of unifying knowledge, Deleuze
    argues that because they are understood on the model of objects of
    experience, they betray the necessary emphasis of philosophy on the
    problem (*DR* 172–74).

BIBLIOGRAPHY

Abou-Rihan, Fadi, *Deleuze and Guattari: A Psychoanalytic Itinerary* (London: Continuum, 2008)

Abraham, Ralph and Shaw, Christopher, *Dynamics: The Geometry of Behavior*, 4 vols. (Santa Cruz, CA: Aerial Press, 1985)

Adler, Alfred and Michel Cartry, "La Transgression et sa derision," *L'Homme*, 11:3 (July 1971), 5–63

Agamben, Giorgio, *Homo Sacer. Sovereign Power and Bare Life* (Stanford University Press, 1998)

Ansell Pearson, Keith, *Germinal Life: The Difference and Repetition of Deleuze* (London and New York: Routledge, 1999)

Viroid Life: Perspectives on Nietzsche and the Transhuman Condition (New York: Routledge, 1997)

Aristotle, *Categories*, in Jonathan Barnes (ed.), *The Complete Works of Aristotle* (Princeton University Press, 1991)

Metaphysics, in Jonathan Barnes (ed.), *The Complete Works of Aristotle* (Princeton University Press, 1991)

The Metaphysics (New York: Prometheus Books, 1991)

Posterior Analytics, in Jonathan Barnes (ed.), *The Complete Works of Aristotle* (Princeton University Press, 1991)

Artaud, Antonin, "Correspondence with Jacques Rivière," in Victor Corti (ed.), *Collected Works of Antonin Artaud*, vol. 1 (London: John Calder, 1968), pp. 25–48

Austin, J. L., *How to Do Things with Words* (Oxford: Clarendon Press, 1962)

Badiou, Alain, *Being and Event*, trans. Oliver Feltham (London: Continuum, 2005)

Deleuze: The Clamor of Being, trans. Louise Burchill (Minneapolis: University of Minnesota Press, 2000)

"Existe-t-il quelque chose comme un politique deleuzienne?," *Cités*, 40 (2009): *Deleuze Politique*, 15–20

Baugh, Bruce. "Transcendental Empiricism: Deleuze's Response to Hegel," *Man and World* 25 (1992), 133–48

Bauman, Zygmunt, *Globalization: The Human Consequences* (Cambridge: Polity Press, 1998)

   Postmodern Ethics (Oxford: Blackwell, 1993)

Beauchard, Jean-Pierre ("David B"), *Epileptic*, trans. Kim Thompson (New York: Pantheon, 2005)

Beaulieu, Alain, "Edmund Husserl," in Graham Jones and Jon Roffe (eds), *Deleuze's Philosophical Lineage* (Edinburgh University Press, 2009), pp. 261–81

   "Gilles Deleuze's Politics: From Marxism to the Missing People," in Constantin V. Boundas (ed.), *Gilles Deleuze: The Intensive Reduction* (London and New York: Continuum, 2009), pp. 204–17

Beistegui, Miguel de, *Immanence: Deleuze and Philosophy* (Edinburgh University Press, 2010)

   "The Ontological Dispute," in Gabriel Riera (ed.), *Alain Badiou: Philosophy and Its Conditions* (Albany, NY: SUNY Press, 2005), pp. 47–58

   Truth and Genesis: Philosophy as Differential Ontology (Bloomington: Indiana University Press, 2004)

Bell, Jeffrey A., *Deleuze's Hume: Philosophy, Culture and the Scottish Enlightenment* (Edinburgh University Press, 2009)

Bell, Jeffrey and Colebrook, Claire (eds.), *Deleuze and History* (Edinburgh University Press, 2009)

Berardi, Franco Bifo, *Félix Guattari: Thought, Friendship, and Visionary Cartography*, trans. G. Mecchia and C. Stivale (Basingstoke: Palgrave Macmillan, 2008)

Bergson, Henri, *Creative Evolution*, trans. Arthur Mitchell (London: Macmillan, 1914)

   Matter and Memory, trans. Nancy Margaret Paul and W. Scott Palmer (Mineola, NY: Dover Publications, 2004)

   Time and Free Will: An Essay on the Immediate Data of Consciousness, trans. F. L. Pogson (New York: Macmillan, 1959)

Birman, Joël, "Les signes et leurs excès: la clinique chez Deleuze," in Eric Alliez (ed.), *Gilles Deleuze: une vie philosophique* (Paris: Institut Synthélabo, 1998), pp. 477–94

Blanchot, Maurice, *The Space of Literature*, trans. Ann Smock (Lincoln: University of Nebraska Press, 1982)

Bochenski, I. M., *A History of Formal Logic*, trans. Ivo Thomas (University of Notre Dame Press, 1961)

Bogue, Ronald, *Deleuze on Literature* (New York: Routledge, 2003)

   Deleuze on Music, Painting and the Arts (New York: Routledge, 2003)

Deleuze's Wake: Tributes and Tributaries (Albany, NY: SUNY Press, 2004)

Bonta, Mark and Protevi, John, *Deleuze and Geophilosophy: A Guide and Glossary* (Edinburgh University Press, 2004)

Bourdieu, Pierre, *Homo Academicus*, trans. Peter Collier (Stanford University Press, 1988)

  The State Nobility: Elite Schools in the Field of Power, trans. Lauretta C. Clough (Stanford University Press, 1988)

Boundas, Constantin, "Heidegger," in Graham Jones and Jon Roffe (eds.), *Deleuze's Philosophical Lineage* (Edinburgh University Press, 2009), pp. 329–38

Bourg, Julian, *From Revolution to Ethics: May 1968 and Contemporary French Thought* (Kingston and Montreal: McGill-Queen's University Press, 2007)

Bourriaud, Nicolas, *Relational Aesthetics*, trans. S. Pleasance and F. Woods (Dijon: Les Presses du Réel, 2002)

Boutang, Pierre-André (director), *Gilles Deleuze from A to Z*, 3-DVD set, trans. Charles J. Stivale (New York: Semiotext(e), 2011)

Braidotti, Rosi, *Metamorphoses: Towards a Materialist Theory of Becoming* (Cambridge: Polity Press, 2002)

  Nomadic Subjects: Embodiment and Sexual Difference in Contemporary Feminist Theory (New York: Columbia University Press, 1994)

  Transpositions: On Nomadic Ethics (Cambridge: Polity Press, 2006)

Brannan, David A., Esplen, Matthew F., and Gray, Jeremy J., *Geometry* (Cambridge University Press, 1999)

Bréhier, Émile, *La théorie des incorporels dans l'ancien stoïcisme* (Paris: Vrin, 1997 [1928])

Bryant, Levi R., *Difference and Givenness: Deleuze's Transcendental Empiricism and the Ontology of Immanence* (Evanston: Northwestern University Press, 2008)

Buchanan, Ian, and Thoburn, Nicholas (eds.), *Deleuze and Politics* (Edinburgh University Press, 2008)

Butler, Judith, *Precarious Life* (London and New York: Verso, 2004)

Canguilhem, Georges, Lapassade, Georges, Piquemal, Jacques, and Ulmann, Jacques, *Du développement à l'évolution au XIXe siècle* (Paris: Presses Universitaires de France, 2003 [1962])

Castells, Manuel, *The Rise of the Network Society* (Oxford: Blackwell, 1996)

Casti, John, *Complexification: Explaining a Paradoxical World through the Science of Surprise* (New York: HarperCollins, 1994)

Caygill, Howard, "The Topology of Selection: The Limits of Deleuze's Biophilosophy," in Ansell Pearson, Keith (ed.), *Deleuze and Philosophy: The Difference Engineer* (London: Routledge, 1997), pp. 149–62

Château, Dominique, *Cinéma et philosophie* (Paris: Nathan, 1996)

Châtelet, François, *Chronique des idées perdues* (Paris: Éditions Stock, 1977),

Choat, Simon, *Marx through Postructuralism* (London and New York: Continuum, 2010)

Clastres, Pierre, *Chronicle of the Guayaki Indians*, trans. Paul Auster (New York: Zone Books, 2000)

Clough, Patricia T., "Introduction," in *The Affective Turn* (Durham, NC: Duke University Press, 2007), pp. 1–33

Cohen, G. A., *Karl Marx's Theory of History* (Oxford University Press, 2000)

Colebrook, Claire, *Deleuze and the Meaning of Life* (Basingstoke: Palgrave Macmillan, 2010)

Collectif A/traverso, *Radio Alice, radio libre* (Paris: Laboratoire de Sociologie de la Connaissance, 1977)

Gilles Deleuze (London: Routledge, 2002)

Critchley, Simon, *The Ethics of Deconstruction* (Edinburgh University Press, 1992)

DeLanda, Manuel, *Intensive Science and Virtual Philosophy* (New York: Continuum, 2002)

"Materialist Metaphysics," in *Deleuze: History and Science* (Dresden: Atropos, 2010)

A Thousand Years of Nonlinear History (New York: Zone Books, 1997)

Deleuze, Gilles, "Cours Vincennes" (14 March–4 April 1978), "Les Cours de Gilles Deleuze," transcripts in translation, www.webdeleuze.com, last accessed June 22, 2011

"De Sacher Masoch au masochisme," *Arguments*, 21 (1961), 40–46

"The Idea of Genesis in Kant's Aesthetics," trans. Daniel W. Smith, *Angelaki: Journal of Theoretical Humanities*, 5:3 (December 2000), 57–70

"Immanence: A Life ...," trans. Nick Millett, *Theory, Culture and Society*, 14:2 (1997), 3–7

"Réponse à une série de questions," November 1981, in Arnaud Villani, *La guêpe et l'orchidée* (Paris: Belin, 1999)

Deleuze, Gilles (ed.), *Instincts et institutions* (Paris: Hachette, 1953)

Derrida, Jacques, "'Genesis and Structure' and Phenomenology," in *Writing and Difference*, trans. Alan Bass (University of Chicago Press, 1978)

Voice and Phenomenon, trans. Leonard Lawlor (Evanston: Northwestern University Press, 2011)

The Work of Mourning (University of Chicago Press, 2001)

Descartes, René, "Rules for the Direction of the Mind," in J. Cottingham, R. Stoothoff, and D. Murdoch (eds.), *Philosophical Writings of Descartes*, vol. 1 (Cambridge University Press, 1985), pp. 7–78

Descombes, Vincent, *Modern French Philosophy*, trans. J. M. Harding and L. Scott-Fox (Cambridge University Press, 1980)

Devlin, Keith, *Mathematics: The Science of Patterns. The Search for Order in Life, Mind, and the Universe* (New York: Scientific American Library, 1994)

Dosse, François, *Gilles Deleuze and Félix Guattari: Intersecting Lives*, trans. Deborah Glasman (New York: Columbia University Press, 2010)

    Gilles Deleuze et Félix Guattari: biographie croisée (Paris: La Découverte, 2007)

    Histoire du structuralisme (Paris: Livre de Poche, 1995)

    History of Structuralism, trans. Deborah Glassman (Minneapolis: University of Minnesota Press, 1997)

Drouet, Dominique, "Index des références littéraires dans l'œuvre de Gilles Deleuze," in Bruno Gelas and Hervé Micolet (eds.), *Deleuze et les écrivains: littérature et philosophie* (Nantes: Cécile Defaut, 2007), pp. 551–81

Duffy, Simon (ed.) *Virtual Mathematics: The Logic of Difference* (Manchester: Clinamen Press, 2006)

Dumm, Thomas, *Michel Foucault and the Politics of Freedom* (London: Sage, 1996)

Feuerbach, Ludwig, "Towards a Critique of Hegelian Philosophy," in Lawrence S. Stepelevich (ed.), *The Young Hegelians: An Anthology* (Cambridge University Press, 1983), pp. 95–128

Flaxman, Gregor, "Plato," in Graham Jones and Jon Roffe (eds.), *Deleuze's Philosophical Lineage* (Edinburgh University Press, 2009), pp. 18–24

Fortes, Meyer, "Colloque sur les cultures voltaïques," in *Recherches Voltaïques* 8 (Paris: CNRS, 1967), pp. 135–37

Foucault, Michel, *The Archaeology of Knowledge and the Discourse on Language*, trans. A. M. Sheridan Smith (New York: Pantheon Books, 1972)

    The Hermeneutics of the Subject: Lectures at the Collège de France, 1981–1982, trans. Graham Burchell (New York: Palgrave Macmillan, 2005)

    Language, Counter-Memory, Practice: Selected Essays and Interviews, ed. Donald F. Bouchard, trans. Donald F. Bouchard and Sherry Simon (Ithaca, NY: Cornell University Press, 1977)

    The Order of Things: An Archaeology of the Human Sciences, trans. anon. (New York: Vintage, 1994)

Franklin, Sarah, Lury, Celia, and Stacey, Jackie, *Global Nature, Global Culture* (London: Sage, 2000)

Freud, Sigmund, *Standard Edition of the Complete Psychological Works of Sigmund Freud*, 24 vols. (London: Hogarth Press, 1953–74)

Gaffney, Peter (ed.), *The Force of the Virtual: Deleuze, Science, and Philosophy* (Minneapolis: University of Minnesota Press, 2010)

Garo, Isabelle, "Deleuze, Marx and Revolution: What It Means to 'Remain Marxist'," in J. Bidet and S. Kouvelakis (eds.), *Critical Companion to Contemporary Marxism* (Leiden and Boston: Brill, 2007), pp. 605–24

Genosko, Gary, "Introduction to the English Translation of Félix Guattari's 'Project for a Film by Kafka'," *Deleuze Studies*, 3:2 (2009), 145–49

Giere, Ronald N., "Constructive Realism," in Paul M. Churchland and Clifford A. Hooker (eds.), *Images of Science* (University of Chicago Press, 1985), pp. 75–98

Gilbert, Jeremy, "Deleuzian Politics? A Survey and Some Suggestions," *New Formations*, 68 (2010), 10–33

Gilroy, Paul, *Against Race. Imagining Political Culture beyond the Colour Line* (Cambridge, MA: Harvard University Press, 2000)

Gilson, Erinn C., "Review of Hallward, *Out of this World: Deleuze's Philosophy of Creation*," *Continental Philosophy Review*, 42 (2009), 429–34

Glissant, Édouard, *Poétique de la relation* (Paris: Gallimard, 1990)

Godard, Barbara, "Deleuze and Translation," *Parallax* 6:1 (2000), 56–81

Goldschmidt, Victor, *Le système stoïcien et l'idée de temps* (Paris: Vrin, 1998 [1953])

Goodwin, Brian, *How the Leopard Changed Its Spots: The Evolution of Complexity* (New York: Charles Scribner's Sons, 1994)

Griffin, Gabriele and Braidotti, Rosi, *Thinking Differently. A Reader in European Women's Studies* (London: Zed Books, 2002)

Grosz, Elizabeth, *Chaos, Territory, Art: Deleuze and the Framing of the Earth* (New York: Columbia University Press, 2008)

   The Nick of Time (Durham, NC: Duke University Press, 2004)

Guattari, Félix, *Les années d'hiver 1980–85* (Paris: Les Prairies Ordinaires, 2009)

   The Anti-Oedipus Papers, ed. Stéphane Nadaud, trans. Kélina Gotman (New York: Semiotext(e), 2006)

   The Guattari Reader, ed. Gary Genosko (Oxford: Blackwell, 1996)

   "Machine and Structure," in *Molecular Revolution: Psychiatry and Politics*, trans. Rosemary Scheed (New York: Penguin Books, 1984), pp. 111–19

   The Machinic Unconscious: Essays in Schizoanalysis, trans. T. Adkins (Los Angeles: Semiotext(e), 2011)

   La révolution moléculaire (Paris: Union Générale d'Éditions 10/18, 1980)

   The Three Ecologies (London: Athlone, 2000)

Guattari, Félix and Negri, Antonio, *Les nouveaux espaces de liberté* (Paris: Dominique Bedou, 1985)

Guattari, Félix, with Rolnick, Suely, *Molecular Revolution in Brazil*, trans. K. Clapshow and B. Holmes (Los Angeles: Semiotext(e), 2008)

Hallward, Peter, *Out of This World: Deleuze and the Philosophy of Creation* (London and New York: Verso, 2006)

Hansen, Mark, "Becoming as Creative Involution? Contextualizing Deleuze and Guattari's Biophilosophy," *Postmodern Culture*, 11:1 (2000), http://pmc.iath.virginia.edu/text-only/issue.900/11.1hansen.txt

Haraway, Donna, *The Companion Species Manifesto: Dogs, People and Significant Otherness* (Chicago: Prickley Paradigm Press, 2003)

Hardt, Michael, *Gilles Deleuze: An Apprenticeship in Philosophy* (Minneapolis: University of Minnesota Press, 1993)

Hegel, G. W. F., *Phenomenology of Spirit*, trans. A. V. Miller (Oxford University Press, 1979)

Heidegger, Martin, *Aristotle's* Metaphysics Θ *1–3*, trans. Walter Brogan and Peter Warnek (Bloomington: Indiana University Press, 1995)

  Being and Time, trans. Joan Stambaugh (Albany, NY: SUNY Press, 1996)

  Contributions to Philosophy (From Enowning), trans. Parvis Emad and Kenneth Maly (Bloomington: Indiana University Press, 1999)

  Identity and Difference, trans. Joan Stambaugh (University of Chicago Press, 2002)

  Kant and the Problem of Metaphysics, trans. Richard Taft (Bloomington: Indiana University Press, 1990)

Hill Collins, Patricia, *Black Feminist Thought. Knowledge, Consciousness, and the Politics of Empowerment* (London and New York: Routledge, 1991)

Hjelmslev, Louis, *Prolégomènes à une théorie du langage* (Paris: Minuit, 1968 [1943])

Holland, Eugene W., "Affirmative Nomadology and the War Machine," in Constantin V. Boundas (ed.), *Gilles Deleuze: The Intensive Reduction* (London: Continuum, 2009), pp. 218–25

  Deleuze and Guattari's "Anti-Oedipus": Introduction to Schizoanalysis (London and New York: Routledge, 1999)

  "Desire," in Charles J. Stivale (ed.), *Gilles Deleuze: Key Concepts* (Montreal and Kingston: McGill-Queen's University Press, 2005), pp. 53–62

  "Infinite Subjective Representation and the Perversion of Death," *Angelaki: Journal of the Theoretical Humanities*, 5:2 (2000), 85–91

  Nomad Citizenship: Free-Market Communism and the Slow-Motion General Strike (Minneapolis and London: University of Minnesota Press, 2011)

Hughes, Joe, *Deleuze and the Genesis of Representation* (New York and London: Continuum, 2008)

Deleuze's "Difference and Repetition": A Reader's Guide (New York and London: Continuum, 2009)

Husserl, Edmund, *Experience and Judgment*, trans. James S. Churchill and Karl Ameriks (Evanston: Northwestern University Press, 1973)

Ideas: General Introduction to Pure Phenomenology, trans. W. R. Boyce Gibson (New York: Collier Books, 1975 [1931])

Ideas Pertaining to a Pure Phenomenology and to a Phenomenological Philosophy, First Book, trans. Fred Kersten (The Hague: Martinus Nijhoff, 1983)

"Philosophy as Rigorous Science," in *Phenomenology and the Crisis of Philosophy*, ed. Q. Lauer (New York: Harper, 1965)

Jones, Graham, "Solomon Maimon," in Graham Jones and Jon Roffe (eds), *Deleuze's Philosophical Lineage* (Edinburgh University Press, 2009), pp. 104–29

Jones, Graham and Jon Roffe (eds.), *Deleuze's Philosophical Lineage* (Edinburgh University Press, 2009)

Jung, Carl, *The Archetypes and the Collective Unconscious: Collected Works*, Vol. IX (London: Routledge, 1968)

"Instinct and the Unconscious," in *Collected Works*, vol. VIII, trans. R. F. C. Hull (Princeton University Press, 1953), pp. 129–38

Kant, Immanuel, *Critique of Judgment*, trans. J. H. Bernard, 2nd rev. edn. (London: Macmillan, 1914)

Critique of Judgment, trans. J. C. Meredith (Oxford: Clarendon Press, 1991)

Critique of Practical Reason, trans. Lewis White Beck (New York: Liberal Arts Press, 1956)

Critique of Practical Reason, trans. Werner S. Pluhar (Indianapolis: Hackett, 2002)

Critique of Pure Reason, trans. Norman Kemp Smith (London: Macmillan, 1929)

Opus Postumum, ed. Eckart Förster, trans. Eckart Förster and Michael Rosen (Cambridge University Press, 1993)

Political Writings, ed. Hans Reiss, trans. H. B. Nisbet, 2nd edn. (Cambridge University Press, 1991)

Kauffman, Stuart, *The Origins of Order: Self-Organization and Selection in Evolution* (New York: Oxford University Press, 1993)

Kerslake, Christian, *Deleuze and the Unconscious* (London: Continuum, 2007)

"Deleuze, Kant, and the Question of Metacritique," *Southern Journal of Philosophy*, 42:4 (2004), 481–508

Immanence and the Vertigo of Philosophy: From Kant to Deleuze
(Edinburgh University Press, 2009)

"The Vertigo of Philosophy: Deleuze and the Problem of Immanence,"
Radical Philosophy, 113 (2002), 10–23

Kline, Morris, *Mathematical Thought from Ancient to Modern Times*, 3
vols. (New York: Oxford University Press, 1972)

Kristeva, Julia, *Pouvoirs de l'horreur* (Paris: Seuil, 1980)

Kymlicka, Will, *Contemporary Political Philosophy* (Oxford University
Press, 2002)

Lacan, Jacques, "Seminar on 'The Purloined Letter'," in *Écrits: The First
Complete Edition in English*, trans. Bruce Fink (New York: Norton,
2007)

Lampert, Jay, *Deleuze and Guattari's Philosophy of History* (London and
New York: Continuum, 2009)

Laplanche, Jean, *Life and Death in Psychoanalysis* (Baltimore and London:
Johns Hopkins University Press, 1976)

Lautman, Albert, *Essai sur les notions de structure et d'existence en mathématiques* (Paris: Hermann, 1938)

Lauzier, Gérard, "Enfin le cri," in *Tranches de vie*, vol. IV (Paris: Les Éditions
Dargaud, 1978), pp. 17–21

Lawlor, Leonard, "The End of Phenomenology: Expressionism in Deleuze
and Merleau-Ponty," in *Thinking through French Philosophy*
(Bloomington: Indiana University Press, 2003), pp. 80–94

"Following the Rats: An Essay on the Concept of Becoming-Animal in
Deleuze and Guattari," in *SubStance*, 117, *The Political Animal*, 37:3
(2008), 169–87

Implications of Immanence (Bronx, NY: Fordham University Press,
2006)

Lecercle, Jean-Jacques, *Badiou and Deleuze Read Literature* (Edinburgh
University Press, 2010)

Deleuze and Language (Basingstoke: Palgrave Macmillan, 2002)

Levinas, Emmanuel, *Alterity and Transcendence* (London: Athlone, 1999)

Levine, Andrew, *A Future for Marxism?* (London: Pluto Press, 2003)

Lévi-Strauss, Claude, *Introduction to the Work of Marcel Mauss*, trans.
Felicity Baker (London: Routledge and Kegan Paul, 1987)

Lewontin, Richard, *The Triple Helix: Gene, Organism, and Environment*
(Cambridge, MA: Harvard University Press, 2000)

Lloyd, Genevieve, *Part of Nature: Self-Knowledge in Spinoza's "Ethics"*
(Ithaca, NY: Cornell University Press, 1994)

Spinoza and the "Ethics" (London and New York: Routledge, 1996)

Lord, Beth. *Kant and Spinozism: Transcendental Idealism and Immanence
from Jacobi to Deleuze* (Basingstoke: Palgrave Macmillan, 2011)

Lucretius, *De Rerum Natura*, trans. W. H. D Rouse (Cambridge, MA and London: Harvard University Press, 1992)

Lundborg, Tom, *Politics of the Event: Time, Movement, Becoming* (London and New York: Routledge, 2011)

Lundy, Craig, *History and Becoming: Deleuze's Philosophy of Creativity* (Edinburgh University Press, 2012)

Mackenzie, Iain and Porter, Robert, *Dramatizing the Political: Deleuze and Guattari* (Basingstoke: Palgrave Macmillan, 2011)

McMahon, Melissa, "Immanuel Kant," in Graham Jones and Jon Roffe (eds.), *Deleuze's Philosophical Lineage* (Edinburgh University Press, 2009), pp. 87–103

Maimon, Solomon, *Essay on Transcendental Philosophy*, trans. Nick Midgley, Henry Somers-Hall, Alistair Welchman, and Merten Reglitz (London: Continuum, 2010)

Malabou, Catherine, "Who's Afraid Of Hegelian Wolves?," in Paul Patton (ed.), *Deleuze: A Critical Reader* (Oxford: Blackwell, 1996), pp. 114–38

Margulis, Lynn, *Symbiotic Planet: A New Look at Evolution* (New York: Basic Books, 1998)

Margulis, Lynn and Sagan, Dorion, *What is Life?* (Berkeley: University of California Press, 1995)

Marks, John, *Gilles Deleuze: Vitalism and Multiplicity* (London: Pluto, 1998)

"Molecular Biology in the Work of Deleuze and Guattari," *Paragraph: A Journal of Modern Critical Theory*, 29:2 (July 2006), 81–97

Marks, John (ed.), *Deleuze and Science*, special number of *Paragraph*, 29:2 (July 2006)

Maturana, Humberto and Varela, Francisco J., *Autopoiesis and Cognition: The Realization of the Living* (Boston: Riedel, 1980)

May, Todd, *Gilles Deleuze: An Introduction* (Cambridge University Press, 2005)

Mengue, Philippe, *Deleuze et la question de la démocratie* (Paris: L'Harmattan, 2003)

Merleau-Ponty, Maurice, *The Phenomenology of Perception*, trans. Colin Smith, rev. Forrest Williams (London: Routledge and Kegan Paul, 1962, rev. 1981)

Metz, Christian, *Film Language: A Semiotics of the Cinema*, trans. Michael Taylor (University of Chicago Press, 1990)

"Interview with Marc Vernet and Daniel Percheron," *Ça Cinéma* (May 1975)

"Interview with Raymond Bellour," *Semiotica*, 4:1 (1971), 1–30

Montebello, Pierre, *Deleuze* (Paris: Vrin, 2008)

Nagel, Ernst and Newman, James R., *Gödel's Proof* (New York University Press, 2001)

Negri, Antonio, "Notes de prison et projet Ulysse," *Chimères*, 39 (2000), 113–25

Nunes, Rodrigo (2010) "Politics in the Middle: For a Political Interpretation of the Dualism in Deleuze and Guattari," *Deleuze Studies*, 4 (Supplement) (2010), 104–26

Nietzsche, Friedrich, *The Anti-Christ, Ecce Homo, Twilight of the Idols, and Other Writings*, eds. Aaron Ridley and Judith Norman, trans. Judith Norman (Cambridge University Press, 2005)

   Beyond Good and Evil: Prelude to a Philosophy of the Future, eds. Rolf-Peter Horstmann and Judith Norman, trans. Judith Norman (Cambridge University Press, 2002)

   Werke: Kritische Gesamtausgabe, ed. Giorgio Colli and Mazzino Montinari (Berlin: Walter de Gruyter, 1969–)

Olkowski, Dorothea, "After Alice: Alice and the Dry Tail," *Deleuze Studies*, 2 (Supplement) (2008), 107–22

   The Universal (In the Realm of the Sensible) (New York: Columbia University Press; Edinburgh University Press, 2007)

Oyama, Susan, *The Ontogeny of Information: Developmental Systems and Evolution* (Durham, NC: Duke University Press, 2000)

Oyama, Susan, Griffiths, Paul, and Gray, Russell (eds.), *Cycles of Contingency: Developmental Systems and Evolution* (Cambridge, MA: MIT Press, 2001)

Parisi, Luciana, *Abstract Sex. Philosophy, Biotechnology and the Mutations of Desire* (London and New York: Continuum, 2004)

Patton, Paul, "Anti-Platonism and Art", in Constantin V. Boundas and Dorothea Olkowski (eds.), *Gilles Deleuze and the Theater of Philosophy* (New York and London: Routledge, 1994), pp. 141–55

   Deleuze and the Political (London and New York: Routledge, 2000)

   "Deleuze's Practical Philosophy," in Constantin V. Boundas (ed.), *Gilles Deleuze: The Intensive Reduction* (London: Continuum, 2009), pp. 186–203

   Deleuzian Concepts: Philosophy, Colonization, Politics (Stanford University Press, 2010)

   "Immanence, Transcendence and the Creation of Rights," in Laurent de Sutter and Kyle McGee (eds.), *Deleuze and Law* (Edinburgh University Press, 2012)

   "Utopian Political Philosophy: Deleuze and Rawls," *Deleuze Studies*, 1:1 (2007), 41–59

Patton, Paul and Protevi, John (eds.), *Between Deleuze and Derrida* (London: Continuum, 2003)

Peffer, Rodney, *Marxism, Morality, and Social Justice* (Princeton University Press, 1990)

Peirce, Charles Sanders, *Écrits sur le signe* (Paris: Seuil, 1978)

Pigliucci, Massimo and Müller, Gerd (eds.), *Evolution: The Extended Synthesis* (Cambridge, MA: MIT Press, 2010)

Plato, *Parmenides*, trans. Mary Louise Gill and Paul Ryan, in John M. Cooper (ed.), *Plato: Complete Works* (Cambridge: Hackett Publishing, 1997), pp. 359–97

   Phaedrus, trans. Alexander Nehemas and Paul Woodruff, in Cooper (ed.), *Plato: Complete Works*, pp. 506–56

   Sophist, trans. Nicholas P. White, in Cooper (ed.), *Plato: Complete Works*, pp. 235–93

   Statesman, trans. C. J. Rowe, in Cooper (ed.), *Plato: Complete Works*, pp. 294–358

Plutarch, *Lives and Opinions of Eminent Philosophers*, trans. C. D. Yonge (London: G. Bell, 1905)

   Plutarch's Moralia, trans. Harold Cherniss, Loeb Classical Library, vol. XIII, part II (Cambridge, MA:, Harvard University Press, 1976)

Protevi, John, "Larval Subjects, Enaction, and *E. coli* Chemotaxis," in Laura Guillaume and Joe Hughes (eds.), *Deleuze and the Body* (Edinburgh University Press, 2011), pp. 29–52

   "Mind in Life, Mind in Process: Toward a New Transcendental Aesthetic and a New Question of Panpsychism," *Journal of Consciousness Studies*, 18:5–6 (2011), 94–116

   "Review of Peter Hallward, *Out of This World: Deleuze and the Philosophy of Creation*," *Notre Dame Philosophical Reviews* (2007), http://ndpr.nd.edu/news/23058-out-of-this-world-deleuze-and-the-philosophy-of-creation/

Rabinow, Paul, *Anthropos Today* (Princeton University Press, 2003)

Rawls, John, *Justice as Fairness: A Restatement* (Cambridge, MA: Harvard University Press, 2001)

   Political Liberalism: Expanded Edition (New York: Columbia University Press, 2005)

Read, Jason, "Fetish is Always Actual, Revolution is Always Virtual," *Deleuze Studies*, 3 (2009), Issue Supplement: *Deleuze and Marx*, ed. Jain Dhruv, 78–101

   The Micro-Politics of Capital (Albany, NY: SUNY Press, 2003)

Rescher, Nicholas, "The Ontology of the Possible," in Michael J. Loux (ed.), *The Possible and the Actual* (Ithaca, NY: Cornell University Press, 1979)

Rorty, Richard, "Unsoundness in Perspective", in *Times Literary Supplement*, June 17 1983, p. 619.

Rose, Nicholas, "The Politics of Life Itself," *Theory, Culture and Society*, 18:6 (2001), 1–30

Salanskis, Jean-Michel. "Idea and Destination," in Paul Patton (ed.), *Deleuze: A Critical Reader* (Oxford: Blackwell, 1996), pp. 57–80

Sander, Klaus, "Entelechy and the Ontogenetic Machine – Work and Views of Hans Driesch from 1895 to 1910," *Development Genes and Evolution*, 202:2 (1993), 67–69

"Hans Driesch's 'Philosophy Really *ab ovo*' or Why to Be a Vitalist," *Development Genes and Evolution*, 202:1 (1992), 1–3

Sauvagnargues, Anne, "De l'animal à l'art," in *La philosophie de Deleuze* (Paris: Presses Universitaires de France, 2004)

Deleuze et l'art (Paris: Presses Universitaires de France, 2005)

Deleuze: l'empirisme transcendantal (Paris: Presses Universitaires de France, 2009)

Schrift, Alan, *History of Continental Philosophy* (University of Chicago Press, 2011)

Twentieth-Century French Philosophy: Key Themes and Thinkers (Oxford: Blackwell, 2006)

Seigworth, Gregory J., "Little Affect: Hallward's Deleuze," *Culture Machine* (Reviews 2007), www.culturemachine.net/index.php/cm/article/view/166/147

Serres, Michel, with Latour, Bruno, *Conversations on Science, Culture, and Time*, trans. Roxanne Lapidus (Ann Arbor: University of Michigan Press, 1995)

Sextus Empiricus, *Adversus Mathematicos*, trans. R. G. Bury (Cambridge, MA: Harvard University Press, 1997)

Shaviro, Steven, "Interstitial Life: Remarks on Causality and Purpose in Biology," in Peter Gaffney (ed.), *The Force of the Virtual: Deleuze, Science, and Philosophy* (Minneapolis: University of Minnesota Press, 2010), pp. 133–46

Shiva, Vandana, *Biopiracy. The Plunder of Nature and Knowledge* (Boston: South End Press, 1997)

Simondon, Gilbert, *L'individu et sa genèse physico-biologique* (Grenoble: Millon, 1995)

Smith, Daniel W., "The Concept of the Simulacrum: Deleuze and the Overturning of Platonism," *Continental Philosophy Review*, 38:1–2 (2006), 89–123

"Deleuze and the Question of Desire: Toward an Immanent Theory of Ethics," *Parrhesia: A Journal of Critical Philosophy*, 2 (2007), 66–78

"Deleuze, Hegel, and the Post-Kantian Tradition," *Philosophy Today* (Supplement 2001), 126–38

"Deleuze, Kant, and the Theory of Immanent Ideas," in Constantin V. Boundas (ed.), *Deleuze and Philosophy* (Edinburgh University Press, 2006), pp. 43–61

"Deleuze's Theory of Sensation: Overcoming the Kantian Duality," in Paul Patton (ed.), *Deleuze: A Critical Reader* (Oxford: Blackwell, 1996), pp. 29–56

"The Doctrine of Univocity: Deleuze's Ontology of Immanence," in Mary Bryden (ed.), *Deleuze and Religion* (London: Routledge, 2001), pp. 167–83

"Mathematics and the Theory of Multiplicities: Badiou and Deleuze Revisited," *Southern Journal of Philosophy*, 41:3 (2003), 411–49

"The Place of Ethics in Deleuze's Philosophy: Three Questions of Immanence," in Eleanor Kaufman and Kevin Heller (eds.), *Deleuze and Guattari: New Mappings in Politics and Philosophy* (Minneapolis: University of Minnesota Press, 1998), pp. 251–69

Smith, Peter, *Explaining Chaos* (Cambridge University Press, 1998)

Somers-Hall, Henry, *Hegel, Deleuze and the Critique of Representation: Dialectics of Negation and Difference* (Albany, NY: SUNY Press, 2012)

"The Politics of Creation: Peter Hallward's *Deleuze and the Philosophy of Creation*," *Pli – The Warwick Journal of Philosophy*, 18 (2007), 221–36

Stewart, Ian and Golubitsky, Martin, *Fearful Symmetry* (Oxford: Blackwell, 1992)

Stivale, Charles J. *Gilles Deleuze's ABCs: The Folds of Friendship* (Baltimore: Johns Hopkins University Press, 2008)

Thoburn, Nicholas, *Deleuze, Marx and Politics* (London and New York: Routledge, 2003)

Thomson, Iain, *Heidegger on Ontotheology: Technology and the Politics of Education* (Cambridge University Press, 2005)

Tonner, Philip, *Heidegger, Metaphysics and the Univocity of Being* (London: Continuum, 2010)

Toscano, Alberto, *The Theatre of Production: Philosophy and Individuation between Kant and Deleuze* (Basingstoke: Palgrave Macmillan, 2006)

Tournier, Michel, *The Wind Spirit: An Autobiography*, trans. Arthur Goldhammer (Boston: Beacon Ness, 1988)

Turner, J. Scott, *The Extended Organism: The Physiology of Animal-Built Structures* (Cambridge, MA: Harvard University Press, 2000)

Van Fraassen, Bas, *Laws and Symmetry* (Oxford: Clarendon Press, 1989)

The Scientific Image (Oxford: Clarendon Press, 1980)

Villani, Arnaud, *La guêpe et l'orchidée: essai sur Gilles Deleuze* (Paris: Belin, 1999)

Watson, Janell, *Guattari's Diagrammatic Thought: Writing between Lacan and Deleuze* (London: Continuum, 2009)

West-Eberhard, Mary Jane, *Developmental Plasticity and Evolution* (New York: Oxford University Press, 2003)

Whitehead, Alfred North, *Process and Reality*, corrected edition, ed. David Ray Griffin and Donald W. Sherburne (New York: The Free Press, 1978)

Whitehead, Alfred North and Russell, Bertrand, *Principia Mathematica*, vol. 1 (Cambridge University Press, 1910)

Widder, Nathan, *Reflections on Time and Politics* (University Park, PA: Pennsylvania State University Press, 2008)

"The Rights of Simulacra: Deleuze and the Univocity of Being," *Continental Philosophy Review*, 31:4 (2001), 437–53

Williams, James, *Gilles Deleuze's "Difference and Repetition": A Critical Introduction and Guide* (Edinburgh University Press, 2003)

Gilles Deleuze's "Logic of Sense" (Edinburgh University Press, 2008)

Gilles Deleuze's Philosophy of Time: A Critical Introduction and Guide (Edinburgh University Press, 2011)

The Transversal Thought of Gilles Deleuze: Encounters and Influence (Manchester: Clinamen Press, 2005)

Wittgenstein, Ludwig, *Philosophical Investigations* (New York: Macmillan, 1958)

Wolfe, Charles T., "Review of *The Anti-Oedipus Papers*," *Metapsychology Online Reviews* 11:35 (August 28, 2007), http://metapsychology.mentalhelp.net/poc/view_doc.php?type=book&id=3790&cn=394

Zabunyan, Dork, *Gilles Deleuze. Voir, parler, penser au risque du cinema* (Paris: Presses de la Sorbonne nouvelle, 2006)

Zahavi, Dan, *Subjectivity and Selfhood: Investigating the First-Person Perspective* (Cambridge, MA: MIT Press, 2005)

Žižek, Slavoj, *Organs without Bodies: Deleuze and Consequences* (London and New York: Routledge, 2004)

Zourabichvili, François, *Deleuze, une philosophie de l'événement* (Paris: Presses Universitaires de France, 1996)

Le vocabulaire de Deleuze (Paris: Ellipses, 2003)

INDEX

Abel, Neils, 230, 231, 233
absurd, 123
actualization, 124, 174, 185, 186, 232–36, 243, 245, 247, 291
aesthetics, 265–83, *see also* art, beauty, the sublime
affect, 4, 25, 148, 175, 177, 184, 191, 192, 236, 251, 282, 304
Agamben, Giorgio, 171, 172
agency, 111, 172, 176, 191, 320
Aion, 70, 72, 124
Alliez, Eric, 54
Althusser, Louis, 4, 43, 130–31
analogy, 93, 338–40, 344, 354
Aristotle, 40, 53, 60, 68, 73, 220, 221, 223, 235, 338–40, 354
art, 25–26, 48, 56, 78, 79, 148, 167, 265–83, 286–305, *see also* aesthetics, beauty, the sublime
Artaud, Antonin, 5, 292, 293, 322
assemblage, 10, 134, 138, 155, 157, 160, 162, 164, 175, 207, 208, 209, 210, 216, 250, 254, 296
attractor, 232, 282
Aumont, Jacques, 147
Austin, J. L., 137, 295

Bacon, Francis, 25–27, 78, 276, 281–83
Badiou, Alain, 9, 11, 21, 32, 80, 180, 198–201, 337, 348–51
Bahktin, Mikhail, 20
bare life, 171, 172, *see also* Agamben, Giorgio
Beauchard, Pierre-François, 152
Beaulieu, Alain, 120
beauty, 271–73, 275, *see also* aesthetics, art

becoming, 77, 180, 301
  animal, 162, 280, 297
  democratic, 166, 212, 213–16
  imperceptible, 301
  intense, 253
  minoritarian, 153, 188, 205–06, 214, 215
  revolutionary, 166, 202, 212, 302
Beistegui, Miguel de, 9, 53, 100
Bell, Jeffrey, 53, 217
Bellour, Raymond, 286, 290
Bergson, Henri, 13, 21, 22–23, 29, 40, 78, 133, 183, 280, 302, 309–10, 319, 320, 323
  duration, 172, 178, 183
  élan vital, 316
Bifo, 153, 154
bifurcation, 28, 232
biology, 44, 214, 239–61, *see also* life, organism
bio-politics, 171
bio-power, 171, 335
Blanchot, Maurice, 44, 118
body without organs, 78, 174, 257–59, 279, 280, 293, 294, 305, 322, 329
the body, 176–78
Bogue, Ronald, 10, 54, 167
Bourdieu, Pierre, 31
Bourg, Julian, 154
Bourriaud, Nicolas, 155
Braidotti, Rosi, 10
Bréhier, Émile, 80
Bryant, Levi, 52, 53, 100

calculus, differential, 223, 224, 347
Canguilhem, Georges, 262

373